DESIGNING SCHOOLS

Designing Schools explores the close connections between the design of school buildings and educational practices throughout the twentieth century to today. Through international case studies that span the Americas, Europe, Africa and Australia, this volume examines historical innovations in school architecture and situates these within changing pedagogical ideas about the 'best' ways to educate children. It also investigates the challenges posed by new technologies and the digital age to the design and use of school places. Set around three interlinked themes – school buildings, school spaces and school cultures – this book argues that education is mediated or framed by the spaces in which it takes place, and that those spaces are in turn influenced by cultural, political and social concerns about teaching, learning and the child.

Kate Darian-Smith holds concurrent appointments as Professor of Australian Studies and History, School of Historical and Philosophical Studies, and Professor of Cultural Heritage, Faculty of Architecture, Building and Planning at the University of Melbourne, Australia. She has written extensively on material culture, memory studies, Australian and imperial history and heritage, with recent publications including *Children, Childhood and Cultural Heritage* (2013) and *Conciliation on Colonial Frontiers: Conflict, Performance and Commemoration in Australia and the Pacific Rim* (2015). Kate is an editor of *Australian Historical Studies,* has served as an adviser to government and cultural institutions and has a long involvement with the international development of Australian Studies.

Julie Willis is Professor of Architecture and Dean of the Faculty of Architecture, Building and Planning at the University of Melbourne, Australia. Her research concentrates on Australian architectural history of the late nineteenth and twentieth centuries. With Philip Goad, she is the editor of *The Encyclopedia of Australian Architecture* (2012), and she was a major contributor to Hannah Lewi and David Nichols (eds), *Community: Building Modern Australia* (2010). Her current research includes writing a new short history of Australian architecture; examining the development of the modern hospital; and, with colleagues from history and education, leading a project examining innovation in the design of twentieth-century schools.

'Discerning and indispensable, *Designing Schools: Space, place and pedagogy* takes us to Australia, Europe, the United States, Africa, and Latin America to learn about school buildings in the twentieth century. This thematically organized and generously illustrated book, written by experts in the field, tracks changes in architectural design, pedagogy, childhood, space, place, technology, and nationality. *Designing Schools* also introduces the teachers, architects, and other adults who wanted to build better schools for an astonishing array of boys and girls – rich and poor, rural and urban, white, Aboriginal, African American, and African children – although the outcomes were not always praiseworthy. A welcome addition to the new and exciting field of children, space, and schools.'

—**Marta Gutman, Professor of Architecture (History & Theory), The City College of New York/CUNY and The Graduate Center/CUNY, USA**

'The wealth of evidence and argument in *Designing Schools* for the cultural significance of school architecture is overwhelming. This book puts the materiality of schooling back into the centre of our efforts to understand how teaching and learning have changed over the last century. Relationships between modernism in school design and efforts to develop progressive pedagogies are only part of the argument. The chapters in this book explore new dimensions of old questions such as the significance of the school in the making of populations conceived in racial, gender and class terms. *Designing Schools* challenges its readers to imagine schools as spaces as much as places, and the meanings they develop within a variety of geographical, cultural and temporal settings that include urban, suburban and rural – national, colonial and post-colonial. *Designing Schools* is significant enough to change the ways we think about schooling.'

—**Craig Campbell, Editor, History of Education Review, University of Sydney, Australia**

DESIGNING SCHOOLS

Space, place and pedagogy

*Edited by Kate Darian-Smith
and Julie Willis*

Routledge
Taylor & Francis Group

LONDON AND NEW YORK

First published 2017
by Routledge
2 Park Square, Milton Park, Abingdon, Oxon OX14 4RN

and by Routledge
711 Third Avenue, New York, NY 10017

Routledge is an imprint of the Taylor & Francis Group, an informa business

British Library Cataloguing in Publication Data
A catalogue record for this book is available from the British Library

Library of Congress Cataloging-in-Publication Data
Names: Darian-Smith, Kate, editor. | Willis, Julie, editor.
Title: Designing schools : space, place and pedagogy / edited
    by Kate Darian-Smith and Julie Willis.
Description: Abingdon, Oxon ; New York, NY : Routledge, 2017. |
    Includes bibliographical references and index.
Identifiers: LCCN 2016013418 | ISBN 9781138886193 (hb : alk. paper) |
    ISBN 9781138886223 (pb : alk. paper) | ISBN 9781315714998 (ebook)
Subjects: LCSH: School buildings—Design and construction.
Classification: LCC LB3221 .D47 2017 | DDC 371.6—dc23
LC record available at https://lccn.loc.gov/2016013418

ISBN: 978-1-138-88619-3 (hbk)
ISBN: 978-1-138-88622-3 (pbk)
ISBN: 978-1-315-71499-8 (ebk)

Typeset in Bembo
by Apex CoVantage, LLC

CONTENTS

FIGURES

ACKNOWLEDGEMENTS

The research for chapters of this book written by Kate Darian-Smith, Philip Goad, Elain Harwood, Sianan Healy, Hannah Lewi, Cameron Logan, Julie McLeod, David Nichols and Julie Willis was supported under Australian Research Council's *Discovery Projects* funding scheme (project number DP110100505, 'Designing Australian Schools: A spatial history of innovation, pedagogy and social change'). Most of the chapters collected in this volume were first aired at an international workshop titled 'School Is Another Place' in June 2013, convened in partnership with the Menzies Centre for Australian Studies at King's College London. We are grateful for the support of Ian Henderson, Carl Bridge and Simon Sleight, all at the Menzies Centre; and the assistance of Laura Douglas, Arts and Humanities Research Institute, King's College London. And we thank all participants of the workshop for their lively exchange of ideas and congenial company.

At Routledge we have been privileged to work with Francesca Ford and Trudy Varcianna, and we appreciate their patience and encouragement throughout this project. At the University of Melbourne, Dr Ann Standish has provided editorial assistance and intellectual and moral support, and her work has been integral to the completion of this volume. We offer her our deepest thanks.

Finally, we are grateful to all the authors of the individual chapters; and to all the photographers, artists and repositories who gave permission for the reproduction of their images, without which the volume would be significantly diminished.

Kate Darian-Smith and Julie Willis
Editors

CONTRIBUTORS

Catherine Burke is Reader in History of Education and Childhood at the University of Cambridge. She is a historian engaged with cultural and material histories of educational contexts and of childhood in the nineteenth, twentieth and twenty-first centuries. Her current research examines the relationship between innovation in teaching and the design of formal and informal learning spaces; the view of the child and young person in the design of education; and the history of twentieth-century school architecture and its pioneers. She edits the 'Sources and Interpretations' section of *History of Education Journal*. Her recent publications include *A Life in Education and Architecture: Mary Beaumont Medd (1907–2005)* (2013).

Kate Darian-Smith holds concurrent appointments as Professor of Australian Studies and History, School of Historical and Philosophical Studies, and Professor of Cultural Heritage, Faculty of Architecture, Building and Planning at the University of Melbourne. She has written extensively on material culture, memory studies, Australian and imperial history and heritage, with recent publications including *Children, Childhood and Cultural Heritage* (2013) and *Conciliation on Colonial Frontiers: Conflict, Performance and Commemoration in Australia and the Pacific Rim* (2015). Kate is an editor of *Australian Historical Studies*, has served as an adviser to government and cultural institutions and has a long involvement with the international development of Australian Studies.

Ning de Coninck-Smith is Professor of History of Childhood and Education, Department of Education, Aarhus University, Denmark. She is the co-editor of and a contributor to a recently published five-volume history of the Danish school. With Marta Gutman she has edited the volume *Designing Modern Childhoods: History, Space and the Material Culture of Children* (2008). Her book *Barndom og Arkitektur* (Childhood and Architecture) (2011) was honoured with the *Årets Historiske Bog*, a prize for the history book of the year, sponsored by, among others, the Danish Ministry of Culture and the Danish Royal Library.

Marco Di Nallo is an architect who studied at the Politecnico di Milano and the Technische Universität Wien. In 2014 he gained a PhD in History of Architecture and Urbanism from the Politecnico di Torino (co-supervised with the Accademia di architettura di

Mendrisio-Università della Svizzera Italiana) with a thesis on Swiss school buildings during the 1950s and 1960s. He is a teaching assistant of Restoration and Reuse of Twentieth Century Architecture at the Accademia di architettura, Università della Svizzera Italiana, since 2011 and in 2015 was a guest lecturer at the Antalya International University in Turkey.

Inés Dussel is a researcher and professor in the Departmento de Investigaciones Educativas del CINVESTAV-IPN, Mexico, and was previously researcher and Director of the Education Area of the Latin American School for Social Sciences (FLACSO)/Argentina. She has undertaken extensive research into the relationships between knowledge, schooling and politics, taking a historical and sociocultural approach. She has published nine books and a great many articles and chapters in academic journals and books, in six languages.

Geraint Franklin works for Historic England as a buildings historian, specialising in postwar architecture. Between 2010 and 2012 he coordinated 'England's Schools 1962–88', a national thematic project on postwar schools. The study is available from http://research.historicengland. org.uk/. In 2012, he also published '"Built-in Variety": David and Mary Medd and the Child-Centred Primary School, 1944–80' in *Architectural History*, vol. 55, and contributed a chapter on the United Kingdom's recent school building program to the collection *School Design Together* (2014).

Philip Goad is Professor and Chair of Architecture at the University of Melbourne. He is an expert on modernism in architecture, and its links to developments in Australia, especially through professional networks, travel, education, design theory, criticism and reception. He is co-author and co-editor of *Modern Times: The Untold Story of Modernism in Australia* (2008) and co-editor of *The Encyclopedia of Australian Architecture* (2012).

Ian Grosvenor is Professor of Urban Educational History at the University of Birmingham, England. He is author of numerous articles and books on racism, education and identity; the visual in educational research; the material culture of education; and the history of urban education.

Dale Allen Gyure is Professor of Architecture at Lawrence Technological University in Southfield, Michigan, USA, and Adjunct Assistant Professor of Historic Preservation at Goucher College. Professor Gyure's research focuses on American architecture of the nineteenth and twentieth centuries, particularly the intersections of architecture, education and society. He has published two books to date: *The Chicago Schoolhouse, 1856–2006: High School Architecture and Educational Reform* (2011) and *Frank Lloyd Wright's Florida Southern College* (2010).

Elain Harwood is a historian with Historic England and worked with Geraint Franklin on the organisation's recent survey of postwar schools. She has published *Space, Hope and Brutalism, English Architecture 1945–75* (2015) and *England's Post-War Listed Buildings* (with James O. Davies) (2015). She has just completed a survey of higher education buildings and is now working on post-modernism and writing a book on new towns.

Sianan Healy is a historian in the field of postcolonial and settler history, with a strong interest in the relationship between Indigenous and settler cultures, and ideas of nationality, citizenship and belonging. Recent publications include articles on representations of Aboriginal children in the Victorian government school reader *The School Paper*, and a survey of the relationship between school design and pedagogy in postwar Australia. Current projects include a study of intersections between the built environment and assimilation policies in Australia from the interwar period to the 1970s.

Martin Lawn is Honorary Professor of Education, University of Edinburgh. He is the founding editor of the *European Educational Research Journal*, and recent books include *The Rise of Data in Education Systems: Collection, Visualisation and Use* (2014), *Europeanizing Education: Governing a new Policy Space* (with Sotiria Grek) (2012) and *Modelling the Future: Changing Education through World Exhibitions* (2009).

Hannah Lewi is Associate Professor in the Faculty of Architecture, Building and Planning at the University of Melbourne. She co-edited and co-authored *Community: Building Modern Australia* (2010). Her current research and publications span Australian and modern architecture history, heritage interpretation and theory, and new media. She is the vice-chair of Docomomo Australia and the historical advisor for the Australian Venice Biennale exhibition and book *The Pool* (2016).

Cameron Logan is a senior lecturer in the Faculty of Architecture Design and Planning at the University of Sydney. He is an urban and architectural historian with a particular interest in historic preservation and the author of *Historic Capital: Preservation, Race and Real Estate in Washington DC* (forthcoming, 2017).

Julie McLeod is Professor, Melbourne Graduate School of Education, and an Australian Research Council Future Fellow (2012–2016). She is Deputy Director of the Melbourne Social Equity Institute and an editor of the journal *Gender and Education*. She researches in the history and sociology of education with a focus on curriculum, youth, gender and inequality. Her books include *The Promise of the New and Genealogies of Educational Reform* (2014), *Researching Social Change: Qualitative Approaches* (2009) and *Making Modern Lives: Subjectivity, Schooling and Social Change* (2006).

David Nichols is a senior lecturer in Urban Planning in the Faculty of Architecture, Building and Planning at the University of Melbourne. He is co-author of the book *Trendyville* (2013), author of *The Bogan Delusion* (2011) and co-editor and co-author of *Community: Building Modern Australia* (2010). His current research and publications span Australian and modern planning history including schools, community, built environment and media representation of community, space and related themes.

Amy F. Ogata is Professor of Art History at the University of Southern California. She is the editor of *Swedish Wooden Toys* (2014) and the author of *Designing the Creative Child: Playthings and Places in Midcentury America* (2013), which won the 2016 Alice Davis Hitchcock Award from the Society of Architectural Historians. *Art Nouveau and the Social Vision of Modern Living: Belgian Artists in a European Context* appeared in 2001.

Ola Uduku is Reader in Architecture at Edinburgh University and has researched the architecture of, and the architectural networks involved in creating, the West African Modern Movement. She is currently involved in the Conserving West African Modernism Project involving universities in Ghana and the United Kingdom. She has an interest in social infra-structure provision for minorities in cities and is a member of the Archi-Africa education committee. Recent publications include 'Designing Schools for Quality: An International Case Study–based Review' (2015) and, as co-editor with Sameer Bagaeen, *Beyond Gated Communities: Urban Gating and Soft Boundaries* (2015).

Amber Wiley is an architectural and urban historian at Skidmore College. Her research interests are centred on the social aspects of design and how it affects urban communities – that is, on architecture as a literal and figural structure of power. She focuses on the ways local and national bodies have made the claim for the dominating narrative and collective memory of cities through design, and examines how preservation and architecture contribute to the creation and maintenance of the identity and sense of place of a city. She also sits on the board of the Vernacular Architecture Forum and is a member of the National Park System Advisory Board Landmarks Committee.

Julie Willis is Professor of Architecture at the University of Melbourne. Her research con-centrates on Australian architectural history of the late nineteenth and twentieth centuries. With Philip Goad, she is the editor of *The Encyclopedia of Australian Architecture* (2012), and she was a major contributor to Hannah Lewi and David Nichols (eds), *Community: Building Modern Australia* (2010). Her current research includes writing a new short history of Australian architecture; examining the development of the modern hospital; and, with colleagues from history and education, leading a project examining innovation in the design of twentieth-century schools.

1

ARCHITECTURE AND THE SCHOOL IN THE TWENTIETH CENTURY

Julie Willis

Across the developed world, and increasingly in the developing world, the school sits at the very heart of its local community. It is not just an institution of learning but a place that shapes and guides the knowledge, capacity and experience of young lives. Schools are places that foster the intellectual, physical and emotional development of children as they are prepared to join society as productive and engaged adults. Modern schools are not only buildings that support the act of teaching; they also are seen as places that must foster effective learning and socialisation. The foundation of progressive and democratised education is the idea of students as learners who are active and dynamic participants in their education. There is also an understanding that the location of learning cannot be confined to a single place – the classroom – but occurs across multiple spaces and places. Schools are thus designed to foster learning and engagement from students, teachers and the community.

But what makes the modern school? What ideas and aspects of architectural design are realised in the design of schools in the later twentieth century? And where and when did these ideas emerge? The concerns that architects have considered important in the design of schools have arisen repeatedly across the nineteenth and twentieth centuries, yet their physical manifestation has changed dramatically over this period. From the mid-nineteenth century, when the design of schools provided teacher-focused environments in which pupils could be effectively taught, it was understood that the relative comfort of children had bearing on their capacity to pay attention, and that the relative hygiene, air quality and light levels of educational spaces were important. By the mid-twentieth century, the concern was more about creating environmentally controlled, flexible, child-centred spaces and environments in which students could effectively learn. Changes to school design were not just a reflection of evolving architectural modes, but demonstrate that pedagogy and design are closely entwined and reflect how, as the conceptualisation of the child as school pupil has changed dramatically over this period, so has the design of the spaces around them.

The design of school buildings developed from the mid-nineteenth century, as various nations began to legislate for universal education as a fundamental social provision; the 1880 amendments to the Elementary Education ('Forster') Act (1870) for England and Wales is just one example. The result was a dramatic increase in the number of school buildings that were constructed, mostly as new buildings. Compulsory education meant that every child and every family gained a direct connection to a new type of public building. The design of schools, therefore, shouldered a significant responsibility in the care and education of its students and the message it conveyed to its wider community.

By the twentieth century, the education of children was seen as essential to a healthy and strong nation. The rise of modern nationalism in the late nineteenth century was encouraged by the development of print culture, with the greater circulation and influence of newspapers, books and other printed media. This corresponded with the increased rates of literacy brought about through mass education and were tied to the national interest. The knowledge gained through education underpinned economic competitiveness and, in industrialising nations, the supply of a skilled workforce. Physical health was also considered important in the nationalist project, where the eradication of slums, reduction of infant mortality rates and the control of disease was seen to enable a fit society, capable of contributing to and building the nation. As architect John J. Donovan wrote in his 1921 book, *School Architecture*, 'The great possibilities before the nation rest entirely upon the opportunities for universal physical and intellectual education, not upon the development of a few prodigies' (Donovan 1921: 1). Donovan's frame of reference was the United States of America, but he could have just as easily been writing about the United Kingdom, France, Germany or many other countries where the circumstances of war had sharpened thinking about the fitness of the next generations to be future citizens. Schooling was not just to be for the privileged few, but for all, as an essential service to the nation.

The idea of healthy children has strongly influenced the design of schools in the nineteenth and twentieth centuries. This is evident in a series of major texts written by architects who advocated the needs and requirements for well-designed and appropriate school buildings (Barnard 1850; Robson 1874; Donovan 1921; Martin 1952; Caudill 1954; Otto 1963). Originally, the concern for health was demonstrated by a suggested amount of airspace per child as the basis for classroom planning, or the requirement for sufficient natural light and ventilation. As early as 1850, Henry Barnard was writing of the need for appropriate natural lighting and adequate ventilation in his *School Architecture or Contributions to the Improvement of School-Houses in the United States*. In his extensive section on ventilation, Barnard quoted scientific studies to demonstrate the need for adequate levels of oxygen and advocated the provision of natural light, to prevent shadows, glare or reflection (Barnard 1850: 41–50). In 1874, E. R. Robson offered an international survey of school buildings within his text *School Architecture, Being Practical Remarks on the Planning, Designing, Building and Furnishing School-Houses*. Robson used German research to support his discussion of adequate lighting and seating (preferably arranged so the light came over the students' left shoulders), ventilation and heating (Robson 1874: 176–9; 263–6). These ideas were articulated regularly by experts advocating healthy environments for schools, so by the early twentieth century school facades were marked by large expanses of windows that could be opened, with accompanying passive ventilation systems. Physical exercise was also seen as important, with experts recommending playgrounds and spaces for athletics and gymnastics, both internal and external, for the use of school pupils (Barnard 1850: 62; Robson 1874: 244–62).

These requirements for appropriate light, ventilation and physical activity had a profound influence on the external appearance of schools and the way they were sited, particularly from the early twentieth century. No other public building had the functional requirement of a curtilage of playgrounds and other spaces for physical activity, nor did they need large banks of windows to illuminate each room appropriately for several dozen occupants. The external stylistic representation of the school ranged from the Gothic Revival (echoing the traditional origins of schools from their church-based beginnings) through to classicism, Romanesque, Edwardian Baroque and various revivalist styles, such as the neo-Georgian, up until at least the 1930s, often reflecting the styles of other, similarly sized public buildings. But regardless of its style, its particular functional requirements made – and make – a school instantly recognisable within the built environment.

As Barnard put it:

> The style of the exterior should . . . be calculated to inspire children and the community. . . . Every school-house should be a temple, consecrated in prayer to the physical, intellec-tual, and moral culture of every child in the community . . . for here the health, tastes, manners, minds, and morals of each successive generation of children will be, in a great measure, determined for time and eternity.
>
> (Barnard 1850: 41)

Barnard's comments pointed to the understanding that the school, and the meanings embed-ded within its architecture, played a critical role in children's development. This view has been remarkably consistent across almost two centuries: architects have returned repeatedly to the idea that school architecture should actively support children's physical, intellectual and moral growth. The exterior of the school was not just a facade, projecting a particular ambition for learning and social improvement: the design of the school building, inside and out, reflected and shaped its educational aspirations. Architects writing on school design noted the impor-tance of translating the school's pedagogy in its design, so that the building as a whole, and its component parts, could best support the teacher and the curriculum being taught. In this they looked at the internal arrangements of classrooms, the design and position of desks, the line of sight for both teacher and pupil, and the apparatus used in the classroom.

In the early part of the twentieth century, the style of the school was also associated with the seniority of the pupils who attended. Architects recommended that architecture for the youngest students at primary or elementary school be simple and pleasing, to facilitate the transition between home and the wider world, whereas those attending secondary schools should be exposed to architecture that spoke of their transition into productive citizens. This is seen in the different scales of buildings, from the intimate spaces of kindergartens and infant schools that often employed domestic references, to the more imposing facades of high schools, with grand entrances and architectural embellishment. Moving from simpler and smaller buildings into larger and more sophisticated edifices as the school students progressed through their education suggested school as place held an important role in introducing chil-dren to and conditioning them for entry into the adult world (Willis 2014).

Increasingly, and in line with modern ideas about pedagogy and child development, the relationship between students and school buildings became more explicit. As Donovan put it, 'the child should be the motive for the architecture of . . . school buildings' (Donovan 1921: 27). This acknowledgement that the needs of children were at the centre of school design was an expression of the wider social shifts that occurred across the later nineteenth century and into the twentieth century. As compulsory education developed the concept of childhood was correspondingly extended. Most notably, in the second half of the twentieth century, the legal age of leaving school was raised, and the period of formal education was lengthened, delaying full engagement with the adult world. Childhood itself was differentiated. In the 1950s the concept of the teenager emerged, where youth between 13 and 18 were considered to be neither child nor adult but a distinct age group of their own.

By the mid-twentieth century, the convergence of ideas about daylight, fresh air, functional spaces and pedagogical principles found a new architectural expression for schools in the clean lines of modern architecture. The principles of modern architecture were founded on functional need, resulting in a universal architectural language that eschewed traditional architectural styles and precedent. This first appeared when architects built social housing projects that focused on providing clean, healthy and functional architecture to the masses, embracing new materials, large windows, open planning and access to fresh air (Le Corbusier 1923). The concern for healthy school children found expression in the open-air schools, beginning in Germany in 1904 and spreading quickly to other parts of Europe, Britain and the United States. Johannes Duiker's design for the *Openluchschool* (open-air school) in Amsterdam of 1930 and Beaudouin & Lods' open-air school at Suresnes, France, 1935–36 (see cover image), exemplified the close connections between modern architecture and the desire to create a healthy environment in the school. In California, Richard Neutra's design for the Corona Avenue Elementary School of 1935 showed a utilitarian architecture, with large sliding glass doors that encouraged a continuum of the classroom between inside and out.

In the United States, modernism was rapidly adopted for school building, with so-called 'finger-plans' (ranges of classrooms opening of a single side of a corridor or breezeway) that allowed for maximum daylight, fresh air and access to the outside, with elevations of unadorned plain-faced brickwork or cement render with large windows and no embellishment, such as Marsh, Smith & Powell's Roosevelt Elementary School in Santa Monica, CA (1935), and Maynard Lyndon & Eberle Smith's Northville Elementary School in Michigan (1936). Further afield, examples such as the Bruderholz School in Basel, Switzerland, by Hemann Baur (1939) and Neutra's San German Home for Girls School in Puerto Rico (1944) included open-air 'classroom patios' (Martin 1952): dedicated external spaces for each classroom. It was not just the overall form of the school that was changing. Internally, arrangements for the students had changed significantly, away from fixed, often shared, desks to individual tables and chairs that could easily be moved and rearranged, along with that of the teacher, enabling flexible and changeable teaching and learning situations and a move from 'formal and directional' instruction to 'a classroom . . . designed to facilitate the learning process . . . so arranged and so equipped that pupils can work in groups and freely communicate with each other' (Caudill 1954: 22–3).

Ideas about appropriate learning environments for children, the connection between pedagogy and architectural space and the new built expression of them had only been realised in relatively few buildings prior to 1945. The conditions in the late 1940s, with rapidly rising numbers of school-aged children coupled with changing legislation, like the Butler Act of 1944 in England and Wales, which enshrined education as a basic provision for children of all ages and the responsibility of the state, saw a dramatic demand for new schools. These were to be efficiently built, well designed and fit for purpose. This boom in school building was not confined to the United Kingdom; it was also evident throughout Europe, the Americas and Australia. Post-World War II restrictions of building materials, coupled with new building techniques developed during wartime, gave architects both challenges and opportunities to reimagine school designs. This resulted in a period of considerable experimentation, which can be seen in examples such as the CLASP (Consortium of Local Authorities Special

Programme) schools in England, the lightweight timber construction (LTC) school designs in Australia and the relocatable prefabricated classroom buildings ('Bristol huts') emerging from repurposed aircraft factories, which allowed for rapid, standardised production of new schools.

Mass education and large numbers of new schools meant that the image of school was reinvented to that of a quintessentially modern building – efficient, utilitarian, functional – and centred on the needs of the child. William Caudill, of well-known US school specialist architects Caudill Rowlett Scott, wrote in 1954 of the 'turning point' in school architecture that had recently occurred, prompted by a series of factors, including changes to city codes governing educational provision. He wrote:

> The 'pupil [centred] approach' insists that school planners should begin with a clear and scientifically accurate realization of the actual physical and emotional needs of the pupil . . . these needs are to be met for the purpose of helping the pupil to perform at peak efficiency in a school designed to function as a positive and flexible aid in the educational process.
>
> (Caudill 1954: 17)

Space and shape were seen to provide the new ways of conceiving the school and its students. School was imagined and realised as locus of community; as a progressive social experiment; as space for diverse educational needs; as mass education; as space for student-centred learning; and as a place for flexible learning. Architects have concerned themselves with many aspects of school design, particularly how to provide what are called 'well-tempered' environments, ensuring the school design reflects its pedagogical intent and understanding the important role a school plays in its wider community. It is the move to a modern child-centred educational model, however, that has wrought the most significant change on the design of school buildings. The modern school does not just provide spaces in which children can be taught. It is a place that actively responds to children's changing needs and development, and it reflects wider social changes.

★ ★ ★ ★

The chapters in this volume speak of the changing nature of school as a socially constructed place in the twentieth century. Across diverse locations and populations, the concerns for education remain remarkably similar. The design of the modern school is founded on ideas that had long been considered, such as healthy spaces, conducive to learning; representing and engaging with communities; reflecting pedagogy; and emblematic of modern ideas about architecture. But the twentieth-century school also saw radical experimentation in classroom pedagogy; new ways of framing the classroom; new technologies that shaped learning; and the increasing importance of the child as learner. The contributors to this volume, *Designing Schools: Space, Place and Pedagogy*, reflect on what makes the modern school through their respective perspectives of architectural, educational and social history.

The volume comprises four parts: 'Lessons from history'; 'School buildings'; 'School cultures'; and 'School spaces'. Part one, 'Lessons from history', includes three short chapters offering distinct perspectives on school design. Ian Grosvenor, in a photographic essay, examines the school as a phenomenon that is both invisible and very present, where designs once considered modern and progressive lose their currency and power over time. Grosvenor encourages us to look at school buildings not just in the present, but 'to recognise that we are looking at what was [once] the future'. Martin Lawn also considers the invisible school – that which is abandoned and derelict. Contrasting the newly built school as a symbol of hope for the future, he sees the abandoned school as failure: 'once beacons of learning. . . . Now they are the sites of the lost ambitions of society'. He exhorts us to understand and value the past, the history, of school design, to understand where its future may lie. Elain Harwood offers a very personal view of post–World War II education through the divergent educational pathways she and her brother experienced, with vastly different places and pedagogical intents. All three authors use the history of schools to suggest what the future may bring for school design.

In part two, 'School buildings', the authors examine changing approaches to the design of school buildings. Philip Goad looks at the development of the ideal learning environment through the work of Ernest Kump, a Californian architect and a prolific school designer from the 1930s to the 1960s who was concerned with ensuring that all aspects of light, ventilation and temperature were perfectly controlled for maximum effect to create the 'well-tempered classroom'. Dale Allen Gyure examines the development of a new type of high school in post-World War II United States, one that moved away from the multi-storey traditionally styled edifices towards schools that were consciously unimposing and more homelike. Reflecting the changing conception of the child, these new 'casual schools' combined modern architecture with new pedagogical approaches, and positioned education as preparing children to be productive adult citizens. Marco Di Nallo further reflects on these themes in discussing Swiss schools in the 1960s, where the school was seen as 'a bridge to the world'. Di Nallo notes the tensions between the creative solutions architects and educators were proposing, through flexible architectural solutions and pedagogical democratisation, and the reluctance of the bureaucracies that governed the school to embrace such reform. The drawing together of architects, educators and administrators to reconsider and re-vision the school environment through the collaborative auspices of the Educational Facilities Laboratories (EFL) in the United States is the subject of Amy Ogata's chapter. She argues that the activities of the EFL from 1958 to the 1970s were an important stimulus of debate and for ideas, including open planning, that fundamentally shaped the post-World War II American school. Cameron Logan also considers the open plan school in his examination of Australian schools in the 1960s and 1970s. Logan posits the open classroom was a response to the challenge to pedagogical authority, 'a crisis in the legitimacy of the school', but one met by resistance by parents and teachers. These chapters explore the advances and limits to which architecture – school design – responded to and engaged with changing educational trends, how they represent the changing position of the child as school student, and acceptance of or resistance to such new ideas.

In part three, 'School cultures', the authors consider the role, and design, of the school within the local community. Ning de Coninck-Smith traces the history of a tiny school in a remote Danish community, where the diverse needs of the local population and the requirements of local authorities were often in conflict over the education of children. Julie McLeod and Sianan Healy examine a community of a different kind in their chapter on the education of Indigenous Australian children at a time when there was increased interest in child-centred and progressive education, yet also government-sponsored assimilationist policies for Aboriginal people. The school thus became a place of mediating and contesting such policies, as educators struggled with the challenge of whether to provide education to Aboriginal children as a distinct group and what effect that should have on pedagogy and school design. Kate Darian-Smith examines how school spaces were provided for vocational education, with a focus on domestic science schools for girls. The relationship between education and the workforce was informed by ideas about gender and class, and the need for skill-based instruction required specialised spaces, such as industrial-style kitchens, in school buildings. The role of school as the locus of community identity is explored by Amber Wiley, in her analysis of the tensions between African American community politics and urban renewal in Washington, DC, in the 1960s and 1970s. New schools in inner urban areas aimed to reinvigorate such places, and were realised in progressive pedagogy and classroom layout, contained in the robust forms of Brutalist architecture: a model school in which the hopes of a community were heavily invested. Ola Uduku continues the theme of model schools in considering the Nigerian 'Unity Schools'. Supported by international development funds, the Unity Schools were initially conceived as modern exemplars of Nigerian secondary education, although as Uduku shows, their realisation was deeply informed by traditional colonial-era ideas about education, as well as British ideas on tropical architecture and school design.

The chapters in part four, 'School spaces', discuss the more intimate aspects of schooling, including quiet spaces and the sensory elements of the classroom. Catherine Burke examines how recognising children's need for quietness and withdrawal influenced the design of English schools. Quietness was not the silence of the old classroom but a space of contemplation for children in an increasingly activity-based curriculum, and further demonstration of the empowerment of the child within education. Geraint Franklin and David Nichols consider another form of sensory engagement in their chapter on Hans Coper and Paul Ritter, who separately created strongly tactile environments for children, in contrast to and as a foil for the utilitarian lines of modern architecture. Their designs sought to encourage and foster children's creativity and imagination within educational settings. David Nichols and Hannah Lewi explore sight and sound through their discussion of audio-visual technology in Australian schools between 1930 and 1980. They examine films as both a medium and a representation of education, where such technology was a means of expressing the progressive nature of the modern school system. Finally, Inés Dussel looks at the impact of the digital revolution in classrooms, through the lens of Argentinian schools participating in a federally sponsored one child–one computer program, to see what attendant changes have occurred in the organisation of space and time within the classroom.

This collection demonstrates that the interconnections between space, place, pedagogy and community have fundamentally shaped the modern school, reflecting the changing position of the child in society. Dussel's chapter suggests a future in which the classroom without walls may well come to pass and our understanding of school as a physical place again undergoes dramatic change. A fully digital classroom is as different to the ones envisaged by architects and pedagogues who promoted open-air schools, then open-plan schools, to replace the traditional classroom of rows of student desks. This echoes Grosvenor's suggestion that all that is now considered old-fashioned and out of date was once seen as highly modern and progressive. Yet the aim to provide children with the best environment in which to learn persists, even if the physical manifestation of what that is continuously evolves.

Acknowledgement

Research for this chapter has been supported by a grant from the Australian Research Council: 'Designing Australian Schools: A Spatial History of Innovation, Pedagogy and Social Change' (DP110100505).

Works cited

Barnard, H. (1850) *School Architecture or Contributions to the Improvement of School-Houses in the United States*, New York: AS Barnes.

Caudill, W. W. (1954) *Towards Better School Design*, New York: FW Dodge.

Donovan, J. J. (ed.) (1921) *School Architecture: Principles and Practices*, New York: Macmillan.

Le Corbusier (1923) *Vers une Architecture*, Paris: C Gres; English translation, Frederick Etchells. London: The Architectural Press, 1927.

Martin, B. (1952) *School Buildings 1945–1951*, London: Crosby Lockwood & Son.

Otto, K. (1963) *School Buildings 1: Examples and Development in Primary and Secondary School Buildings*, London: Iliffe Books.

Robson, E. R. (1874) *School Architecture, Being Practical Remarks on the Planning, Designing, Building and Furnishing of School-Houses*, London: John Murray.

Willis, J. (2014) 'From Home to Civic: Designing the Australian School', *History of Education Review* 43, 2: 138–51.

PART I

Lessons from history

2

FROM LOOKING TO SEEING, OR THIS WAS THE FUTURE . . .

Ian Grosvenor

School buildings hold many secrets. They are repositories of thousands of memories of events that took place in them. They hold within their walls the spaces in which learning happens. Birmingham, like other major cities in the United Kingdom, is full of such buildings and memories. Schools are everywhere in the cityscape, still operating as schools or occupied by new learning agencies or even commercial enterprises (see Figures 2.1, 2.2 and 2.3). Sometimes they are broken and abandoned to the elements; sometimes they have been transformed into expensive apartments (see Harwood 2010). They are or have been little beacons in their areas, pulling people in everyday and accumulating generations of meaning. Yet because they are so commonplace, these sites of memory are often invisible.

This invisibility of the school is not just an English phenomenon, as the American writer and poet Philip Lopate observed in the early 1970s when describing Public School 70 in New York City where he was going to work as writer in residence:

> P.S. 70 might just as well be invisible. Most neighbourhood people don't even see it. Three stories high, built of administrative red brick, as easily mistaken for a bus depot as a public school, it seems to urge you not to notice it, like a stalled driver who waves the other cars past. . . . With so much to look at, why would anyone want to bother with a low brick box, overpowered by apartment houses, upstaged even by the emaciated trees with fences around them.
>
> (Lopate 2007: 3)

But to return to the cityscape of Birmingham and its schools, in 2001 I walked around the city in the company of the Portuguese photographer Paulo Catrica. He was working on a project with Martin Lawn, funded by the Gulbenkian Foundation, to 'make legible, through a particular approach, a vast and rich subject matter – the Birmingham schools' (James 2004: 3; see also Catrica 2005). One of the schools he photographed that day was Floodgate Street School (see Figure 2.4).[1] This photograph, along with others, was exhibited in Birmingham in the spring of 2004 and was used as the front cover for the accompanying exhibition publication.

FIGURE 2.1 The 'abandoned school': Steward Street School, opened 1873, closed 1969, was at the centre of the Ministry of Education pamphlet *Story of a School* (see Burke and Grosvenor 2013).

Photograph: Ian Grosvenor

FIGURE 2.2 The school as art gallery: Oozell Street School, built and opened in 1878, is now the IKON Contemporary Art Gallery.

Photograph: Ian Grosvenor

FIGURE 2.3   The school as apartments: Seven Street School opened as the Royal Lancastrian Free School in 1809 and was sometimes called Birmingham British School. It closed in 1933 and was turned into apartments and offices in 2007.

Photograph: Ian Grosvenor

FIGURE 2.4   From Moores Row, Floodgate Street Board School, 26 July 2001.

Photograph: Paulo Catrica, reproduced with permission

The German art historian Paul Frankl insisted that to understand a building

> we must get to know it as a whole by walking through it from end to end, from cellar to roof, through all its outstretching wings. The entrance, the vestibule or passage leading to courtyard or stair, the connections between several courtyards, the stairs themselves and the corridors leading away from them . . . like the veins of our bodies – these are the pulsating arteries of a building.
>
> (Frankl 1968 [1914]: 79)

Catrica's making legible the story of Birmingham schools also involved stepping inside them. On another occasion he photographed the interior of Somerville Junior and Infant School (see Figure 2.5). Prior to the Birmingham commission Catrica had worked on another assignment to photograph Portuguese liceus (grammar schools), and in a commentary on this photographic project the historian Antonio Novoa observed:

> Paulo Catrica's photographs are fragile. They do not impose themselves as illustrations. They suggest a space for relationships and dialogue. They do not exist without the attention of the viewer who reads them.

FIGURE 2.5   Classroom 5P, Somerville Junior and Infant School, 27 July 2001.

Photograph: Paulo Catrica, reproduced with permission

It is not a matter of discovering what is invisible, but rather of allowing ourselves to be instructed by what we see. Images are there to question us, and to be questioned by us in turn.

(Catrica 2005: 76)

So when we look at these two images, what questions do they ask us and what can we see?

The school dominates its surroundings, which appear to press in on it from all sides restricting the structure and forcing it to push upwards. This impression is enhanced by the church-like tower which sits atop of the school as though squeezed between two adjoining roofs, the angle of the photograph and the sharp lines of the building captured against a washed-out sky. The building is three-storeys high and built of red brick. Large windows dominate the building on one side, and again their height is exaggerated by the camera angle. Terracotta mouldings frame windows and decorate the masonry and the roof cresting. When we move through the internal spaces of the school, we notice among other things that the large windows seen from the outside were over a metre off the classroom floor level, to prevent children being distracted by events outside, while classroom door handles were positioned at a height suitable for children. In the second image, no children or adults are present. Yet what it presents is so familiar in both its form and its function that we can quickly populate it from our memories, conjuring up the activities, the movements and the soundscapes of classrooms we have known. Look deeper and we can see the past and the photographic present caught in the same image. The physical space has not changed, but the material world within it has, as new pedagogic practices demanded different forms of storage and furniture configurations.

If we look at gazetteer of all the schools built in Birmingham before 1964, the entry for Floodgate tells us it was a Victorian board school which opened in 1891 to accommodate 1,115 children and infants. A bathroom was added in 1906, and the school was reorganised in 1931 as a senior mixed and infant school. It closed in 1940, and it became an annexe for a nearby Roman Catholic school. Somerville was also a board school. It opened in 1894 to accommodate 960 children and infants. The infant part of the school was enlarged in 1901. It was reorganised in 1931 into a junior mixed school. In 1961 its accommodation consisted of 16 classrooms (Reynolds 1964: 512, 539). The architectural histories of Birmingham's Victorian and Edwardian buildings additionally tell us that both schools were designed by the Martin and Chamberlain architectural partnership. Martin and Chamberlain were the leading practitioners of Birmingham's 'terracotta schools'. Their schools built in the Gothic style were characterised by red brick, terracotta facings and the use of towers (Holyoak 2009: 170–81; Shackley 2009: 340–5). Chamberlain believed that school architecture should contribute to the aesthetic sensibility of the children and offer them 'some compensation for the drab homes from which they came' and argued that Gothic was the only true vernacular style for England (Seaborne and Lowe 1977: 4, 31).[2] Today, while Floodgate Street has been physically integrated into a college of further education, Somerville Road School is a thriving primary school.[3]

All of this additional contextual information helps us to further interpret what we see in the photographs, but what neither the photographs nor the texts announce or suggest is that what is on view is in fact a modern school, a school for the future. When they were built the design of these two schools was innovative and modern, the materials used were of the highest quality, the physical items inside the school were newly manufactured and the learning spaces they contained were ready to witness teachers using modern pedagogical practices to produce the modern school(ed) child. Floodgate and Somerville were Birmingham equivalents of Conan Doyle's 'big, isolated clumps of buildings', rising high above the slated roofs of the London skyline like 'a brick island in a lead-coloured sea'. There were board schools, light-houses and beacons of the future, 'capsule[s]' containing 'hundreds of bright little seeds . . . out of which will spring, the wiser, better England, of the future . . . ' (Conan-Doyle 1893: 257–8). Similarly, Lopate's PS 70 was also a school of the future, as he wrote:

> the building must once have been spanking new. It must once have been a lighting-rod connecting all the high-minded hopes of parents and community. . . . The cornerstone says: Erected 1950. If you wanted to you could consider it a modern schoolhouse. Or you could think of it as stylistically congruent with the Korean War.
>
> (Lopate 2007: 3)

Birmingham had a national reputation for the design and quality of its board schools, and in 1896 the *Pall Mall Gazette* compared London schools unfavourably with those built in Birmingham:

> In Birmingham you may generally recognise a Board school by it being the best build-ing in the neighbourhood. With lofty towers which serve the utilitarian purpose of giving excellent ventilation, gabled windows, warm red bricks and stained glass, the best Birmingham Board schools have quite an artistic finish. . . . In regard to light and air, the worst schools are equal to the best in London.
>
> (Seaborne and Lowe 1977: 10)

Birmingham schools were designed to be 'fitting and congruous to their noble purpose' (Seaborne and Lowe 1977: 10), and the opening of a new one was a major local event involving an official opening, public addresses by local dignitaries and a report in the press. Reported speeches and press articles invariably framed the event as being future focused. A report on the opening of Sherborne Road School in 1889 included references to the school buildings being 'inspected and admired by crowds of residents, whose children will be accommodated there', and noted that nothing 'calculated to promote the comfort and con-venience of teachers and scholars' had been neglected and the arrangement and the furniture of the rooms was 'complete and of modern design'. The chairman of the school board stated they had 'considered future as well as present needs' and that the school was 'as perfect as . . . [it] could be' (School Clippings File 1889).

Externally, schools such as Floodgate show over time the wear and tear of history, but there is no obvious sign of change and adjustment to new educational futures. The original design features remain, but internally the layers of habitation that can be seen in the photograph of the Somerville classroom reflect new pedagogical practices and point to the gradual transforma-tion of a space from being something new to becoming something sedimented. The interior captured in this photograph is inscribed with educational ideas and practices. The photograph both presents and represents chronicles of change and use: 'marks of use, building alterations, plans versus usage, professional "satisficing" of spaces, technology and fabric interface, national and local regulations' all worked upon the sites of schooling (Lawn and Grosvenor 1999: 391).

Schools are invisible in the cityscape because they are so familiar, and just as they can go unnoticed so too can their histories. When we look at school buildings, we need to be con-scious not only of their present but of their beginnings, to see a school as others did when it was being designed and built, to recognise that we are looking at what was the future. But can what was once modern, but was designed in the past, still be a school of the future?

At the end of the 1930s, Impington Village College in Cambridgeshire, England, stood boldly for all that was progressive in school building. Designed by the Bauhaus architect Walter Gropius and the British architect Maxwell Fry, the college was an elementary school for boys and girls aged 11 to 14 during the day and an adult education centre for nearby villages in the evening. Gropius had met Henry Morris, Cambridgeshire's chief education officer, in 1934, and their meeting was described at the time as follows: 'Enlightened architect met enlightened educationist: result: organism'. The college design was variously described as 'superb: a veritable architectural seduction, chaste and severe, but intense', 'one of the best buildings of its date in England, if not the best' and as 'practical, functional and beautiful . . . a demonstration of idealism in education . . . a rallying point for all reformers who realize the importance of the environment and the functional structure of the school' (Burke and Grosvenor 2008: 86–8).[4] Herbert Read, the public intellectual, poet, art educator, literary critic and anarchist, believed Impington offered a vision of the future and devoted a chapter to the school in his book *Education through Art* (Read 1943: 290–5). More recently, in the year of its seventy-fifth anniversary, the school has been described as 'an exemplar of humanist modernism: an essay in genteel grandeur, with barely perceptible curves, local yellow bricks, ribbon windows and a fan-shaped hall' (Bennett 2015), and Rowan Moore, architectural critic of *The Observer*, identified it as one of the ten most outstanding schools in the United Kingdom (Moore 2015). What is most significant about the school and its continuing success is that the design 'still works . . . it is not quaint or delicate. The central long promenade is light and inviting. You never feel hemmed in' (Bennett 2015, quoting the current principal of the college, Robert Campbell). The design still works because Morris's educational vision of education as 'knowledge exchange' and the school as a place where 'life is lived' remains deeply embedded within the ethos of the school.[5]

Notes

1 Many thanks to Paulo Catrica for permission to reproduce his images. A complete set of Catrica's Birmingham photographs is held in the Birmingham City Archives.
2 Complaints were made in the late 1890s that Martin and Chamberlain had a virtual monopoly as Birmingham Corporation architects (Shackley 2009: 345).
3 Floodgate was used as a delegate site visit as part of the International Standing Conference for History of Education in July 2001.
4 The quotes, in order, are from Jack Pritchard, the designer who was instrumental in bringing Gropius out of Nazi Germany; Henry Morris; Nicholas Pevsner, the art historian; and Herbert Read.
5 Morris's vision of a school as a place where 'life is lived' predates Henri Lefebvre's observation, 'This space was produced before being read; nor was it produced in order to be read and grasped, but rather in order to be lived by people with bodies and lives in their own particular urban context' (quoted in Forty 2000: 84).

Works cited

Bennett, O. (2015) 'Bauhaus and Moral Purpose: The Very Model of Modern Community Schools', *The Guardian*, 17 November 2015, available at: http://www.theguardian.com/education/2015/nov/17/bauhaus-community-schools-village-colleges-cambridgeshire (accessed December 2015).

Burke, C. and Grosvenor I. (2008) *School*, London: Reaktion Books.

Burke, C. and Grosvenor, I. (2013) 'The Steward Street School Experiment: A Critical Case Study of Possibilities', *British Educational Research Journal* 39, 1: 148–65.

Catrica, P. (2005) *Liceus*, Lisbon: Assírio & Alvim.

Conan Doyle, A. (1893 [1950]) 'The Naval Treaty', in *The Memoirs of Sherlock Holmes*, Harmondsworth: Penguin: 238–82.

Forty, A. (2000) *Words and Buildings: A Vocabulary of Modern Architecture*, London: Thames and Hudson.

Frankl, P. (1968 [first published in German in 1914]) *The Principles of Architectural History: The Four Phases of Architectural Style*, Cambridge, MA and London: MIT Press.

Harwood, E. (2010) *England's Schools: History, Architecture and Adaptation*, Swindon: English Heritage.

Holyoak, J. (2009) 'John Henry Chamberlain', in P. Ballard (ed.) *Birmingham's Victorian and Edwardian Architects*, Birmingham: Victorian Society: 153–81.

James, P. (2004) *The White Room Series: Photographs by Paulo Catrica*, Birmingham: Birmingham Libraries and the University of Birmingham.

Lawn, M. and Grosvenor, I. (1999) 'Imagining a Project: Networks, Discourses and Spaces: Towards a New Archaeology of Urban Education', *Paedagogica Historica: International Journal of the History of Education*, New Series 35, 2: 381–94.

Lopate, P. (2007) *Being with Children: A High Spirited Account of Teaching Writing, Theater and Videotape*, New York: The New Press.

Moore, R. (2015) 'The 10 Best School Buildings', *The Guardian*, 2 January, available at: http://www.theguardian.com/culture/2015/jan/02/the-10-best-school-buildings (accessed December 2015).

Read, H. (1943) *Education through Art*, London: Faber and Faber.

Reynolds, S. (1964) 'Schools', in W. B. Stephens (ed.) *A History of the County of Warwick, Volume VII The City of Birmingham*, London: Oxford University Press: 501–48.

School Clippings File (1889) Birmingham: Library of Birmingham.

Seaborne, M. and Lowe, R. (1977) *The English School: Its Architecture and Organization, Volume II 1870– 1970*, London: Routledge & Kegan Paul.

Shackley, B. (2009) 'Frederick William Martin', in P. Ballard (ed.) *Birmingham's Victorian and Edwardian Architects*, Birmingham: Victorian Society: 520–3.

3

BUILDING RUINS

Abandoned ideas of the school

Martin Lawn

> *Ruins are the visible symbols and landmarks of our societies and their changes, small pieces of history in suspension. The state of ruin is essentially a temporary situation that happens at some point, the volatile result of change of era and the fall of empires.*
>
> (Yves Marchand and Romain Meffre 2010)

> *The ideas ruins evoke in me are grand. Everything comes to nothing, everything perishes, everything passes, only the world remains, only time endures.*
>
> (Denis Diderot 1767)

Introduction

In this short piece, I reflect upon the contributions to this collection to introduce a number of points about school buildings, their social context and their imagined processes. These points are cast as a set of musings on school buildings and the passage of time and purpose, and start with an interest in the dominance of the architect–planner alliances which determined how we are meant to 'see' their work in designing and constructing schools.

School building in Western countries appears to be episodic, reflecting economic and social difficulties or 'boom' periods, and often spurred by population or reconstruction crises. Yet this history of the surge and decline of school provision, of investment and economy, and of industrialisation and deindustrialisation, is overlaid by powerful rhetorics about the progress and design of education. The 'future of society' rhetoric is aligned closely with school building, and to examine buildings over time, and their processes of construction and decay, is to raise questions about this rhetoric. Modernism, as a movement in school building processes and architectural ideas, does not look back, but the researcher has to. The problem that researchers have is that we tend to become absorbed in the aims and intentions of the new school, its innovations in structure and content, its pedagogical designs, and its significance at the time. But now the future seems to have broken down again, and the state's vision for the future is limited to acts of individual progress or delegation to private actors.

So, to stop looking forward for the moment, and take the reverse direction to most future-focused education writers, I would like to express an interest in twentieth-century schools that were the product of modernity but were left behind with it. As their usefulness ended and buildings became inadequate or damaged, they were closed, abandoned or deserted. The opportunity to look at abandoned schools and classrooms breaks the natural links between the educational researcher and education. We are looking not at key contemporary terms in education, like improvement and development, but at unfamiliar terms, such as destruction, abrupt departure and decay. Objects are revealed not within a happy, working classroom or on an engaging website but as abandoned, left behind without a backward look. There is a disconnection between the acts of construction in school architecture, which are positive and future oriented, and the decline and decay of buildings representing past versions. The merging of different approaches and stories, located in different parts of human experience – the discursive history of the professional architect, the history of schooling and subterranean studies of the abandoned school – need to be brought into conjunction. School demolition, derelict schools and abandoned school sites are an expression of the profound relation between buildings and education. The abandoned school may represent catastrophes, population mobility and severe decline, and even signify the collapse of education.

Images of the school are quite limited and often closely associated with new school buildings. Images of decaying and collapsed school buildings are unexpected and disconcerting. Images should be of light and curves, of modernity, hope, and the future. In the twentieth century, they always symbolised society. Since the 1940s in the United Kingdom and the United States of America, at least, the straight line or the curves of the wall, the windows, the desks and the amenities of the new building have been lovingly produced to show the advances of education in society, represented in the form and function of the new building. The image is evidence and not just illustrative; it is the discursive home of the future. The image was well lit; the sun shone upon it and so upon us. If this interpretation stands, then how can we view the image of the abandoned school, the school in ruins? The Spanish historian of education Agustin Escolano points the way towards the semantics of signs and their relation to the objects they show:

> the history of school architecture has to transcend physicalist, topographical and ecological approaches, to go in search of the anthropological–cultural explanations of the meanings of the symbolic spaces that are dedicated to teaching.
>
> (Escolano 2003: 60)

Rising

The twentieth century was the century of the school. Societies work at different speeds, but in European societies the school was viewed as a key feature of development in the twentieth century. Schools and their images are interesting and, at different times, show the quite different emphases the buildings and their work display. The late nineteenth-century Victorian schools are less well represented now, but exist through contemporary photographs of ordered classrooms and pedagogical objects. These schools are built of brick both inside and out, and have high ceilings and poor natural light; classrooms have either part glass partition walls (looking into a shared hall) or plain brick walls, and are filled with mass-produced desks. Society will be as ordered as the subjects in these images.

The contemporary English primary school, usually in the city suburbs, was built in the building boom of the 1950s and 1960s using the material innovations of aluminium, fibre panelling and shaped wood. Images of such schools are numerous and signify the postwar rebuilding of society with children playing and working in sunlight in friendly classrooms.

They are used as evidence of how state education has developed, and of its place as a significant force in the growth of the state. They represent modernity and modernism. The nation can be viewed as maturing and strengthening, and becoming disciplined and organised in new ways. Citizens are being cared for and over time can be seen to be well fed and clothed. The future is bright.

To build schools, architects, manufacturers and educationalists developed models that integrated new structural forms and ways of teaching and learning, all within strong financial controls. In the United States, contractors and school planners also made contributions, and the power of each partner varied at different times and places. Sometimes the architect was viewed as a synthesiser and sometimes as a crucial organiser and catalyst (Reeder 1927; Smith 1939; McClure 1942; Johnson 1964). They built the school as a symbol, the 'critical site in the project of making postwar culture' (Ogata 2008: 585), endowing 'the material and spatial qualities of the postwar schoolhouse with social and psychological importance' (Ogata 2008: 575).

At different times and places in the twentieth century, schools were erected to rebuild societies, and these buildings were endowed with enormous representative power, reflecting significant positive changes in their societies. For example, the postwar primary school had light, easy access to the exterior, natural landscaping, good access to child welfare services (school nurse, dentist and so on), and flexible spaces. These schools promised more than the older elementary schools did, not least about children's future in the new society.

Ruins

Schools are becoming redundant in every state. Sometimes, but not always, they are inhabited by new purposes; for example, they are used commercially, converted into residences or absorb new public service functions. But dereliction is present in many places and not just extreme cases, like Chernobyl and Detroit. Following Escolano, we need cultural analyses of these symbolic spaces when they crash and burn. I would argue that abandoning a school symbolises a failing society, a weakening education service and the end of a vision. It creates the negative image of its early design and build stage. This might be the case only in very particular areas or regions, but, if a new school stands for the future, doesn't a ruin of a school stand for decline and degeneration? The future is frozen in time when a ruined school is looked upon. Society is rendered immobile, faith in the future is crushed, and the state is vaporised. An abandoned school draws our attention to the often-vacuous rhetoric of the school as a site of education and learning, certainly the school as a force of moral suasion and discipline, and definitely to the disappearance of the future.[1]

The United States is a major site for school ruins, but they exist in many other places – in Ukraine (particularly the Chernobyl zone), in the United Kingdom, in Belgium and in Germany. They are abandoned because of population movements, budgetary crises, school desegregation and underperformance. Current school closures are dramatic. According to the American Association of School Administrators, about 6 per cent of schools were closed or consolidated in 2009/10, compared to 3 per cent in 2008/9. In 2011, Detroit planned to close a quarter of its schools (about 44), following the closure of 29 schools the year before. Kansas City voted to close half its schools (30) to avoid bankruptcy. Milwaukee has closed six schools a year since 2005, and Cleveland planned to close a third of its schools (Martinez 2011: 71–2). In a survey of over a thousand US school systems, there was a total of 801 abandoned secondary and elementary schools (Morgan and Morgan 1972: 213). Schools in the United Kingdom tend to continue to be used way beyond their planned life. Public (that is, state) schools have been studied that are still in operation 130 years after they were built. It is uncommon for major shifts of population to leave them behind. Smaller school populations might mean that some become redundant, but, whether in the city or the country, the buildings become converted to other uses, increasingly into housing. But it is still possible in the city to see the now unloved Victorian school, empty and ignored, with broken tiles, smashed windows and weed ridden.

These schools had previously cost the city large amounts of borrowed capital and were state of the art once. What is interesting about the abandoned schools is the way they become treated. Often they are locked and left. Libraries, laboratories and classrooms are left suddenly, as if a catastrophe has struck. Through the effect of rain and ice, or of intruders and 'scrappers', chaos arrives inside the building: books are strewn around, classrooms turned over and walls and doors smashed. Images of these buildings over time, sometimes after only a few years, show collapsed roofs, broken windows, thick mould and graffiti walls. As a symbol of the new modern education system fostered by the state, it is now useless, and its association with the optimism of past learning theories is broken. It has to be shunned. Its presence cannot become an embarrassment; it has to be stripped of its meanings.

The school ruin does not appear to be a place of meditation on the decline of the future, yet in the nineteenth century the idea of the picturesque ruin was part of the Romantic idea of the folly or aesthetically pleasing collapsed building, which gave onlookers pleasure, as Rose Macaulay pointed out:

> down the ages men have meditated before ruins, rhapsodized before them, mourned pleasurably over their ruination, it is interesting to speculate on the various strands in this complex enjoyment, on how much of it is admiration for the ruin as it was in its prime.
>
> (Macaulay 1953: xv)

This was the ruin as the past, and the decline and the fall of once mighty empires or over-bearing and imperious individuals was a subject to be observed. The ruin signifies hubris. For example, the British Empire, and its centre, London, was imagined in the nineteenth century as ruined: would London become like once powerful Rome, a set of ruins? In viewing the ruin, the viewer would introduce a sense of foreboding and fate, and the confidence of the Empire or the Reich could not still the voice of presentiment. The twentieth century is full of ruins, often the result of deliberate acts of destruction, caused by war or neglect or natural disaster. The ruin is among us and constantly produced by privatisations, population move-ments and mergers. If ruins are allowed to exist, it is clear that they will become dangerously derelict and scavenged.

Older pupils might be upset by the school ruin; others be pleased. But those who believed in education and life in an educational community can miss them. They regret the passing of their school. Two former pupils revisit their past on a school closure day:

> During the graduation breakfast . . . I figured no one would miss me for 10 minutes while I walked through every memory-filled classroom. So I slipped away from the school breakfast and tearfully wandered the halls for a personal recess from reality.
>
> Along the way, I paused at important places – the top of the staircase where I'd heard the news that President John F. Kennedy had been assassinated, the fine Victorian desk where I learned reading and arithmetic.
>
> . . .

Before the bulldozers arrived, they left with souvenirs: the roll-up map of the world left behind in an abandoned classroom and a section of slate blackboard. Later, I arranged to buy the wooden cabinet where our school textbooks were stored. . . . The classrooms, library, chapel and garden have disappeared. My set of highly emotional memories have not.

(Kelly 2010)

The town or city views the ruin not as romantic but as a problem and a danger. The closure and consequent dereliction of a school does have its own sense of foreboding, but why? Is it more than just a ruin?

The larger ruins are more sad; they have lost more. Nothing can have been more melancholy than the first shattered aspect of the destroyed abbeys before they took on the long patience and endurance of time; they were murdered bodies, their wounds gaped and bled.

(Macaulay 1953: 454)

There is nothing more desolate than a factory or shopping mall in ruin, unless it is a school. For a while the ruined school produces a melancholic gaze. Like the destroyed abbeys, there is a sense that something more than a school building has been destroyed.

For I would argue that ruined schools epitomise the dismantling or collapse of the education system, and, even if there are contradictory signs of merged schools and new buildings, the ruins now exist within powerful discourses of the end of education, the rise of individualised learning and the privatisation and consumption of schooling. They no longer have champions or close links with the expansion of the mind or of society. They are embarrassing leftovers from a thoughtful past. They represent a time of investment, of the public, of the local and of the civic. They were once beacons of learning, in Conan Doyle's phrase. Now they are the sites of the lost ambitions of society:

Dilapidated classrooms, chalkboards with their last lessons visible in dusty white smudges, vacant chairs haphazardly arranged, books and globes left behind to teach no one in empty classrooms. . . . The schools are left with hollow lockers, bookless libraries and childless classrooms and the smell of grease still hangs thick in the air of the lunchrooms . . . these were once bustling places for children to grow and learn, they now contain only remnants of that past.

(Greathouse 2007: 2)

A derelict school can be a shocking sight to an ex-pupil or an educator. To see books, toys and chalkboards lying around, broken and rotting, is deeply disturbing. School libraries are shown with their books catalogued as if still waiting for readers, and also as piles of mouldering books, a result of water and vandal damage. These are not picturesque ruins or places of meditation. Instead scrap merchants or night crawlers on ghost tours break into them and create new meanings for them, as sources of value or excitement.

But following Escolano, an optimism about the future, epitomised in the new buildings of the present, has to be connected with a pessimism about the future, epitomised by the derelict school buildings. A contemporary discourse of school improvement and performance has become so powerful that even new architecture is cloaked in it, and old schools, once the future, are rendered invisible. It is not possible that we should continue to celebrate the future and not recognise the lessons of the past. One lesson would be that the state and its education systems are fragmenting, just like the schools they built. Empires are passing; everything perishes.

Seeing an image of her old school in Baton Rouge, now derelict, an ex pupil, who attended it when it was new in the 1950s, said that once it looked like the school of the future, now it is the school of the past.

And that's my point. The future looks to be behind us now.

Note

1   It is not possible to reproduce the internet images of school dereliction across many countries in this chapter. But there are interesting collections and examples available. See, for example:

http://www.detroiturbex.com/content/schools/index.html
http://weburbanist.com/2010/06/02/abandoned-schools-out-for-summer-schools-out-forever/
http://villageofjoy.com/chernobyl-today-a-creepy-story-told-in-pictures/
http://abandonedbatonrouge.typepad.com/abandoned_baton_rouge/2009/07/lee-high-school.html
http://opacity.us/site11_bennett_school_for_girls.htm
http://opacity.us/site17_salesian_school.htm
http://opacity.us/site115_jacob_tome_school_for_boys_bainbridge_usntc.htm
http://opacity.us/site249_horace_mann_school_kc.htm
http://www.urbanghostsmedia.com/2013/07/9-abandoned-schools-universities/8/Taiwan.

Works cited

Diderot, D. (1767 [1995]) *Diderot on Art*, Volume II, *Salon of 1767*, ed. and trans. J. Goodman, New Haven and London: Yale University Press.

Escolano, A. Benito (2003) 'The School in the City: School Architecture as Discourse and as Text', *Paedagogica Historica: International Journal of the History of Education* 39, 1: 53–64.

Greathouse, L. Q. (2007) 'Hallowed Halls: Abandoned Schools of Louisiana', available at: http://etd.lsu.edu/docs/available/etd-04122007.

Johnson, M. R. A. (1964) 'How the Architect Works', *ALA Bulletin* 58, 2 (February): 109–11.

Kelly, J. (2010) 'School Day Memories Never Fade', available at: http://articles.baltimoresun.com/2010–03–06/news/bal-md.kelly06mar06_1_graduation-day-roland-park-nuns, 6 March (accessed 5 November 2014).

Macaulay, R. (1953) *Pleasure of Ruins*, London: Weidenfeld and Nicolson.

Marchand, Y. and Meffre, R. (2010) *The Ruins of Detroit*, Göttingen: Steidl.

Martinez, M. (2011) 'Learning Deserts', *The Phi Delta Kappan* 92, 5 (February): 72–3.

McClure, W. (1942) 'Trends in the Construction of School Buildings', *Review of Educational Research* 12, 2 (April): 191–202.

Morgan, T. E. and Morgan, M. J. (1972) 'Empty Schools: Myth or Reality?', *The Phi Delta Kappan* 54, 3 (November): 213–14.

Ogata, A. F. (2008) 'Building for Learning in Postwar American Elementary Schools', *Journal of the Society of Architectural Historians* 67, 4 (December): 562–91.

Reeder, W. G. (1927) 'School Architectural Service', *Educational Research Bulletin* 6, 11 (25 May): 221–8.

Smith, H. D. (1939) 'Trends in School Architecture and Design', *Review of Educational Research* 8, 4 (October): 443–50.

4

POSTWAR SCHOOLS

A personal history

Elain Harwood

I was born in 1958. I belong to the generation that struggled behind that which came of age in the 1960s, which seemed to have broken down society's traditional barriers and bagged all the interesting jobs – one of Richard Hell's 'blank generation' who wallowed in punk and unemployment as Margaret Thatcher set out to unravel the welfare state. Or so it seemed when in 1980 I was thrown off the conveyor belt of education and had to find a job. With hindsight, however, the balance of idealism and angst of the late 1970s seems a truly creative time in which to have attended university, the first of my family to do so: student grants were never so good again, and I had been suited to a schooling that had directed me exclusively to that end. Mine was a very exam-focused, classroom-based education that had survived virtually unaltered since my schools were built, all of them in the 1950s. My brother, eleven years younger (I was planned), had a very different experience. Between us we span the history of local authority education in a working-class suburban area from the early 1960s to the mid-1980s.

My first school was Trent Vale Infant School (see Figure 4.1), built in 1948–49 as Beeston Rylands Infant School, the name referring to low-lying meadows north of the River Trent that was developed from the 1900s with housing and factories, the latter for the manufacture of motor cars, boilers and telephones. Boots took a large site in the 1920s on its eastern boundary, where Sir E. Owen Williams provided the area's outstanding buildings, which I became aware of only much later. Trent Vale set the standard for my entire school education, for the Nottinghamshire county architect, E. W. Roberts, produced a design that was repeated around the county until his retirement in December 1954 (Nottinghamshire County Council 1955). Its strong proportions and blond brickwork were impressive – and remain so despite window replacement – comprising a single-storey range of six classrooms, with an assembly hall and dining hall forming a long south elevation facing a large playing field, backed by boys' and girls' cloakrooms and lavatories in wings off the corridor to the rear. Such a finger plan must always have been expensive to heat. Its light steel frame was clad in brick, with large south-facing windows and doors opening onto a terrace that provided an overflow space for more ambitious model-making activities by the bigger boys. A retaining wall and some flowerbeds provided a psychological barrier to the playing field, which was used only in the summer term. The classrooms were high and light, very large for their small clientele, with a sink for paints but otherwise entirely regular. We huddled round small tables, or perhaps groups of desks in the top classes, moving round the room in groups with our peers rather than personal friends. The white table really was white, and there sat the youngest children; I remember feeling smug when I was advanced to the dizzy heights of the yellow table where the better readers sat, but which class was that?

In the summer holidays between infants and junior school – that is, when I was seven (and still blissfully an only child) – my parents moved about three miles so that I could avoid the Rylands Junior School, a timber structure of the 1930s. Its reputation for poor results and indiscipline rested on the character of the headmaster, by turns idiosyncratic and lazy, rather than the dilapidated green and black huts, yet how often do the two seem to go hand in hand? My contemporaries loved their cosy huts; I got a primary education of ruthless efficiency led by its headmaster, Mr Ellis, with children pushed for the 11-plus intelligence tests that were our entry to grammar school. Built in 1950–52, College House in sprawling, suburban Chilwell (little more than a hamlet before 1900) repeated the formula of Trent Vale almost exactly, save for the addition of a second storey that included six more classrooms (see Figures 4.2a and 4.2b). A line of disused storerooms provided furtive fascination at break times. With more and larger children running around, it always looked tired, its exposed internal brickwork painted in bright gloss yellows and blues that dated rapidly. Standing today behind its large playing field next to a small 1950s Anglican church, however, it appears the solid heart of a chaotic piece of unplanned suburbia, created as Beeston expanded rapidly westwards after the two world wars.

FIGURE 4.1   Trent Vale Infant School, Beeston.

Photograph: Elain Harwood, 2016

FIGURE 4.2A   Chilwell College House, Chilwell.

Photograph: Elain Harwood, 2015

FIGURE 4.2B   Chilwell College House, Chilwell.

Photograph: Elain Harwood, 2014

Nottinghamshire County Council embraced with gusto R.A.B. Butler's Education Act of 1944, which established free secondary schooling for all in a three-tier system of grammar, technical grammar and secondary modern schools. It needed to, for at that date there were no grammar schools in the western half of the county, where new coal mines were being sunk and light engineering was expanding rapidly. Even in the city of Nottingham, a separate education authority, only 6.4 per cent of its children went on to grammar schools in 1944 compared with a national average of 14 per cent; of the other two smaller education authorities within the county abolished in 1944 (when their schools were transferred to the county council under the Education Act), the mining town of Mansfield did surprisingly better, the market town of Newark significantly worse (Ingles nd). With only a few scholarships to Nottingham schools available to children living in the county, it is unsurprising that my parents never got to a grammar school, but that lack led them to focus their ambitions on me.

After the war the county was one of the few to build technical schools in parallel with its grammar schools (in response to the local industries). Entrance to the technical schools was by the same intelligence test at eleven rather than by a later assessment of technical skills, so in practice they served as second-string grammar schools. Many were on shared sites, ensuring that access roads and sports facilities were not duplicated. One pair was at Worksop, where the technical school opened in 1956 and the grammar school in 1962; another was at Carlton Le Willows, east of Nottingham, where the grammar school of 1952–54 was followed by a technical grammar school to one side in 1962. The third was to the west at Bramcote, where the county council bought a country house estate in 1947, part of which was laid out as a public park and where swimming baths opened in 1965; a straggling single-storey secondary modern school for boys built in 1949 in a concealed hollow across the park quickly seemed old fashioned. The technical school opened in 1956, and the grammar school I attended followed in 1958, set proudly on rising land above the main A52 road linking Nottingham and Derby, again facing due south and with rolling grounds that included an athletics track (see Figures 4.3a and 4.3b). The technical school is also prominent from the north where there were extensive rugby and hockey pitches. (The A52 itself achieved fame in 2005 when it was named Brian Clough Way in memory of the football manager's connection with both cities; the road signs soon vanished.)

The technical grammar school was much the larger of the two, with an extra storey of classrooms and a long range of workshops and drawing offices. Its buildings were big-boned and austere, but Mr Clements the headmaster was popular and the school was relaxed – the girls wore pretty open-necked check shirts rather than the formal gold blouse and blue/grey striped tie inflicted on us. The uniform reflected the difference in tone; there was nothing relaxed about our headmaster, the grave Mr Lyons, who had ruled the school since its opening – we called him 'Ben', though in the 1970s we had no idea of the radio program 'Life with the Lyons' that had given him this epithet since it had ended in 1961.

The grammar school was architecturally smarter than the 'tech'. It was built with a mixture of concrete and concealed steelwork, clad in brick but with some timber fascias. A sixth-form privilege was to use its broad entrance, flanked by the staff room and rose bushes. A large, light foyer had stairs on either side ascending to two storeys of classrooms, gloriously bright at the front, incredibly gloomy at the rear and some even with frosted glass as the brick wall of the dining and hall range was only a few feet away. These two large spaces were linked by the stage, curtained off when not needed for overflow lunches; a brick wall was put in permanently when rising costs reduced the numbers taking school dinners. Steps led down to

FIGURE 4.3A   Bramcote Hills Grammar School, the main entrance.

Photograph: Elain Harwood, 2006

FIGURE 4.3B   Bramcote Hills Grammar School, the art and woodwork block, the art rooms with classrooms on top. The windows had been changed by the time this photograph was taken in 2006.

Photograph: Elain Harwood, 2006

the hall and down again to a large (usually freezing) gymnasium, at its most lively when used for exams. In the other direction, a dark corridor with lavatories on one side and a charming library on the other led to a loosely planned range containing two large classrooms that were the focus of geography and history teaching, and smaller classrooms set over the cookery and needlework rooms (where my career was ignominious and short-lived). A separate building linked by a covered way contained laboratories for chemistry, biology and physics, with a couple more classrooms. The limited art budget bequeathed us two faded prints, one of Albrecht Dürer's rabbit, the other a Gauguin with impossibly pink sand. The plans, dating from 1954, showed that a further block was to be added later as a sixth form (Roberts 1954). What they did not reveal was that for speed the builders used high alumina cement, so that in the middle of an extensive repair program the school closed suddenly in 2009 and these buildings were demolished. New glazing and red cladding panels, a general air of neglect and in particular a high, very blue security fence close round the school had already destroyed its character for me.

Between 1944 and 1955 the County Architect's Department under E. W. Roberts built 54 new schools, a teacher training college and two technical colleges – no mean feat (Ingles nd). Roberts was succeeded in February 1955 by Donald Gibson, formerly the dynamic chief architect of Coventry, where a dispute with his councillors led him to take the far less prestigious job at Notts. He did not stay long, but his response to the schools shortage and mining subsidence transformed not only the Notts program but changed the pattern of school building across England within two years, something not achieved by the Ministry of Education's Architects and Building Branch in nine.

In 1955, with an annual school capital budget of about £1 million, Nottinghamshire's building program was in crisis. Schools were taking up to three years to build, partly because of a shortage of bricklayers and plasterers, while up to 10 per cent of their cost went on reinforcement in case of subsidence where coal was to be extracted from beneath them – although Gibson found they were still liable to serious damage ('The Story of CLASP' 1961). He initiated a temporary program, using private architects and proprietary building systems while he brought in a new team and conducted investigations with the Ministry of Education that led to the county's own method of prefabrication, the Consortium of Local Authorities Special Programme, or CLASP, so called because he brought in other authorities to develop the program and because it was not intended only for schools. This system was devised to ride mining subsidence, thanks to a cold-rolled, pin-jointed steel frame supplied by the West Midlands firm of Brockhouse, already used by Gibson in Coventry and by the Ministry of Education for a school at Belper, Derbyshire, which the Notts team braced with springs and set on raft foundations, with a light cladding of glass and tile hanging. Henry Swain, recruited from Hertfordshire, was the leading designer. The resulting brown and cream buildings looked invitingly warm and friendly, although when pushed to two or more storeys for secondary schools, the use of different materials could look bitty; later versions of CLASP used concrete panels that were often dull, while a program for works of art did not long survive Gibson. However, small early examples of the system could be attractive, as shown by the model primary school exhibited at the 1960 Milan Triennale, labelled Mark 2 as the Brockhouse prototype was allowed to be Mark 1 (Meikle 2012).[1]

The program for 1958–59 included the additional block for Bramcote Hills, with two art rooms tucked below a group of small classrooms and a music block that was set into the steep hillside so that both floors could be accessed at grade. The classrooms were hot in summer, and the art rooms, which never caught the sun, were freezing cold in winter, while the walls were constructed of a form of plasterboard that cracked fairly easily under boy pressure and was found to be infilled with cardboard that could be chucked around the room. But they had something that the rest of the school (and my previous schools) lacked. They had style. The Mark 2 CLASP had delicate framed timber windows with complex upper lights incorporating louvres (hence the cold). The classrooms and upper cloakroom had thick, soft rubber flooring. Above all, money was spent on the internal fit-out, with built-in cupboards around the art room walls and timber floors and a stage in the music room. Cheaper windows later caused problems, but these rooms were beautiful, something never normally mentioned in relation to CLASP. The most common response is that typified by N. R. Goodwin, who wrote in 1964:

> CLASP is a heap of parts intended to be put together in many diverse ways, good or bad, but mainly indifferent. This is where the architect makes his greatest contribution, always remembering that while architecture is not an end in itself, it is not to be subordinated to the expression of the building technique alone.
>
> (Goodwin 1964: 621)

My brother's schooling was very different, save for the four years of junior school, where he too went to College House. My infant school had formal classrooms; he attended a new school built in CLASP that was entirely open plan. From the first, the brief for primary schools in CLASP allowed more space for children's activities by reducing circulation areas, encouraging a more domestic and child-sized atmosphere than hitherto. A letter of 24 May 1956 to Swain from Mary Crowley recorded that 'it is most encouraging to see you and your advisers and teachers have confirmed many of the principles that seemed to emerge from our own investigations at Amersham' (Crowley to Swain 1956).[2] The letter concentrates on planning matters, such as the size of halls and dining areas (she encouraged a larger hall – 2000 square feet – for free movement) 'and the value of moveable locker units as space dividers. The move towards open plan had its origins in Amersham Primary School, designed by Mary and David Medd for the ministry, with its defined but linked classrooms. They further developed this style in schools for Oxfordshire County Council and in designs by David Medd and John Kay at Eveline Lowe for the Inner London Education Authority in tandem with the Plowden Report of 1965. Open planning at Notts seems to have followed this common descent, suggesting that it was here rather than in its experiments with building systems that the ministry's team had its greatest influence.

Most early CLASP schools gathered classrooms around a central hall in the common 'hen and chicken' formation, but in the late 1960s the classrooms began to be broken down and team teaching in larger spaces took their place. Alderman Pounder Infants' School (see Figure 4.4) was built in Chilwell in two phases, in 1970 and 1971–72, and my brother started there at the age of five. My mother would help with the children's sewing classes occasionally, and once reported how disruptive children could run round and round the building, disturbing every class. Her memories are more nuanced now. There was a central hall for activities, with areas for assemblies, physical education and dining, flanked by two large carpeted classroom spaces for children of all ages, where they often sat on the floor, with little cubicles on the sides for individual lessons or for reading, divided by curtains. It was thus a poor relation of the larger and grander school built by West Suffolk County Council at Great Waldingfield in 1969–71, where two teaching areas flank a main hall under a space-frame roof, rather than the complex layout by Derbyshire County Council advised by the Department of Education and Science of 1972 for Chaucer Infant School, Ilkeston, Derbyshire, with its deep plan interrupted by tiny internal courts (since infilled) and light-scoops. Built of CLASP Mark 4B and clad in brick and tile, with wooden fascias and large areas of glass, Alderman Pounder School was striking for its very small size and the way in which its structure was entirely exposed; in the absence of walls, the children's art was suspended from the curtains or furniture. The children had the same teacher for their entire time at the school, in my brother's case a Mrs Davies. All the teachers were in their forties; most had had families of their own and come back to teaching – what they made of the new form of school planning we never knew.

For his secondary education, my brother got another new school. Nottinghamshire's first comprehensive school had been built in 1961–63, but a program of reorganising all its secondary education was only completed in 1978 when the three schools at Bramcote Hills and other nearby secondary moderns were paired up into split-site comprehensives. Chilwell already had a purpose-built comprehensive, however, which had taken its first students in 1970 (see Figure 4.5); had I been a year younger, my parents might have moved again, such was their wariness of mixed ability teaching. My parents' expectations for my brother were as high as, if not higher than, they had been for me, but he seemed unwilling to shine and was happy enough with the 'comp' with its excellent sports facilities. 'He's not Elain', said

FIGURE 4.4 Alderman Pounder Infants' School, Chilwell.

Photograph: Elain Harwood, 2016

FIGURE 4.5 Chilwell Comprehensive School.

Photograph: Elain Harwood, 2013

Mrs Langley, the one teacher who taught us both; even the most experienced teachers seem unable to spot late developers.

Two features made the Nottinghamshire comprehensive schools distinctive. One was the development in tandem of community sports facilities, partly as a response to the growth in adult education and leisure hours. The idea of shared facilities had begun in the 1930s with Henry Morris's village colleges in Cambridgeshire, but Nottinghamshire's model was Wyndham School in Egremont, Cumberland, built for the children of the scientists working at Sellafield. At Notts the accent on shared sites was strongly weighted towards sport, encouraged by David Barnes, the county's gifted chief adviser on physical education. He believed that PE had become dominated internally by Scandinavian gym equipment, such as expensive climbing frames and beams, and externally by team games; he sought a wider concept of physical education that would be of greater value to students in later life. The Department of Education and Science issued a circular in 1965 exhorting authorities to use expensive education buildings more widely, which, coupled with Circular 10/65 calling for comprehensive schools, prompted Swain to work with the education officer W. G. Lawson and the small second-tier authorities to build sports facilities that could be used by the adjoining new school in the daytime and by the whole community in the evenings. The first of these paired complexes of school was at Bingham, where a swimming pool and sports hall was opened in 1969 by the Minister for Sport, Dennis Howell. It was followed by a similar development at Carlton Cavendish School in the outer Nottingham suburbs in 1970.

The other, less distinctive, feature at Notts's comprehensives was the building of separate blocks for the first two year groups – that is, for children aged eleven to thirteen. This was a clever way of enlarging an existing grammar or secondary modern for the bigger intake required by comprehensives or, as at Chilwell, of building a school in phases, while breaking down the scale of a very large school and easing in the younger students by degree. The main part of Chilwell Comprehensive was built in 1969–71 between Chilwell and a smaller village called Attenborough; it remains cut off by unattractive roads and fields from other buildings, and its site is always muddy despite a new drainage pond. The main school is a smaller version of Bingham, as is the sports hall – there is no swimming pool here. Far more interesting is the lower school built of CLASP Mark 5, completed in 1978 but used for its proper purpose of housing the first and second years only in 1980 – my brother's intake. Mark 4 had first pushed CLASP to use storey-high concrete panels that gave it a more sophisticated look, for offices and for York University as well as for schools. Mark 5 was cheaper, with fewer components and simpler site operations than Mark 4, yet was more sophisticated in appearance, developed with computer-aided design in mind and with projecting 'oriel' windows in addition to the pyramidal roof lights developed for York and a feature of larger CLASP buildings in the 1960s. Mark 5 was first used at Dalestorth Primary School at Sutton-in-Ashfield in 1971–72; 80 per cent of its buildings were clad in concrete panels, given a white, red, grey, brown or green aggregate finish in the casting, with plastic coated windows from the first, designed for ease of maintenance (*CLASP Fifteenth Annual Report* 1972: 19–21).

The lower school at Chilwell has all these features, including the bay windows and pointed rooflights (see Figure 4.6). It was also open plan, developed around a central resource centre on two levels, with five areas for team teaching gathered round it and separated, specialised laboratories for science beyond. In 1980 the staff introduced an integrated studies course for the first years, incorporating elements of history, geography, religious studies and English, to exploit the possibilities of the layout, arranged so that parallel forms follow the course at the

FIGURE 4.6   Chilwell Lower School.

Photograph: Elain Harwood, 2013

same time in three adjoining bases under three or four teachers, to encourage team teaching, the formation of groups of varied size and practical or investigatory work by the students (Burns 1980: 983–97). Yet as early as 1984 this was abandoned and the building became a sixth form, until 2008 known as Lakeview College, and this is why, uniquely, the open plan survives. Students work on computers and laptops, with books and other resource material to hand, without disturbing those engaged in tutorials round large tables on the upper floor, each one visibly in sight of the next. It succeeds because sixth form groups are small, and the murmur of lessons distils a working ethos across the computer areas. The staff and students are unusually proud of their building, by Nottinghamshire standards, because of the rare formal quality to the elevations (which show Mark 5 at its best), their relationship to the adjoining pond and the careful detailing of the central area, particularly the open stairwell with its fine handrails.

My little brother was thus educated while open planning was at its height in a moderately progressive local authority, but these methods were already coming into question. The Labour Prime Minister Jim Callaghan in 1976 commissioned a 'Yellow Book', *School Education in England: Problems and Initiatives*, which studied progressive reforms in primary schools in the face of the series of 'Black Papers' produced by right-wing educationalists and politicians from 1969 (the last of the five, reinforcing earlier demands for more parental choice in education, appeared only in 1977) that were widely disseminated in the right-wing national press. Neville Bennett's report on primary school teaching methods in Lancaster, *Teaching Styles and Pupil Progress*, in 1976 concluded that whole class teaching, regular testing and competition produced better results than those taught using informal methods. Its conclusions caught the headlines when staff at William Tyndale School in north London lost control of their pupils, leading a public inquiry to conclude that teachers should be made more accountable.

A green paper in 1978, 'Education in Schools: A Consultative Document', concluded that 'in the right hands [the so-called child-centred approach] has produced confident, happy and relaxed children, without any sacrifice of the 3Rs or other accomplishments – indeed, with steady improvement in standards'. But it suggested that some teachers had insufficient experience or ability to make the system work (Gillard 2015).

My brother got the last laugh. After leaving school aged sixteen with no qualifications and little career guidance, he thrived at the local college of further education, completing an Ordinary National Diploma (OND) in computing with flying colours, and after more advanced technical training he is now technical director of a leading firm of surveyors.

Notes

1   I am grateful for background information from a conversation with Alan Meikle, formerly deputy county architect to Henry Swain.
2   The letter is also notable for questioning the appropriateness of separate handicraft activities for boys and girls, and for being signed Mary Crowley rather than Mary Medd.

Works cited

Burns, Peter (1980) 'Building Study: Chiwell Lower School, Nottinghamshire', *Architects' Journal* 172, 47 (19 November): 983–97.
CLASP Fifteenth Annual Report (1972) Nottingham: Nottinghamshire County Council.
Crowley, Mary to Henry Swain (1956) CC/AR/4/1, Nottinghamshire Archives.
Gillard, Derek (2015) 'Education in England, a Brief History', available at: http://www.educationeng land.org.uk.
Goodwin, N. R. (1964) 'The Role of the Architect in CLASP', *The Builder* 206, 6305 (20 March): 620–3.
Ingles, R. E. (nd) 'The Development of Education in Nottinghamshire over the last One Hundred Years', unpublished history, CC/ED/5/35/13, Nottinghamshire Archives.
Meikle, A. (2012) Personal Conversation with the Author (16 January).
Nottinghamshire County Council (1955) Sites and Buildings Committee CC3/12/20/1, Nottinghamshire Archives.
Roberts, E. W. (1954) Plans of Bramcote Hills Grammar School CC/AR/2/5, Nottinghamshire Archives.
'The Story of CLASP' (1961) *Architects' Journal* 133, 3454 (29 June): 953–60.

PART II
School buildings

5

THE CLASSROOM IS ANOTHER PLACE?

Ernest J. Kump's 'ideal' learning environments for Californian schools 1937–1962

Philip Goad

What constitutes the ideal learning environment? This question preoccupied many school designers for the first half of the twentieth century. One of these designers, the American architect Ernest J. Kump Jr (1911–99), made the search for an optimised classroom space an integral component of his long career of designing elementary and secondary schools in the US state of California. From the mid-1930s until the early 1960s, despite postwar shifts in educational pedagogies that had radical implications for how the classroom as a learning environment was conceived, Kump's 'finger plan' schools came to define the typical image of the postwar Californian school. Further, they also represented the sometimes uneasy meeting of an environmental idealism in relation to the individual classroom with the hard-nosed rationalism of efficient, economic construction techniques and the contingencies of a large-scale, expandable school campus.

Kump's dual interests in standardisation and repetition and the environmentally 'perfect' classroom were pursued to a logical endpoint – to the extent that by 1964, with the opening of the Henry Gunn Senior High School in Palo Alto, Kump's ideal classroom comprised a fully air-conditioned space with no windows. It was a long way from where Kump had begun. This chapter outlines the genesis of Kump's search, from the translation of a Utopian ideal where teacher and pupil interacted in an indoor–outdoor experience and where contact was made with sun, shade and nature, to its complete obverse some thirty years later.

A modernist ideal

In 1926, Viennese émigré modernist architect Richard Neutra (1892–1970), then resident in Los Angeles, designed a hypothetical ideal metropolis, Rush City Reformed. In striking counterpoint to his vision of marching high-rise slabs, elevated pedestrian bridges and ramped highways, Neutra set an accompanying vision of an ideal school within a separate verdant landscape complete with watercourse and winding paths (Hines 1982: 61). The design with its oval plan of linked classrooms, labelled as Ring Plan School (*Ringplanschule*), also featured in Neutra's book *Amerika: Neues Bauen in der Welt* (1930) and was included in the New York Museum of Modern Art's seminal 'Modern Architecture: International Exhibition' in

1932 (Neutra 1930). Key to Neutra's school was its series of open-air classrooms, each with clerestory lighting and access to individual outdoor teaching spaces connecting to the natural world.

Neutra's design determinants for the individual classroom, largely environmental rather than pedagogical, were not new. As Anne-Marie Châtelet has described, the development of open-air schools from the 1890s was driven by a focus on sunlight, air and ventilation with the aim of fostering a healthy body – which by the 1930s came also to be associated with a healthy mind (Châtelet 2008: 108; see also Kinchin and O'Connor 2012: 88–107). Neutra's ideas were realised in the seven classrooms added to the Corona Avenue School in Bell, Los Angeles, in 1935. A celebrated aspect of Neutra's addition was the use of lightweight timber and steel construction, although this choice was externally determined. The passing of the Field Act in April 1933, following the devastating Long Beach earthquake the month before, mandated that all school buildings be earthquake resistant and gave rise to an extensive program of new school building and upgrades across California. Most were single storey, and most employed lightweight construction, all seismically determined (Alquist 2007: 7).

Neutra's classrooms at Corona Avenue School were innovative in their combination of progressive design elements: spaces were ventilated and lit from two sides (hence the term 'bilateral' lighting) via clerestory windows above an open-air covered way on one side and on the other by full-height sliding glass walls. Adjustable roll-down blinds controlled direct sunlight, and each classroom opened onto its own 'garden' classroom. Widely publicised at the time of its completion and since, Neutra's classrooms had national and international impact: Neutra built versions of his open-air schools in Puerto Rico and Guam in the 1940s and early 1950s; Texas architect and educational specialist William Caudill used Neutra's ideas as an exemplar in his internationally influential studies, 'Space for Teaching' (1941) and *Toward Better School Design* (1954) (Caudill 1941, 1954); and their influence was evident in numerous examples illustrated in Swiss architect Alfred Roth's multiple editions of *The New School* (Roth 1950).

Variation on the model

However, not all architects accepted Neutra's model uncritically. One of these was Berkeley- and Harvard-trained Ernest J. Kump Jr, son of an architect who also specialised in schools ('Some Recent Work of Mr Ernest J. Kump' 1916). Kump's connection with Richard Neutra is difficult to ignore. In 1937, in Bakersfield, Kump's hometown, Neutra had completed the Davis house at 2914 West 21st Street. Just a block away at 3109 West 20th Street, Kump had designed the Sill house (1938), for the client of his much larger Sill commercial offices (1938) in downtown Bakersfield. It is almost certain that Kump knew of the Davis house and especially the school work of its architect. Neutra's experimental school in Corona Avenue, Bell, Los Angeles, had been published in *Architectural Record* in June 1936 and a year earlier in *Architect and Building News* ('Experimental School, Bell, California' 1936: 453–6; 'Public Elementary School, Los Angeles' 1935: 226–7).

Between 1937 and 1942, the Fresno-based firm of Franklin & Kump reconfigured Neutra's model classroom in a series of important but little known modernist schools for the agricultural communities of Reedley, Teague and Fowler near Fresno in California's San Joaquin Valley. The most important of these was Fowler Elementary School (1938) (see Figures 5.1 and 5.2[1]), which replaced the earlier Fowler Grammar School that had been destined for destruction since the 1933 earthquake because it did not meet the new regulations (*Fowler Ensign* 1938; McFarland

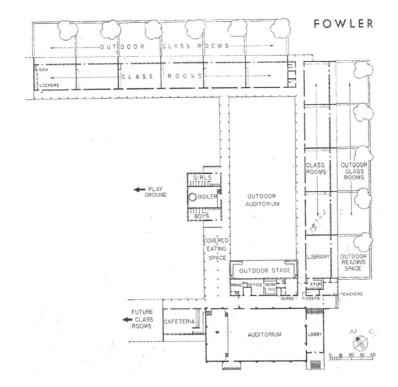

FIGURE 5.1   Plan, Fowler Elementary School, Fowler, California, USA, 1938.

Architect: Franklin & Kump

Source: 'Fowler Elementary School, Fowler, California' (1939)

FIGURE 5.2   Street view, Fowler Elementary School, Fowler, California, USA, 1938.

Architect: Franklin & Kump

Photograph: Philip Goad, 2010

1972: 34). The new school was planned around a central grassed courtyard, which doubled as an outdoor auditorium ('Fowler Elementary School' 1939: 120–2). Two 'finger' wings, each of five classrooms, formed an L-shape and half the quadrangle enclosure. The other half was formed by a covered way, with girls' and boys' bathroom blocks attached, and the final leg of the L completed by administrative offices, a nurse's station and an outdoor stage for the quadrangle auditorium. Key aspects of Kump's future school designs are present. An indoor auditorium and cafeteria were then attached to the administration block, and the school's main entry was at the corner where the two elements met.

At this point, it is useful to compare Kump's 1938 school with that of Neutra's 1935 Bell school. Both were single storey, and both adopted structural systems designed to cope with seismic disturbance. Both employed the so-called 'finger plan', but the Bell school was much smaller. Both had standardised classroom sizes (Neutra's $23 \times 38 \times 12$ feet high [$7 \times 11.5 \times 3.65$ metres]; Kump's based on 4-foot [1.2-metre] modules, essentially $24 \times 40 \times 12$ feet high [$7.3 \times 12.2 \times 3.65$ metres]). Both had two doors per classroom providing access from an open-air corridor. Because construction at Fowler was based on the 4-foot module, all cross partitions were non-load-bearing, thus permitting intermediate classroom partitions to be interchangeable.

In design, Kump had adopted Neutra's section. Both schools had bilateral natural lighting, open corridors and major expanses of glazing on the other side of the classroom from the corridor entry. Both had clerestory lighting (hoppers at Bell, louvres at Fowler) above the external corridor canopy. Both had wings with walls that extended out and implied an outdoor teaching space, suggested on Neutra's plan and labelled as 'outdoor classrooms' on Kump's. On the generously glazed window wall of the classroom, both schemes had vertical adjustable drop shades or blinds. Neutra employed steel sash and frame glazing, with a huge sliding panel to allow the classroom to open up to the outdoors. There were no windows that could be opened in the fixed multi-paned areas of glass. Kump employed two French doors, framing and sashes were in timber, and his glass wall had multiple opening sashes; below sill level were panel radiators and a sub-floor service trench for future maintenance and upgrading. There was no indication of heating in the Bell school and probably no need given the climate in Los Angeles. Neutra's roof had a deep section formed by a timber truss with a suspended ceiling. Kump's, by contrast, was slimmer in section, also ventilated and insulated, but sloped to follow the roof pitch. Both had sloping eaves.

Where the two schools differed was in orientation. Neutra faced his classrooms with the major glass wall to the west. Kump, by contrast (and he was to make much of this in subsequent writings), more practically, faced his classrooms to the north or east. This reduced direct sunlight and glare, maximised indirect light and reduced the need to provide internal curtains. What Kump had achieved at Fowler was to make a practicable system of the Neutra model. It was this systematising and economic rationalisation of the structure and idea that made the Neutra model ultimately flexible and allowed it to be developed further. The key advances made by Kump were that he had transformed Neutra's concept into a workable constructive solution and that he was able to foresee the need for larger planning and site-related consequences of school plant growth.

Refining the new model

For Kump, then, Neutra's work represented a model to be critically tested and re-evaluated again and again. In all his subsequent school designs, Kump placed particular emphasis on

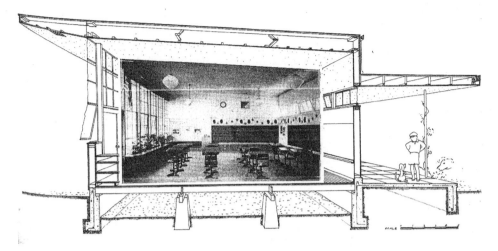

FIGURE 5.3   Sectional perspective, Ducor Elementary School, Ducor, California, USA, 1938.

Architect: Franklin & Kump

Source: 'Elementary School, Ducor Union School District, Ducor, California' (1943)

refining the building section and its construction, and optimising natural lighting, heating and ventilation.

For example, at Ducor Elementary School (1939–40), also in California's San Joaquin Valley, Kump changed the section, placing clerestory windows under the corridor roof to achieve construction economy (see Figure 5.3). Inside, built-in lockers, sink and bench spaces, as well as a built-in planter box and bookshelves and a private study alcove, suggested that the classroom might function in the John Dewey sense of 'learning by doing' as an activity space and not simply as a traditional classroom ('Manufactured, Prefabricated, Classroom-office-kindergarten Units' 1943: 64–7). These features all indicate Kump's emerging dedication to notions of flexibility in space and time as related to a curriculum that might also be flexible and dynamic. Kump sought a generic classroom space that could realistically accommodate several different pedagogical approaches.

With each new school design, Franklin & Kump progressively moved beyond the Neutra diagram, using the firm's growing experience, the changing needs of school clients and technological developments in the construction process to work through design issues. Kump's design efforts were directed towards perfecting an idealised learning space that was environmentally controlled in all aspects: light, air, temperature and ventilation.

From model to module

By 1942, as the United States was being drawn further into World War II, Franklin & Kump had redefined the face of educational infrastructure for California's San Joaquin Valley. However, it was a school on the outskirts of San Francisco that would bring Kump national attention, largely because of its size, completeness, refinement and the adaptability of its 'flexible' classrooms. As a completely new stand-alone plant, it was a highly organised diagram of accommodation and circulation, similar to the rational organisation accorded at the time to a hospital or factory ('Advanced California School Meets Limited Budget' 1941: 82–7; *Architect and Engineer* June 1941: 32–3; 'Pioneer School has proved the Value of its Scientific Design' 1949: 104–6).

Completed in late 1940, the first stage of Acalanes Union High School (1939–40) at Lafayette, just east of the Berkeley hills, was the apotheosis of the finger plan school. A series of finger wings with external corridors were oriented *Zeilenbau*-style (ribbon-like) with all classrooms facing north and each finger bisected by low-roofed connecting walkways. Classrooms featured bilateral lighting, steel-framed windows, acoustic ceilings, linoleum floors and the typical steel-framed 'loft' construction sitting above a suspended concrete slab, which allowed easy access and upgrade of services. All planning conformed to the 4-foot module, and a further innovation was that dividing partitions between each classroom were standard 4-foot (1.2 metre) wide and 10-foot 6-inch (3 × 0.15 metre) high natural plywood clad panels, able to be moved at will should classroom sizes change. Kump had systematised almost every element of the building, a strategy that he would shortly put to use during wartime in his school for the new township devoted to defence industries at Carquinez Heights (1941) ('War Needs Community Facilities' 1942: 47–8) and his self-patented Pre-Built Schools for the Standard Engineering Corporation (1945) ('Manufactured, Prefabricated, Classroom-office-kindergarten Units' 1943: 52–5; 'Building with Wood' 1944–45; 'Prefabricated Schoolhouse' 1945: 182). Prefabrication, modular planning and the efficient construction of a school as if it was a barracks or military hospital were the natural outcome of wartime circumstance; it was a case of production over pedagogy.

By 1946, *Architectural Record*'s editor Douglas Haskell summarised Kump's design approach as a 'full service [that] involves *system* as the first pre-requisite, and the outstanding characteristic of Mr Kump himself is the ability, *by clear-headed analysis, to reduce intermediate steps to a routine*, so that attention can be focussed on special problems and on new creation' (Haskell 1946: 85; italics in original). Haskell was referring to Kump's belief in providing an educational space that was completely flexible and enabled students to learn in any way the teacher desired. As Amy Ogata has observed, the term 'flexibility' became a leitmotif in US school design in the immediate postwar period (Ogata 2008: 568–9; see also Ogata 2013: 115–16). However, the idea of 'flexibility' did not reflect any specific change in educational pedagogy. Rather, the concept of 'flexibility' largely came to stand in for and justify the repetitive outcomes of the dramatic postwar boom in school construction across the United States, a demand that matched in scale and need the postwar demand for housing.

Kump's schools fitted the bill. His standardised structural grid (4 feet [1.2 metres]), his 'loft' spaces capable of re-division in any manner, a plan that did not interfere spatially with structure and windows and doors which were interchangeable, comprised an ideal kit of parts. Educational equipment was not attached to essential structure (not even the chalkboards). Further to this, the idea that the teacher might not need to control light, heat or ventilation meant that Kump was searching for an idealised environment within which anything might take place. It was a goal that Kump would pursue over the next twenty years: the creation of a universal space for teaching that was environmentally and spatially flexible.

However, one school stands out as a final tribute to the Neutra model before Kump began to refine his model classroom. In 1944, Kump was commissioned to design White Oaks Elementary School at San Carlos on the San Francisco Peninsula (see Figure 5.4). Here Kump outdid Neutra. He oriented the single finger wing so that the large steel-framed classroom windows faced north, meaning there was no need for retractable blinds and no problem with glare. Each classroom, including the kindergarten room, had its own dedicated garden, an outdoor shelter with benches and outdoor sinks. Each classroom was 30-foot (9.15-metre) square, giving ultimate teaching flexibility, and each had radiant heating by copper piping

FIGURE 5.4   Classroom courtyard, White Oaks Elementary School, San Carlos, California, 1944.

Architect: Ernest J. Kump Co.

Photograph: Philip Goad, 2010

in the floor slabs, a first for the Kump office. Each classroom had bilateral lighting, and here Kump employed the tactic he'd earlier used at Carquinez Heights School, largely for economic expediency: a single roof covered the outdoor corridor, the classroom and part of the outdoor classroom, overlapping with the lower child-scaled parasol roof of the outdoor classroom. The structure was an elegant frame of steel Lally columns that sat free of the walls and steel beams that cantilevered and tapered to a point, thus eliminating the need for columns at the outer edge of the external corridor. It was a simple but extremely effective section, reducing even further the structural lightness of Neutra's (and Kump's for that matter) earlier designs. With White Oaks, it seemed that Kump had realised his perfect finger plan and classroom type ('First Postwar Schools' 1946: 100–7).

From bilateral to trilateral

After 1945, Kump began to hatch other ideas: a series of schools that combined a single roof form, the introduction of what Kump called 'tri-lateral lighting', refinements in heating and ventilation, and efficiencies in construction aimed at achieving a fully controllable learning environment. Franklin, Kump & Falk's Laurel Creek Elementary School in San Mateo (see Figure 5.5) was designed in 1945, and even as it was being constructed in 1947 it attracted national attention. Touted as 'a school type so different as to be virtually new', the school had a number of innovations ('"Tri-lateral" Lighting, Panel Heating' 1947: 93). For his ideal

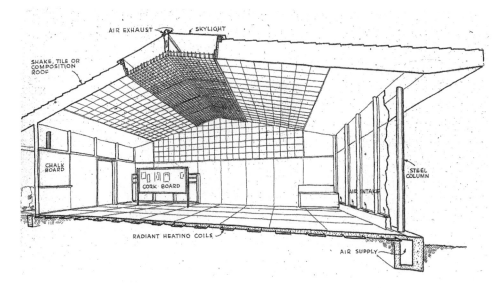

FIGURE 5.5   Sectional perspective, Laurel Creek Elementary School, San Mateo, California, 1945–8.
Architect: Franklin, Kump & Falk
Source: 'Tri-Lateral Lighting, Panel Heating' (1947)

32-foot (9.75-metre) deep, almost square in plan, classrooms, Kump needed additional natural light. His solution was direct: a skylight running down the centre of the classroom's length, in addition to light from both sides (from the corridor clerestory and the major glazed wall to the north) – hence Kump's newly coined term, trilateral lighting.

The design was predicated on Kump's finger plan, a single-loaded corridor and a single-storey building. Kump folded the flat roof of the White Oaks cross-section into a gable while retaining the covered way to the south and large areas of glass to the north. He then inserted the linear skylight following the ridge of the classroom ceiling. The loft construction principle was retained, and the skylight was given a white painted plywood eggcrate diffusing grid, which followed the ceiling line. The room could also be widened, potentially achieving better educational outcomes, according to the faith at the time in the pedagogical virtues of the square planned classroom, where teacher visibility, auditory access and flexible furniture arrangement could be maximised.

The other innovation at Laurel Creek School was the heated and fully air-conditioned classrooms – creating a hermetically sealed and controlled learning environment. This predates the Belaire Elementary School, San Angelo, Texas (1955), claimed by Ogata to be the first elementary school to be air-conditioned in the United States (Ogata 2013: 131). All windows were fixed with provision for fully automatic ventilation as well as heating. Laurel Creek was the sixth Kump school to have radiant heating coils placed in the slab. Air outlets were located in the low window sills with air supply (for cool or supplementary warm air) provided by a duct within a long edge beam along the major window wall, and the newly featured skylight had an extra function. A linear vent at the apex of the gable served as the air exhaust for the classroom. Heating was zoned for individual classrooms, and a pneumatic thermostat operating a pneumatic bypass valve could control temperatures. Kump argued for this feature on the basis of teachers' freedom; avoiding issues of lighting and temperature control enabled students to have a completely controlled environmental experience in which the brain might develop ('"Tri-lateral" Lighting, Panel Heating' 1947: 93).

In examining better techniques for providing natural light in the classroom, Kump was, of course, not alone. The problem of adequate lighting was seen as a key element in the provision of ideal learning conditions, and it was discussed constantly in various US school building forums, and especially within professional and educational journals. Maynard Lyndon, who had a practice in Michigan and designed many schools there before moving to Los Angeles in 1942, directed much of his attention towards mediating the strength of the Californian sun. In 1946, he also was exploring trilateral lighting through the use of louvres and baffles to diffuse light evenly across the square classrooms that had come to be the acceptable shape of a teaching space. He proposed, for example, at Saugus Union School in Santa Clarita, California, the use of a very large skylight (half the roof area), which was louvred immediately inside the glass then had a large ceiling space before an eggcrate grid was inserted at ceiling level ('A Radical Departure in Daylighting' 1946: 120–1). Indeed, Lyndon's experiments should be seen as precursors to Kump's later development of his 'Environmental Control Grid' in 1960. By 1949, Perkins & Will had developed their 'Louverall' egg-crate ceiling at Lincoln School, Park Ridge, Illinois (c. 1948) (Perkins and Cocking 1949: 150–1). At Laurel Creek School, photographer Roger Sturtevant could not help but comment on the teacher wearing sunglasses inside. She had forgotten to take them off given the brilliant lighting in the classroom ('A New School Cycle Gracefully Begun' 1948: 85). Today, almost all Kump's gable line roof lights have been covered over because of perceived excessive brightness and glare.

Kump's office subsequently produced numerous elementary and high schools on the San Francisco Peninsula and in regional California that adopted the finger plan, gable roof and new trilateral lighting, heating and ventilation.[2] Various modifications were made, but on the whole this type, for the moment, satisfied Kump's eagerness to keep inventing. Between 1938 and 1950, Kump's office completed more than fifty schools. In British school architects C. G. Stillman and R. C. Cleary's internationally influential book, *The Modern School* (1949), among other images of Kump-designed schools, Stillman used the kindergarten room of Laurel Creek Elementary School as the final image in his account of contemporary school design; he captioned Kump's school as an exemplar of 'adequate light, spaciousness and interior finish' (Stillman and Cleary 1949: 150). That same year, Kump's Acalanes Union High School, Carmel High School, Antioch High School, Sunnybrae School and Laurel Elementary School also featured in Lawrence Perkins's (of Perkins & Will) important postwar book, *Schools* (Perkins and Cocking 1949).

A shift in approach: the cluster

In October 1953, *Architectural Forum* published the outcomes of a forum its editor, Douglas Haskell, had organised among school architects and educators. Kump was notably absent, away on holiday in Europe. It is almost certain, however, that he took significant notice of the outcomes of the discussions, because by 1955 he had completely discarded the finger plan. *Architectural Forum* gathered together in New York a group of architects, engineers, school consultants, city and state school officials, and representatives from industry and academia for a meeting on school economy at a time of mass growth in the school system. Key figures in this informal national network of school design were present: William Caudill, Lawrence Perkins, Donald Barthelme and John Lyon Reid (who had worked in Kump's office) were among the architects; there was also the well-known acoustics engineer Robert Newman (of Bolt, Beranek & Newman) and N. L.

Engelhardt Jr (a prominent educational consultant and author).[3] Haskell presided over the event. The group came up with a detailed list of cost-cutting measures, but what was more interesting was the series of case studies following the group's conclusions and its '50 ideas for school house economy'. There was also an important announcement: 'The cluster is 1953's biggest news in schoolhouse planning (forecast in AF, Oct. 52). This is the approach that pioneering thinkers in design and education are exploring today beyond all else' ('Cluster Plan' 1953: 127). The growing interest in the 'cluster', the tendency to create separate 'houses' of one to eight rooms, was a pedagogical and spatial reaction against the grouping of classrooms along corridors – in short, a reaction against the finger plan which Kump had perfected as a type and helped popularise. Administration, general activities and other much larger spaces like auditoria and gymnasiums were located in a 'main house' or series of larger, scaled-up versions of 'houses'.

Architectural Forum succinctly listed the advantages of the cluster: child-size scale; intimacy; a non-institutional, unregimented atmosphere; grouping into 'age' neighbourhoods; and the semi-isolation of disparate activities. The planning and construction approach was simple: lighting, ventilation, grading and framing were all potentially more economical. Ceilings could be lowered, there were no corridors to build, and one could have units independently heated and cooled. It was a combination of moves towards a child-centred pedagogy and the attractive prospect of saving money in design.

The magazine published a series of examples to prove their point, notably Caudill, Rowlett, Scott, Neff & Associates' Phyllis Wheatley Elementary School, Port Arthur, Texas (1952–53), where a cluster consisted of four square-planned back-to-back classrooms with a central heating and plumbing core. A second cluster was separated by a broad breezeway, and over the two clusters a 'big inexpensive umbrella' – an all-encompassing and simple flat roof – was slung. Other examples illustrated were by John Carl Warnecke for additions to White Oaks School (which must have riled Kump); Heathcote Elementary School at Scarsdale, New York, by Perkins & Will; and a prefabricated school in Kidderminster, England, by Yorke, Rosenberg & Mardall. All indicated a new architectural freedom for the publicly funded school, and an opening up of architectural possibilities as well as a loosening of the determinism of the teaching space. It also meant the possibility of a cluster comprising one very large teaching space. The cluster in many respects harked back to the idealism embodied in the Crow Island School of 'little houses' in Winnetka, Illinois (1940), designed by Perkins, Wheeler & Will and Eliel and Eero Saarinen. Here, the small buildings grouped together fostered individuality and easy access to outdoor space – and the promise that the complex could be extended. While *Architectural Forum* described three other types of school design – the loft plan, the core plan and the zoned plan[4] – it was the cluster concept that would interest Kump most and where his energies would be focused in his next sequential modification of his own personalised system of school building. By publishing Kump's 'regionalism' of school form (where he advocated single-level finger plans for elementary schools and multistorey schools for older students) in the same issue, the journal and the mini-symposium had virtually laid down a challenge to which Kump could not help but respond ('Cluster Plan' 1953: 166–71).

In 1955, when *Architectural Forum* published another issue devoted to school building design, titled 'Schools: A Look Backward and Forward', it undertook a detailed design evaluation of the Crow Island School, outlining its positive and negative attributes and hailing its relevance to contemporary school design. The article described it as 'the most influential school of modern times' ('Editorial. Schools' 1955: 129). The Kump office was represented in the same issue by the gable-roofed, trilaterally lit North Hillsborough School, described as 'another mature and accomplished performance' and 'the culminating school, the most refined example to date of the leading plan type of the forties: the finger plan and its adaptations'. Such backhanded praise, which in effect suggested he was almost a decade out of date, would have stung Kump, especially as in the next breath the journal stated that the classroom additions to the Jane Phillips Elementary School, Bartlesville, Oklahoma, by Caudill, Rowlett, Scott & Associates (also shown in the same issue) 'represents the emergence of what promises to be the dominant scheme in the fifties: the quadruplex cluster'. A further comparison between a finger plan school and one 'for come what-will in educational policy' clearly indicated a shift in American thinking about high school pedagogy and planning towards the notion of a campus, indicative not just of gradually relaxing attitudes towards the economics of school building but of a greater embrace of the student experience of the complete environment of the school and its grounds. The aerial photograph of Ketchum, Gina & Sharp's Senior High School at Northport, Long Island, emphasised *Architectural Forum*'s view that '[f]or the campus plan, outdoors is the matrix; the important focal points move indoors' with discrete 'clusters' of six classrooms, separate large 'houses' accommodating the auditorium and another housing the gymnasium. The library was given honorific form as a circle in the plan and was the focal point of landscape fully designed by landscape architects Tregenza & Briglia. Significantly, the Northport school held a glimpse of what Kump and landscape architects Sasaki Walker would later achieve in their masterwork, Foothill College, Los Altos (1958–62) (see Figure 5.6), which was not a high school but a community college campus that comprised

FIGURE 5.6   External view, Foothill College, Los Altos, California, USA, 1958–62.

Architect: The Office of Ernest J. Kump

Photograph: Philip Goad, 2010

discrete clusters of seminar rooms and lecture theatre buildings integrated and unified by a sophisticated landscape design and which architectural critic Allan Temko would describe as the 'Acropolis of the West' (Temko 1962: 54).

Kump's clusters and the 'Environmental Control Grid'

It did not take long for Kump to respond to this change of mood in school planning. In 1957, the Miramonte High School in Orinda, California (see Figure 5.7), was completed, the first of what Kump called his basic space module (BSM) schools, where he used 'big units of space as his building blocks' ('The Space-module School' 1957: 124–7). These 'big units' were 56-foot (17-metre) square. Each could be subdivided into four standard classrooms, left completely open internally or in various internal combinations, and then arranged in rows, clusters or mall schemes depending on topography or educational requirements – for example, when larger spaces were needed for science laboratories, domestic science rooms, libraries and art rooms. The key behind Kump's idea was that the basic space module could be square, round or rhomboidal and that any structural, mechanical or modular component design could be used so long as it was completely flexible inside ('The Space-module School' 1957: 124–7). Overhead at Miramonte, low-pitched gable roofs cantilevered to form covered ways without the obstruction of columns, and the major structural element was a central steel girder forming the ridge beam and supported by two reinforced concrete 'hollow' piers that contained mechanical and service areas. The principle was in essence a highly serviced parasol roof, complete with louvred skylights supplemented by linear banks of fluorescent lighting.

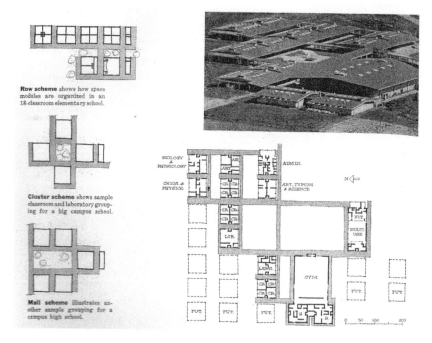

FIGURE 5.7   Kump's 'Basic Space Module' at Miramonte High School, Orinda, California, USA, 1957.

Architect: The Office of Ernest J. Kump

Source: 'The Space-module School' (1957)

The logical next step for Kump was to develop an entire system where most of the environmental servicing for the classroom interior would be delivered from above. By July 1962, Kump had sought patents for what he called the 'Environmental Control Grid', a completely integrated suspended three-dimensional lighting, air-conditioning and electrical service grid that could be fitted into new or existing buildings, of any building type (see Figure 5.8). The development of the ceiling system had been sponsored by the Ford Foundation's Educational Facilities Laboratories (EFL) and was tested in a 35 × 48 foot (10.66 × 14.6 metre) classroom at Cubberley Hall, Stanford University, in December 1962 ('Western Sky Industries' 1962; see also 'An "Environmental Grid"' 1962) and later at San Jose East Side Union High School. Kump's system, based on a 4-foot square modular grid, allowed for complete flexibility in that demountable and operable walls could be readily used within the system:

> Any loft space divided by walls or partitions, regardless of the dimensions, will result in the space so divided, having all of the proper environmental conditions required. This provides the utmost of flexibility and keeps operating costs under control.
>
> ('Western Sky Industries' 1962)

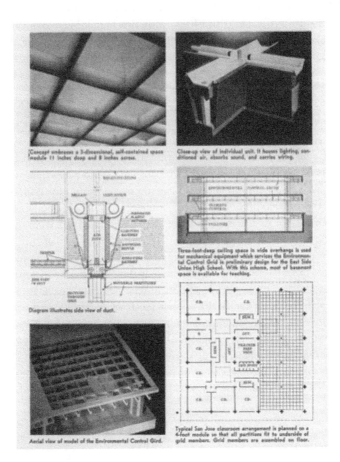

FIGURE 5.8 Details of Kump's 'Environmental Control Grid' patented in 1962.

Architect: The Office of Ernest J. Kump

Source: McDonald (1967)

Kump claimed in 1967 that the Environmental Control Grid could be utilised 'not just in school or university buildings but in almost any type of structure' and could also 'be used successfully in remodeling older buildings' (McDonald 1967: 32). Later marketed as 'Enviro-Grid', the system was employed by architects Albert A. Hoover & Associates on specialised space plans for seventh and eighth grades in schools in Los Altos, where it was claimed the rooms 'will become laboratories where teaching and learning will prove the worth of space and equipment flexibility in school structure' ('For the First Time Complete Classroom Flexibility' nd).

By 1962, Ernest Kump appeared to have 'perfected' his environmentally controlled classroom. His technical ideas for systemising school construction and providing mechanical and electrical services, developed over the previous twenty-five years, predated the subsequently well-publicised and highly feted ideas of Ezra Ehrenkrantz and Schools Construction Systems Development (SCSD), also sponsored by EFL but based across the bay at University of California, Berkeley (Marks 2001). In many respects, it could be argued that Kump's most recent technical ideas, despite the external pedagogical engagement with Stanford and San Jose East Side Union High School, were taken as the basis for SCSD to develop a far more sophisticated and complete systems approach that also embraced the pedagogical trend towards the open-plan school that had been emerging in the United States since the late 1950s (Farmer and Weinstock 1965; see also EFL 1973; Ogata 2013: 140–6). It is also highly likely that the prolific nature of Kump's school practice, which dominated the postwar Californian scene, was the target of EFL president Harold B. Gores's derogatory term 'egg-crate plans' and the brace of US school architects that largely excluded Kump from their supportive network (Gores 1959: 154–8).

The simple fact was that Kump and his school clients did not engage with the pedagogical shift towards the open-plan school. His practice had already moved on from one specialty to another: from elementary and high schools from the 1930s to the 1950s to the new demand for community colleges in the late 1950s. Kump's BSM was deployed at a large scale from 1958 in the new educational form of the community college, specifically at Foothill College, Los Altos (1958–62), with its clusters of four top-lit (and windowless except for a clerestory strip) classrooms also serviced from above. The aesthetic and professional success led to larger commissions, not just for community colleges but also for university buildings.

The classroom designs of Ernest Kump between 1937 and 1962 were thus symptomatic of a phase of modern school design in the United States where the demands of building production were combined with the belief in and pursuit of complete environmental control – the architecture of the well-tempered classroom – as the provision of an apparently perfected neutral container available to any mode of educational delivery. This phase had, by the early 1960s, almost totally inverted the health-giving ideals of the 1930s and not always for the better. The largely windowless, environmentally controlled learning space of the open-plan school would find its architectural parallel in the hermetically sealed, air-conditioned, open-plan workplace of the 1960s office. Kump's career-long critique of Neutra's Ringplan school, based on the search for the ideal learning environment, would be the prelude and the prototype for the classroom's complete dissolution. It had become not another place, just an open space.

Acknowledgements

The research for this chapter was supported under the Australian Research Council's Discovery Projects funding scheme (DP110100505) and a sabbatical undertaken by the author at University of California, Berkeley, in 2010. The assistance of Glen Billington (principal, Fowler Elementary School), Waverly Lowell (Environmental Design Archives, UC Berkeley), Marilyn McDonald (archivist, Foothill College), Marc Treib, Jeffrey Turnbull and Elizabeth Veal (principal, White Oaks Elementary School) in the research for this chapter is gratefully acknowledged.

Notes

1 Every reasonable effort has been made to identify the owners of copyright for figures 5.1, 5.2 and 5.3. Errors or omissions will be corrected in subsequent editions.
2 Kump-designed schools with trilateral lighting included the Barstow Union High School, Barstow (1945); music building, high school, Hollister (1946); Jefferson Union Elementary School, Lawrence St, place unknown (1946–50); Borel Elementary School, San Mateo (1945–50); Charter Street School, Redwood City (1946); Lincoln Elementary School, Redwood City (1946); Broadway Elementary School, San Jose (1947); Alum Rock Elementary School (1947); Lawrence Elementary School, San Mateo (1947); Clayton Valley Elementary School (1947); John Gill School, Redwood City (1945–50); Fitzuren Elementary School, Antioch (1947); and additions to Wasco Union High School, Wasco (1947).
3 The ten architects present were Donald Barthelme (Texas); William Caudill (Caudill Rowlett Scott & Associates, Texas); Alonzo J Harriman (Maine); William Lyles (Lyles Bisset Carlisle & Wolff, South Carolina); John McLeod (AIA School Committee, Washington, DC); Lawrence Perkins (Perkins & Will, Illinois); Michael Radoslovich (Chief Architect, New York City Board of Education); John Lyon Reid (California); Stanley Sharp (Ketchum, Gina & Sharp, New York); and Walter Taylor (Director, AIA Department of Education & Research).
4 The loft plan school was planned as a compact, short periphery block that made extensive use of top-lit interior space and internalised streets, almost like a city grid. A hypothetical scheme drawn by Matthew Nowicki (1949) is a good example. The core plan school was planned as a series of classrooms placed back to back and side to side, shortening the exterior wall and sharing a centralised run of plumbing, heating and electrical lines. An example is the Foster Junior High School, Seattle, by Ralph H. Burkhardt (*Architectural Forum*, May 1953). The zone plan school comprised areas, wings or levels zoned according to noise, use and age groups. It is not as easily identified architecturally as the loft plan and core plan schools as both types could also be zoned. *Forum* listed a school by TAC and Johnson as an example ('Should the Design of Today's School Be Domestic or Institutional?' 1953: 152).

Works cited

'Advanced California School Meets Limited Budget' (1941) *Architectural Record* 89, June.

Alquist, A. E. (2007) *The Field Act and Public School Construction: A 2007 Perspective*, Sacramento, CA: California Seismic Safety Commission.

'Building with Wood' (1944–45). Exhibition #267, MoMA 14 November 1944–1918 February 1945, New York: Museum of Modern Art.

Caudill, W. W. (1941) 'Space for Teaching: An Approach to the Design of Elementary Schools for Texas', *Bulletin of the Agricultural and Mechanical College of Texas* 12, 9: 715–20.

Caudill, W. W. (1954) *Toward Better School Design*, New York: F. W. Dodge Corporation.

Chatelet, A-M. (2008) 'A Breath of Fresh Air: Open-Air Schools in Europe', in M. Gutman and N. de Coninck-Smith (eds) *Designing Modern Childhoods: History, Space and the Material Culture of Children*, New York: Rutgers University Press: 103–17.

'Cluster Plan: The "Little House" or "Campus" Idea' (1953) *Architectural Forum* 99, October.

'Editorial. Schools: A Look Backward and Forward' (1955) *Architectural Forum* 103, October.

EFL (Educational Facilities Laboratories) (1973) *Five Open Plan High Schools: A Report*, New York: EFL.

'Elementary School, Ducor Union School District, Ducor, Calif.' (1943) *Pencil Points* 24, September.

'An "Environmental Grid"' (1962) *Architectural Forum* 117, August.

'Experimental School, Bell, California: Richard J. Neutra, Architect' (1936) *Architectural Record* 79, June.

Farmer, M. and Weinstock, R. (1965) *Schools Without Walls*, New York: EFL.

'First Postwar Schools' (1946) *Architectural Record* 99, March.

'For the First Time Complete Classroom Flexibility' (nd), brochure, Ernest Kump Collection, Environmental Design Archives, UC Berkeley.

'Fowler Elementary School, Fowler, California' (1939) *Architectural Record* 85, February.

Fowler Ensign (1938) 2 June quoted in J. R. McFarland (1972) *Village on the Prairie: the story of Fowler's First 100 Years*, Fowler, CA: Ensign Publishing Co. and the Fowler Mothers' Club: 34.

Gores, H. B. (1959) 'Educational Change and Architectural Consequence', *Architectural Record* 126, December.

Haskell, D. (1946) 'The Architects in Action on Schools', *Architectural Record* 99, March.

Hines, T. S. (1982) *Richard Neutra and the Search for Modern Architecture*, New York: Oxford University Press.

Kinchin, J. and O'Connor, A. (2012) 'Light, Air, Health', in J. Kinchin and A. O'Connor (eds) *Century of the Child: Growing by Design 1900–2000*, New York: The Museum of Modern Art: 88–119.

'Manufactured, Prefabricated, Classroom-Office-Kindergarten Units' (1943) *Pencil Points* 24, September.

Marks, J. (2001) 'The Educational Facilities Laboratories (EFL): A History. National Clearing House for Educational Facilities', December, available at: http://crs.arch.tamu.edu/media/cms_page_media/713/eflhistory.pdf.

McDonald, K. R. (1967) 'Environmental Control Grid Developed: System Houses Lighting, Wiring, Conditioned Air, and Absorbs Sound' *Lighting and Electrical Design* 83, 9: 32–3.

McFarland, J. R. (1972) *Village on the Prairie: The Story of Fowler's First 100 Years*, Fowler, CA: Ensign Publishing Co. and the Fowler Mothers' Club.

Neutra, R. (1930) *Amerika: Neues Bauen in der Welt*, Vienna: Verlag Anton Schroll.

'A New School Cycle Gracefully Begun' (1948) *Architectural Record* 103, January.

Nowicki, M. (1949) *Architectural Forum* 91, October.

Ogata, A. (2008) 'Building for Learning in Postwar American Elementary Schools', *Journal of the Society of Architectural Historians* 67, 4: 562–91.

Ogata, A. (2013) *Designing the Creative Child: Playthings and Places in Mid-Century America*, Minneapolis: University of Minnesota Press.

Perkins, L. B. and Cocking, W. D. (1949) *Schools*, New York: Reinhold.

'Pioneer School has Proved the Value of its Scientific Design in Eight Years of Orderly Growth and Educational Progress' (1949) *Architectural Forum* 91, October.

'Prefabricated Schoolhouse' (1945) *Architectural Forum* 82, February.

'Public Elementary School, Los Angeles: Architect Richard Neutra' (1935) *Architect and Building News* 144, 22 (November): 226–7.

'A Radical Departure in Daylighting' (1946) *Architectural Record* 99, March.

Roth, A. (1950) *The New School*, Zurich: Girsberger (republished in 1957, 1961, 1966).

'Some Recent Work of Mr Ernest J. Kump' (1916) *The Architect and Engineer* 46, 3 (September): 38–55.

'Should the Design of Today's School Be Domestic or Institutional?' (1953) *Architectural Forum* 99, October.

'The Space-module School' (1957) *Architectural Forum* 107, December.

Stillman, C. G. and Cleary, R. C. (1949) *The Modern School*, London: Architectural Press.

Temko, A. 'Foothill's Campus Is a Community' (1962) *Architectural Forum* 116, February.

'"Tri-lateral" Lighting, Panel Heating' (1947) *Architectural Record* 101, January.

'War Needs Community Facilities' (1942) *Architectural Record* 91, May.

'Western Sky Industries' (1962) (US Patent Application Ser. No. 211350, Filed July 20, 1962) Environmental Control Grid brochure, Ernest Kump Collection, Environmental Design Archives, UC Berkeley.

6

EDUCATIONAL FACILITIES LABORATORIES

Debating and designing the postwar American schoolhouse

Amy F. Ogata

Educational Facilities Laboratories, or EFL, was an independent voice in the American debate on postwar education and architecture, and a force behind the adoption of the open school. Founded in 1958 as a collaboration between the Ford Foundation, the American Institute of Architects and Teachers College of Columbia University, EFL enjoyed immediate visibility, and its influence grew substantially throughout the next twenty years. EFL not only granted funds for the study of facilities-related problems, new buildings and building types but also brought architects, administrators and industry leaders together to discuss the problems of school building and American education. These collaborative endeavours, from academic conferences to workshops and charrettes, made EFL a unique node in the larger conversation about school architecture and an active agent in stimulating new ideas. In this chapter, I examine how the organisation established a language of change, how it nurtured experimentalism and how it transformed school buildings. The rich debate and an open-ended process of design helped shape the material reality of postwar American schools.

Educational Facilities Laboratories

The Ford Foundation created EFL as a separate non-profit institution with an initial grant of US$4.5 million in January 1958.[1] After World War II, the foundation was reorganised to become a national presence in philanthropy devoted to human welfare and the strengthening of democracy. Improving public education was a central part of the foundation's concerns. Since it was already committed to educational causes through the Fund for the Advancement of Education, the Ford Foundation used EFL to address the school shortage crisis and provide a voice for wide-ranging discussions on schoolhouse design over the next twenty years. The president of EFL was Harold B. Gores, who had been superintendent of schools in Newton, in suburban Boston, Massachusetts, for ten years and had gained a reputation for relishing experimentation. Gores was not only an effective administrator; he also possessed a strong interest both in the physical form of schools and in a participatory culture. His ethos of open experimentalism and his conviction that design changes in the school plant would affect learning became the central achievements of EFL.

Gores was often quoted as saying, 'If I can kick it, I can fund it' (Marks 2009).[2] Yet many of the grants and projects that EFL supported existed only as ideas. EFL's general philanthropic practice was to grant money, often in small amounts, to specific groups to tackle problems that had implications for widespread change, and to disseminate these ideas through its publications. As a publisher, EFL produced thousands of illustrated soft-bound reports and documents that reached school administrators, district superintendents and architects throughout the country and extended its influence from school architecture proper to questions about the broader environment of learning, including childcare centres, museums and playgrounds. Thus, in addition to granting money for specific projects, it was the sketch and the pamphlet that represented the EFL outlook and furthered its ideological aims.

EFL was founded at the height of the baby boom, a moment of anxiety about the rising American birth rate and the reality of providing sufficient facilities for the growing population, a chronic teacher shortage and underlying concerns about curriculum. After World War II, American schools gained unprecedented attention. Schools and schooling were at once a national and a local issue because in the United States individual states regulated educational decisions and the largest source of revenue, which paid for new buildings, came from local property taxes and voter-approved municipal bonds. Debates on education and building were covered in both professional and popular publications, in exhibitions and in local conversations held in towns and cities across the country. The surge of new births and significant population growth (in 1949/50 there were 25.1 million children enrolled in American public schools; by 1971 it was 46 million) meant that at the end of the war the demand for new classrooms collided with a limited and outdated stock of school buildings (Ogata 2008). In 1955, editors at *Architectural Forum* worried: 'every 15 minutes enough babies are born to fill another classroom and we are already 250,000 classrooms behind' ('Schools' 1955: 129). Along with insufficient numbers of school seats, the looming question about American education was the relationship between the individual and society, and the role of the school as an agent in the cultivation of democracy. The Cold War suspicion that an American-educated populace might not be able to meet a future Soviet threat enhanced the need for new models of learning and buildings that would reinforce values of individuality and autonomy. 'Education', Gores observed in 1959, 'is in a period of ferment' (Gores 1959: 154).

The New Schools for New Education conference, 1959

From the beginning, EFL was concerned with the relationship between school architecture and emerging educational theories. One of EFL's first projects, held in October 1959, was to bring architects, educational researchers and administrators together to discuss secondary schools, which were about to experience the stress of the baby boom. The New Schools for New Education conference was planned by Gores and his staff and hosted by the University of Michigan, which housed a school-planning laboratory and an academic school of education. EFL invited ten architects to debate new research on high school education conducted by J. Lloyd Trump of the University of Illinois. Trump's report, *Images of the Future* (1959), which was referred to as the 'Trump Plan' throughout the conference, was also produced with funds from the Ford Foundation.

Trump, working with data gathered from a national group of high school principals, advocated reorganising the modes of instruction, with flexibility in class schedules and staffing, and use of technological aids. He suggested that students would benefit from increased individualisation by having a selection of large classes in addition to smaller discussion groups, as well as studying alone with 'teaching machines'. To meet these demands, schools would have to disrupt the rigid age-graded courses and class schedules, and increase the variety of room sizes. The spatial demands included small individual spaces where a student might read independently and keep materials but also engage with aural recordings or television; classrooms for small group discussions of 12 to 15 people; and rooms for large groups of 200 or more.

The ten school architects invited by EFL to explore and respond to Trump's ideas at the conference included John C. Harkness of The Architects Collaborative (TAC), William Brubaker of Perkins & Will, William Caudill of Caudill Rowlett Scott, Donald Barthelme and John Lyon Reid. These five architects were respected figures of postwar American school building, representing a wide geographic span and the most densely populated areas of the United States. The other participants – which included Trump himself as well as educators, school administrators, deans of university faculties, architectural critics, medical practitioners and psychologists from across the country – debated the forms and ideas that the architects introduced. Each firm was allotted an hour and a half to present a project that was intended to be a 'generalized architectural solution' to the spatial challenges Trump's pedagogical theories posed (EFL 1959a: 17). With the ideal of stimulating a conversation about school building and new educational programs, the architects were encouraged to be experimental. Most of the projects existed only in plans, and several firms delineated only a set of general principles.

Brubaker, of Perkins & Will, introduced the concept of the Q-Space to satisfy the high school student's need for individual study. With 'Q' standing for 'quest', Brubaker argued for a carrel-like space fitted with a desk, a bookshelf, file storage and even a television. It aimed to encourage individualised learning and to disrupt the age-grade ladder of education currently in place in secondary schools. The Q-Space resembled college-level autonomy for students, but the individual units were situated within a larger classroom. The discussion at the workshop raised questions about relative levels of maturity needed to achieve independent learning in these circumstances.

William C. Caudill's presentation on behalf of his firm Caudill Rowlett Scott was likewise a set of ideas rather than a conventional architectural plan. He presented a graphic narrative of a teacher breaking out of a box-like space (a classroom with 25 pupils) to embrace a large loft-like space that could accommodate a variety of smaller areas (see Figure 6.1). Having dismissed the rectangular 'sacred cow' of schoolhouse architecture, Caudill's ideal was the barn. In the final drawing, he envisioned a space that was economical, adaptable and 'creative'. As he described it:

> The last drawing suggests a new kind of learning space, at least new to the public schools, but certainly familiar to boys and girls who have a nook in their attic, garage, or barn which they can call their own and in which they can pursue creative learning activities. It advocates the use of an enormous barn; good, cheap space that provides a large number of nooks, crannies, and cubicles for independent research projects. In essence, this barn for learning is a place in which to exercise creativity.
>
> (Caudill, in EFL 1959b: 18)

At once familiar and unconventional, Caudill's space was a proposal to consider the more general notion of openness. Since the early 1950s, his firm had advocated a move away from the rectangular box of the classroom to an ideal spatial arrangement of larger spaces, transoms, freestanding room dividers and doorless spaces in both elementary and high schools. Openness enhanced the sense of curricular possibility, as Caudill commented, of *'learning by doing* instead of *learning by listening'* (Caudill 1941: 42; italics in original).

Each project at the New Schools conference represented a departure from the established norms of school planning. The complex needs of the secondary school posed significant problems to the architect who aimed, as Reid stated, 'to provide a framework in which all learning experiences can be synthesized in a meaningful whole' (Lopez 1956: 253). Large comprehensive high schools of the postwar era required increasing numbers of specialised rooms for science and subjects that were no longer considered purely vocational, such as shop (technical subjects from woodworking to automotive repair) and home economics. School buildings with long corridors – and classrooms located on one side, or both sides – were now derided at the conference as 'egg-crates', or a 'cells and bells' approach to education. What the designers, superintendents, educators and psychologists debated at the conference in 1959 was a way of opening up the process of learning and teaching and engaging different types of spaces as active agents in the students' intellectual and social life.

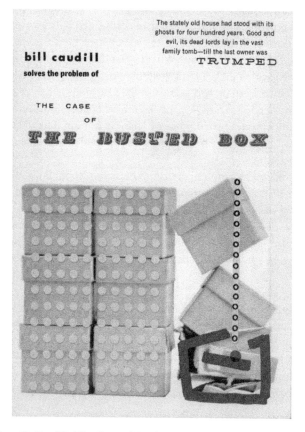

FIGURE 6.1 William C. Caudill, 'The Busted Box', 1959.

Source: New Schools for New Education (New York: EFL, 1959)

The most current embodiment of the new thinking about flexible schedules and decentralised planning was TAC's Wayland Senior High School, in Wayland, Massachusetts, designed between 1958 and 1959 and at the time of the conference just beginning construction (it opened in 1960). John C. Harkness presented the plans and drawings for the building, which was located on more than 90 acres of open farmland 16 miles from Boston. Wayland Senior High School was the result of a year-long examination and reconsideration of the relationship between educational process and architectural form (Anderson 1963). To accommodate large and small group meetings, team teaching, independent study and the use of media in the classroom, TAC created six clusters of subject areas with classrooms grouped around a reference centre, a library-like space with subject-specific information and resources. Instead of uniform classrooms strung along a corridor, TAC designed a variety of learning spaces – from large lecture halls to small conference rooms – and relegated the open corridors to the exterior. With the reference centre as the focal point of each cluster, the school more closely resembled a tertiary college campus with its varied disciplinary nodes ('High School Plan Has Campus Look' 1959: R8) (see Figure 6.2). This, it was thought, would enhance student identification with particular subjects and teachers. The designers and educators believed small conference rooms grouped together with specialised lab or media spaces (the school had a closed-circuit television system) would not only enable, but *insist* upon, individualised instruction. The smaller scale of each subject cluster and the building's non-monumental, mostly one-storey construction, arranged around landscaped courtyards and open corridors, was also designed to play an active role in engaging the students and teachers in a collaborative relationship.

FIGURE 6.2   The Architects Collaborative, Rendering of Wayland Senior High School, c. 1958.

Source: New Schools for New Education (New York: EFL, 1959)

If Wayland High School represented a 'transitional' understanding of Trump's ideas, then the renovation John Lyon Reid presented in plan for Mills High School in San Bruno, California, as a 'totally flexible' loft plan was the most literal incarnation of Trump's educational philosophy. Described as 'a space platform to be used as a navigational aid for charting courses on the turbulent sea of education', Reid's design was emphatically experimental for 1959 (EFL 1959b: 30). He proposed transforming the existing school away from rows of classrooms and toward large open areas with columns and moveable partitions, marking 28-foot (8.5-metre) bays – light wells – with interchangeable windows and doors. The plan pushed 'instructional areas' (he did not use the word 'classroom') to the interior in proximity to spaces used for large groups and listening booths, and removed the distinction between shop, home-making, music and science rooms.

Even more dramatically futuristic was Donald Barthelme's design submission to the New Schools conference. He described this as 'not a school building at all . . . it is a lot of units, an organism with parts – an ant colony or a series of beehives – with a panoramic pattern of people finally providing the architecture'. 'Buildings', he argued, 'should get out of the way of people' (EFL 1959b: 50). This ostensibly anti-architectural position was evoked in a series of striking spaces: a sequence of sky domes, a maze and an egg-shaped soundproof enclosure, into which materials from the stacks could be mechanically lifted. The domes enclosed 'work rooms' with individual student workstations similar to a drafting room, and access to the outdoors. Instead of following Trump's specific themes of age-grade separation, flexible scheduling and differentiated spaces, Barthelme evoked its general principles. He argued, however, that his design followed a 'situations method', a model that seemed based, if only loosely, on the architecture school where large open spaces and relative autonomy were the organising agents.

The ideal of design flexibility coupled with student individuality and self-discovery pervaded the discussions at the New Schools conference. EFL encouraged the architects to think in both visionary and practical terms about the pedagogical needs they anticipated for the future. As architects wrestled with the grand concepts of educational principles and theories and visually inspiring spaces, they also considered the importance of acoustics, insulation, lighting and structural questions. The conference served not only as a set of guidelines for individual local government districts considering how to provide effective high school education, but became a blueprint for the aspirations of the EFL itself. Indeed, many of the ideas debated in 1959 were central to the questions the organisation continued to pursue well into its second decade.

Significant schools and educational television

Around the same time they were planning the New Schools for New Education conference, EFL initiated several series of publications, including the Profiles of Significant Schools series. These in-depth studies explored the planning of an institution and its architectural and curricular aims. The publications were inexpensively produced in typescript with clear photographs and plans, and were available at no cost from EFL (see Figure 6.3). By 1961 there were 12 profiles, and in 1972 there were 21. That same year EFL estimated that a total of 735,000 copies had been distributed. The institutions that were profiled ranged from elementary schools to high schools. Perkins & Will, John Lyon Reid & Partners, TAC and Caudill

Rowlett Scott, the most prominent architectural figures at the New Schools conference, all had their work profiled in the first year of the series.

The Profiles of Significant Schools provided fully realised examples of the kinds of architectural and educational ideas that EFL supported, which were considered daringly experimental at the time. These publications joined a vast literature addressing the concept of excellence in school design that flourished in the United States throughout the postwar era. Yet while many architectural press compendia emphasised the aesthetic and practical dimensions of the school plant, EFL's publications also explained the pedagogical rationale of design and the collaboration between architects, teachers and communities. The Profiles series served, according to EFL, as 'the armchair equivalent of a trip around the country to see some of the more important American school buildings' (EFL 1961: 31).

Technology in the classroom was another theme EFL identified as a new issue affecting schools. Television was identified as an educational tool in Trump's plan, and its inclusion in school design was a sign of openness to new methods of teaching and a promising solution to a teacher shortage. The presence of a television set was an index of forward-thinking model classrooms of the mid-1950s. At the University of Michigan's Model Classroom (1954), a television set was surrounded with heavy curtains to block light. Around the same time, the Los Angeles firm of Smith, Powell, Morgridge rendered a model classroom with a built-in television set for the Schoolroom Progress USA exhibition, a project of the Henry Ford Museum and the *Encyclopedia Americana*, which travelled the country by railway. In 1959, EFL spent

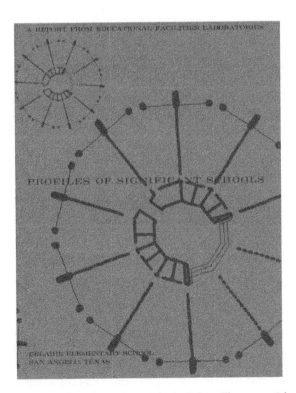

FIGURE 6.3   Evans Clinchy, *Profiles of Significant Schools: Belaire Elementary School, San Angelo, Texas* (New York: EFL, 1960).

FIGURE 6.4 *Design for ETV: Planning for Schools with Television* (New York: EFL, 1960).

US$60,000 to study educational television (ETV) in the classroom, which it estimated was already in use in 569 public school districts (EFL 1959a: 32).

EFL worked with Chicago industrial designer Dave Chapman, a contract designer for the Brunswick furniture company, to develop ways for school facilities to support the use of educational television and thus waded into the specifics of classroom and furniture design, and televisual equipment (EFL 1960: 5). What it produced was a set of ideas, a few guidelines and a publication illustrated with sketches demonstrating how educational television might be integrated into both existing and new classroom spaces (see Figure 6.4). EFL had proposed the 'significant schools' as 'real' models of new architectural and educational excellence rather than just the fanciful notions of architects (as had largely been the case at the New Schools conference). Nonetheless, they continually underscored the importance of identifying and imagining new types of spaces for shifting educational, economic and social circumstances.

The open school

Although the term 'open schools' gained widespread use in the late 1960s, the fundamental spatial, pedagogical and technological questions were already under debate in sketches and proposals at the New Schools conference in the late 1950s. EFL is closely associated with the experimental open school movement of the 1960s and early 1970s. The open school was an attempt to deinstitutionalise schools according to a belief that children gained increased agency in spaces that allowed them to see other teachers and pupils, that relinquishing age-graded levels would benefit both advanced and slower learners, and that free movement around the classroom and use of media could stimulate children's attentions and curiosity. Spatially, the open schools relied on grouped classrooms divided by folding partitions and few walls and doors.

EFL put significant effort into sponsoring and then promoting open school building systems, giving abstract ideas a physical manifestation. With its Stanford Planning Laboratory, which joined EFL as a West Coast wing in 1959, EFL sponsored research that resulted in the School Construction Systems Development (SCSD) corporation, a project to build several California schools from standardised component parts. By 1962, SCSD had secured agreements from 12 California public school districts to create a flexible system of building with standardised parts that could be combined and configured according to the needs of each district. SCSD aimed to save costs by large-scale purchasing of modular systems that could be erected in many different interchangeable configurations depending on the specific site requirements. In addition to economical construction, the designers of SCSD hoped to create schools to meet the needs of a rapidly changing curriculum, with open spans of 60 to 70 feet (18.2 to 21.3 metres) that could be easily partitioned and modified without a monotonous row of classrooms strung along a corridor. The SCSD system allowed for internal flexibility and variety of room configurations, and the structures built encompassed small elementary schools as well as large high schools (EFL 1967).[3] Nonetheless, the open school idea was more often envisioned as a space for elementary-aged children than it was for older pupils (EFL 1973).

Architects had been experimenting with hexagonal classrooms since the early 1950s, but classroom shape became a preoccupation in the early 1960s. Gores and EFL pursued the idea of domed space for open schools. Caudill recounted: 'Gores asked us what we knew about domes. He said that sooner or later we had better start studying curvilinear form as related to some newer educational techniques' (Caudill 1960). With money from EFL, Caudill Rowlett Scott developed a huge concrete dome floating on glass walls with no fixed interior walls for a school system in Port Arthur, Texas (Clinchy 1960) (see Figure 6.5). When the municipal bond issue for the Texas school failed and could not be built, this model, which the firm called the 'Dome School', was adapted for several locations (Ogata 2013: 142–4). It is clear that Gores was instrumental in making high-level introductions in New York City, where the 'Dome School' was finally realised in 1962 as the Paul Klapper School (Public School 219), a demonstration school for the City University of New York's Queens College. Public School 219 offered an example of how open schools might work in an urban context, another of EFL's central concerns. Like Donald Barthelme's futuristic domes, Caudill Rowlett Scott believed that the circular form could better enhance the practice of team teaching and learning activity. According to Caudill, 'the uniqueness is that there will be a CONTINUOUS movement of children' (Caudill 1960). Under the dome, the low dividers created four classrooms that could be combined into a single space. A freestanding mezzanine placed just off centre made use of the vertical space for a second-storey research centre and created a curtained assembly area beneath. Beyond the dome were four outdoor courts for studying natural science, gardening, arts and crafts, and maths and social science.

The planning of the open school was described as 'a physical expression of today's academic dedication to the individual student' (*The Open Plan School* 1970: 12). Rephrasing the notion of individualised student learning in spatial terms, EFL promoted both the pedagogical and the architectural dimensions of the open schools. When EFL co-hosted a conference with the Institute for the Development of Educational Activities (IDEA) around 1970, it attracted educators and school superintendents who sought new ways of updating their ageing institutions

FIGURE 6.5 *The Things of Education: A Second Report from Educational Facilities Laboratories* (New York: EFL, 1961).

to meet changing curricular ideals. As new ideas met a stagnating American economy, school districts struggled to create open schools without building new structures. Schools from the early postwar era were now called the 'new old', and editors deemed them 'left behind by rapidly changing educational thinking' ('C.P.' 1971: 88). Echoing EFL language and doctrine, Colorado Springs architect Lamar Kelsey dismissed the 'old cells and bells school' and aimed to 'break out of the classroom box without breaking up the budget at the same time' ('C.P.' 1971: 88). He proposed an eight-step design of a remodelled elementary school near Denver that would remove non-load-bearing walls, doors and fixed casework to create open spaces with carpeting, moveable storage, supergraphics and places for television and film.

A plan for action, 1972

In 1972, the city of Crystal Lake, Illinois, faced a similar dilemma of desiring to adopt open school principles without having the funds to build one from the ground up. It was a growing suburban town, absorbing population from nearby Chicago, and had recently added three new schools to three older ones. The disjuncture in educational models both spatial and curricular across the district troubled the superintendent, Corbin Hamby, who desired cohesion among the six schools. EFL provided money for a two-day charrette to turn the three older Crystal Lake schools (built in 1906, 1952 and 1953) into open schools through low-cost solutions. Without an immediate means of raising funds for substantial renovations, the district asked EFL to help them redesign their schools and permit a consideration of the open school model. Nine architects from across the country were grouped together (three to a site) to redesign the three existing schools.

If the New Schools for New Education conference sponsored by EFL 14 years earlier had lavished attention upon architects' visionary plans and produced a sleek catalogue with detailed textual explanations, the Crystal Lake school project did the opposite. Instead of fantasy projects and experimental schemes created in advance and unveiled at the conference, this project was focused on developing, in the space of 24 hours, practical applications for the individual problems of a specific place. The resulting report, pages stapled together, offered three approaches for realising the principles of open schools – increasing children's agency in the classroom, providing spaces for projects and activities and the flexibility to change depending on the immediate needs of the group – within the existing spaces.

Each architectural team was paired with groups of administrators and teachers to develop a set of ideals and drawings. William Brubaker of Perkins & Will, the only architect who was involved in both this project and the New Schools conference, was part of a team that redesigned the South School. Since the original symmetrical building was conceived and built in three stages in the mid-twentieth century, with a steel-truss structure, minimal bearing walls and extensive windows, the building could be transformed to accommodate several different learning schemes. The group drew up six themes including integrated age groups, learning centres, self-contained and open plan classrooms and what they called a 'community' model, which was a collaborative rather than teacher-led environment. They identified their solution as a shell that could accommodate a rolling program of these options through both open and semi-open spaces.

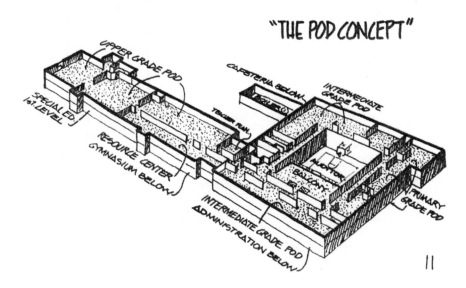

FIGURE 6.6 *A Plan for Action or How to Change Old Schools into Open Space Schools without Any Money!* (New York: EFL, 1972).

The other groups worked according to established open school models. For the Central School, which had been built in 1906 with later additions, the architects decided to 'try a minimum of wall breakdowns and achieve maximum change with furnishings, pillows, interior decoration, etc' (*A Plan for Action* 1972: 9). They decided on a pod model of mixing ages and grades, and began with one for grades one through three with a team of three teachers. Replacing walls with retractable dividers that made the three classrooms into one large L-shaped space, the primary grade pod not only benefited from graphics, colour and furniture but also spaces for groups, individual study carrels and a room for projects (see Figure 6.6). For the North School, with its double-loaded corridors and self-contained classrooms, the aim was to 'de-institutionalise' the school; following aspects of the other two, the group devised pods according to broad age groups and multiple uses.

Conclusion

At the New Schools conference of 1959, John Lyon Reid remarked: 'Education is a creative, thoughtful method of learning and is a fluid activity. A fluid might be said to take the shape of its container. If that is true, I think we might also say that the container should change its shape when required' (EFL 1959b: 31). EFL facilitated the notion that buildings had to change to meet the shifts in educational research and the debates and conversations around education and school building in postwar America. With the conviction that children could meet their potential in spaces designed to enhance their experience of learning, the group ceaselessly promoted new spaces and new forms for the American schoolhouse, along with the furnishings and technology that raised the educational standard. I have argued elsewhere that educational progressivism, while tempered among the American public, was resurgent among American architects after World War II (Ogata 2008). EFL was central to this debate and fully embraced the ideals of modernism and educational progressivism.

Considering its history in retrospect, James W. Armsey observed that the Ford Foundation's Fund for the Advancement of Education was interested in 'ridding the education establishment of its attachment to forms and methods that they believed were hamstringing the teaching-learning process'. Transforming the school plant, he argued, was easier than changing people's minds about learning (Marks 2009: 1). If we re-examine the questions the organisation faced, it is clear that the values of openness and the discourse of individualism mirrored EFL's own culture of experimentation. EFL rephrased an optimistic, modernist outlook that understood both education and building technology in terms that were liberating. Because it was vested with funds from Ford, its ideas were taken seriously and its numerous publications were disseminated in large quantities. The organisation was nimble in its adaptation of emerging educational and architectural ideas and canny about choosing key figures to support its platform of research. There is, of course, much we do not know about the real effects of EFL's discourse upon architects beyond the immediate EFL circle or the legacy of the projects it funded, or their effect upon the children who attended those schools. But if we can begin to explore the ways that these ideas were presented and represented, we can also begin to understand why that 'other' place we understand as the postwar school took the shape it did.

Notes

1 By 1972, EFL had partnerships with the Commonwealth Fund, Kettering Foundation, I/D/E/A, Rockefeller Brothers Foundation, American Conservation Association and the US Government.

2   Gores was also quoted as describing schools and the interest of EFL as 'the things in education that you can, with impunity, kick with your foot' (Reif 1966).
3   The promotion of the SCSD program reached a national audience, and it attracted considerable attention. Although many praised the notion of component systems, the feasibility did not necessarily reduce overall costs. The California districts did not build cheaper schools. However, EFL argued that they received more comprehensive buildings of better quality. Thirteen, rather than the initially projected 22, schools were erected with SCSD components, but aspects of the design were installed in industrial buildings, and similar programs for school building were developed in Canada and Florida through the late 1960s. There were also related projects in Toronto, in Montréal and at the University of California.

Works cited

Anderson, E. J. (1963) 'How We Made the Change-Over', *Life* 86 (22 March): 85–7.

Caudill, W. W. (1941) 'Space for Teaching', *Bulletin of the Agricultural and Mechanical College of Texas* 12, 9: 42.

Caudill, W. W. (1960) 'Eggcrates, Eggheads and Eggshells', Address Given at the Sarasota Conference, Sarasota, Florida, 17 November, CRS Archives Document 1079.0102, CRS Archive Center, Texas A&M University.

Clinchy, E. (1960) *Wayland Senior High School, Wayland, Massachusetts, Profiles of Significant Schools Series*, New York: Educational Facilities Laboratories.

C.P. (1971) 'Breaking out of the Box: The New Old School', *Progressive Architecture* (February): 88–91.

EFL (1959a) *Here They Learn: First Annual Report*, New York: Educational Facilities Laboratories.

EFL (1959b) *New Schools for New Education*, New York: Educational Facilities Laboratories.

EFL (1960) *Design for ETV: Planning for Schools with Television*, New York: Educational Facilities Laboratories.

EFL (1961) *The Things of Education: A Second Report from Educational Facilities Laboratories*, New York: Educational Facilities Laboratories.

EFL (1967) *SCSD: The Project and the Schools*, New York: Educational Facilities Laboratories.

EFL (1972) *A Plan for Action or How to Change Old Schools into Open Space Schools Without Any Money!* New York: Educational Facilities Laboratories.

Gores, H. B. (1959) 'Educational Change and Architectural Consequence', *Architectural Record* 126 (August 1959): 154–8.

'High School Plan Has Campus Look' (1959) *New York Times* (26 April): R8.

Lopez, F. G. Jr (1956) *Schools for the New Needs: Educational, Social, Economic*, New York: F. W. Dodge Corporation.

Marks, J. (2009) *A History of Educational Facilities Laboratories (EFL)*, Washington, DC: National Clearinghouse for Educational Facilities.

Ogata, A. F. (2008) 'Building for Learning in Postwar American Elementary Schools', *Journal of the Society of Architectural Historians* 67, 4 (December): 562–91.

Ogata, A. F. (2013) *Designing the Creative Child: Playthings and Places in Midcentury America*, Minneapolis: University of Minnesota Press.

The Open Plan School, Report of a National Seminar (c. 1970), New York and Florida: EFL and I/D/E/A.

Reif, R. (1966) 'The Ford Foundation is Helping Schools Build for Tomorrow', *New York Times* (12 January).

'Schools' (1955) *Architectural Forum* 103 (October).

Trump, J. L. (1959) *Images of the Future: A New Approach to the Secondary School*, Urbana, IL: National Association of Secondary School Principals, Commission on the Experimental Study of the Utilization of the Staff in the Secondary School.

7

CREATING FRIENDLY SCHOOL ENVIRONMENTS

'Casual' high schools, progressive education and child-centred culture in postwar America

Dale Allen Gyure

Two quotations about children and school buildings are particularly illuminating for the insights they bring into the world of postwar education in America. The first is from famed childcare specialist Dr Benjamin Spock: 'The tendency is for American parents to consider the child at least as important as themselves – perhaps more important' (Spock 1946: 11). The second was written by educational architect William W. Caudill: 'The good school building is child-centered. The child is the yardstick by which the effectiveness of the building and its equipment is gauged' (Caudill 1951: 19). Taken together, these statements reveal the emergence of a new attitude toward children and adolescents which had important repercussions for the country's educational system and its architecture. During the immediate postwar era, American public schools engaged in a remarkable nationwide trend in which schools began to be designed – for the first time – with the aim of making children psychologically and physically *comfortable*. Educators and architects attempted to create school surroundings that were relaxing and nurturing rather than impressive or imposing, in marked contrast to their predecessors. Educational historian Robert Hampel has aptly described this generation of postwar schools as 'casual' (Hampel 1986). Their design and decoration resonated with the ideals of a society obsessed with children and their well-being.

This chapter adopts Hampel's notion of the 'casual school' as a useful construct for examining American secondary education in the decades immediately following World War II. It will describe how this educational movement toward informality and comfort and a cultural fascination with child raising manifested itself in school buildings, and interpret some of the educational, cultural and architectural influences that shaped these schools. Although casual schools appeared at both primary and secondary levels of education, the chapter focuses on public high schools and adolescents. And while educators constructed hundreds of casual school buildings in urban, suburban and rural settings throughout all regions of the United States, the chapter will provide examples from Chicago's public schools in an effort to localise this national phenomenon.

What were casual schools?

What was a 'casual' school? Visitors to many newly built public schools around America between 1945 and the late 1960s certainly would have experienced something very different from the palatial school buildings of the early century – namely, a prevalent sense of archi-tectural casualness and informality in the school environment. Designers of the new casual high schools rejected the monumental schools' size and institutional character. Many of these casual school buildings were low-profiled, spread out on the site and unimposing in nature, in stark contrast to the earlier generation's lofty, attention-grabbing monuments (Gibbons and Hereford 1955). Apart from the large masses of the auditorium and gymnasium, few casual school buildings stood taller than two storeys (see Figure 7.1). Bilateral symmetry, so prevalent in the plans and elevations of previous schools, became less common. Also, instead of a single building, the gymnasium, auditorium, classroom and administration spaces, and perhaps shop classes, sometimes occupied separate structures, attached to each other by glass-enclosed walkways, in what was commonly known as the 'campus plan' (Ireland 1952; see Figure 7.2).

Inside the buildings, large expanses of glass let in natural light and provided views of landscaped courtyards, while classrooms often allowed direct access to the outdoors. Spa-cious lobbies with built-in seating and greenery-filled planters appeared (see Figure 7.3). Lower ceilings in classrooms and hallways, curtains, bright and cheerful colour schemes and lightweight, moveable furniture all contributed to a casual ambiance that tried to reference students' homes rather than impersonal institutional buildings (Clapp 1956; Caudill 1963). Hampel vividly described the contrast between these postwar schools and their predecessors:

> The new citadels offered friendlier settings than the old museums of virtue. . . . The buildings conveyed the impression of greater accessibility than the schools of early

FIGURE 7.1 William J. Bogan High School, Chicago, Illinois, 1959.

Architect: Naess & Murphy

Source: Chicago Board of Education Archives

FIGURE 7.2   Loy Norrix High School, Kalamazoo, Michigan, 1961.

Architect: Perkins & Will

Photograph: Dale Allen Gyure

FIGURE 7.3   Spring Grove Joint Senior High School, York County, Pennsylvania, 1953, lobby.

Architect: Lester L. Buchart

Source: American School Board Journal 129, September 1954

years. . . . On the surface, the architecture announced ranch house ease more than cathedral-like solemnity, third-grade playfulness more than college seriousness.

(Hampel 1986: 56)

Educational origins of the casual school

The casual schools of the 1950s and 1960s had their roots in progressive education reforms dating back to the late nineteenth century. American educational pioneers like Francis Parker, inspired by European pedagogues such as Johann Pestalozzi and Friedrich Froebel, began to experiment with an alternative mode of education that attempted to match the learning process to children's innate interests and abilities. The leading American figure in what became known as 'progressive education' was John Dewey, who proposed as early as 1900 that the public education system was misguided. In traditional education, he wrote, 'the center of gravity is outside the child. It is in the teacher, the text-book, anywhere and everywhere you please except in the immediate instincts and activities of the child himself'. This approach, Dewey hoped, would be replaced by a better way of thinking about education. 'Now the change which is coming into our education is the shifting of the center of gravity', he wrote.

> It is a change, a revolution, not unlike that introduced by Copernicus when the astronomical center shifted from the earth to the sun. In this case the child becomes the sun about which the appliances of education revolve; he is the center about which they are organized.
>
> (Dewey 1959 [1899]: 52–3)

More than a half-century later, this 'student-centred' approach continued to have its champions. 'It is apparent even to perceptive laymen that a student may be expected to work harder and achieve better results in an activity which bears a relationship to the pupil's life', claimed a study of American high schools, 'and that the closer this relationship is to the pupil's present activities, the more effective the learning' (French 1967: 11–12).

The progressive reformers' main target was the physical and psychological formality of classrooms, stressful places which had changed very little in centuries. Traditional classrooms – still ubiquitous after World War II – saw students seated at orderly ranks of desks (often bolted to the floor to prevent movement) for most of the day, standing to respond to questions from a teacher whose own desk, in a forthright exhibition of authority, was raised on a platform. This centuries-old autocratic system emphasised memorisation and recitation with very little critical thinking and no consideration for children's curiosity or abilities; additionally, it was daunting for many children. As progressive educators pointed out, this atmosphere hindered learning. As an alternative, reformers like Dewey proposed radical changes, including, among other things, allowing children to help select subjects, emphasising active learning through hands-on activities instead of passive learning through reading or listening, cooperative and group activities instead of individual recitation, class and small group discussions, and relating subject matter to family and community life (Ravitch 1985: 44–5; see Figure 7.4). Relocating the centre of the educational process from the subject to the child would allow teachers to access a wide range of effective new techniques. All these activities would ideally occur in an atmosphere where both the physical environment and teacher–student interactions were relaxed and happy rather than intimidating and anxiety provoking.

FIGURE 7.4 Abington Township Senior High School, Abington, Pennsylvania, mid-1950s, class-room suite.

Architect: Joseph Wigmore Jr

Source: American School Board Journal 135, July 1957

The child-centred society

Educational critics seeking a student-centred curriculum and pedagogy would soon receive reinforcement from psychologists and childcare experts. In America after World War II, a number of factors combined to create a 'child-centred' society that increasingly viewed children as special and requiring extra care and attention. Charles Strickland and Andrew Ambrose used the phrase 'child-centred' to describe the 'high degree of parental preoccupation with the needs and interests of their children' by parents who 'placed the welfare of the children at the center of family life' (Strickland and Ambrose 1985: 538). For the purposes of this chapter, two particular aspects of America's child-centred society are most significant: rising birthrates after World War II and the extraordinary proliferation of published childcare advice. The postwar 'baby boom' produced 70 million American babies between 1946 and 1964. During the Great Depression, birthrates had averaged approximately 18 or 19 per 1000 people; by the peak of the baby boom the rate rose to 26.5 births per 1000 people (Colby and Ortman 2014: 2). Eighteen straight years of elevated fertility rates produced an unprecedented number of children, which in itself would have spurred popular interest in childcare and educational practices. Suddenly there were more children than ever before, and their parents tended to be more concerned with their offspring's psychological well-being than their own parents and grandparents had been.

This in turn gave rise to a set of beliefs and practices shaped by the rapid multiplication of childcare publications. The most notable figure in this area was paediatrician Benjamin

Spock, whose 1946 *Common Sense Book of Baby and Child Care* argued in favour of showering children with affection and forging close emotional bonds; it became one of the best-selling books of all time in the United States (Spock 1946). His simple message – to 'trust your instincts' when parenting – and commonsense advice contrasted sharply with childrearing guides of the past. Previous generations of child-development researchers had advocated a strict hand, warning parents against the dangers of coddling their children. Popular manuals such as *Infant Care* (1914) and *Psychological Care of Infant and Child* (1928) had stressed the importance of rigid feeding and toilet training schedules, leaving crying babies alone and avoiding close physical contact like kissing, cuddling and tickling (West 1914; Watson 1928). Spock's book, which argued the opposite, rode the crest of a wave of child-raising literature. Never before had there been such an outpouring of information about children and parenting. In popular magazines, newspapers and books, experts assailed parents with 'scientifically' supported information about how to raise their children with a gentler approach than in the past, focusing on positive parent–child interactions. When combined with a cultural fascination with psychoanalysis that had been developing for decades, this resulted in a dizzying array of advice designed to help anxious parents fashion pleasant and carefree childhoods for their progeny. Although the professional opinions sometimes conflicted, the underlying message was consistent: parents needed to pay more attention to their children's needs, desires and interests if they wanted to raise happy and well-adjusted future adults (Hulbert 2003; Stearns 2003).

The birth of the casual school

The widespread changes proposed by the student-centred reform movement and the child-centred culture merged to give birth to the casual school. The process was rapid but did not occur overnight. Some commentators in the architectural world had already begun to speculate on how traditional school buildings might be altered. In 1942, for example, New York's Museum of Modern Art (MOMA) sponsored an exhibition of 'Modern Architecture for the Modern School', which included a section titled 'School Architecture Begins to Catch Up with New Educational Methods'. In a press release for the exhibition, Elizabeth Bauer Mock, head of MOMA's Department of Architecture and Industrial Design, optimistically stated: 'The purpose of this exhibition is to show that the elementary school should be designed in relation to the child's psychological as well as his physical needs'. She advised that 'the really modern school should be a rambling, child-scaled, one-story building, gay and friendly, direct and unpretentious, that welcomes the outdoors as enthusiastically as the old-fashioned school sought to exclude it' (Museum of Modern Art 1942). Mock proved to be prescient; she perfectly captured the essence of the soon-to-be-developed casual schools.

The MOMA exhibition showcased a handful of mostly American school buildings constructed since the mid-1930s which, taken together, indicated a new direction for educational architecture. At the same time, many commentators attacked contemporary schoolhouses for their intimidating mood and unpleasant appearance. In Chicago, for instance, a 1946 editorial in the *Chicago Tribune* titled 'Must Schools Be Ugly?' undoubtedly touched a chord with many readers with its criticism of high-ceilinged classrooms, 'cold and uninviting' spaces and monumental facades ('Must Schools Be Ugly?' 1946). Similar sentiments could be found in the journals targeting school administrators and designers. While the issue of the schoolhouse's image concerned both groups, their critiques of school architecture at this time were just beginning to move beyond discussions of orderly floor plans, calculations of proper air and light per classroom, and cost effective construction techniques to embrace the significance of the school building's aesthetic appearance and psychological impact. Commentators began to extol the virtues of less institutional and more 'homelike' designs for schools.

The term 'homelike' had dual meanings in the postwar era. On one hand, it could stand for architectural elements similar to those found in houses, like steeply pitched roofs, decorative tiles along corridor walls or fireplaces in the kindergarten room (Busselle 1921: 51). Of greater importance, however, was its broader sense; 'homelike' came to represent an abstract concept of home as a locus of comfort and safety. Translating the casual coziness of domesticity to a school setting was the goal of casual school proponents (Ball 1948; Cannon 1951; Tomancik 1954). 'At present there are well defined trends toward the design of school buildings which are informal, friendly to children, and less monumental than the mass block type of buildings of the last 30 years', wrote Caudill (Caudill 1949: 102). Just a few years later the Chicago public schools' *Annual Report* described the 'ideal school' as 'cheerful, friendly, and attractive both inside and outside', and a place where students could work and live together 'in the climate of the "good life"' (Chicago Board of Education 1954: 29). By 1958, Chicago Superintendent Benjamin Willis opined: 'There has been a trend away from monumental features of buildings and toward more simplicity in exterior and interior design. The net result is less cost, a building with a friendly atmosphere, and an increase in the value of all other property in the community' (Chicago Board of Education 1958: 9; see Figure 7.5). Words like 'friendly', 'homelike', 'informal' and 'casual' occurred more frequently in educational and

FIGURE 7.5   George Washington Elementary and High School, Chicago, Illinois, 1957.

Architect: Perkins & Will

Source: Chicago Board of Education Archives

architectural articles, curriculum textbooks and school reports (Jacobek 1950; Fay 1958). By 1963, for example, the Chicago schools' *Annual Report* explained how design innovations in the past decade had created a 'more friendly school environment' (Chicago Board of Education 1964: 33). And a popular text on high school curricula offered this commonly held viewpoint (which would have been anathema to nineteenth-century educators): 'The appearance of the school should give the impression that the school is a place where it would be fun to live and work' (Wiles 1963: 185).

The initial attempts to fashion casual, pleasant environments for students appeared in elementary schools in the 1940s (Otto 1946; Vincent 1947). Schools like the Crow Island Elementary School (1940) in the Chicago suburb of Winnetka, Illinois, offered early demonstrations of casual school principles in action. Architects Eliel Saarinen and Perkins, Wheeler & Will lowered ceilings, ordered smaller furniture, allowed classrooms to open to a grass-filled courtyard and punctuated the building with whimsical decorative sculptures. The premise behind these experiments was that comfortable and unimposing surroundings, like young children were used to at home, would make them more amenable to learning. Soon, however, educators and architects recognised the casual atmosphere's benefits for high school students as well. In an article in *The Nation's Schools*, a school administrator explained the rationale:

> Elementary children particularly need a relaxed and cozy atmosphere. The high school student with his paper-thin sophistication also adjusts better and maintains a better temperament for learning in a setting not too different from the one to which he is accustomed.
>
> (Hughey 1957: 73)

Caudill echoed this sentiment, claiming that

> high school sophistication is, after all, a pretty thin veneer. In some ways the emotional needs of the older children are greater. . . . The older child does not have exactly the same emotional needs that the younger child has, but he does need a cheerful, clean, and wholesome atmosphere in the school just as much as he needs it at home.
>
> (Caudill 1954: 9)

Such considerations of students' psychological welfare marked an important advance for American education.

Adapting the casual approach to high school buildings and older students presented architects with different challenges from those faced at the elementary level, given adolescents' maturation and the more differentiated curricula available in secondary education. An article co-written by Caudill and Hollis Moore, superintendent of the Tyler, Texas, schools, provides insight into the attempt to harmonise teenagers with their school buildings. The duo began by listing 'eight characteristics of teenagers' encompassing their cognitive, social, physical and psychological needs and desires. Then they considered how each of these characteristics affected architecture. For example, because teens were faced with 'rapid and profound bodily changes', wise planners would recognise that teaching spaces 'should be designed to give release from nervous tension as far as possible' by being 'pleasant and restful'. Comfortable equipment and furniture, and using glass in all four walls of a classroom, could accomplish this aim, while abundant mirrors would also be helpful. Acknowledging that 'there should be a close relation between the home and school', Moore and Caudill addressed teenagers' need for a school to have 'human values' expressed through 'warm, friendly architecture' (Moore and Caudill 1955: 57). In the junior high school featured in the article, the authors believed they expressed such human values through an attractive grouping of colourful buildings with glass-walled classrooms, united in form, residential in nature and sympathetic to the terrain, with room for both social and recreational activities on the grounds.

Architectural pedigree

The casual schools, though innovative, had an architectural pedigree rooted in earlier developments at the elementary school level. One of their salient traits – buildings with a relationship to the outdoors – can be traced back to European 'open-air' schools of the 1900s for children suffering from, or at risk for, tuberculosis (Châtelet 2008). The first of these schools-without-walls materialised in Germany, but they quickly spread through Western Europe and across to the United States before World War I. In England, educators, architects and medical practitioners, worried about the widespread lack of hygiene in the schools, saw the beneficial health effects of fresh air and cross-ventilation on tubercular students and sought to apply them to public elementary schools with the so-called veranda-type school building. Deviating from the popular central-hall plan, these buildings lined classrooms in rows and employed folding doors opening out to verandas, combined with clerestory windows in the opposite wall, to guarantee continuous airflow. By the 1920s architects were replacing the verandas with grassy courtyards, further strengthening the indoor–outdoor connection (Seaborne and Lowe 1977). At roughly the same time in Frankfurt, Germany, Ernst May and his team of architects created 'pavilion schools' as a part of their reformist social agenda. May's school buildings featured lower, horizontal profiles; glass-walled classrooms opening onto student gardens; and small, lightweight, moveable furniture (Henderson 1997). The integration of school buildings with nature was seen as a vital component of the curriculum, and outdoor activities were encouraged.

Many of these same elements would later be found in the school buildings of European émigré architects practicing in California, such as Richard Neutra and Albert Frey, along with local architects like Ernest J. Kump, Jr. Their pre–World War II school designs took advantage of the region's warm and sunny climate to open buildings to the outdoors through patios or play areas directly accessible from classrooms, external covered walkways rather than indoor hallways, and larger than normal windows. These architects also continued a tradition of verandas and outdoor corridors dating back to Californian schools from decades earlier (Donovan 1921).

English postwar school architecture also influenced many American educators and designers, particularly in the area of economics. Because of extreme material shortages, British architects had been forced to contrive a new vocabulary of school design that relied on prefabricated parts, minimal structure and small scale; this method produced a series of school buildings that attracted international attention. American educators struggling to construct schools fast enough to house the Baby Boomers found English solutions attractive. But beyond cost-saving measures, some reformers viewed English schools as an exemplar for integrating educational programs with school buildings. A study of British schools in an American architectural journal, for example, lamented that 'Britain concentrates on child environment, while US architects busy themselves with the school lighting mania' (Part 1952: 126–7).

Schools and suburbs

Casual schools appeared in a culture where social norms were changing, and some of the schools' defining attributes paralleled those of contemporary suburban homes. At the same time that the public schools were moving toward informality, family and social relations, manners and fashion were becoming noticeably less constrained. The relaxed postwar atmosphere was especially visible in the design of the American home, where the increasing popularity of 'family rooms' and 'recreation rooms' in middle-class houses signalled a casual, more easy-going lifestyle (Jacobs 2006). Most of these houses were constructed in the suburbs, where residents were devising novel forms of popular entertainment centred on patios, backyards, televisions and recreation rooms. One advocate for casual school design in the mid-1950s challenged traditionalist opponents by referencing this lifestyle: 'But is our way of life today based on formality? Isn't the present pattern of living (outdoor barbeques, do-it-yourself projects, the flight to the suburbs) quite the opposite?' he asked. 'If our present living pattern expresses itself through informality, do we really wish to surround our children with a physical school environment that appears to oppose their pattern of living?' (Rogers 1956: 83).

Casual schools and suburban houses shared another commonality. Both types of structures indirectly participated in a bizarre Cold War–era conflation of architecture, landscapes and democracy. In a period when every aspect of cultural production was politically charged, even something as innocuous as the view out a window could be interpreted as reinforcing Western democratic principles. As Sandy Isenstadt has pointed out, the growing popularity of spaciousness, views and picture windows in postwar suburban houses was part of a larger cultural phenomenon wherein unobstructed landscape views came to symbolise democratic openness and political freedom. This led to a situation where 'liberty and freedom were

FIGURE 7.6   Steven Tyng Mather High School, Chicago, Illinois, 1959.

Architects: Loebl, Schlossman, Bennett & Dart and A. Epstein & Sons, Inc.

Source: Chicago Board of Education Archives

analogized, indeed, literalized with a scene of open space' (Isenstadt 2006: 255). The casual schools' abundant windows, glass walls and landscaped courtyards served this cause just as well as the suburban house's picture window and backyard (Kane 1961). Some schools – both in the suburbs and in urban areas – were even placed in or adjacent to open parks. In Chicago, the public school system partnered with the Chicago Park District from the 1940s on to provide parks for its new schools. By 1958, 35 of these 'school-park' cooperative efforts had been constructed or developed (Chicago Board of Education 1958: 24–5; see Figure 7.6).

Tensions and conflicts

Student-centred notions of educating children with regard for individual interests and abilities fostered an alternative secondary curriculum called 'life skills' or 'life adjustment' by the late 1940s. The life adjustment movement's non-academic courses were designed to be appealing to teenagers and more relevant to their lives because they emphasised individual fulfilment and societal roles over mental training or mastery of particular subject matter. A major presumption of the life adjustment curriculum was that most students were not talented enough to complete a college preparatory course of study and uninterested in the specificity of vocational training, and therefore needed an undemanding general education. A US Office of Education pamphlet explained this rationale: 'Most boys and girls are headed for jobs that require little training. These youth need and want an invigorated *general* education that relates to their everyday lives' (Rummel 1950: 5; italics in original). Proponents believed the life adjustment curriculum was better adapted to adolescents' special needs. 'If the products of our schools turn out to be healthy and patriotic citizens who are good husbands, good wives, good fathers, good mothers, good neighbors, good workers, good employers, wise spenders of income, wholesome users of leisure time and so forth', boasted the Illinois Superintendent of Public Instruction, 'we know that our schools are good' (Nickell 1949: 154).

Life adjustment curricula, tailored to students' interests and real-life situations, meshed perfectly with the notion of the casual school. However, this shift toward student-centred curricula was not accompanied by a corresponding change in the pedagogical methods used to teach high school students. Evidence suggests that teachers working in casual high school buildings largely used the same teacher-centred tactics as their predecessors, including recitations of memorised material, daily assignments from textbooks and extreme disciplinary control. While some of the innovative teachers employed alternatives such as audiovisual technology, individualised instruction, group discussions and active learning, the truth was that secondary school teaching showed little influence from a half-century of progressive innovations (Cuban 1986: 142–4). 'Basic teaching procedures reflect to a large degree the prescientific era when learning was regarded as a passive process and education was directed toward disciplining the "mind"', admitted the authors of a 1962 textbook on the high school curriculum (Alberty and Alberty 1962: 13). Many teachers even rejected the fresh possibilities offered by the casual schools; for example, educational and architectural journals of the period are filled with photographs of students sitting in moveable desks that have been arranged into orderly ranks, mimicking the old-fashioned classroom with its seats bolted to the floor.

Thus, the freedom implied by the casual schools' informal ambiance often was contradicted by the austere reality of their formal pedagogies. But this was not the only contradiction visible in the casual high schools. The entire educational system was enmeshed in a conflict between child-centred concepts and student-centred environments, on the one hand,

and age-old paternalist practices, on the other. The social construction of adolescence, begun early in the century, was fully developed by the 1950s. For the first time, teenagers, being a mere step away from adulthood, were widely recognised as having unique interests, needs and pressures (Coleman 1961). Statistics concerning Americans' average age of marriage and childbirth confirmed these impressions: most men married by age 23 and women by 21, and they began having children shortly thereafter, with many starting their new families soon after high school graduation (May 2008: 3). Despite this sprint into adulthood, teenagers were *not* treated as young adults in the public schools. The strict schedules, social rules and rigid pedagogical techniques of previous generations continued even as school architects strove to make buildings more casual. Although their high school curricula became increasingly oriented toward courses emphasising their imminent roles as parents and workers in a free, democratic society, high school students remained relatively infantilised, with their movements, clothing and behaviours tightly controlled by adults. A book on American high schools reminded readers that 'dreary institutions and mediocre teachers can combine to break the free spirit' of teenagers, and it reprinted a student's poem to give a sense of the typical school's repressive atmosphere:

> No freedom in the classroom
> No freedom in the hallways
> Herded and hounded the day throughout
> From 8 to 4 this school is a gaol,
> No doubt

The authors agreed, complaining that 'rigid, regimented, routinized programs, coupled with dreary and obsolete buildings' did not 'personify the American dream of education for all youth' (Taylor, McMahill and Taylor 1960: 395). Similarly, a report generated by the Educational Facilities Laboratories (EFL) – a non-profit corporation funded by the Ford Foundation to revitalise school architecture – inveighed against the schools' stern formality. In calling for educators and architects to 'de-juvenilise' the high school, the EFL looked forward to a day when 'not only will the environment encourage the student to hasten his maturity but the management of students will move toward a more adult relationship with the student'. In these future schools

> the bells will cease to ring, the more mature and responsible students will be 'de-scheduled' from the close control and maximum security regulations in force for the more immature and irresponsible, and students will confront the prescribed bodies of knowledge ... when they are ready to profit from such study and not just when the subjects are offered in the course of study.
>
> (EFL 1960: 134)

Despite the best intentions of their designers, the casual school buildings facilitated administrators' ability to control students as much as the monumental generation of schoolhouses. As the buildings became increasingly transparent with the popularity of glass walls and larger windows, they also became more open to surveillance. Architects designed the schools without spaces the students could consider their own or places to congregate outside the watchful eyes of their teachers. 'There were no places that the students "owned"', noted Hampel.

'Long straight corridors banked with rows of lockers emphasised the lack of space belonging to students. An area for quiet reflection was not a priority' (Hampel 1986: 56–7). Sometimes the much-lauded landscaping was just a tantalising dream viewed by students through the big windows – students who were often unable to access the courtyards and gardens. The authoritarian attitude found in some circumstances ran counter to the advice of advocates like Earl Wiltse, who claimed high school buildings 'should be planned and equipped in such a way that the students will consider it the most desirable place in the community to learn, work, and play together' (Wiltse 1955: 33). In reality, the casual high schools could be deceptive; the buildings' casual atmosphere disguised the institution's strict formal nature.

Conclusion

Casual school design and life adjustment curricula were heralded in their day as brilliant advances which improved the educational experience for millions of students. But that day was rather brief. The casual schools' convergence of architecture, education and culture was affected by the Soviet Union's launch of the Sputnik satellite in 1957. This seminal event resulted in a widely shared belief in the United States that the public education system had failed, particularly in teaching science and mathematics, thus allowing the Soviets to gain scientific supremacy. By the late 1950s many school systems were already reverting back to more traditional academic subjects in response to this crisis, hastening the demise of the less-rigorous life adjustment movement. Student-centred methods, however, became more common, even as the curriculum retreated. Architecturally, the casual schools' transparent openness and smaller scale gave way to a new aesthetic by the end of the 1960s, characterised by concrete sturdiness, a greater sense of enclosure and less sprawling footprints. But aspects of the casual school continued on, most notable in the on-going popularity of interior courtyards and open plans, the persistence of moveable furniture and reconfigurable rooms, and the overall attempt to make the school's physical environment upbeat and pleasing. In the last quarter of the twentieth century, American public education struggled to find the proper balance between student-centred practices and child-oriented buildings, as the union of curriculum, pedagogy and environment that first appeared in the casual postwar schools – however tenuous – remained the somewhat elusive goal of school administrators, theorists and educational architects across the country.

Works cited

Alberty, H. B. and Alberty, E. J. (1962) *Reorganizing the High-School Curriculum*, 3rd edn, New York: The Macmillan Company.
Ball, L. F. (1948) 'Providing a Homelike Atmosphere', *The Nation's Schools* 42 (September): 58.
Busselle, A. (1921) 'Domestic Quality in School Design', *Architecture* 43 (April): 121.
Cannon, Jr, J. W. (1951) 'Tomorrow's School Plant Will Be a Child's School', *The Nation's Schools* 48 (December): 60–1.
Caudill, W. W. (1949) 'Toward Better Schools', *Architectural Forum* 91 (October): 94–102, 170, 174.
Caudill, W. W. (1951) 'What Characterizes a Good School Building?', *The School Executive* 70 (June): 19–22.
Caudill, W. W. (1954) *Toward Better School Design*, New York: F. W. Dodge Corporation.
Caudill, W. W. (1963) 'Fourteen Ways School Design Has Responded to Modern Education', *The Nation's Schools* 71 (January): 52–63.

Châtelet, A-M. (2008) 'A Breath of Fresh Air: Open-Air Schools in Europe', in M. Gutman and N. de Coninck-Smith (eds) *Designing Modern Childhoods: History, Space, and the Material Culture of Children*, New Brunswick, NJ: Rutgers University Press: 103–17.

Chicago Board of Education (1954) *Annual Report of the General Superintendent of the Chicago Public Schools*, Chicago.

Chicago Board of Education (1958) *Annual Report of the General Superintendent of the Chicago Public Schools*, Chicago.

Chicago Board of Education (1964) *Annual Report of the General Superintendent of the Chicago Public Schools*, Chicago.

Clapp, W. F. (1956) 'Trends in School Building: The Atmosphere', *The School Executive* 75 (August): 70–2.

Colby, S. L. and Ortman, J. M. (2014) 'The Baby Boom Cohort in the United States: 2012 to 2060', available at: https://www.census.gov/prod/2014pubs/p25–1141.pdf (accessed 1 June 2015).

Coleman, J. S. (1961) *The Adolescent Society*, New York: The Free Press.

Cuban, L. (1986) *How Teachers Taught: Constancy and Change in American Classrooms 1890–1990*, 2nd edn, New York: Teachers College Press.

Dewey, J. (1959 [1899]) 'The School and Society', in *Dewey on Education*, New York: Teachers College Press.

Donovan, J. J. (ed.) (1921) *School Architecture: Principles and Practices*, New York: The Macmillan Company.

EFL (1960) *The Cost of a Schoolhouse*, New York: Educational Facilities Laboratories.

Fay, L. C. (1958) 'Unenclosed Classrooms Create Atmosphere of Family Living', *The Nation's Schools* 61 (May): 57–60.

French, W. M. (1967) *American Secondary Education*, 2nd edn, New York: The Odyssey Press.

Gibbons, K. and Hereford, K. (1955) 'A Panorama of 100 New Schools', *The School Executive* 74 (April): 70–101.

Hampel, R. L. (1986) *The Last Little Citadel: American High Schools Since 1940*, Boston: Houghton Mifflin Company.

Henderson, S. R. (1997) '"New Buildings Create New People": The Pavilion Schools of Weimar Frankfurt as a Model of Pedagogical Reform', *Design Issues* 13, 1: 27–38.

Hughey, R. H. (1957) 'Entire Building is for Living and Learning', *The Nation's Schools* 60 (November): 72–3.

Hulbert, A. (2003) *Raising America: Experts, Parents, and a Century of Advice About Children*, New York: Alfred A. Knopf.

Ireland, D. B. (1952) 'Campus Type of Senior High School', *The Nation's Schools* 50 (September): 65–73.

Isenstadt, S. (2006) *The Modern American House: Spaciousness and Middle-Class Identity*, New York: Cambridge University Press.

Jacobek, A. (1950) 'Practical Materials Give Wilmette Elementary School Home-Like Atmosphere with Low Maintenance Costs', *The Nation's Schools* 49 (June): 58–9.

Jacobs, J. A. (2006) 'Social and Spatial Change in the Postwar Family Room', *Perspectives in Vernacular Architecture* 13, 1: 70–85.

Kane, W. J. (1961) 'Thoughts on the School Courtyard', *American School Board Journal* 142 (January): 32–3.

May, E. T. (2008) *Homeward Bound: American Families in the Cold War Era*, New York: Basic Books.

Moore, H. A. and Caudill, W. W. (1955) 'Designed for the Early Teen-Ager', *The Nation's Schools* 55 (January): 56–64.

Museum of Modern Art (1942) 'Modern Architecture for the Modern School', press release, available at: https://www.moma.org/pdfs/docs/press_archives/821/releases/MOMA_1942_0063_1942–09–24_42914–57.pdf?2010 (accessed 10 June 2015).

'Must Schools Be Ugly?' (1946) *Chicago Daily Tribune*, 5 December.

Nickell, V. L. (1949) 'How Can We Develop an Effective Program of Education for Life Adjustment?', *Bulletin of the National Association of Secondary-School Principals* 33 (April): 153–6.

Otto, H. J. (1946) 'Designing Elementary School Classrooms for General Use', *The School Executive* 66 (November): 53–7.

Part, A. (1952) 'What Can Be Learned from Britain's New Schools?', *Architectural Forum* 97 (October): 126–8, 170, 172.

Ravitch, D. (1985) *The Troubled Crusade: American Education 1945–1980*, New York: Basic Books.

Rogers, A. C. (1956) 'Toward an Expressive School Architecture', *The Nation's Schools* 57 (March): 81–4.

Rummel, F.V. (1950) *High School: What's in it for Me?* Washington, DC: US Office of Education.

Seaborne, M. and Lowe, R. (1977) *The English School: Its Architecture and Organization Volume II 1870–1970*, London: Routledge & Kegan Paul.

Spock, B. (1946) *Common Sense Book of Baby and Child Care*, New York: Duell, Sloan and Pearce.

Stearns, P. (2003) *Anxious Parents: A History of Modern Childrearing in America*, New York: New York University Press.

Strickland, C. E. and Ambrose, A. M. (1985) 'The Baby Boom, Prosperity, and the Changing Worlds of Children, 1945–1963', in Joseph M. Hawes and N. Ray Hiner (eds) *American Childhood: A Research Guide and Historical Handbook*, London and Westport, CT: Greenwood Press: 536–62.

Taylor, L. O., McMahill, D. R., and Taylor, B. L. (1960) *The American Secondary School*, New York: Appleton-Century-Crofts.

Tomancik, M. (1954) 'Twin Schools Exemplify New Meaning of "Homelike"', *The Nation's Schools* 53 (May): 63–70.

Vincent, W. S. (1947) 'Tomorrow's School Building', *School Executive* 67 (November): 25–7.

Watson, J. B. (1928) *Psychological Care of Infant and Child*, New York: W.W. Norton.

West, M. M. (1914) *Infant Care*, Washington, DC: US Government Printing Office.

Wiles, K. (1963) *The Changing Curriculum of the American High School*, Englewood Cliffs, NJ: Prentice-Hall.

Wiltse, E. W. (1955) 'Before the Architect Begins', *American School Board Journal* 130 (January): 33–4.

8

OPEN SHUT THEM

Open classrooms in Australian schools, 1967–1983

Cameron Logan

Introduction

The decade from the late 1960s to the late 1970s was a watershed for school design in Australia. The influential Plowden Report was tabled in the United Kingdom in 1967 (Plowden 1967), precipitating major changes to educational procedure and learning spaces in that country. This had an immediate impact on educational leaders in Australia, some of whom travelled so they could observe international changes in situ. A. W. (Alby) Jones, a senior education bureaucrat in South Australia in the period and Director General of Education in the state from 1970 to 1977, as well as a member of the Australian Schools Commission from its inauguration in 1972, was particularly influential. Jones was convinced that the hierarchical and authoritarian aspects of state schooling had to be reformed and that rigid school spaces and timetabling needed to be broken down if students and teachers were to be given greater input into the content and form of education (Jones 1977). Reflecting a global trend, a growing number of educational leaders and school designers in Australia in the period shared Jones's view that the conventional organisation of schools around individual, enclosed classroom units was outmoded and educationally counterproductive. Consequently, various versions of the open classroom idea flourished in the period as each state and territory adopted some version of it, rethinking the design of classrooms and schools, while loosening grade-level divisions and encouraging collaborative teaching and problem-based learning. This chapter examines that moment of educational and architectural transformation, and it considers how educational and architectural objectives coalesced into a distinctive new type of school that, broadly speaking, embraced open planning and encouraged spatial fluidity.

Open planning in architecture, which involves the removal or minimisation of internal partitions with the intent of creating a more 'harmonious' or 'organic entity', was a central reforming ideal of modernism in the twentieth century. It was promoted by the leading figures in the modern movement beginning with Frank Lloyd Wright in the 1910s and was gradually adopted for a whole range of building types, including schools.

In the twenty-first century, open-plan models of workplace design have gained traction with hip start-ups and the tech industry championing the idea; architects and their clients have highlighted increased user interaction, informality and flexibility as benefits. Frank Gehry's new campus for Facebook in Silicone Valley, which has been described by Facebook founder and CEO Mark Zuckerberg as 'the largest open floor plan in the world' (Kaufman 2014), has magnified and focused this debate. Both proponents and critics of open planning, however, have discussed the issues mostly without recalling the strengths and failings of earlier models.

Open planning was tried and modified or rejected in schools and workplaces in many parts of the world in the 1950s, 1960s and 1970s. German management consultants and organisational theorists developed the idea of the Bürolandshaft – or office landscape – in the 1950s, based on a more egalitarian and flexible concept of workplace interaction. Child-centred or progressive pedagogues highlighted similar values in arguing for a change in the way schools were organised across the twentieth century. By the 1970s, educational decision-makers began to adopt such an approach on a wide scale (Ogata 2008: 585).

Australian schools did not lead this change, but the Australian state school systems provide a clear index of international trends in the late 1960s and 1970s (Cuban 2004). The structure of public schooling in Australia, which is planned and managed in each of the eight states and territories individually, means that such trends reverberated widely. The extensive resources of the state-based public works departments and their architectural departments were deployed to implement new spatial models. Consequently, hundreds of schools were physically transformed or created from scratch in the late 1960s and 1970s in ways that reflected new ideas about the best environments for learning. But that trajectory, and the mingling of architectural and educational thinking that it involved, has been little discussed and is poorly understood.

The progressive background

At mid-century, most schools in Australia did not reflect the ascendant values of progressive educators, or the new models of spatial planning associated with modern architecture. The rectangular classroom, arranged along corridors or opening onto cloisters or continuous verandas, remained the organising unit for the school plan and the basic experience of Australian schoolchildren (see Figure 8.1). Some forms of flexibility and openness in school design were trialled in the postwar decades. Large doors and folding partitions were introduced into a limited number of government schools in the state of Victoria in the late 1940s (Goad 2013). But a more radical rethinking of the school environment was not yet apparent. Such a transformation would depend on more than just shifts in architectural thinking and practice. School design is an institutional apparatus that depends on the assumptions and values of educators, bureaucrats and parents as much as architectural designers. Opening up the school plan, therefore, required a deliberate reform of education and new conceptions of how to use learning spaces.

The realisation of open-space school buildings in the late 1960s and 1970s was the crystallisation of progressive ideals in both architecture and education. Those parallel progressive cultural movements – referred to in the middle decades of the twentieth century as 'the new architecture' (Miller-Lane 1968) and 'the new education' (Cremin 1958; Boyd and Rawson 1965) – shared important values. Progressive is a somewhat loose term, but it captures the commonality of effort among those who directed their energies towards an ideal of social progress and against the reproduction of traditional meanings and procedures. The progressive movement in schooling and pedagogical theory was concerned with nurturing the individuality and curiosity of the child in contrast to a focus on the traditional disciplines of knowledge. Proponents of a 'new architecture' highlighted their concern with function and with

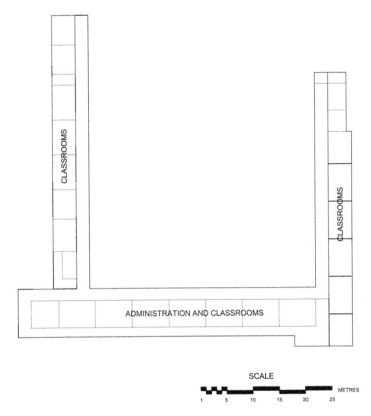

FIGURE 8.1   Redrawn plan of Yokine Primary School, Western Australia, showing the standard finger or quadrangle plan of the postwar decades with its series of box-like spaces.

social utility over the formal expression of social hierarchy and the other codes embedded within the traditional stylistic languages of architecture.

Modern architecture and progressive education both had intellectual roots in the ideals of the eighteenth-century Enlightenment. Architecture's modern structural and spatial rationalism was based on an Enlightenment myth of primitive constructional simplicity (Rykwert 1972), while educational progressivism was deeply rooted in Rousseauian romanticism about the simplicity and goodness of the child and a Lockean commitment to the value of empirical observation (Butts and Cremin 1953). But their full emergence as coherent ideologies did not occur until the twentieth century. Indeed, both educational and architectural modernism or progressivism emerged as powerful influences in the interwar decades when they established strong organisational apparatuses enabling the ideas of charismatic individual propagandists to achieve programmatic force (Boyd and Rawson 1965). But despite this parallel development, the two did not coalesce in schools, at least not across entire school systems or districts.

Modernism and the school

There were experiments in school design in the 1920s and 1930s that suggested a break with the conventional image and spatial arrangements of the school. But they were limited in number, isolated in application and did not initiate major changes in mass schooling. The best known are Richard Neutra's schools in Southern California; the Crow Island School in Winnekta, Illinois, by Perkins and Will in collaboration with Eero and Eliel Saarinen; Walter Gropius and Maxwell Fry's Impington Village College in England; and Richard Duiker's Open Air School in Amsterdam (Roth 1950; Gutman and de Coninck-Smith 2008; Harrod, Hoch and Kinchin 2012; Ogata 2013). These architects did not have an immediate impact on the school building policy of large school districts or at the regional or national level, but they introduced the ideas of modern architecture to the problem of the school for the first time.

In the postwar years that tentative introduction blossomed into a more thoroughgoing relationship. In Australia and elsewhere a reductive or minimal approach to applied ornament became the norm, and the authoritative, traditional architectural languages that had been used for school buildings – collegiate gothic and various iterations of the classical language, especially the Georgian – were cast aside. Designers of new schools in the middle decades of the twentieth century in Australia, the United Kingdom and the United States, many of them working within public works departments, for school districts or local authorities, placed great emphasis on simplicity and utility in construction and looked to prefabrication and other means to systematise and rationalise the school building process (English Heritage 2012; Goad 2010; Burke 2013). School architects and planners of this period also emphasised the importance of light and fresh air (Ogata 2008). By the middle decades of the twentieth century, designers of new schools assumed the importance of first *two* of the three great values of modern living expressed in Sigfried Giedion's formulation, 'Licht, Luft und Oeffnung' (Light, Air and Openness) (Giedion 1929; Overy 2007). The third of these values, openness, was not as obviously a part of modern school design. The rectangular separate classroom was usually presumed to be a norm around which the design and activities of the school revolved. But during the 1970s openness would become a keyword in the educational lexicon. Alby Jones noted in the mid-1970s: 'almost any discussion or piece of writing on education features the word *open*' (Jones 1977: 57; italics in original). He went on to cite a series of terms, many of which referred directly to the ideal of open planning in schools. These included open space, open flexible plan, open school, open-area classroom and open education (Jones 1977: 57). Something had happened in the 1960s and 1970s that initiated this shift towards openness and began devaluing enclosure, boundary and separation.

Freedom and authority in the schools

Many pedagogues, child psychologists and social scientists had long argued for a move away from the standard procedures and conventional spatial arrangements of schools. But familiar practice was hardy. Alby Jones noted in 1968 that while many practitioners of earlier years had been 'fired with enthusiasm' about progressive educational ideals, 'the statement of high aims had not been converted into classroom practice for them, nor had the necessary services been provided' (Jones 1968: 4). In other words, progressive aspiration had been blunted by official indifference, conventional procedure and the obdurate quality of existing school buildings.

It was only with a wider questioning of traditional forms of authority in the latter part of the 1960s and into the 1970s that the broad ideals of the new education movement of the 1920s and 1930s were animated and articulated to a fundamentally new spatial and architectural model in schools. That is, progressive education and architecture required a third force, a social catalyst, to realise their latent commonality. This was provided by the youth movements and counterculture of the late 1960s, with their intense expressions of opposition to conventional, institutional schooling. Teachers, activists and students articulated such opposition in a variety of ways, including through radical school magazines, documentary films and the formation of new organisations. Radical educators in Australia formed The Open Book for a Free Educative Society, a journal and network of teachers, academics and parents committed to rethinking the system of education. High school students joined the anti-war movement and the radically focused groups that grew out of universities in the period. Subsequently, high school students formed their own groups modelled after the radical university groups (*A Moment of Brightness* 1969; Hannan and Hannan 1972–1975).

The trenchant critique of conventional, institutional arrangements that emerged from this period of intense questioning and anti-authoritarianism also exercised some influence within the state departments of education in Australia. During the premierships of Don Dunstan (1967–1968, 1970–1979), South Australia enjoyed a period in which explicitly progressive politics were ascendant. It was in this context that South Australia assumed leadership among Australian states in promoting the renewal of state education. Soon after becoming Director General of Education in 1970, Alby Jones issued a memorandum to the heads of all department schools in the state with the title 'Freedom and Authority in the Schools'. He instructed heads that within the 'broad framework' of the Education Act and the approved curriculum:

> you have the widest possible liberty to vary courses, to alter the timetable, to decide the organisation of the school and government within the school, to experiment with teaching methods, assessment of student achievement and in extra-curricular activities.
> (Jones 1970a: 1)

He went on to suggest, in particular, that 'block timetabling' and 'ungrading' would be acceptable as would 'co-operative teaching, team teaching, tutorials and independent study' (Jones 1970a: 1). The memo thus mandated a move away from the conventional 50- to 60-minute, disciplinary-oriented and teacher-focused sessions, controlled by a single teacher in a room containing 30 or 40 pupils, towards a more open-ended, problem-focused mode of inquiry. Invoking the central progressive shibboleth of 'student centredness', Jones reminded principals that such experiments with teaching methods could only be justified in relation to the general well-being and education of students. Moreover, key decisions about how the school was governed, he asserted, should 'make provision, especially in secondary schools, for student opinion to make itself known' (Jones 1970a: 2). The memorandum thus made a powerful case for devolving power and introducing more democratic and inclusive modes of decision-making in South Australian state schools.

But Jones's memorandum went beyond asserting the desirability of decentralised decision-making. It also provided a clear indication of what he thought were the most urgent tasks in the reform of schooling and, therefore, the best ways for school heads and teachers to utilise their new-found freedom. If it was not already clear, the second to last paragraph of the memorandum leaves little room for doubt. 'Finally, the sooner the old concept of the fixed timetable and strictly regulated movement as the blueprint for the school day disappears, the better' (Jones 1970a: 2). While the memorandum did not inspire the first use of open-space classrooms in South Australia – a prototype, the Burnside Unit, was trialled in 1969 – Jones's conviction underpinned the implementation and rapid expansion of South Australia's far-reaching program during his tenure as director general in the 1970s. Other states would soon follow suit, though mostly in more limited ways and without the coherent, progressively oriented vision outlined by Jones.

Open-space school buildings

In the late 1960s a number of Australian educational bureaucrats travelled overseas to examine innovations in education, including in the design of schools. In 1968 the Director of Education in Western Australia, Henry Dettman, returned from a study tour to the United Kingdom firmly convinced of the efficacy of eliminating the conventional divisions between learning areas (Gregory and Smith 1995). This was connected with a wider set of reforms and ideas that were shaping the educational discourse in the United Kingdom in the wake of the Plowden Report. By 1970 both South Australia and Western Australia were very explicit in pursuing new policies towards school buildings and classroom spaces. Other states would soon follow.

The cover of the 1969 annual report for the WA Department of Education carried a photograph of one of the new open-space classrooms that had been completed and utilised that year (WA Department of Education 1970). The picture shows a teacher's desk, though no teacher, in the centre of a large classroom – which is in fact two classrooms joined via a folding partition. What is notable about the image, probably staged as an illustration of new methods, is the obvious absence of a single focal point in this learning area. The children pictured are focusing on a number of different points. Some are looking past the camera at an undisclosed activity, others are watching or learning from other children, and some pupils are working on their own. The picture is an illustration of the contemporary pedagogical aspiration to take the focus of classroom activity away from the teacher through implementing new modes of learning in different kinds of learning spaces.

The same annual report noted that 11 new schools had been completed that year, six of them developed according to the new 'cluster plan'. That plan was enabled by new furnishings, especially trapezoidal desks, and directed towards providing a new sense of flexibility in which 'fixed class sizes would become less relevant' (WA Department of Education 1970: 4). The report further observed: 'Teaching groups may be expected to vary from period to period, subject to subject and school to school according to the learning content or activity, and the techniques of instruction employed' (WA Department of Education 1970: 4). By the end of 1970, 50 cluster schools were either in operation or nearing completion.

In 1970 South Australia trialled the Cowandilla Demonstration Unit, its second open-space prototype ('S.A. Open Plan' 1974). Alby Jones pointed to the completion of six new open-space units in primary schools with many more to follow, including several whole new schools to be built on the same model. Even more than in Western Australia, South Australian education reoriented the school environment away from the traditional classroom to enable alternatives to grade-level distinctions and discipline-based teaching (Jones 1970b).

The details of how progressive educational thinking was translated into specific built forms in South Australia was determined by an interdepartmental working group formed in 1968. The Building Consultancy, as it was known, was made up of educationalists from the Education Department as well as architects from the Public Buildings Department and a consulting architect from the United Kingdom, Peter Falconer. Falconer was a successful commercial architect who specialised in industrial warehouse design and logistics, but his firm had also developed a secondary specialty in schooling in the 1960s through several projects for Catholic schools in the United Kingdom ('S.A. Open Plan' 1974; Falconer 1964).

The brief that the consultancy developed for Cowandilla and subsequent open-space schools in South Australia called for the following:

- a large open teaching space to permit large and small group activity or individual study;
- ready availability of water, gas and electrical services for art, craft, science and mathematics;
- an acoustically isolated withdrawal room for either noisy or quiet activities;
- and outdoor covered work areas leading to semi-enclosed courtyards ('Cowandilla Primary School' 1971: 448).

The brief was an architectural distillation of a progressive program in education. Students should be able to move in these rooms; they should be able to do hands-on work in art and science (learning by doing); the group size should fit the activity, not the division of rooms and the conventional organisational structure of the school; the new arrangements, with their smaller withdrawal rooms, should allow for different noise levels; and the new planning approach should provide ready access to outdoor learning areas and a richer connection to the natural settings of the schools (see Figure 8.2).

By 1973, the South Australian education department had also opened new high schools in the Adelaide suburbs of Para Hills and Para Vista based on the 'open space flexible' model

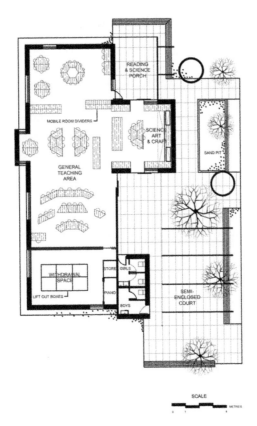

FIGURE 8.2 Redrawn plan of the Cowandilla Demonstration Unit, South Australia, 1970.

(Condous 1978). By 1977 there were 14 more secondary schools with open-space learning areas operating in South Australia, and any additions to existing schools were planned around open-space units. In a paper reflecting on the use of open-space units at the high school level, South Australian education bureaucrat Jack Condous acknowledged that some teaching innovations associated with the new model were not successful. He insisted, however, that the values of flexibility and experimentation were key. The point of the new model was that the schools, the teachers – in concert and individually – and the students could all play a role in determining how the school day was to be conducted. Physical constraints of building and room, he insisted, 'should not determine the mode of education' (Condous 1978).

The South Australian redesign of classrooms was the furthest reaching in Australia at this time. But during the same period, New South Wales and Victoria, the largest states in Australia with the biggest school systems, also established special interdepartmental working groups to look at how they could update their school facilities and integrate the thinking of designers and educationists. In Victoria the state government established the Educational Facilities Research Laboratory (EFRL), clearly echoing the Ford Foundation's Educational Facilities Laboratory (EFL). While the impact of the EFRL fell well short of the internationally influential EFL, it was a mechanism for putting Victorian Education Department personnel into more direct contact with the state's Public Works Department. Moreover, the very title of the group expressed the prevalent aspiration to connect education research and thinking to the design of school facilities.

In New South Wales, the Schools Building Research and Development Group, formed in 1967, was likewise intended to utilise contemporary educational thinking and research (NSW Government Architect's Branch 1979; Jack 1980). The Development Group focused on bringing progressive strands of educational thought into the provision of school buildings and grounds. In 1968 the NSW Public Works Department introduced their cluster schools – and in 1970 a more economical version, the I70 or K schools. These designs included folding partitions and withdrawal spaces to allow greater flexibility in learning group size. The schools group within the Government Architect's Branch also created six experimental school designs in the early 1970s, with five of them built in outer suburban and regional areas: Toongabbie North (later renamed Winston Heights), Briar Road Pubic School at South Campbelltown, Newling Public School at East Armidale, Widemere Public School at Merrylands West and Murray Farm at North Rocks, an addition to an existing school. A piece in *NSW Builder* from December 1973 highlighted the educational objectives embedded within this group of experiments. The schools made it possible, it was claimed, 'for teachers to share resources, to work together and to provide both small and large, group and individual instruction'. The emphasis on 'practical activities', 'integrated programs' and 'unlimited opportunities for individual expression' were also noted (Jack 1980: 128).

Those schools, while experimental in plan, maintained the vocabulary that had been devised by the NSW Government Architect's Branch in the 1960s and did not look especially different on the outside from the previous generation of schools. They were constructed from the same palette of materials – exposed brick walls, tile roofs and timber panels on the inside – and did not break from the overall rectilinear form of traditional schools. However, the next group of NSW primary schools, the '75 brief' schools, took the open-space ideas considerably further. At Kelso Public School (1976), for example, the fractured forms, clerestory lighting, and irregular and flexible internal spaces created a very distinct image and experience. As in other states the architects justified their choices in terms of the standard ideals of progressive educational thinking, highlighting student-centredness and greater informality as key objectives. In a publication produced by the NSW Government Architect's Branch in the late 1970s, architect Philip Rose noted that the broad objective of most architects in the schools section was to create school environments that were 'casual, unforbidding [*sic*] and non-institutional' (NSW Government Architect's Branch 1979). While debates within the NSW Government Architect's Branch were heated about just how much informality could be introduced before the buildings ceased to be architecture, the shared ethic was certainly one that opposed traditional institutional associations and traditional formal devices related to thresholds and spatial hierarchy. The focus instead was on openness and fluidity of learning spaces as well as the frank expression of key structural elements. In many of the schools, open steel trusses are visually prominent aspects of the interiors. Yet this structural expressiveness was not an end itself and was accompanied by a very overt commitment to defining interesting, playful spaces. At Hampden Park Public School (1976), for example, architect Chris Johnson included a small loft area, accessible by ladder (see Figure 8.3). It was an idea that had been championed in the United Kingdom in the 1960s by influential school architects David and Mary Medd and also incorporated into the work of Melbourne architect Kevin Borland in the early 1970s. Borland's designs for Preshil, the progressive private school in the Melbourne suburb of Kew, were widely published in Australia.

By the end of the 1970s, flexible and open-space learning areas enjoyed wide acceptance among school architects in Australia, and by 1976 every state and territory had utilised

FIGURE 8.3   Loft area at the Hampden Park Public School, New South Wales, 1976. The image highlights the effort to create playful, dynamic spaces that are not merely open spaces.

Architect: NSW Government Architect, Project Architect: Chris Johnson

Source: David Moore Photography

some version of them. From the extensive rollout of open-space schools and classrooms in South Australia, where they found a place in both primary and secondary schools, and where teaching and learning were explicitly oriented towards their use, to their more limited application in some states where such progressive educational ideas had not been embraced so wholeheartedly, this different model of schooling had a major impact on the character and spatial quality of school environments. But while architects generally endorsed this approach to school design in the 1970s and progressive educators saw open-space learning areas as a vital means to cast off unnecessary restrictions on educational practices, they did not achieve anything like universal acceptance.

Evaluation and reassessment

The search to legitimise open-space planning models and modes of teaching saw the new programs subjected to extensive evaluation by education departments and by university-based researchers. In South Australia such evaluations were conducted very widely at both primary and secondary levels. Teachers, pupils and principals were all surveyed as part of the process in the early years of the implementation of open-plan school models, between 1969 and 1975 (Lambert 1973; Lefleur 1973; Lovegrove 1974; 1975). The conclusions drawn from these studies broadly supported the direction of the changes to the school environment despite some equivocal responses. However, this soon changed. In 1979, two University of Western Australia education academics, Peter Hill and Max Angus, undertook a broad survey of such evaluations around the country from the preceding decade, 1969–1979 (Hill and Angus 1980). By that time some of the evaluations included not only user feedback, the basis of most of the South Australian research, but also standardised testing data. Hill and Angus concluded from their research that while many students were often as happy, or more so, in open-area classes, statistically they were performing worse than those learning in traditional classrooms. While Hill and Angus did not condemn the open classroom outright, they did suggest that the implementation of the idea in Australian schools had not been based on adequate consultation with school users, especially the teachers (Hill and Angus 1980: 3).

By the time Hill and Angus published the conclusions to their study in a 1980 paper, it was quite clear that the open classroom's legitimacy was already being widely questioned by teachers, designers and researchers in many parts of the world. The annual review of school designs in the technical review section of the British *Architect's Journal* charts waning confidence in open-space models of school design in the United Kingdom (Fitzsimmons and Loosely 1977: 18–19). The 1976 review noted that the coming period would be one of 'appraisal and consolidation' of the recent wave of innovation in school design focused around the rethinking of the classroom unit. This circumspect assessment presaged a more fundamental reappraisal of the legitimacy of open-space ideas. In 1977 Roger Fitzsimmons and George Loosely, who worked for Peter Falconer, identified the historical and social forces that were now working against the more idealistic and progressive currents within education. They observed:

> There is a widespread feeling now that education for personal fulfilment must be complemented by education to produce a viable economic society. The pressures of competitive attainment are also beginning to become apparent with the increase in unemployment among school leavers. Further study may therefore be expected of the

effectiveness of methods of teaching and assessment of standards achieved, especially in literacy and numeracy.

(Fitzsimmons and Loosely 1977: 18)

The implications for school design, they believed, were fairly clear:

> Findings to date suggest that the child-centred approach, with individual or small group learning, is effective under a skilled teacher but may be a trap for the inexperienced or less able teacher. Effective teaching is possible with both formal and informal methods; and the teacher should be allowed to choose. The buildings, therefore, should be designed to allow either formal or informal methods, class or co-operative teaching and vertical or horizontal grouping.

(Fitzsimmons and Loosely 1977: 19)

Such equivocation pointed to the waning influence of the open-space classroom internationally. Without the passionate conviction that education must change and that its modes of authority, its procedures and its spaces must be rethought, the project of redesign was almost bound to falter. The gradual turn away from open-space planning ideas and the return to more traditional procedures was not trumpeted as a new direction. Nevertheless, the retrenchment of those ideas was clear and inexorable. By the end of the 1980s the excitement and energy that had driven the shift towards open-space learning areas in the late 1960s and early 1970s was a distant memory. Some of the physical remnants remained. The discussion pits or kivas, the withdrawal areas and large open-plan spaces were occasionally still evident in schools built in the 1970s. But the educational procedures that justified them were mostly discarded.

The historian of school reform and classroom technology Larry Cuban has argued that in the United States the retrenchment of the progressive tendency in education, and especially its spatial elements, which occurred in the 1980s was part of a broader conservative reaction to the social and political upheavals of the 1960s and 1970s (Cuban 2004). This is a nice simple story that makes perfect sense in relation to well-established, globally resonant accounts of the period between the early 1960s and 1990. That narrative describes an ascendant liberal progressive reform agenda that, among other things, offered young people greater autonomy and a less disciplinary school regime. But widespread social anxieties based on economic insecurity and the perception of growing social disorder encouraged a strong push back from conservative social and political forces.

This broad political reading of the rise and fall of the open-space classroom works quite well in relation the 1960s, 1970s and 1980s, but it is fairly obvious that spatial arrangements in themselves do not have a political content. Critics of the recent vogue for open planning in workplace design have noted, for example, that management is usually very enthusiastic about the benefits of removing partitions and opening up offices, but workers much less so (Kauffman 2014). Critics of recent school reform ideas have similarly noted that it is the advocates of increased privatisation and opponents of teachers' unions who have been most enthusiastic about innovative facilities and learning technologies. Indeed, some left-leaning teachers, such as Megan Erickson in the United States, have made spirited defences of teaching and learning in ordinary places and artificially structured situations, of tolerating dull routine and unimaginative buildings (Erickson 2012). Where teachers' unions and the progressive left initiated major changes to school procedures and environments in the 1960s and 1970s, today corporate capitalism has taken on the task of cheerleader for 'reform'.

Conclusion

This combined story of architecture and education casts new light on the parallels between these two domains in the twentieth century and highlights how long it took for fundamental reforming tendencies to come together to remake the school environment. In the postwar years, Swiss architectural critic Alfred Roth emphasised the importance of the school as a 'type' for progressive architecture and urban planning (Roth 1950). Yet the Australian example shows that neither educational progressivism nor architectural modernism was sufficient in itself to transform the basic architectural template for mass schooling. It was only with the widespread challenge to traditional forms of authority in the late 1960s and 1970s that public school systems saw the need to explore a more radical departure from their familiar spaces and procedures. But just as greater openness and flexibility in attitude by teachers and educational authorities would not solve persistent problems of social disadvantage and youth alienation, open-space classrooms could not alone unshackle latent curiosity and creativity in school children. Predictably, unfamiliar methods and environments caused anxiety and were associated with a loss of order and standards. It also seems certain that the potential benefits of greater openness and flexibility in spatial arrangements were not sufficiently understood by teachers to be realised.

In Australia, the decade from the late 1960s was the only period in which there was such an intense interaction between architecture and education. The open classroom, although flawed in many of its manifestations and arguably misunderstood in its educational potential, was the most tangible outcome of that interaction. Understanding what motivated educators and architects to pursue this new model of school planning provides us with a powerful example of how people at this time believed education might change and how architecture might serve that process of change. While that potential clearly no longer exists and the political dynamics around public education now are very different to those of the 1960s and 1970s, it would be wrong to dismiss this whole episode as a case of simple naivety or excessive optimism. Some of the changes that occurred in education in the period have had a lasting impact. Moreover, reforming ideas in education tend to be cyclical and generational. The story of what happened in public education in South Australia and elsewhere in Australia during the 1960s and 1970s does not have any direct applicability for today, but it does provide a stark example of the possibility of transformative episodes of change.

Acknowledgement

Research for this chapter has been supported by a grant from the Australian Research Council: 'Designing Australian Schools: A Spatial History of Innovation, Pedagogy and Social Change' (DP110100505).

Works cited

Boyd, W. and Rawson, W. (1965) *The Story of the New Education*, London: Heinemann.
Burke, C. (2013) *A Life in Education and Architecture: Mary Beaumont Medd*, Farnham, Surrey: Ashgate.

Butts, R. and Cremin, L. (1953) *A History of Education in American Culture*, New York: Holt Reinhart and Winston.

Condous, J. (1978) 'Open Space Flexible Schools', *Pivot* 6, 1 (January): 25–6.

'Cowandilla Primary School' (1971) *Architecture in Australia* (June): 446–51.

Cremin, L. (1958) *The American School*. Madison, WI: The Americana Press.

Cuban, L. (2004) 'The Open Classroom', *Education Next* 4, 2 (Spring), available at: http://educationnext.org/theopenclassroom/ (accessed 13 October 2015).

English Heritage (2012) *England's Schools 1962–1988: A Thematic Study*, Research Report Series 33, London: English Heritage.

Erickson, M. (2012) 'The Case for Cinder Blocks', *Jacobin Magazine* 6 (Spring): 64–66.

Falconer, P. (1964) 'St. Peter's', *Interbuild* (March): 34–6.

Fitzsimmons, R. and Loosley, G. (1977) 'School Design', *Architect's Journal* (January): 18–19.

Giedion, S. (1929) *Befreites Wohnen*, Zurich: Orell Füssli Verlag.

Goad, P. (2010) 'Making the Modern Californian School: The Educational Buildings of Ernest J. Kump 1937–1962', unpublished research paper.

Goad, P. (2013) 'Preserving Perfect Plans: Percy Everett's Polygonal Classroom Designs for Victorian Schools 1947–1952', Proceedings of the 12th International Docomomo Conference: The Survival of Modern from Coffee Cup to Plan, Brussels: Docomomo.

Gregory, J. and Smith, L. (1995) *A Thematic History of Public Education in Western Australia*, Perth: Building Management Authority, Centre for Western Australian History.

Gutman, M. and de Coninck-Smith, N. (2008) *Designing Modern Childhoods: History, Space and the Material Culture of Children*, New Brunswick: Rutgers University Press.

Hannan, W. and Hannan, L. (1972–1975) *The Open Book: For a Free and Educative Society*, Melbourne: Self-published.

Harrod, T., Hoch, M. and Kinchin, J. (2012) *Century of the Child: Growing by Design 1900–2000*, New York: Museum of Modern Art.

Hill, P. and Angus, M. (1980) *The Theory Practice Nexus: A National Case Study of a School Building Innovation*, Perth: Research Branch, Education Department of Western Australia.

Jack, R. (1980) 'The Work of the NSW Government Architect's Branch: 1958–1973', M.Arch thesis, University of New South Wales.

Jones, A. W. (1968) 'Individual Differences', unpublished opening address, South Australian Education Department Conference, Goolwa SA, 20 September, Folder 5, Box 2, A. W. Jones – Manuscript Records, PRG 1501, State Library of South Australia.

Jones, A. W. (1970a) 'Freedom and Authority in the Schools', Folder 2, Box 2, A. W. Jones – Manuscript Records, State Library of South Australia (SLSA) PRG 1501.

Jones, A. W. (1970b) 'Developments within Divisions Since the Last State Conference', Folder 1, Box 2, A. W. Jones – Manuscript Records, PRG 1501, State Library of South Australia.

Jones, A. W. (1977) *Ebb and Flow*, Adelaide: Education Department of South Australia.

Kaufman, L. (2014) 'Google Got It Wrong: The Open Office Trend is Destroying the Workplace', *Washington Post* blogs, 30 December, available at: https://www.washingtonpost.com/posteverything/wp/2014/12/30/google-got-it-wrong-the-open-office-trend-is-destroying-the-workplace/ (accessed 29 September 2015).

Lambert, T. (1973) *Feedback: A Post Test*, Adelaide: Education Department of South Australia.

LeFleur, C. (1973) *Evaluation as Feedback: Children's Feelings about Their Open Space Unit*, Adelaide: Education Department of South Australia.

Lovegrove, E. (1974) *Recent Trends in Secondary Schools: With Particular Reference to the South Australian Open Space Secondary Schools*, Adelaide: Education Department of South Australia.

Lovegrove, E. (1975) *Secondary Open Space Teachers Study*, Adelaide: Education Department of South Australia.

Miller-Lane, B. (1968) *Architecture and Politics in Germany 1918–1945*, Cambridge, MA: Harvard University Press.

A Moment of Brightness (1969) dir. Peter Drummond, 16mm film, Melbourne: Beaumaris Production Company and Victorian Secondary Teachers' Association Production Company.

New South Wales Government Architect's Branch (1979) 'Schools', *Newsletter* 3 (April), held by The Australian Institute of Architects (NSW) (n.p.).

Ogata, A. (2008) 'Building for Learning in Postwar American Elementary Schools', *Journal of the Society of Architectural Historians* 67, 4 (December): 562–91.

Ogata, A. (2013) *Designing the Creative Child: Playthings and Places in Midcentury America*, Minneapolis: University of Minnesota Press.

Plowden Report (1967) *Children and Their Primary Schools: A Report of the Central Advisory Council for Education (England)*, London: Her Majesty's Stationery Office.

Roth, A. (1950) *The New School / Das neue Schulhaus / La nouvelle école*, Zurich: Girsberger.

Rykwert, J. (1972) *On Adam's House in Paradise: The Idea of the Primitive Hut in Architectural History*, New York: Museum of Modern Art.

'S.A. Open Plan' (1974) *Architecture in Australia* (October): 67–70.

Western Australian Department of Education (1970) *Annual Report*, Perth: WA Department of Education.

9

THE BALANCE BETWEEN INTIMACY AND INTERCHANGE

Swiss school buildings in the 1960s

Marco Di Nallo

In 1969, in their book *New Directions in Swiss Architecture*, Jul Bachmann and Stanislaus von Moos qualified Swiss architecture as 'modest', despite its refinement and the high standard of the average Swiss building (Bachman and von Moos 1969). This modesty, which in the eyes of the Swiss critics was the price paid for the complicated distribution of competences in the democratic system, was, in international comparison, actually one of its most appreciated features. When applied to school building, particularly, it led to 'the intimacy of scale and friendly homelike atmosphere' typical of the Swiss approach (Kidder Smith 1950: 151).

In 1966 the Swiss architect Alfred Roth, one of the main international actors in debates about school building, published an updated version of his famous trilingual book *The New Schoolhouse*. The theoretical corpus was almost unchanged from the original, published in 1950, while, 'of the thirty-two examples of the third edition, eleven are replaced by fifteen new case studies'. These changes revealed a new concern with the relationship between school and community: 'the school must become more and more an "open house", a community centre ... and counteract the dehumanizing influences of today's society' (Roth 1966: 6). While in the first edition of the book most of the case studies of schools were pavilion or corridor-type school buildings, the following editions introduced new trends in the layout and grouping of classrooms. The plans were characterised by separate areas for different teaching activities and by the concentration of buildings around a distinctive centre, usually the assembly hall. Solutions of this type were first developed in England (Roth 1966: 36). The multipurpose hall fulfilled one of the main principles of education: to promote community spirit and communal activities.[1]

Since the mid-1950s, apart from standard issues such as square classrooms, bilateral lighting and movable furniture, one of the main points of the international debates about school buildings concerned the sense of community and the idea of the school as a 'bridge to the world' (Füeg 1966: 123). The social and political changes of the 1960s pushed towards pedagogical reform, and with it came a reconceptualisation of the school building. On one side, architects and educators demanded and conceived more flexible approaches and the democratisation of teaching methods; on the other side, Swiss educational institutions and bureaucracies hesitated in applying any reform. This hesitancy was in part also because the Swiss education system is very diverse, with the authority for the school system largely delegated to the cantons or member states. In Switzerland, this decentralisation led to uneven school planning and to a tendency towards conservatism in the education system, particularly when compared to other Western countries such as the United Kingdom, where important education reform was already underway in 1944 with the Butler Education Act.

This chapter deals with the complex interaction of technical concerns, educational theory and social forces that during the 1960s enlivened international debate on the school and, specifically, its consequences for school design in Switzerland. Using journals and official documents from the period, it discusses not only the effects of socioeconomic change and teaching reform on Swiss school building but also the role Swiss architects played in these reform processes.

One of the terms that recurs most often in reference to the Swiss cultural and socio-political context is 'compromise'. The impact of compromise is clear also in architecture, and in particular in school building: the interesting architectural interplay between intimate learning spaces and public-access zones is permanently embedded as an image in the minds of many Swiss architects. The balance – or, rather, the compromise – between intimacy and interchange played an essential role in the design principles of the 1960s, a period when the traditional classroom started opening up, and the once self-contained square space, dominated totally by the teacher, became just a part of a larger series of spaces.

The other teaching rooms

> The community of people is a fundamental topic in the new architecture . . . in modern architecture the openness appears not only in form and space, but also in the handling of functional and constructive aspects of the building project, so that Modern Architecture should actually be called 'Open Architecture'.
>
> (Füeg 1961: 4)

On the occasion of a public lecture titled *Schulbau als Abbild einer Gemeinschaft* (School Building as a Reflection of Community), the Swiss architect Franz Füeg wondered what impact this tendency towards openness might have on school building.[2] In his essay *Die Welt der Augen* (The World of the Eyes) the Swiss anthropologist Adolf Portmann observed how the first year of our contact with the environment builds our own world (Portmann 1958). Educators and designers agreed that the child experiences school as a community, and that this community should be adapted to the ability of the child. In designing school buildings, Füeg believed that to create a sense of community, beyond the inevitable obligations, a considerable measure of freedom should also be guaranteed. Therefore the environment and the layout of a school building should both allow and stimulate the child into open decisions. Füeg observed: 'Our school buildings are still improperly conceived regarding the act of connecting, encountering and meeting. The interior of school buildings is usually a set of boxes, even staircases and corridors' (Füeg 1961: 4). In the late 1950s and early 1960s, despite the lack of change in building programs or teaching regulations, experimental proposals began to give new impulses to school buildings. Architects' attention moved from classrooms to what Füeg (1966) defined as 'the other teaching rooms': playgrounds, halls and stairwells. In these 'encounter places' pupils could gather in groups, but they could also isolate themselves. In building programs these places were often absent or included only as 'secondary rooms', but educators and architects considered them fundamental for a lively school environment. In recreation halls and in playgrounds, playing, fighting and shouting were the relief valves for students who were under pressure during regular teaching activities. The recess period was also considered to be a learning time; it is in recreation time that a child first learns to socialise with and separate from others, allowing opportunities for voluntary gender and age-level association.

In some examples, with particular technical and design solutions, the schoolyard was conceived as an open-air theatre; corridors became larger and began to be used for recreation and as reading areas, and the staircase became a stage for recitals or concerts. Füeg put into practice many of these ideas in the primary school in Kleinlützel (see Figure 9.1), completed in 1960 in canton Solothurn (Joedicke 1962). A central open-air recreation yard, laid out in the middle of the four main buildings of the complex, and two smaller open areas, sheltered from the wind, were conceived so 'the little [children] could isolate from the older and the girls from the boys' (Füeg 1966: 126). The classroom wings and the facilities pavilion were connected by glazed corridors, opening the view to the surrounding landscape. The assembly hall was the core of the whole complex and was conceived with multiple uses: as a recreation hall in bad weather, for cinema and slide shows, and for lectures and exhibitions. During special occasions, the glazed walls could be opened to both the outside and the corridor, creating spatial, not just visual, continuity (Füeg 1966: 127).[3] Through a sophisticated three-dimensional entanglement of space, Füeg created a building that was unpretentious from the outside, but

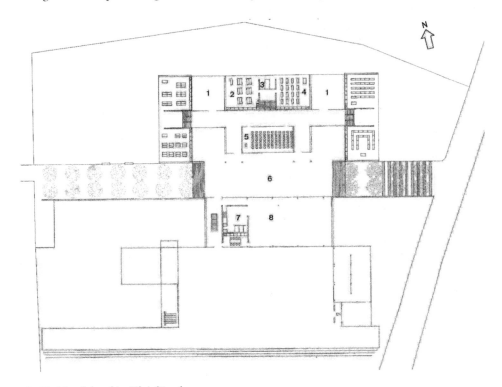

FIGURE 9.1 School in Kleinlützel.

Entrance floor: 1. small recreation yard; 2. wood and metal workshop; 3. storage; 4. needlework; 5. assembly hall; 6. recreation yard; 7. gymnastic equipment; 8. gym-hall

Architect: Franz Füeg

Source: Archives de la construction moderne, Ecole Polytechnique Fédérale de Lausanne, Fonds Franz Füeg

which at the same time had an inner quality that exuded 'an unexpected elegance and light-ness' (Graser 2014: 229). The whole complex was in every corner a physical representation of openness and interpenetration of space; what Füeg called *Durchdringung* (interpenetration) (Füeg 1981: 54).

The physical openness of space is the basis of the idea that the school building should have multiple aims, or rather that openness actively contributes to freer teaching methods and a more flexible use of space. Since the late 1950s, Swiss educators, sociologists and architects had firmly supported the principle of die *Schule als offenes Haus* (the open house school), the idea of a school open to the community, able to fulfil at once teaching requirements and the increasing demand for leisure facilities – a school conceived not only as a place for children's education but also as a recreation centre, for sports events, meetings, theatre and hobbies.[4] In the 1960s, new designs were conceived to combine leisure and educational activities, in extensions to existing schools and in completely new school buildings equipped with recrea-tional facilities for the entire community. Resistance to reform from the school as an institu-tion hampered these developments.

Modernity and the stalemate of reform

During the 1960s, the lively debate on school building in Switzerland was characterised by discussion of educational reform and the positive mood of architects, on the one hand, and reluctance to consider educational change from canton educational authorities, on the other. Since an exhibition held in 1953, *Das neue Schulhaus* (The New School Building), calls had been made by educators for team teaching and a child-centred school, but these found little resonance in educational praxis or building programs. A clear example of this discrepancy is the comparison between the Zurich building regulations and the recommendations of the 5th International Congress on School Building and Open-air Education, held in Zurich in 1953, on the occasion of the aforementioned exhibition. The latter asserted: 'The class unit, its shape, its size and its equipment should match the different child development stages' (Empfehlungen II des V. Internationalen Kongresses 1953). Each level, according to those recommendations, should correspond to a different spatial configuration of the class unit, the recommended size of which should be minimum two square metres per child, or about a quarter more than the amount of 1.6 square metres for primary and secondary school stu-dents indicated in the Zurich school building regulations (Gross 1963). While education and school building regulations varied little in those years, Swiss architects looked for new forms of expression and layout. Since most school building projects were awarded via competitions, architects were given the opportunity to experiment with several solutions, and lesser-known firms were also able to participate. Each new proposal unveiled new spatial layouts, exploring corners for group activities, open working areas and flexible or communicating classrooms.

In the early 1960s, Swiss architecture magazines published several articles pleading for educational reforms and recognition for the role of architects in carrying out these reforms. In 1960, in an essay titled 'Planning Requirements for Secondary Schools, Today and Tomorrow', Werner M. Moser observed that school buildings of the early 1950s, especially those for the secondary-level students, were no longer suitable for current pedagogical notions. He called for the individualisation of teaching programs, referring to examples in the United Kingdom and the United States where 'the individual curriculum for each student requires more floor space than a school built according to current standard. In England and in the United States a large part of the usual circulation area are successfully converted in useful area' (Moser 1960: 971). The ability to teach small groups as well as large groups, and to attend to social education, became increasingly important. The consequences for school building were evident.

Moser also observed positive solutions in Switzerland, especially for dealing with the increased attention to the social aspects of schooling and to opening the school to the community. Beyond the positive approach of the city of Zurich to the issue of leisure and in promoting the combination of school buildings and recreation centres, Moser praised two projects in particular.[5] These were the competition project for a school complex with physical education facilities and a parish centre in Rapperswil-Jona (1958–59) – designed by Moser and his colleagues Max E. Haefeli and Rudolf Steiger – and the middle school of Locarno, designed by Dolf Schnebli (1959–64; see Figure 9.2).[6] The latter is characterised by a cluster of classrooms with skylights, distributed along a corridor that is not a long and narrow space, but which rather widens and narrows the space so it can be used for team-working, for individual learning or as a recreation hall. This distribution space became a sort of 'urban interior', a reminder, in different form, of the school buildings designed by Hans Scharoun, where the circulation areas promoted the social life of children ('Ginnasio Cantonale di Locarno' 1960; 'Gymnasium Locarno und Bünzmattschulhaus in Wohlen AG' 1966).

During the 1960s, a period of rapid social change, teaching methods became increasingly diverse, complex and specialised. 'Does it make any sense to create spatial solutions for a teaching method that is absolutely not yet supported [by reform]?' Roland Gross wondered rhetorically (Gross 1961: 274), comparing the futility of the question to the 'chicken and egg' problem. Despite the great uncertainty of educational reform and the rapidity of social changes, the strong optimism of architects and their firm belief that 'through architecture, they

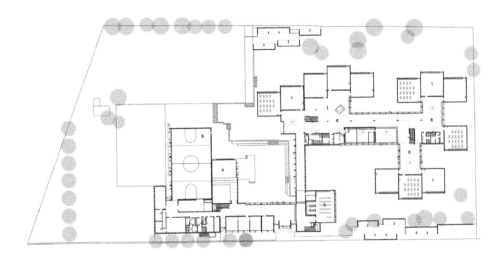

FIGURE 9.2 Middle school in Locarno.

Ground floor: 1. classroom; 2. workshop; 3. drawing classroom; 4. music classroom; 5. gym-hall; 6. hall.

Architect: Dolf Schnebli

Source: Redrawn by author

could change education, and through education the world' (Dangel and Kurz 2004: 78) led them to experiment further with different design solutions.

Swiss architects involved in the debate about school building saw the need to invent a different type of school and envisaged a much more flexible layout that made it possible for classrooms to work in differentiated groups, with teachers rotating through classrooms rather than students changing rooms for every class. The elimination of special classrooms would lead to financial savings; at the same time each classroom would become in and for itself a unit capable of future adjustments.

In the early 1960s the most popular school model was the one composed of normal and special classrooms, but increasing specialisation of knowledge led, theoretically, to a school building where the class lost its sense of social group, and where all the classrooms were specialised rooms within which the students went and came from hour to hour depending on the subject. This kind of pedagogy drove the need for specialist classrooms, but the inter-relationships between scientific, technical and humanistic knowledge became increasingly evident and complex, providing a strong argument in support of flexible classroom spaces that didn't separate knowledge strands into distinct silos.

On the basis of this new conception of knowledge and learning, architects and educators highlighted the need to create a different type of school with a new level of flexibility. Two tendencies became apparent. One was towards complete flexibility of the schools' interior layout, leading to an almost radical surrender of the architectural form in favour of a structural grid that could be freely arranged. The other was the definition of a new class unit composed of two or more classrooms that shared a multifunctional space for teamwork, crafts or individual study.

The *Abschlussklassenschule* and a new model of school building

In the early 1960s an additional educational stage between primary and secondary school was established in the first step towards a complete review of the education system in Switzerland.[7] The *Abschlussklassen* – literally 'final classes' – was designed for students between the seventh and ninth grade (that is, aged thirteen and fifteen years) and was initially conceived for those who were considered more suitable for practical training than for intellectual studies. The addition of this stage represented a fast track for disseminating methods and objectives of the modern teaching (Schohaus 1958; Stieger 1962). Fundamental to the *Abschlussklassen* was practice-oriented teaching and the autonomy of the student; particular importance was given to teaching in groups and teamwork, and knowledge was transmitted in different units, with a vocational focus (Gross 1964b).

The 1962 competition for the *Abschlussklassenschulhaus* in Frauenfeld demonstrated that the holistic education embodied in this educational stage required a new kind of architecture. The well-structured competition program required several special classrooms for teaching different subjects and for numerous work-oriented activities. Further, one of the most interesting requirements was for a team-working space for every two classrooms, of the same dimensions as a normal classroom (Joedicke 1962). Proposals by Peter Disch and Max Graf, respectively awarded the second and third prizes, presented very complex solutions that looked to a direct transposition into architecture of the functional program. The winning design by Alfons Barth and Hans Zaugg proposed instead a model marked by an extreme spatial freedom and characterised by large glazed buildings ('Abschlussklassenschule Frauenfeld' 1969). The building, completed in 1968 following the competition entry design faithfully, dealt with technical problems similar to those of an office or industrial building, where the priority is to maximise clear-span space to allow the most flexible floor layout. The project increased the potential for varying spaces (with movable partitions, modular furniture and so on) while at the same time reducing to a minimum fixed elements like columns, staircases and facilities (see Figure 9.3). The project by Barth and Zaugg, as illustrated in the competition drawings, allowed infinite possible layouts: enclosed classrooms with shared areas for individual learning, enclosed classrooms linked with team-working areas, bigger classrooms for tutorial teaching and even larger spaces for big groups created by removal of all the partition walls.

Although the *Abschlussklassenschulhaus* model was inspired by the requirements of a specific educational stage, its pedagogical and architectural ideas proved to be relevant also for primary and secondary schools. Educators and architects tried to push the principles of the *Abschlussklassenschulhaus* towards a comprehensive reform both of education and of school building (Gross 1963: 211; 1967).

In Switzerland in the second half of the 1960s, research into flexible designs with a clear distinction between served (main) and servant (ancillary) spaces, and the use of industrialised systems and movable partitions, became fundamental to debates on school buildings. In 1969, on the occasion of the competition for the school complex of Mesocco, architect Giancarlo Durisch proposed a radical project in which the only clearly defined elements were six blocks containing staircases and ablution facilities. The rest of the space was completely free and could be arranged according to any requirements (Institut für Bauplanung Stuttgart 1970). The project was not awarded a prize, but the specialised press paid it some attention and the following year, in a restricted competition for the Oberstufenschulhaus in Buchs, Roland Gross proposed a solution that recalled the same distinction between served and servant spaces and the great flexibility of the interior (see Figure 9.4). This design won the first prize ('Oberstufenschulhaus "Petermoos" in Buchs ZH' 1971; Von Moos 1978).

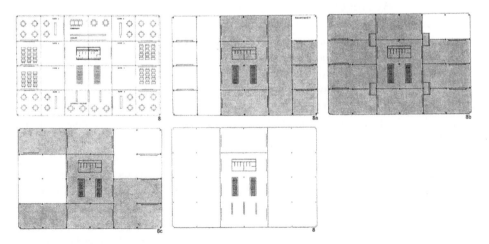

FIGURE 9.3 *Abschlussklassenschulhaus* in Frauenfeld, plan of the competition project and diagrams of possible layouts.

Architects: Alfons Barth, Hans Zaugg

Source: gta archives, ETH Zurich, Bequest Barth-Zaugg

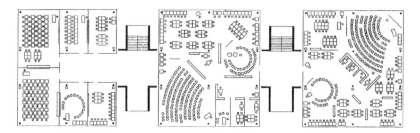

FIGURE 9.4 Petermoos school in Buchs, floor plan, possible layouts.

Architect: Roland Gross

Source[8]: Schweizerische Bauzeitung 38, 1971

Rotational symmetry as formative and constructional aid

A more comprehensive educational system in Switzerland, along with the uncertainty of the reform and the social revolution of the 1960s, meant flexibility became an even more central issue in school building. A certain versatility seemed to be the *conditio sine qua non* for good architecture. Moreover, the increasing need for spaces in school buildings for team-teaching, individual learning and leisure activities led to greater land consumption. For social and economic reasons, such as increasing land prices, particularly in urban areas, Swiss architects developed new solutions for concentrated educational complexes. From the late 1950s a layout based on a 'windmill plan' (a central core, with radiating wings) had begun to catch on, especially because it combined a concentrated and therefore economically viable solution with spaces suitable for new pedagogical needs.[9]

In the mid-1950s the work of German mathematician Hermann Weyl on symmetry and that of his Swiss colleague Andreas Speiser on group theory also aroused interest among designers (Weyl 1952; Speiser 1956). Symmetry leads to linear alignments, scatter effects, blanket arrangements and pyramidal developments, systems that can be easily applied to design. The shapes generated by central symmetry have indeed many different possibilities of application; they are not only limited to school buildings, but can also be found in many office buildings and housing projects of this era, including the Price Tower by Frank Lloyd Wright (1952–56), Hans Scharoun's 'Romeo and Julia' in Stuttgart (1954–61) and the Hochhaus zur Palme in Zurich (1955–64) by Haefeli, Moser, Steiger. Although symmetry as an architectural principle is much older than the mid-1950s, in this period many architects played with the potential of rotational symmetry, following a sort of fractal layout, to increase the frontage of a building and therefore its natural lighting and ventilation.

In 1964, in the pages of the architecture journal *Das Werk*, Roland Gross analysed the potential offered by rotational symmetry in school buildings (Gross 1964a). Classrooms arranged according to rotational symmetries were clustered around a centre. This was not only symbolic; the central hall played an important role in the community life of the school and offered possibilities for new teaching methods. It could be equipped with facilities for manual work and small presentations, which meant some activities requiring a special room could be carried out partially in the hall, bringing important economic and pedagogic benefits.

Gross tested these possibilities in several different competition projects. In his proposal for the school Sonnenberg in Adliswil (1964; see Figure 9.5), he designed a plan consisting

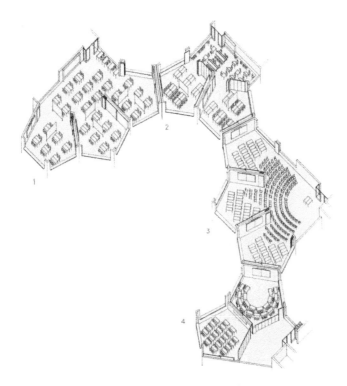

FIGURE 9.5   Sonnenberg School in Adliswil, competition project.

Isometric view of possible layouts: 1. team working, separation of groups through light partition walls; 2. hand working in the hall; 3. large lecture class; 4. as individual class

Architect: Roland Gross

Source: Schweizerische Bauzeitung 14, 1965

of four 'pedagogical units', each one composed of two or three pentagonal classrooms and a multipurpose hall. Movable partitions between classrooms and halls allowed multiple spatial configuration ('Schulhauswettbewerb "Sonnenberg" in Adliswil' 1965). In contrast to other layout principles, which were theoretically repeatable *ad infinitum*, rotational symmetry allowed just a small number of classrooms to be arranged around the central hall – usually no more than six. This unit proved to be a manageable size for teaching purposes, and it was also seen as appropriate to the scale of the child.

In the competition project for the school in Zurich-Witikon (1960), the same principle of rotational symmetry was applied – *mutatis mutandis* – not just to a single building but to the layout of the whole complex. Instead of arranging the different grades along an axis with the community centre at its head, as was usual in school plans of the time, Gross proposed to arrange the space around a centre formed by common facilities. The complex appeared as a physical representation of a living community, a hierarchically structured organism that could be identified from every point as a whole and that could be perceived by the child as his or her own habitat (Gross 1964a: 200).

The large number of architectural competitions, which in Switzerland are the only way for an architect to be commissioned with public works, were an ideal testing ground for devising new architectural and pedagogical solutions. In the early 1960s, the competition for the school complex Loreto in Zug (1964) was one of the most important both for the complexity and innovation of its building program and for the quality of the proposals. The school complex, the size of which was unusual in Switzerland, consisted of two secondary schools (one for boys and one for girls), a school for graduating students (*Abschlussklassenschule*), physical education facilities, an indoor swimming pool and a recreation centre. The projects that won first, second and third places – by R. Limburg and W. Schindler, Leo Hafner and Alfons Wiederkehr, and Tanner & Lötscher, respectively – and one by Roland Gross that received a special mention, were all based on rotational symmetry ('Schulanlage Loreto in Zug' 1964).

Not every Swiss school building of the 1960s was designed according to rotational symmetry, of course, but this kind of layout and the research on geometry as a formative and constructional aid were prominent during that time, not only in Switzerland, and inspired other ideas such as the 'field theory' developed by Walter Netsch (North Western University Library 2009). When compared with other possible layouts for schools, such as the classical linear organisation of rooms, the cluster plan or the grid or pyramidal disposition, rotational symmetry seemed best to provide a good balance between intimacy and social relations, and to offer spatial solutions suitable for the new teaching methods.

The social revolution: repercussions for schools

During the 1960s, Swiss school building represented a very interesting experimental enterprise even without any real education reform to drive it. Swiss architects conceived school design solutions that were ahead of their time, especially compared with progress in education and public administration. It is possible that the absence of reforms, along with the system of open competitions, inspired such architectural innovation.

By 1968, however, social questions, rather than didactic or architectural factors, finally awakened Swiss political awareness on education reform. Two decades of economic boom from the 1950s had notably changed the country, and the great social and cultural revolutions of the time that had so changed the world also had clear repercussions in Switzerland. The school was under attack from all sides: the segregation of knowledge into discrete areas was debunked as undemocratic and inefficient, and a call went out for more porous models of teaching at secondary level. New technical aids like language laboratories, learning programs and school televisions offered undreamt-of possibilities for instruction. Anti-authoritarian pedagogy challenged the teacher's identity: the teacher was no longer considered to be the master who provides all knowledge, but rather a tutor who should help students learn by themselves (Dangel and Kurz 2004: 80).

Questions around schools opening up to the outside world had already been debated, but the events of the late 1960s emphasised the gap between social expectation and the school system. During the 1960s, important sociological research highlighted problems related to learning not being democratised and to the concept of education demonstrating an authoritarian order of society, which contributed to criticism of schools and educational bureaucracy as an institution.

In 1967, in the pages of *Das Werk*, the Swiss sociologist Lucius Burckhardt demanded the activation of latent reserves of talent in students, a new principle of selection which did not only rely on students 'repeating a year' and 'failing', the introduction of uniformity in academic requirements and in examinations throughout the country, and new teaching methods to prepare pupils for modern teamwork and lifelong learning (Burckhardt 1967).

The theoretical output of these years was stoked by the protests across Europe in 1968, which involved many, uneven, social movements. Students were central to these protests, calling into question the authority of the school as an institution and, consequently, also its architecture. On January 1968, four months earlier than the famous protests in Paris, students of the teacher training college of Locarno wrote in the journal of their union: 'The culture of our school is almost completely useless, bookish, fake, hypocrite, dehumanised' ('Rivista del circolo studentesco Magistrale Locarno' 1968).

According to Burckhardt, and many others, larger and more centralised school complexes and the comprehensive school were the way of the future. Comprehensive schools were considered able to fulfil, all at once, most points of the reform agenda: 'Democratisation, equal opportunities, differentiation and individualisation of teaching, introduction of new technical tools, and new subjects' (Institut für Bauplanung Stuttgart 1970). In architectural journals, interest shifted from architectural questions to terms such as structure, process, program, project management, cost planning, systematic construction methods, flexibility, adaptability and other similarly abstract values.[10] In view of the rapid and unpredictable changes occurring, it was questioned whether architecture in the traditional sense was even possible. 'The shape cannot be conceived just according to the current requirements: therefore [the solution is] a big undifferentiated space, which could be arranged as freely as possible' (Institut für 1970: 512). However the open-plan school did not spread in Switzerland as it did in some other countries.[11]

The big comprehensive school complexes, called for by Burckhardt and many others, were also rarely realised in Switzerland. The 1973 oil crisis put a swift end to the belief in technological solutions, and the emergence of the motto 'Small is Beautiful' worked against the idea of the large educational complex (see Schumacher 1973). Indeed, Swiss school buildings were characterised not by a single model but by a variety of solutions that played with the balance between intimacy and interchange. Swiss school buildings during the 1960s, and in the following decade, were in general open but manageable units, clustered around a centre (usually with a rotational symmetry layout) or freely arranged within a compact and regular building – such as in the *Abschlussklassenschulhaus* in Frauenfeld. While waiting for comprehensive educational reform, the compromise reached by architects and educators was a school building where signs of life were perceptible, but where, at the same time, concentrated instruction could also take place.

Notes

1 The multipurpose central hall was also a recurring theme of Scandinavian modernism in the 1930s. First developed in Denmark (Oregard Gymnasium, Gentofte, 1924; architects G.B. Hagen, E. Thomsen), the hall-school, departing from the single-wing formation, consists of a big central roofed court around which all class and service rooms are grouped. The design was motivated by the desire to have a large covered general assembly or recreation area without the accompanying expense of full cubature. These buildings were usually big and multistorey, while the British model mentioned by Roth was arranged according to a cluster layout.

2 On Franz Füeg see Graser (2014).

3 The alternation of these kinds of spaces – open, covered, closed – where people could meet or be alone according to the spatial arrangement also characterised other projects by Füeg. The competition project for the primary school in Dornach (1958), for example, featured two small outside covered recreation halls, two open-air recreation areas, and a large recreation yard at the centre. The latter was conceived in continuity with the auditorium and could be covered by a moveable roof.

4 Already in 1953 part of the exhibition 'Das neue Schulhaus', curated by Alfred Roth in Zurich, was devoted to the relationship between leisure and education, in particular through the topic of modern playgrounds and the concept of the school as neighbourhood centre.

5 On the combination of schools and leisure centres see Di Nallo (2013).

6 The project in Rapperswil is remarkable for two main reasons: it combined different buildings and functions in a community centre very well – the assembly hall could be used both for school activities and for liturgy – and has a windmill layout to its classrooms extending from a central hall, which established an important model for the following years. See Weiss (2007).

7 See the agreement about education coordination of 29 October 1970: *Konkordat über die Schulkoordination vom 29. Oktober 1970.*

8 Every reasonable effort has been made to identify the owners of copyright for Figures 9.4 and 9.5. Errors or omissions will be corrected in subsequent editions.

9 See, for example, the competition project of 1953 by Haefeli Moser Steiger for the school Chriesiweg in Zurich and the school complex Riedenhalden in Zurich-Affoltern by Roland Gross, Hans Escher and Robert Weilenmann (1957–59) (Roth 1966); Zwölf Architekten entwerfen für die Stadt Zürich ein neues Primarschulhaus: zu den Projekten für das neue Schulhaus am Chriesiweg in Zürich-Altstetten ('Zwölf Architekten entwerfen für die Stadt Zürich 1955: 77–85); and Gross (1962).

10 In 1972 the Organisation for Economic Co-operation and Development (OECD) founded the Program on Educational Building (PEB) devoted exclusively to buildings for education. A report published on 1976 dealt mainly with the concepts of flexibility and adaptability (OECD 1976).

11 In Switzerland the open-plan school had been a much-discussed issue, especially on architectural reviews, but few were actually built. The exceptions were a very small number of buildings conceived with a very flexible design such as the previously mentioned *Abschlussklassenschule* Frauenfeld by Alfons Barth and Hans Zaugg or the competition project for the new Magistrale in Locarno by Luigi Snozzi (see Maurer 2015). On the open-plan school in other countries, see, for example, in this volume, the chapters by Amy F. Ogata on the Educational Facilities Laboratories and the open school in the United States and by Cameron Logan on Australian schools. See also, for the Swedish case, Britt and Mühlestein (1975).

Works cited

'Abschlussklassenschule Frauenfeld' (1969) *Das Werk* 56, 7: 475–7.

Bachmann, J. and Von Moos, S. (1969) *New Directions in Swiss Architecture*, New York: George Braziller.

Britt, M. and Mühlestein, B. (1975) 'SAMSKAP – ein schwedische Schulbauprogramm für "offene" Schulen', *Das Werk* 62, 1: 73–80.

Burckhardt, L. (1967) 'Schulhäuser', *Das Werk* 54, 7: 393.

Dangel, K. and Kurz, D. (2004) '100 Jahre Reformdiskussion / A Century of Discussion on Reform', in Kurz, D. and Wakefield, A. (eds) *Schulhausbau, der Stand der Dinge: der Schweizer Beitrag im internationalen Kontext / School Buildings, the State of Affairs: The Swiss Contribution in an International Context*, Zurich: Birkhäuser: 68–85.

Di Nallo, M. (2013) 'Die Schule als offenes Haus: School Building and Leisure in Switzerland during the 1950s and 1960s', *Journal of Architecture* 18, 5: 647–71.

Empfehlungen II des V. Internationalen Kongresses (1953) für Schulbaufragen und Freilufterziehung über 'Das neue Schulhaus', typescript in ETH Zurich, gta Archiv, Alfred Roth bequest, 131-S-33-1.

Füeg, F. (1961) 'Schulbau als Abbild einer Gemeinschaft', *Bauen & Wohnen* 15, 8: 1–5.

Füeg, F. (1966) 'Die anderen Unterrichtsräume', *Bauen & Wohnen* 20, 4: 123–9.

Füeg, F. (1981) 'Durchdringungen' *Werk, Bauen & Wohnen* 68, 7/8: 54–9.

'Ginnasio Cantonale di Locarno' (1960) *Schweizerische Bauzeitung* 78, 21: 346–7.

Graser, J. (2014) *Gefüllte Leere das Bauen der Schule von Solothurn Barth, Zaugg, Schlup, Füeg, Haller*, Zurich: gta Verlag.

Gross, R. (1961) 'Neue Ziele der Schule', *Bauen & Wohnen* 15, 8: 271–4.

Gross, R. (1962) 'Schulanlage Riedenhalde in Zürich-Affoltern', *Das Werk* 49, 2: 58–60.

Gross, R. (1963) 'Pädagogischer Schulbau', *Das Werk* 50, 6: 213.

Gross, R. (1964a) 'Drehsymmetrien im Schulbau', *Das Werk* 51, 6: 197–203.

Gross, R. (1964b) 'Neue Tendenzen im Schulbau', *Schweizerische Bauzeitung* 82, 28: 489–97.

Gross, R. (1967) 'Pädagogischer Schulbau', *Element – Inhalt, Aufbau, Form des Bauwerks* 15: 13–31.

'Gymnasium Locarno und Bünzmattschulhaus in Wohlen AG' (1966) *Das Werk* 53, 8: 311–16.

Institut für Bauplanung Stuttgart (1970) 'Zur Planung von Gesamtschulen', *Das Werk* 57, 2: 77–80.

Joedicke, J. (1962) 'Schulhaus in Kleinlützel', *Bauen & Wohnen* 16, 7: 275–81.

Kidder Smith, G. E. (1950) *Switzerland Builds*, New York, Stockholm: Albert Bonnier.

Maurer, B. (2015) 'Hallers Traum: Die Schule als "allseitig offenes Systrem"', in Stalder, L., Vrachliotis, G. (eds) *Fritz Haller Architekt und Forscher*, Zurich: gta Verlag: 54–77.

Moser, W. M. (1960) 'Voraussetzungen der Planung von Mittelschulen Heute und Morgen', *Eternit im Hoch-und Tiefbau* 55 (August): 967–78.

North Western University Library (ed.) (2009) *Walter A. Netsch, FAIA: A Critical Appreciation and Sourcebook*, Evanston: Northwestern University Library.

'Oberstufenschulhaus "Petermoos" in Buchs ZH' (1971) *Schweizerische Bauzeitung* 89, 38: 954–7.

Organisation for Economic Co-operation and Development (OECD) (1976) *Pourvoir aux changements futurs: adaptabilité et flexibilité dans la construction scolaire*, Paris: OECD.

Portmann, A. (1958) 'Die Welt der Augen', *Die Ernte* 40: 131–59.

'Rivista del circolo studentesco Magistrale Locarno' (1968) *Il Conciliatore* (January).

Roth, A. (1966) *The New Schoolhouse / Das Neue Schulhaus / La Nouvelle École*, Zurich: Verlag für Architektur.

Schohaus, W. (1958) *Aufgabe und Gestaltung der Abschlussklassen*, Frauenfeld: Erziehungsdirektion des Kantons Thurgau.

'Schulanlage Loreto in Zug' (1964) *Schweizerische Bauzeitung* 82, 26: 461–71.

'Schulhauswettbewerb "Sonnenberg" in Adliswil' (1965) *Schweizerische Bauzeitung* 83, 14: 222–33.

Schumacher, E. F. (1973) *Small is Beautiful: A Study of Economics as if People Mattered*, New York: Harper and Row.

Speiser, A. (1956) *Die Theorie der Gruppen von endlicher Ordnung*, Basel: Birkhäuser.

Stieger, K. (1962) *Die Schule als Brücke zur modernen Arbeitswelt*, Stuttgart: E. Klett.

Von Moos, S. (1978) 'Notizen zu einigen neuen Schweizer Schulbauten', *Werk-Architese* 65, 13/14: 23–8.

Weiss, D. (2007) 'Primarschule mit Turnhalle und Kirchgemeindehaus', in Hildebrand, S., Maurer, B. and Oechslin, W. (eds) *Haefeli Moser Steiger – Die Architekten der Schweizer Moderne*, Zurich: gta Verlag: 408–9.

'Wettbewerb für ein Abschlußklassenschulhaus in Frauenfeld' (1962) *Bauen & Wohnen* 16, 11: XI 37.

Weyl, H. (1952) *Symmetry*, Princeton: Princeton University Press.

'Zwölf Architekten entwerfen für die Stadt Zürich ein neues Primarschulhaus: zu den Projekten für das neue Schulhaus am Chriesiweg in Zürich-Altstetten' (1955) *Das Werk* 42, 3: 77–85.

PART III

School cultures

10

MAKING SCHOOLS AND THINKING THROUGH MATERIALITIES

Denmark, 1890–1960

Ning de Coninck-Smith

Introduction

In the autumn of 1939 Mr Christian Jørgensen, a carpenter from the village Sjunkeby on the island of Lolland, was busy. He had been asked by the Kappel parish council to design and build a school for ten children at the tip of the Albue peninsula (The Elbow), located at the western end of Nakskov Fjord. In those days the peninsula was almost an island, since the ocean had cut a wide passage across it.[1] Only a narrow and dangerous strip of land was left to walk on, and most people made the crossing by boat (see Figure 10.1). Building materials for the school were also taken by boat to the isolated site, where about ten families, headed by pilots and fishermen, were living. It was expected that the school building would be finished at the beginning of 1940, at which stage the existing school could move from the attic of one of the pilot's homes, where The Elbow's children had been taught for the previous four years (Aalbæk Jensen 1981: 34–64; Nellemann 2000).[2]

A purpose-built school had long been wished for by the parents and teachers. Since 1889 the pilots had been asking various authorities for a specific school space. By 1939, drawings had finally been approved by Thomas Havning, the advisory architect of the Danish Ministry of Education (see Figure 10.2). Havning's office needed to ensure the plans complied with national regulations about sanitation, heating, light and space; if they met these, the local authorities could then apply to the Danish government for funding for the school to be built.

The whole enterprise of building a school at The Elbow was extraordinary. For one thing, the location was remote and very windy, and the local population included only a very small, and fluctuating, number of children. Another problem was the money available for education; the responsible parish was already burdened by the expected growth of schools at the nearby villages of Kappel and Langø. Because of these circumstances, there were some unusual aspects to the school plans at The Elbow. The school would be built out of wood, rather than brick, which was the standard building material at the time, and the building would be smaller than most.

Havning made few comments about the drawings. Normally, he would have made sure the toilet facilities were in accordance with a circular from 1938 and had separate sections

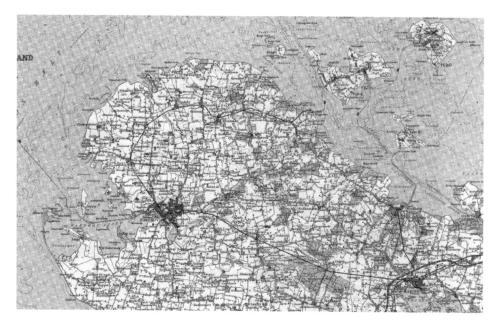

FIGURE 10.1   Map of Lolland, 1956. The city of Nakskov and Nakskov fjord can be seen to the left. The Elbow (Albuen) is located at the very end of the fjord, and the village of Kappel is to the south of The Elbow.

Source: Kort 1411 Nakskov. Geodætisk Institut. København 1956.

for boys and girls, running water, enough seats, and wash basins – a more recent demand that meant all children could wash their hands after using the toilets and before dining (which took place in a separate area that was not their classroom) (Havning 1942). But there was no running water at The Elbow. The locals collected rainwater in big tanks and used outhouses. Because of this, the architect gave approval for two outdoor privies, one for boys and one for girls, and did not mention the basins. His comments were limited to the need to prevent draughts coming from the floors and to make sure the walls were properly insulated. Havning also made a few technical comments to confirm that the roof would not fly off in a storm and that the chimney would not catch fire.[3]

There is no doubt that the situation at The Elbow stood out among Danish school design at this time because of its isolated location and the limited number of children. Quite how exceptional it was, however, is now difficult to define. In 1935 Denmark counted 490 small and big islands, of which, according to the national statistics, only 108 were inhabited (Danmarks Statistik 1939: table 4, 4). Surprisingly little is known about schools that may have operated on the many islands that had in the past supported small communities. Local history studies indicate that the education of children in these small communities was a constant challenge, and that parents sought help from the relevant authorities as early as the eighteenth century (Hummelmose 1973; Jonasen 1989). Sometimes a public school was built, but at other times a private solution had to be found. These ranged from parents teaching their own children or paying for a teacher themselves, to engaging the church clerk to teach. In some cases, such as on Femø, an island not far from The Elbow, the job was undertaken by

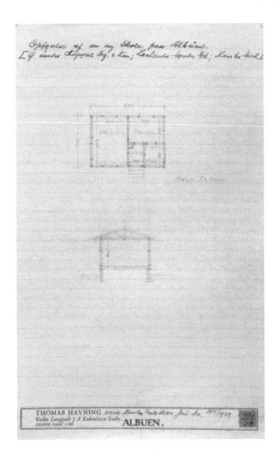

FIGURE 10.2   Drawing of the school at The Elbow – originally by carpenter Christian Jørgensen, and copied by Thomas Havning, the consultant architect in the Ministry of
Education.

Source: The National Danish Archives

Photograph: Ning de Coninck-Smith

local men when they were at home in winter, having spent the summer working as sailors
(Geertsen 2003: 12).

In 1814 King Frederik VI signed five laws that made it obligatory for all children in Denmark to be taught at the elementary level. After this, schools were gradually built all over the
country, and also on some of the smaller islands. Even though the law demanded that teachers
be trained at a 'seminarium', many teachers at the small communities had no training at all. At
the beginning of the 1920s on the island of Rågø, north of The Elbow, where another pilot
station was located, the teacher was the wife of one of the pilots.

It was not unusual for teaching on the smallest islands to take place in existing buildings
rather than purpose-built schools. On the islands of Hirsholm to the north of the Danish
mainland, school was held in the local inn up until the 1950s, and on the island of Æbelø
during World War II a school for five children was established in what had been a ranger's
home (Omø Jensen 2004).[4] In 1944 a newspaper claimed this was the smallest school in the
country, which was not completely true. The school at The Elbow had the same number of

students, though by this time they were taught in an actual school building.[5] Nor was the timber construction of The Elbow's school unprecedented. On the island of Saltholm, outside Copenhagen, schools built in 1912 and 1927 were both constructed of timber (Kjær Jansen, Zimling and Bo Schmidt 1999).

Part of what makes the school at The Elbow so interesting is this mixture of the usual and the unique. The small size of the community makes it possible to follow the connected, entangled and conflicting processes, social and educational, which materialised in the school building. In turn, this allows us to see and think about school architecture as processual, transformative and in dialogue with the surrounding landscape. At The Elbow, the school moved between three locations at different sides of the bay. Each location made a difference to the school space depending on whether it was a private home belonging to a pilot or a fisherman, or a public building. The school at The Elbow was literally on the move during much of its existence.

The debate over the school building at The Elbow took place during a period that encompassed two world wars, and which also saw the beginning of the welfare state in Denmark and the start of a process of urbanisation, even though most of the Danish population still lived in rural areas (Petersen et al. 2012). On a very small scale, the events at The Elbow illustrate how these sweeping political and social changes were translated and interpreted by the people and the local school authorities in a countryside region a full day's travel from Copenhagen, the capital.

Making educational spaces

This chapter's exploration of the school at The Elbow draws upon an understanding of the school space as a material-discursive phenomena. As American theoretician Karen Barad has conceived it, such space is a material dynamic of interactivity between humans and non-human agents and a 'rather specific material (re)configurations of the world through which local determinations of boundaries, properties and meanings are differently enacted' (Barad 2003: 828).

Matter, writes Barad, is not a fixed essence but a substance in its intra-active becoming – not a thing but a doing, 'a congealing of agency' (Barad 2003: 828). For architectural history and the history of school design, these ideas imply a greater occupation with the processes involved, particularly complex creative processes, rather than the final product or building. In relation to the school at The Elbow, these processes involve the move from drawings of the school to bills from craftsmen; from the school's design to its construction from mortar, timber, nails and glass; from the external to internal spaces of the school; from the building to the landscape and community where it was situated; and from political discourses to everyday visions and wishes, emotions, conflicts and negotiations – and from the intended outcomes to unintended events, the moments when things just happened (de Coninck-Smith 2011; de Coninck-Smith et al. 2015).

This path follows a dichotomy set up by the anthropologist Tim Ingold, where it is the *making* of educational spaces and not the *designing* of them that is foregrounded. At the centre of such a making are the many entangled and conflicting micro-processes, involving humans and non-humans, which together, at different times, created a school at The Elbow.

The purpose of this chapter is not to open up the 'black box' of the everyday existence of the classroom as others have done through the use of photos, memoirs, films or schoolbooks and other 'stuff' (de Paepe and Simon 1995; Grosvenor et al. 1999; Braster et al. 2011). I have instead tried to put my ear to the walls of The Elbow's 27-square-metre red wooden school building and listen to the many stories about materiality and class that are embedded within it, framed by a rough, windy and isolated landscape. Why and how did this school building matter so much to the community? To find out, I have undertaken an 'art of inquiry' where, to quote Ingold, 'the art of thought goes along with, and continuously answers to, the fluxes and flows of the material with which we work'. 'These materials think in us', he continues, 'and we think through them' (Ingold 2013: 6).

In my research process, I have sensed the landscape by rowing, hiking and driving through it and staying overnight in the room that at the end of the 1930s belonged to the teacher. Reading memoirs and talking to locals have filled my imagination with stories about ghosts, poverty and illegitimate children, as well as big storms and peaceful springtimes, when The Elbow was dressed in pink flowers. I have been surprised many times in the archives, when the lid was taken off boxes left by the Pilotage Authorities (*Lodsdirektoratet*), Maribo County (*Amt*) or the advisory architect of the Ministry of Education. Through my research journey I have pursued 'an archaeology of the small and ordinary', and connected traces in the landscape with records, which have been left from the pragmatics of life and the regularities of power. This is inspired by the work of Mímisson and Magnússon, who advocate an 'inward focus' and that we look for meaning within each event and object of research – and thereby honouring singularities and how they can reassemble into composite entities like practices, events or persons – in contrast to trying to make meaning from a larger narrative (Mímisson and Magnússon 2014).

Education at The Elbow

The schooling situation at The Elbow differed little from that of other small communities on islands in many parts of Denmark. Families with children needed to make sure their children got a basic education, and their attempts to do so started early. In 1834, according to the census of that year, a private teacher was living with one of the pilot families at The Elbow and instructing eight school-aged children. By the next census in 1840, the teacher was gone, and there were only six school-aged children left.

During the 1860s, parents at Rågø and Vejrø, two islands not far from The Elbow, had asked the County School Board for public assistance in educating their children, but before 1889 the sources do not mention any demands from the parents at The Elbow.[6] In that year, a lengthy correspondence began between the pilots, local school authorities, the Pilotage Authority and the Ministry of Education in Copenhagen. From these letters it becomes clear that the community's children were being taken by boat to the village school at Langø, located about three kilometres in a straight line into Nakskov Fjord.

This was not a satisfactory solution for the pilots, who now wanted to build a proper school at The Elbow and hire a pedagogically trained teacher. The building they proposed would be an addition to one of the existing pilot houses, and the school would also include a private room for the teacher and a kitchen with a stove heating all the rooms, so precious fuel could be spared. The cost of rent and the salary of the teacher would be split between the local authorities and the Pilotage Authority. The parents would pay for the firewood.

Teachers in the countryside were usually men, but the parents at The Elbow planned to hire a woman, since her salary would be lower and she could supplement her income by doing needlework – she would have enough time to do so, they argued, because there were so few children to teach.[7] This plan never materialised, partly because of financial disagreements but also because it was impossible to find rooms for both the school and the teacher, as all the private homes were fully occupied. The children, therefore, had to continue sailing every other day to the school at the half island of Langø (see Figure 10.3).

In 1899 a new and energetic inspector from the Pilotage Authority, Oscar Hansen, visited the pilot station, and again the question of a school at The Elbow was raised. Pilot Hans Kristian Mogensen, who had five children, explained that not only was the landing at Langø very difficult but also, 'at winter, when the sea freezes, it is very difficult to get the children to Langø and many times, the weather gets rougher during the day' – which meant he could not get his children home and they had to rely on 'good humans' in Langø. In addition, Mogensen had incurred fines because of his children's absences from school, and risked spending time in jail because he could not pay.[8]

These irregularities were not good for either the children or the pilotage, especially with the growing importance in Denmark of the traffic of goods and people by the sea. Inspector Hansen started a series of negotiations with the county and parish about setting up a school at The Elbow. On 2 April 1900, a little school located in chief pilot Hans Krøyer-Hansen's home was inaugurated by the pastor from the Kappel church, members of the school board and the pilots' and fishermen's families. An existing room had been equipped with a bigger window, a plastered ceiling and a rail for hanging the children's overclothes.[9] From the start, this was a school for children of the pilots, the fishermen and the families who stayed at The Elbow over summer. The parents would pay for the fuel, the books and the rent of the room, while the Pilotage Authority, the county and the parish paid the teacher's salary.[10]

FIGURE 10.3 Photos from a Trøst-Hansen map of Kappel Parish, made during World War I. Seira Krøyer-Hansen and Elna Gunnersen appear in the bottom row of people. The old and new schools at Langø, which children from The Elbow sailed to before 1901 and after 1946, can be seen in the bottom left.

Source: Trøst-Hansen no. 2659, AU Library, DPB

The first teacher was 17-year-old Seira Krøyer-Hansen, the chief pilot's daughter. She had been allowed by the chairman of the local parish council to order everything necessary to equip the school: two sets of benches; a wooden blackboard; school books for Danish, writing, history, maths and geography; a songbook; a bible history and a Testament; and rulers, pens and ink. It was a while before the children received exercise books, and later the school was also provided with a map of Denmark and 'the world'. Even though Seira asked the authorities for educational wall charts, a new addition to the turn of the century curriculum, this request does not seem to have been successful.

After consultation with the principal of the city school in Nakskov, Seira set up a weekly schedule. The most important subject was religion, followed by history, then reading and writing. Once or twice a week she held spelling exercises with the youngest children. In contrast to other schools in the countryside, children came to the school six days a week, although the youngest seem only to have attended the school in the afternoon.[11] This reflects the limited need for children's labour at The Elbow. Apart from weeding the potatoes and gathering seagull eggs – and seaweed for insulation – girls would assist their mothers in the homes, while boys had few chores until they turned twelve and were old enough to go to sea with their fathers.

Seira Krøyer-Hansen had not been the first choice of teacher. The pilots had wanted a pedagogically trained teacher, and the prefect and the pastor, who had most likely confirmed Seira, both expressed strong reservations about her intellectual competencies. However, the alternative was worse. As Inspector Hansen stated in front of the prefect, 'a modest but continuous teaching [is] better than a much more qualified but irregular teaching'. Seira was probably told to do her very best, and in one of the few surviving letters from her to Hansen she promised to practise before she started teaching.[12]

Major reservations were eventually put aside, after Inspector Hansen, the prefect and the pastor visited the new school on various occasions. The prefect found Seira to be intelligent and clever, the inspector praised the punctuality of the school, and the pastor commented that the children had learned a lot. It was suggested Seira would benefit from some training, with Hansen observing that while she maintained punctuality and industry among the children, she was quite 'un-pedagogical' in her examination of their learning.[13]

But not all parents were as satisfied. The pilot family of the Mortensens, who had two of the four children in the school, complained about Seira keeping their son and daughter in for half an hour after school as a punishment for not doing their homework and for being absent without a legal reason. Mrs Mortensen had even threatened to carry the complaint all the way to Copenhagen and have Seira dismissed from her position. 'If I cannot punish them this way, how should I keep order at the school?' Seira wrote in a letter to the inspector.[14] His answer is not available to us, but things seem to have solved themselves. The next event of note happened in September 1903, when Seira married and left The Elbow. All the school equipment, which now also included a stove and gymnastic apparatus, was transported to the home of the new teacher, Elna Gunnersen, who was also the aunt of the two other children in the class.[15] Not only was the school on the move, but its properties, boundaries and meanings had also to be re-enacted.

Lines of quarrel

The house to which the school was relocated was not, in fact, Elna's own. It was the home her brother Adler had built for himself, his mother and Elna (see Figures 10.4a and 10.4b). Later,

FIGURE 10.4A The Gunnersen house – where Elna Gunnersen kept school between 1903 and 1936 in 1980 (left). Note the tube and the tank for collecting rainwater.

Source: George Nellemann, *Lollands Albue: set i historisk perspektiv*, 2000, p. 25

FIGURE 10.4B The Gunnersen house – where Elna Gunnersen kept school between 1903 and 1936 in 2015.

Photograph: Ning de Coninck-Smith, July 2015

another brother, Gerhard, returned to The Elbow from sailing on the big oceans and moved into the home's loft. The Gunnersen family was descended from the first Gunnersen recorded at The Elbow, who was registered as a pilot in 1630.[16] Since then the pilots had lived on a stretch of land owned by the king and later the state, while the fishermen lived across the bay on land that belonged to the Gottesgabe Manor. Not all sons could inherit the job of pilot from their fathers, and those like the Gunnersen sibling household, who did not inherit pilot positions and did not leave the community, had to make their living from fishing.

The change of location that came with the change of teacher meant the school had moved from the pilots' side of the bay to that of the fishermen. Consequently the pilots' children had much further to walk along the shore of the inner bay to get to school, which was especially hard during winter. Because of this, the inspector from the Pilotage Authority told Elna to give the children a two-hour lunch break so they could go home for lunch. School should begin at 8.30 in the morning and end at 3.30 in the afternoon. She was advised to consult the parents to find out when they needed the children for outdoor work and indoor housekeeping. The inspector also requested that Elna not require too much rote learning from the children. It was more important, he claimed, that things were properly explained and the children understood them thoroughly, than that they merely memorised the curriculum.[17]

Elna's brother Adler had initially been willing to host the school, but became increasingly unhappy with the arrangement. On several occasions between 1918 and 1927 he nearly evicted his increasingly desperate sister and the school from the house, before changing his mind soon after and signing formal agreements to keep the school in his home. According to the census, in 1921 his sister was living on her own, while by 1925 she had moved back in with her two brothers. Story has it a shed was used as a school for a time, possibly during these years of intense quarrelling.

Adler's opposition to accommodating the school was partly based on his need for more space for fishing gear, but primarily it was over how much the parents should pay to send their child to the school. The parish and state authorities were co-funding the school, which meant it had to be open for all the children at The Elbow. However, the income of fishermen was insecure, and when illness struck these families could not always pay their share of the school rent and fuel. This angered Adler greatly, and in one case he banned the son of a fisherman from coming to the school. For Elna, this sort of action could potentially lead to the loss of her job, since the school could not be maintained without public support. The problem escalated. The pilots were getting older and no longer had school-aged children, while the fishermen were younger and did have children attending the school – as did some families who came and stayed over the summer, thus offering only a temporary financial contribution.[18]

Alongside these financial problems, Elna frequently complained to authorities about her low salary, especially during World War I when the cost of living skyrocketed. In 1923 the school board granted her a stay at a Danish folk high school to regain her energy and soothe her nerves. During these conflicts about the school, class interests clashed, and the authorities in Copenhagen tried to negotiate a solution that could be accepted by both pilots and fishermen. The idea of constructing a school building that stood alone, independent from any private dwelling, began to resurface. 'I would be satisfied with the smallest', Elna Gunnersen wrote to the inspectorate at the Pilotage Authority in Copenhagen in 1918. Two pilots, Valdemar Gunnersen and August Hansen, who both had children at the school at the time, explained to the Pilotage Authority in 1922 that if a state loan could be granted, the parents would be willing to help construct a little school with three small rooms and a kitchen.[19]

But these were the years of economic crisis – and nothing happened, apart from the number of students dwindling. According to the teacher's diary, in 1924 there were seven children of different ages in the classroom. By 1931, there were four students and soon after only three. The continuing existence of the school was in doubt. The arrival of new school children, like the boy Børge in the spring of 1932 – born out of wedlock in 1925 to Anna Mathea Gunnersen (a niece of Elna), who had come back to live with her parents and siblings – raised hopes that the school could survive. These hopes increased when two young families moved into the pilot houses in 1934 and started the process of renovation, which included an extension of one of the apartments. When their two sons entered the school in 1936, the number of students doubled – and it was expected that with young couples moving into the area, even more children would follow.

According to the teachers' diary, which began in 1900 and was kept until the retirement of Elna Gunnersen in April 1936, few children ever missed school. If they did, it was because they were ill, had to go to Nakskov for treatment or were in their last year of school and had to see the pastor at the church of Kappel twice a week to be prepared for the Lutheran confirmation. Exams were held annually in the presence of the parish school board of three members, chaired by the pastor. In general, the board was satisfied with what it observed of the children's writing and needlework.[20] A few notebooks from the early years of Elna's teaching have survived in the cupboard of a former pilot's homes (see Figure 10.5). They contain

FIGURE 10.5 Notebooks with ink blots and school books can be found in a cupboard at the museum at The Elbow.

Photograph: Ning de Coninck-Smith, May 2014

children's essays describing ice skating in wintertime and the longed-for visits from cousins and friends over summer. Ink blots tell their own story about children struggling to learn to write, while religious sentences repeated many times over bear witness to the importance of religion not only at school, but also in the life of families at The Elbow.

Temporariness, unexpectedness and movement across a class-divided landscape were built into the walls of the school at The Elbow. While pilots and fishermen argued, the female teacher was caught in between. Making a school was obviously not only a matter of economy or demography; it was just as much a question of making sense of the conditions of life.

From private to public

The two newcomer fathers, however, did not find Elna Gunnersen's teaching acceptable. They wanted a proper school building and a trained schoolmistress who could teach the children until they were 14 or 15 years old, not just in their first years at school. They also wanted the school to be completely free and public as was the case on nearby islands like Rågø and Enehøje.[21]

When Elna Gunnersen retired in 1936, on a small yearly pension, the pilots hired a young female teacher straight out of teacher training college.[22] The school was now moved to another pilot's home. This time the schoolroom was installed in the loft of the house, next to the teacher's bedroom. The room was equipped with a stove, a kitchenette and a cupboard. The loft was long and narrow, and the children sitting at the back could hardly see the blackboard. It was stifling during summer and freezing cold in winter. In 1937 a new door was fitted and an extra layer of glazing added to the windows to prevent draughts.[23]

The first young teacher soon left, and a new one, Miss Larsen, arrived during the summer of 1938. New subjects like biology and geography were introduced, the children practised 'indoor gymnastics', and plans were laid for a separate school building. The pilots had calculated how many students would be expected to attend the school in the future – and, importantly, how many of them would be children of the pilots, given the pilots had far more say in the 'school case' than the fishermen. The final estimate was that a total of six children would attend the school in 1941–42, with one or two of these being the children of pilots.[24]

Finally, the local authorities, the Pilotage Authorities and the Ministry of Education agreed to build a school during the autumn of 1939. The parish paid for construction of the building and an outhouse, and the state offered the land free of charge (see Figures 10.6 and 10.7). Parents would continue to pay for the school's fuel and the books, as well as provide a living room outside the school for the teacher. The school had to move for the third time since 1900.[25]

It was not coincidental that it was in the late 1930s that the authorities gave in to the ongoing agitation by the pilots to build a stand-alone school at The Elbow. First, Denmark needed to keep the pilots on side. They were crucial for patrolling the strait of Langeland and the entry to German waters, and this was even more important after the declaration of World War II in September 1939. Further, from 1937 new national school reforms had made it mandatory for parishes to equip schools with gym halls and dedicated rooms for teaching woodwork and sewing. The Social Democratic–Social Liberal government believed children in the countryside should have the same educational opportunities as children in cities, particularly the ability to continue their education by proceeding to middle (*Real*) school – and eventually high school. It was also proposed that special education be introduced for children with learning difficulties (Gjerløff et al. 2014).

FIGURE 10.6 The school built at The Elbow during the winter of 1939/40.

Photograph: Ning de Coninck-Smith, May 2014

FIGURE 10.7 View from the school, when it was located in Elna Gunnersen's home. The new school was built next to the lighthouse which can be seen in the distance, as can the pilot's home next to it.

Photograph: Ning de Coninck-Smith, July 2015

In response to these various factors, the parish council of Kappel began to look into the future of the three schools in the parish, at Kappel, Knuppelykke and Langø. In 1943, the school at Knuppelykke was closed, and it was decided that only the school at Kappel should be equipped with classes for home economics and woodwork. Parents from the Langø school protested and demanded that the parish pay for the bus transport this arrangement entailed. It was also proposed that a new wing be added to the school at Kappel, originally built in 1901, for the special classes and apartments for housing the extra teachers. The community hall would be used for gymnastic lessons.

The advisory architect of the Ministry of Education, Thomas Havning, feared the village church in Kappel would be dwarfed by the new buildings but generally accepted the remodelling of the old buildings. The German occupation of Denmark from April 1940 to May 1945, followed by the lack of building materials in the postwar period, delayed the process of constructing an addition to the existing school at Kappel. In 1953 it was decided to instead build a completely new 'central school' at Kappel. This would have three separate classrooms, a gym hall, various special teaching rooms and homes for the teachers. During the same year, the school at Langø was extended with a gym hall and a second classroom. The number of school children at The Elbow was dropping, but across the parish enrolments were rising due to a baby boom at the end of the war, and the central school at Kappel became age graded in 1960, when a new extension was built. Around this time a school reform of 1958 put a definitive end to the old system where children in the countryside attended school only every other day. From then on, children had to go to school six days a week, and it was expected that education should be their prime activity. This also put a pressure on the school buildings (de Coninck-Smith 2011).[26]

The old school at Kappel was turned into a public library (see Figure 10.8) – and the new school was built in a field to the east of the village.[27] The location signalled that the school was no longer 'the daughter of the church' but had its own identity rooted in the new educational sciences (Appel and Fink-Jensen 2013). Teachers were no longer expected to serve as church clerks or as church singers, and the school inspections by pastors, as chairmen of the school board, had been replaced by professional educational inspectors (Gjerløff et al. 2014).

The development of the schools in the Kappel parish mirrored what was happening across Denmark. More than 600 village schools disappeared during the second half of the 1950s. In many places, as in Langø, parents fiercely resisted their closure. This resistance, combined with the impact of the war and the lack of teachers, put a brake on the centralisation process. In 1957 only a third of the parishes in the countryside had a school system adapted to the new demands (Nørr 2008: 196). The contested central schools came to play a key role in the so-called educational explosion that hit Denmark after World War II, where a still growing number of children passed a middle school or *Real* exam (the equivalent of a British 'O Level'). During the 1960s and 1970s the percentage of a youth cohort who left school with the white student cap on their head after completing 12 years of education rose from 7 per cent to 25 per cent (Undervisningsministeriet 1978: 24).

Small scales and large blend and slide in the story of the school at The Elbow. Teachers were no longer chosen from among the women of the community, but arrived from the outside with a teaching diploma in their suitcase; the old families of pilots, who had been pilots over many generations, were supplemented by newcomers, who brought new ideas about the importance of education – and the parish as well as the Ministry of Education raised their engagement by supporting the construction of an independent school building. Things mattered differently.

FIGURE 10.8   Kappel Church and its rectory with Kappel school next door to the left. Pastors from the parish church came on annual visits to the school at The Elbow to examine the children.

Photograph: Ning de Coninck-Smith, May 2015

'A sad affair'

One issue, which at The Elbow had mattered since Elna Gunnersen's retirement, was where the teacher would live. According to the Pilotage Authority, the new school building at The Elbow should have contained an apartment for the teacher. This was completely in line with how other schools in the countryside had been built since the 1720s, when the first wave of school building took off.[28] But the locals understood it differently. When the building was ready around New Year 1940, there was only one small room for the teacher of about six square metres; the rest was made up of a classroom, a cloakroom and a tea kitchen. The existing arrangement, where the teacher slept at the loft of one of the pilot's homes, had to continue.

Miss Larsen, the teacher (see Figure 10.9), must have found a way to deal with having her private living quarters split between two locations a two-minute walk apart. In the summer of 1943 she lent out her room in the attic, although to whom is not known. The consequences require some explanation. Fresh water is scarce at The Elbow. During high tide, wells became contaminated with salt water, and it would take at least a month before the water became drinkable again. Therefore rainwater was collected in big tanks or brought to the islands in jugs, and showers and flush toilets were never installed. The person who had borrowed Miss Larsen's room in the summer of 1943 had been informed of these challenges, which involved using a chamber pot, the contents of which was not to be thrown out the window. Despite this, waste from the chamber pot was thrown outside, and ended up contaminating the rainwater tanks and drinking water. In an effort to prevent the school from being closed after this incident, fisherman Sigurd Gunnersen wrote in a letter to the Pilotage Authority that a 'sad affair' had occurred, 'but it will never happened again, especially if the drainpipe is turned to the side'.

Mr Mogensen, the pilot who housed the teacher – who, in contrast to Gunnersen, had no children at the school – insisted the teacher leave his house, although he took two years to send his complaint to the Pilotage Authority. When it was received, Larsen was reprimanded and told never to lend out her room again. It is not clear why it took so long for the complaint to be heard. It may have been that someone connected to the German forces had used the room, and so nobody could speak up about it during the years of occupation. Just as likely the fishermen and one of the other pilots, who had children at the school, were satisfied with Larsen's teaching and feared it could be difficult to replace her if she was dismissed.[29]

A year after her reprimand, in October 1946, Miss Larsen took up a teaching position at Nakskov, and the parents at The Elbow had to look for a replacement. Denmark had a shortage of trained teachers at this time, as the number of school-aged children was growing, and more were staying on in school after confirmation to take middle school exams. No teacher could be found who was prepared to accept the tough and primitive conditions at The Elbow or the low salary on offer.[30]

Once again, the school children who remained at The Elbow had to travel by boat to the school at Langø. The arrangement lasted until 1959, when the pilot station at The Elbow was

FIGURE 10.9   Miss Larsen and her students Kirsten, Bodil, Jens, Svend and Calle at the school building at The Elbow, during the years of the German Occupation, c. 1941.

Photograph: Ib Egebjerg Nielsen, private collection, reproduced with permission

moved to the enlarged harbour at Langø. This time, however, the children's trip to school was not a private arrangement taken on by their families. A newspaper article from the mid-1950s titled 'Expensive Boys' told the story of Arne, son of the pilot at The Elbow, and Finn, son of the inspector at the island of Enehøje, who were sailed to school every day by two local fishermen. This transport was compared to public school buses, which had been introduced by parishes across the country. When the children were at school, the fishermen went to sea to look after their fishing net. The head teacher, Mr Carl Dahl-Hansen, conveyed the local community's pride in this system:

> Even though we are a farming parish, and to many very isolated, we have a completely modern school system, also for 'eremite' ['isolated'] children, who get the same opportunities of education as all other children – even though they have to spent many hours in the boats.
>
> (Grandt nd)[31]

His comments reflect the investment made during the same years by Kappel parish with the rebuilding of his own school at Langø and the building of a central school at Kappel as well as a belief that education in the countryside would survive in a modernised form since the number of school children was on the rise again.

But people were on the move – like Miss Larsen, who in 1946 had left for the city of Nakskov. At the end of the 1950s the number of industrial workers was for the first time greater than the number of people working in agricultural production. Denmark was becoming industrialised (Rasmussen and Rüdiger 1990: 90). Things would never be the same, and the school at The Elbow was a thing of the past.

End of story

In this chapter, teaching spaces have been viewed as 'spaces on the move', and as material-discursive phenomena where human and non-human agents blend in contingent, emotional, connecting and crossing ways. The material-discursive creative processes, the 'doing' and 'making' of school in The Elbow – and the connected stories, the unforeseeable, the unin-tendedness and the interaction between human and non-human agents, like the chamber pot being thrown out of the window on a rainy summer night in 1943 – have taken the narrative in unexpected directions.

Over nearly 50 years, the teacher, the children and the 'stuff of school' at The Elbow moved from one private home to another, having their own building only between 1940 and 1946. No matter where the school was located, the walls echoed the class conflicts in the little community at The Elbow, where pilots held the social and cultural upper hand and the fishermen were pressed by the weather conditions, insecure incomes and, at times, many children. The story about the school thus turns into a history of strong emotions and fights between parents and non-parents as they were played out within an isolated and at times rough environment. Throughout, authorities from the Pilotage Authority and the Ministry of Education, as well as the prefect, the pastors, the school board and the parish council, tried – sometimes in vain, at other times more successfully – to negotiate and to align this private teaching arrangement with village schools at the mainland through annual exams and inspections.

Between 1900 and 1946 the public engagement in the schooling of the children at The Elbow grew from financial support and annual exams and inspections to the construction of a dedicated school building. Despite the unique qualities of this story, it therefore also reflects the growing welfare state involvement in the education of all children in Denmark, whether they lived in cities or in the countryside. The symbols of this were the rise of the new central schools with the consequent closure of many village schools and transportation of children to school by bus.

These developments were anchored in a new understanding of the importance of education to the lives of children living in the countryside. When two young pilot families moved to The Elbow in 1934, they brought these new ideas with them, and an old dream of a school building and hiring a trained teacher became a reality. Paradoxically, the same ideas also led to the school being closed in 1946: teachers were needed in cities and at the new central schools, and there were not enough to also serve the isolated country areas. Another unforeseen event had crossed the history of the school at The Elbow, and the few remaining school-aged children had to be sailed to the school at Langø – just as the custom had been 50 years earlier.

Notes

1 The name Albuen (in English, 'The Elbow') refers to the shape of the stretch of land, which resembles an elbow. In Statistisk Aarbog 1939, The Elbow is listed as an island, and in 1935 there were 36 people living there. (Danmarks Statistik 1939: table 4, 4).
2 The fieldwork for this research was carried out at The Elbow in 2013, 2014 and 2015, and at the Local Archives of Rudbjerg and Nakskov in May 2015. The archives of the Kappel parish council have not survived. For more information on the records used, see the list of archival sources. Box is 'kasse'; file is 'læg'.
3 See letters in Kappel school, kasse 1: 410–34.
4 See also Hirsholm school, kasse 67.
5 See newspaper clipping, Albue Lodseri, læg Albue skole.
6 See Maribo Amt, Amtsskoledirektion, forhandlingsprotokol 24 April 1860, 24 April 1862, 19 April 1864 and 28 May 1881.
7 Albue Lodseri, læg Albue skole letters 15 August 1889, 20 August 1890 and 10 October 1890.
8 Beretninger 15 May 1899.
9 Beretninger 2 April 1900.
10 Albue Lodseri, læg Albue skole letter 24 October 1924.
11 Albue Lodseri, læg Albue skole letters 5 December 1899, 19 March 1900, 25 March 1900, 18 April 1900, 8 October 1900, 25 December 1900.
12 Albue Lodseri, læg Albue skole letter 27 April 1900.
13 Beretninger 11 June 1901, 21 April 1901.
14 Albue Lodseri, læg Albue skole letter 2 March 1903.
15 Albue Lodseri, læg Albue skole letters 31 August 1903, 5 September 1903, 30 September 1903 and 19 October 1903.
16 See Slægtsoptegnelse over familien Gunnersen (Gunnersen family records).
17 Dagbog letter 6 December 1903.
18 Albue Lodseri, læg Albue skole agreements 1918 and 1920; letters 10 June 1918, 17 November 1919, 21 December 1921, 29 October 1920, 3 November 1920, 28 April 1922, 28 October 1924, 7 October 1927, 10 October 1927, 16 October 1927, 21 October 1927 and 27 October 1927.
19 Albue Lodseri, læg Albue skole letters 10 June 1918 and 28 April 1922.
20 Albue Lodseri, læg Albue skole indberetninger 1930–32; letters 30 April 1935, 8 April 1937.
21 Maribo Amt, Amtsskoledirektion letter 6. September 1934; Albue Lodseri, læg Albue skole letters 28 April 1934, 11 March 1935, 20 December 1935 and 9 December 1935.
22 Albue Lodseri, læg Albue skole letters 20 July 1936, 16 July 1936, 1 September 1936.
23 Albue Lodseri, kasse 2 letter 1 June 1937; bill 22 May 1937.

24 Albue Lodseri, læg Albue skole letter 21 April 1937.
25 Albue Lodseri, læg Albue skole, letters 14 April 1939, 27 April 1939 and 5 October 1939.
26 See also Kappel school; Langø school.
27 Maribo Amt, Amtskoledirektion: kasse 3: Kappel.
28 Albue Lodseri, læg Albue skole letters 14 April 1939 and 5 October 1939.
29 Albue Lodseri, læg Albue skole letters 22 June 1945, 13 June 1945, 1 June 1945, 23 June 1945, 8 October 1945.
30 Albue Lodseri, læg Albue skole letter 3 September 1946.
31 See also Albue Lodseri, læg Albue skole letters 18 October 1946, 20 April 1948, 22 May 1948 and 3 July 1948.

Works cited

Aalbæk Jensen, E. (1981) *Livet på øerne: Smålandshavet og Nakskov Fjord*, København: Gyldendal.
Appel, C. and Fink-Jensen, M. (2013) *Da læreren holdt skole: Tiden før 1780*, Dansk skolehistorie bind 1, Aarhus: Aarhus Universitetsforlag.
Barad, K. (2003) 'Posthumanist Performativity: Toward an Understanding of How Matter Comes to Matter', *Signs* 28, 3: 801–31.
Braster, S., Grosvenor, I. and del Mar del Pozo Andrés, M. (eds) (2011) *The Black Box of Schooling: A Cultural History of the Classroom*, Brussels: PIE Peter Lang.
Danmarks Statistik (1939) *Statistisk Aarbog 1939*, København: Gyldendal.
de Coninck-Smith, N. (2011) *Barndom og arkitektur: Rum til danske børn gennem 300 år*, Aarhus: Klim.
de Coninck-Smith, N., Rosén Rasmussen, L. and Vyff, I. (2015) *Da skolen blev alles. Tiden efter 1970*, Dansk skolehistorie bind 5, Aarhus: Aarhus Universitetsforlag.
de Paepe, M. and Simon, F. (1995) 'Is There Any Place for the History of "Education" in the "History of Education"? A Plea for the History of Everyday Educational Reality In- and Outside Schools', *Pedagogica Historica* XXXXI, 1, 9–16.
Geertsen, J. (2003) *Skolen på Femø*, Snekkersten: Forlaget Kurs.
Gjerløff, A. K., Faye Jacobsen, A., Nørgaard, E. and Ydesen, C. (2014) *Da skolen blev sin egen, 1920–1970*, Dansk skolehistorie bind 4, Aarhus: Aarhus Universitetsforlag.
Grosvenor, I., Lawn, M. and Rousmanière, K. (eds) (1999) *Silences and Images: The Social History of the Classroom*, New York: Peter Lang.
Havning, T. (1942) 'Landsbyens byggeproblemer', *Den danske Skolehaandbog*, Copenhagen: E. Suenson & Co.
Hummelmose, M. (1973) *Gammeltid på Fejø*, Fejø, Denmark: Self-published.
Ingold, T. (2013) *Making: Anthropology, Archaeology, Art and Architecture*, London: Routledge.
Jonasen, O. (1989) *Drejø 'øen midt i Verden'*, Svendborg: Skrifter for Svendborg og omegns museum, bind 28.
Kjær Jansen, I., Zimling, H. and Bo Schmidt, S. (1999) *Saltholm*, Tårnby: Kommunes Lokalhistoriske Samling.
Mímisson, K. and Gylfi Magnússon, S. (2014) 'Singularizing the Past: The History and Archaeology of the Small and Ordinary, *Journal of Social Archaeology* 14, 2: 131–56.
Nellemann, G. (2000) *Lollands Albue: kystkultur i historisk perspektiv*, Nykøbing Falster: Museet Falsters Minder.
Nørr, E. (2008) 'Hvorfor blev skoleloven af 1937 først gennemført i 1950'erne og 1960'erne?', in E. Hansen and L. Jespersen (ed.) *Samfundsplanlægning i 1950'erne: Tradition eller tilløb?* København: Museum Tusculanum: 153–225.
Omø Jensen, P. (2004) 'Livet på Æbelø i 1950'erne', *Sletten årsskrift for nordfynsk lokal- og kulturhistorie* 9: 66–74.
Petersen, J. H., Petersen, K. and Christiansen, N. F. (ed.) (2012) *Velfærdsstaten i støbeskeen*, Dansk velfærdshistorie, bind 3, 1933–1956, Odense: Syddansk Universitetsforlag.
Rasmussen, H. and Rüdiger, M. (1990) *Danmarks historie*, Copenhagen: Gyldendal.
Undervisningsministeriet (1978) U 90 *Samlet uddannelsesplanlægning frem til 90'erne*, bind 1, Copenhagen: Statens Informationskontor.

Archival sources

Albue Lodseri 1889–1983. Udtagne sager vedrørende Albue Lodseri, kasse 1 (læg: Albue skole) og kasse 2, læg Albuen Lodseri. Lodsdirektoratet (The Pilotage Authority). Rigsarkivet (The Danish National Archives).

Albuen skole: kasse 1, 401/34. Den rådgivende arkitekt i skolebygningssager/Hans Henning Hansens arkiv (HHH). Undervisningsministeriet (Ministry of Education). Rigsarkivet (The Danish National Archives).

Andersen, A. (c. 1951), memoir. Rudbjerg lokalhistoriske arkiv (Rudbjerg Local History Archive).

Beretninger om inspektioner (inspector's reports) m.m. 4 November 1898 to 23 May 1902. Sjællands Overlodsdistrikt (The Inspector of the Pilotage Authority), Rigsarkivet (The Danish National Archives).

Dagbog Skolen på Albue (school diaries) 27 April 1900 to 27 October 1924; 14 December 1927 to 29 April 1936. Ib Egebjerg Nielsen (private loan).

Folketællinger (census), 1901, 1906, 1911, 1916, 1921, 1935, 1930, available at Arkivalier.online: https://www.sa.dk/brug-arkivet/arkivalieronline.

Frederiksen, D., f. Gunnersen (c. 1901), memoir. Rudbjerg lokalhistoriske arkiv (Rudbjerg Local History Archive).

Frederiksen, H. El. (c. 1951), memoir. Rudbjerg lokalhistoriske arkiv (Rudbjerg Local History Archive).

Grandt, W.h (nd) *Nogle dyre drenge* (np). Rudbjerg lokalhistoriske arkiv (Rudbjerg Local History Archive).

Hirsholm skole: kasse 67, 1595. Den rådgivende arkitekt i skolebygningssager/ Hans Henning Hansens arkiv (HHH). Undervisningsministeriet (Ministry of Education). Rigsarkivet (The Danish National Archives).

Kappel skole: kasse 14, 401–455B, kasse 1, 401–79, kasse 46, 401–1145, kasse 138, 401–2438, kasse 67, 401–1593. Den rådgivende arkitekt i skolebygningssager/ Hans Henning Hansens arkiv (HHH). Undervisningsministeriet (Ministry of Education). Rigsarkivet (The Danish National Archives).

Kirkebøger (parish registers): Kappel sogn and Maribo sogn, various years, available at Arkivalier.online: https://www.sa.dk/brug-arkivet/arkivalieronline.

Langø skole: kasse 14, 401–455A, kasse 46, 401–1122. Den rådgivende arkitekt i skolebygningssager/ Hans Henning Hansens arkiv (HHH). Undervisningsministeriet (Ministry of Education). Rigsarkivet (The Danish National Archives).

Letters relating to Elna Gunnersen's employment and retirement (copies). Ib Egebjerg Nielsen (private collection).

Maribo Amt: Amtsskoledirektion (County school board) Forhandlingsprotokoller (proceedings) 1856–1934. Rigsarkivet (The Danish National Archives).

Maribo Amt: Amtsskoledirektion (County school board) Sager vedr. de enkelte skoler kasse 1–9. 1930–1970. Rigsarkivet (The Danish National Archives).

Maribo Amt: Amtsskoledirektion (County school board) Skoleplaner 1930–1970. Rigsarkivet (The Danish National Archives).

Slægtsoptegnelse over familien Gunnersen (Gunnersen family records). Rudbjerg lokalhistoriske arkiv (Rudbjerg Local History Archive).

11

DOMESTIC SPACES AND SCHOOL PLACES

Vocational education and gender in modern Australia

Kate Darian-Smith

In 1924, an extraordinary experiment in outreach education was launched in Australia when the Better Farming Train undertook its first tour of country towns across the state of Victoria. An engine towed 15 carriages, all painted bright orange, carrying livestock, pasture plots, fertilizers, farm equipment and various displays. The train also transported 80 staff, including experts across a range of areas to provide lectures and demonstrations and teach classes to adults and youth. The Better Farming Train was described by an enthusiastic press as a novel 'college on wheels' ('Better Farming Train' 1925: 2) or, as the Hobart *Mercury* put it, 'like a big rolling stone, going around the country increasing efficiency amongst primary producers' ('Work and Production' 1925: 5).

The train was the initiative of Harold Clapp, the dynamic chairman of the Victorian Railway commissioners, and was run in collaboration with the Department of Agriculture. Clapp had spent some years in the United States, where he became aware of the use of special trains to promote the latest farming practices: in 1909 in Ohio, and between 1914 and 1922 throughout the Canadian province of Saskatchewan (Tiffany 1999: 24). Clapp extended these North American models for Australian conditions. At a time when automobiles were scarce, and many farmers could not attend government sponsored field days, the Better Farming Train could promote the latest information on scientific agriculture, home economics and public health to rural communities (Elvery 2006). Its educational importance was bolstered by an upsurge in farming ventures under the Soldier Settlement Scheme, which granted blocks of land to around 40,000 ex-servicemen under a nation-wide World War I repatriation program. Some allocations were on remote or unsuitable land, presenting the soldier farmers, their wives and their families with environmental challenges and leaving them eager for support and instruction.

Over its operational life, the Better Farming Train made 38 extensive rural tours, stopping at 390 towns throughout Victoria, and conducting one circuit through South Australia. The tours cut back during the economic downturn of the 1930s, and reluctantly disbanded in 1935. The government of New South Wales also ran its own customised train with great success from 1927 to 1929, when it too was discontinued due to the financial stringency of the Depression. Throughout the time of their operation, the arrival of these trains was a major local event, attracting up to 2,000 visitors at each country town: in Victoria alone, at least 250,000 people attended demonstrations and lectures (Tiffany 1999: 24). These were aimed not only at adults but also at older boys and girls, many of whom had only limited access to formal schooling and training in practical skills.

There were specific carriages on the Better Farming Train dedicated to women and girls. These offered information and classes on cooking, childcare and sewing, and proved to be enormously popular. There was a focus on hygiene in rural areas, with magic lantern slides and films on such topics as 'The Spread of Disease' and 'The Danger of Flies'. In advocating the science of modern home management, the train's educational program positioned women as the 'leading crusaders against germs and disease' in rural Australia (Lake 1987: 184). Maternal and child health services were also promoted. A report in 1926 to the Victorian Minister of Public Health on the welfare of women and children noted the success of the 'mothercraft' lectures and the special car devoted to maternal and child health:

> In all, fourteen tours have been undertaken, in which ten included the whole train, and four the women's section only, by special request. By this means visits have been paid to 105 different places, where the lectures and demonstrations have been given. At least 20,000 women have attended . . . they frequently travel 20–30 minutes at great personal inconvenience to attend these lectures.
>
> (Main and Scantlebury 1926: 240–2)

Despite its numerous tours, and the copious publicity they received at the time, the Better Farming Trains – with their fitted-out mobile classrooms – are now largely forgotten by educational and social historians. Yet they were part of vigorous efforts by Australian authorities, dating back to the colonial period, to provide vocational education to rural and urban populations alike. Such 'practical' instruction required customised learning spaces in schools, including laboratories and workshops, which have seldom been discussed in histories of educational design.

In the twentieth century, the relationship between school education and the workforce was strengthened, notably with the establishment of technical schools and vocational streams within comprehensive high schools. With the introduction of mass education, vocational schooling was seen to be primarily, if not exclusively, for students from working-class families, and its curriculum reflected the gendered divisions that existed in the workforce. Boys received instruction in technical, mechanical and agricultural skills, and were steered towards apprenticeships. Girls were taught cookery, needlework and clerical subjects, and attained skills that were seen to be as useful in the home as in employment. By the 1920s, the development of domestic science schools reflected the growth of an ideological and pedagogical approach that transformed the home into a domestic laboratory, and the housewife or domestic servant into a skilled manager and practitioner. Modern ideas about domestic science (also known as home economics or domestic arts) were to become influential in the new professions of public health and social welfare. They also determined parental and government attitudes towards the education of girls, who were often directed to the domestic science schools and later to vocational streams in high schools. Indeed, until the 1980s, girls lagged well behind boys in the completion of the senior years of secondary school and in entrance to universities (Teese 1989: 248–9).

This chapter traces the evolution of vocational education for girls across the mid decades of the twentieth century, and in doing so explores how social expectations about class and gender were reflected through the curriculum and its perceived relevance to the future role of girls as workers, wives, mothers and citizens. 'Practical' subjects like cookery, needlework and typing required specialised facilities and spaces, including rooms and buildings designed for purpose, and the prevailing assumptions about appropriate education for girls shaped their design and use. From the mobile classrooms of the Better Farming Train to the establishment of model single-sex domestic science schools, these unconventional places of learning were aligned with the post-school world of employment and national economic development.

Vocational education

The 'spatial turn' in the history of education has resulted in greater consideration of the relationship between the policies and practices of educational pedagogy and the design intent of classrooms and schools. The materiality and the sensory dimensions of everyday school life, the shifting conception of the child and the adolescent, and the evolving culture of the school as a distinctive social institution (see, for instance, Burke and Grosvenor 2008) highlight the spatial dynamics of schooling (Healy and Darian-Smith 2015). Histories of education in Australia, however, have been more concerned with policy and curriculum, and the colonial origins and development of today's state-based educational bureaucracies (Blake 1973; Barcan 1980; Marginson 1993; Marginson 1997; MacKinnon and Proctor 2013; Campbell and Proctor 2014). The social context of vocational education, and its technological needs, however, bring to the fore the issue of classroom equipment and design and its relationship to social and educational values.

From the early nineteenth century, in a transplanted settler society, the acquisition of technical and agricultural knowledge was important to the economic development of the Australian colonies. Instruction in these topics, mainly for male adults and youth, was provided through institutions imported from Britain: the mechanics institutes, schools of arts and workingmen's colleges (Murray-Smith 1966; Goozee 2001). Compulsory education for children to an elementary level was introduced in the various Australian colonies from the 1870s, and vocational subjects were soon evident in schools. By Federation in 1901, leading educationalists agreed on the value of technical education to the creation of a skilled male workforce. This had been highlighted during the economic crash of the 1890s, which sparked a Royal Commission on Technical Education in each of the most populous states of Victoria and New South Wales. Their recommendations led to a reorganisation of vocational teaching within the education system. In Victoria, for example, agricultural high schools were opened in rural areas, and junior technical schools in the cities. The industrialist H.V. McKay donated land and buildings for a boys' technical school, which opened in 1913 adjacent to his Sunshine Harvester factory in Melbourne's working-class western suburbs. The factory manufactured farming equipment, and the proximity of the school made the link between education and work blatant (Spaull 2005).

Each state developed a mix of intermediate schools, high schools and technical schools during the first half of the twentieth century. Technical schools were particularly prominent in Victoria, which maintained a separate technical branch up to the 1980s. In high schools, vocational subjects were generally available alongside academic ones, with block timetabling often placing students in dedicated streams for the entirety of their school education. The technical schools and the vocational streams in the high schools, whether in the government or non-government sector, were strictly gendered. Agricultural and mechanical skills were taught to boys, and home economics, cookery, needlework, typing and shorthand to girls. This division reflected historical and social attitudes towards the acquisition and application of technical skills, and the status of occupations within the workforce. The education of children and adolescents was thus critical to the gendering of work.

As vocational education became more prominent in the interwar years, so too did ideas about child-centred pedagogy and active learning practices and the belief that education could be transformative not only for the individual but for society as a whole. Citizenship education in Australia was influenced by new international understandings of adolescent psychology and a more child-focused curriculum (McLeod and Wright 2013). It recognised the individual's relationship to Australia's distinctive national character, as well as the need for a more expansive 'world-mindedness'. In the classroom, however, citizenship education was 'often mundane, personal and domestic in nature' and included preparation for adulthood and the workplace (McLeod 2012: 343). This nexus between the individual and the nation provided a rationale for vocational schooling. While the intention of the cookery or woodwork lesson was to further individual learning, collectively these endeavours were of national benefit because they produced the workforce for a modern industrialised economy. Training for post-school employment contributed to the institutional role of the 'socially useful' school (Campbell and Proctor 2014: 118–59).

Although the colonial impetus for extended technical education was to ensure male employment, it soon extended to the private and feminised sphere of home and family. From the late nineteenth century, the domestic science movement 'deliberately set out to construct a new model of the efficient housewife' (Reiger 1985: 8), drawing on the latest theories about motherhood, nutrition and hygiene, and elevating housework by equating it with 'science' and 'economics'. Women in Australia, as in other industrialised nations, were at the forefront of the promotion of domestic science and its inclusion in the school curriculum. While there were variations between each state, domestic science classes for girls were held in elementary, intermediate and secondary schools. Such instruction was always informed by understandings of class. The concern that middle-class girls needed to learn how to be skilled wives and mothers drove the curriculum at private girls' schools and colleges. Nonetheless, the majority of government-funded domestic science schools established from the 1920s were located in working-class suburbs. They were seen to address social problems by equipping girls with the practical knowledge to improve the living and moral standards of working-class families (Campbell and Proctor 2014: 118). They also trained girls for entry into domestic-oriented employment, such as dressmaking and domestic service or, increasingly, to work in factories, retail and commerce – even if this was intended for only a short period before marriage.

The supply of qualified domestic science teachers was a priority, and post-secondary colleges for this purpose attracted government and philanthropic funding. A bequest from Sir William McPherson, a businessman and politician who served as the treasurer and premier of Victoria, established perhaps the largest in Australia: the Emily McPherson College of Domestic Economy in central Melbourne. It was launched with great fanfare by the Duchess of York in 1927, indicating the importance given to its purpose. The elegant three-storey building was in Greek Revival style, designed by the chief architect of the Public Works Department, E. Evan Smith, and reflected the values of simplicity, cleanliness and modernity that defined the domestic science movement. While some graduates of 'Emily Mac' and similar colleges worked as demonstrators or in advertising for the manufacturers of modern household appliances (Dickenson 2016: 96–7), most carved out careers in education.

As new domestic science schools multiplied in metropolitan areas, there was also a commitment to providing opportunities for rural girls. The spaces to teach domestic science in some country schools were often rudimentary, with older equipment such as wood-stoves rather than the latest electric or gas ones. In Queensland, where remote towns were separated by vast distances, railway schools were introduced and remained in service until the 1960s. Like the Better Farming Trains, these had carriages fitted out as demonstration classrooms (Logan: 1981) (see Figure 11.1).

More generally, state departments of education struggled to meet the costs of equipping the buildings and rooms required for vocational education, particularly during the Depression when student demand soared. While all schools and teaching practices are shaped by technologies of learning (Lawn 1999), vocational school education required specialised equipment, classrooms and workshops. Customised kitchens suitable for teaching groups, for instance, were expensive. Some schools attempted to recoup these establishment and running costs by selling food products and fancywork to the public and by relying on the labour of students for the daily cleaning and upkeep of school buildings. Businesses sometimes assisted with the donation of items they wished to promote, such as Pyrex glass or china.

By the 1930s, there were over 40 girls-only domestic science schools in New South Wales. There were also four domestic central schools which offered a more extended curriculum,

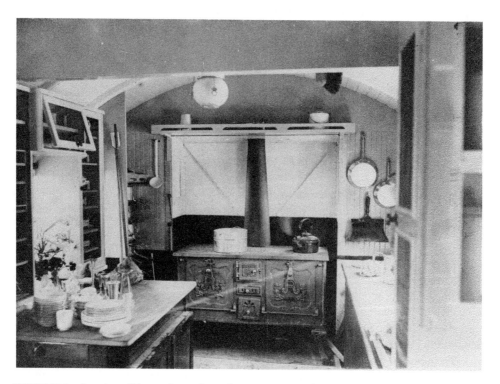

FIGURE 11.1 Interior of domestic service railway car, Queensland. This was in use until 1967.

Source: John Oxley Library, State Library of Queensland, negative no. 22607

with a dedicated commercial stream that prepared girls for 'secretarial, clerical and welfare positions'. In 1933, the state's governor, Sir Philip Game, visited Burwood Central Domestic Science School in Sydney, and found it to be 'a perfect school'. An enthusiastic report by a journalist from the *Sydney Morning Herald* wrote that '[i]f the main function of a girls' school is to provide the conditions and environment most favourable to their mental, physical and aesthetic development', then this was fulfilled 'naturally and delightfully' at the Burwood school (*Sydney Morning Herald* 22 August 1933: 10). Girls were observed cooking in three kitchens, each fitted with 16 gas stoves, though it is likely that some students had no access to such modern equipment at home. There were other specialised workrooms for laundry (with a boiler and mangle) and ironing. Older girls learnt shorthand, or typed in unison to music played on a gramophone (Figures 11.2 and 11.3). These practical lessons were accompanied by general education subjects taught in conventional classrooms decorated with pictures of countries around the world or literary greats such as Shakespeare.

In Victoria, domestic science enrolments and specialised schools increased significantly in the interwar years. In the early 1930s, two new schools exemplified the link between the education of girls and broader social reform. Both were funded by male philanthropists and were located within walking distance from each other in a working-class area on the southern fringe of central Melbourne. The first, the J. H. Boyd Domestic College, opened in 1932 in a Tudor-revival building, originally designed in 1885 by the Department of Education's

FIGURE 11.2 Instruction in cleaning bathrooms, Burwood Girls High School (then Burwood Domestic Science School), New South Wales, c. 1930.

Source: State Records NSW: NRS 15051, Digital ID: 15051_a047_002113

FIGURE 11.3   Cooking class and classroom, Burwood Girls High School (then Burwood Domestic Science School), New South Wales. c.1930.

Source: State Records NSW: NRS 15051, Digital ID: 15051_a047_002111

chief architect, Henry Bastow, as a co-educational primary school. The building was remodelled to meet the high demand for domestic science education, and a 1930s wing was added with state-of-the art facilities. Students also practised their skills in a model cottage, where the headmistress lived; indeed, model homes were to be found in many domestic science schools. A bequest from a wealthy grazier, James Hill Boyd, to support a 'School of Domestic Economy, Cookery and Housework' in perpetuity provided additional funds for scholarships for 'capable' girls to undertake a full domestic science curriculum to intermediate level, enabling working-class girls to remain at school. The bequest also allowed for tennis courts and a gymnasium to be built in the late 1930s, and these facilities situated the Boyd Domestic College as a pioneer providing modern 'physical culture' for girls (Darian-Smith and Henningham 2014: 154–6).

In 1934, the self-made confectionary tycoon Sir MacPherson Robertson contributed £40,000 towards a girls' high school as a centenary gift to the City of Melbourne. A design competition was held, with the winning entry by Norman Seabrook conveying a bold civic presence for the school. The building had a vertical clock tower shaft, with a horizontal blade roof and flagpole to distinguish its entrance. These elements emulated Willem Dudok's design of the Hilversum Town Hall in the Netherlands, and indeed Dudok's work had inspired the architecture of several schools built in Britain (Harwood 2013: 193; Willis 2014: 145). The interior fit-out was modern, with an industrial aesthetic, and there were open-air classrooms

THE ROSE SERIES/P. 2611   SECTION OF MacROBERTSON GIRLS' HIGH SCHOOL, MELBOURNE, VIC.
COPYRIGHT

FIGURE 11.4   The MacRobertson Girls' High School, Melbourne, Victoria, designed by Norman Seabrook, c. 1934.

Source: Rose Stereograph Co., State Library of Victoria H32492/3781

(Phillips 2012) (see Figure 11.4). Named MacRobertson Girls' High School, the flagship school offered an academic curriculum and a pathway towards university entrance for girls whose families could not afford private school education.

The physical proximity of these two modern girls' schools meant that from the 1940s a stream of academically orientated girls transferred from Boyd Domestic College to Mac-Robertson Girls' High (Darian-Smith and Henningham 2014: 159). Despite the differences in their vocational and academic curriculum, the dedicated female staff at Boyd Domestic College and 'MacRob' shared a commitment to the post-primary education of girls when this was not always the priority of parents or communities. By the 1940s and 1950s, however, the skills needed in the workforce were changing, and this brought about shifts in domestic science schools and their curriculum, and the places of learning for girls.

Expanding educational opportunities

The relationship between education and work in Australia was most explicit during periods of high unemployment, when schools were blamed for failing to prepare young people to successfully enter the workforce (Blackmore 1992: 353). During the 1930s Depression, there was a marked retreat from the comprehensive high school in Australia and a concentration of enrolments in vocational education. In Victoria, fees were reintroduced for the senior years of high school to allay government expenditure, and consequently technical schools became even more entrenched in working-class areas (Teese 1989: 249).

In the post-World War II reconstruction of Australian society, the existing educational facilities were seen as woefully inadequate for the development of the nation and its young people. The demand for schools was high and would continue to grow throughout the 1950s and 1960s in line with rapid population growth. This was due to the rising birthrate of the baby boom and the mass migration scheme that brought millions of new arrivals, many in family groups, to Australia. In addition, in the new suburbs that now ringed the cities, the school was central to both the ideology and the infrastructure of the community (Lewi and Nichols 2010). As government expenditure on schooling increased, education was seen as 'an engine of economic growth and an agent of social welfare' (Mackinnon and Procter 2013: 440). The expansion of the secondary school sector was dramatic: in Victoria, the number of secondary schools increased between the mid-1940s and mid-1960s from 46 to 227 (Teese 1989: 242).

The relationship between school and employment remained strong in Australia during the immediate postwar decades, with a raised leaving age, a climbing school retention rate and, externally, a long boom where full employment was the norm. In this context, vocational education remained important, and was to expand nationally. A comparison with the situation in Britain at the end of World War II indicates a similar acknowledgement of the importance of vocational school education, but in this case there were limited resources to realise its potential. The 1944 Butler Education Act in England and Wales had established the principle of educational access for all. It split the division between primary and secondary education at the age of 11, when an examination determined a child's educational path; the minimum school leaving age was raised in 1947 to 15 years. The tripartite system for secondary education in England consisted, in principle, of grammar schools, secondary modern schools and secondary technical schools. The technical schools were modelled on earlier forms of vocational instruction in Britain and were intended to serve industry through the provision of scientific, mechanical, artistic, agricultural and other skills.

In their 1947 book *The Modern School*, the most authoritative text at the time on Britain's proposed expansion of schools, educational architects C. G. Stillman and R. Castle Cleary noted that specialised teaching rooms and equipment represented 'the largest and most costly part of the building programme' (Stillman and Castle Cleary 1947: 85). These facilities were essential to technical education. For girls, where a 'sound training in housecraft is a sure foundation in right standards of living', they recommended that a school of 450 pupils required a purpose-built 'housecraft room, a needlework room, a unit kitchen and a complete flat or bungalow' (Stillman and Castle Cleary 1947: 94). Indeed, a small house of up to 11,000 square feet (1,022 square metres) was seen as an excellent space to teach girls the complexities of household management. Recommendations were given on the size, ventilation, light and equipment needed for instructional kitchens and sewing rooms, with these design features allowing teaching for both individual and group work. Specifications and equipment – filing cabinets, a duplicator and a gramophone – were likewise listed for the ideal typewriting room. *The Modern School* also contained detailed plans for the technical education of boys. Five 'shops' aimed at a class of 20 students, covering woodwork, carpentry, engineering, general metal trades and general building trades, were recommended. The plans account for noise and safety issues, with drawing offices located nearby (Stillman and Castle Cleary 1947: 101–3).

Between 1945 and 1970, over 11,000 new schools were built in England and Wales. However, only a tiny number were secondary technical schools. This was partly because of the lack of resources, especially in rural areas, and the difficulty of converting existing building stock to the specialised classroom requirements of technical education. It was also compounded by a shortage of vocational teachers. In some local government areas, however, two of the three types of secondary education were combined, and the London City Council merged all three types of secondary schools on the one site. Such comprehensive schools, which included some rooms used for vocational subjects, consisted of 'vast single blocks, with only halls and/or workshops areas set separately' (see also Saint 1987; Harwood 2010: 77).

In Australia, while the emphasis was on a more general and flexible system of secondary schools, vocational subjects continued to have a secure place in the curriculum. Specialised institutions such as the technical schools or domestic science schools in Victoria were retained, and their provision was extended. At Boyd Domestic College, as in other girls' vocational schools, the scope of vocational education was changing to meet workplace demands. In 1940, a full commercial stream was introduced and gained prominence as more jobs opened up for women in secretarial work and office administration. The graduate destinations of students at Boyd Domestic College reveal that by the 1950s the majority were entering what they described as 'office work', a clear departure from their employment as dressmakers or domestic duties in earlier decades (Darian-Smith and Henningham 2014: 160). By the 1960s, the school had introduced further academic subjects such as French, and, although its emphasis continued to be on preparing girls for work, it also offered a pathway for final year matriculation into tertiary education.

By the 1960s, Boyd Domestic College was increasingly catering to the daughters of migrants who had settled in its surrounding working-class suburbs because of opportunities of employment in the nearby port and factories. A significant proportion of the girls came from non-English-speaking backgrounds, particularly from Greece and, slightly later, Turkey and Vietnam. This meant that the college, and many other primary and secondary schools across Australia located in suburbs where new migrants concentrated, introduced English-language instruction and prepared students for an 'Australian way of life' and national values as well as the workplace. The single-sex and vocational orientation of Boyd Domestic College was particularly attractive to some migrant families. It continued to use the financial scholarships which had been bequeathed in the 1930s to encourage girls to remain longer in education.

Nonetheless, the idea of girls' domestic science education was becoming increasingly outmoded, and the technical schools more generally were seen to be of a lesser status than the more comprehensive high schools. These ideas were fed by broader social change and economic upheaval, and the influence of second-wave feminism on a new generation of teachers was to be reflected in progressive ideas about girls' education and gender equity. In 1968, a new domestic science wing was added to the school, with specialised classrooms and industrial-style kitchens. A former student recalled that the building had 'beautiful, state of the art kitchen facilities' and a fully furnished lounge room 'so that you could learn how to vacuum, how to dust and how to polish'. It was probably the last purpose-built facility of this size constructed in Victoria. That same year, the Department of Education was to reclassify the college as a general girls high school, signalling the demise of the distinctive domestic science schools for girls in Australia (Darian-Smith and Henningham 2014: 162).

Conclusion

In an analysis of the dominant themes in school architecture across Australia between 1900 and 1980, Julie Willis has argued that the school was successively conceived of as a home, a civic structure, a factory and a town (Willis 2014). These design elements reflected the changing place of the school within Australian society, and the aspirations that communities held for their students. With the post–World War II democratisation of education, the school campus and its buildings increasingly resembled a small town, with varied but related activities dispersed across learning spaces. Across this period, vocational education was a key component of the school system, although its narrow focus on training for manual and semi-skilled jobs and the entrenched gendered nature of its curriculum became increasingly problematic. The federal Karmel Report into equality and educational opportunity was published in 1973 and concluded that girls and non-English-speaking migrants were educationally disadvantaged (Karmel 1973). The report also found that the school environment and philosophy was crucial in influencing parents about the educational and occupational expectations of their children. In this wider context, girls' education could no longer be linked to a domestic science or commercial training, and by the 1980s Victoria's separate technical schools were transformed into comprehensive high schools.

By the late twentieth century, the expectation that secondary education served to prepare students for future employment was being addressed not just with on-site teaching and classrooms but with the integration of external work experience into the secondary curriculum. This typically involved the 'middle-school students, aged fourteen or fifteen and looking towards the job market, to spend a week in a shop or factory', but also enabled greater vocational awareness and a greater understanding of the relevance of school to the wider world (Schoenheimer 1980: 145). By 2000, girls were completing secondary school at a rate that equalled or exceeded that of boys, and were a majority in undergraduate tertiary courses. Across the twentieth century to the present, the education of girls has been crucial to changing understandings of gender relations, equity and occupational expectations. Despite the limitations they clearly offer from today's perspective, the specialised spaces and places of girls' vocational education in schools were seen, at least until the 1960s, as providing new opportunities for girls to participate in the workforce and as contributing to the social transformation of modern Australia.

Acknowledgement

Research for this chapter has been supported by a grant from the Australian Research Council: 'Designing Australian Schools: A Spatial History of Innovation, Pedagogy and Social Change' (DP110100505).

Works cited

Barcan, A. (1980) *A History of Australian Education*, Melbourne: Oxford University Press.
'Better Farming Train' (1925) *North Eastern Ensign* (Benalla) 14 August: 2.
Blackmore, J. (1992) 'The Gendering of Skill and Vocationalism in Twentieth-Century Australian Education', *Journal of Education Policy* 7, 4: 351–77.
Blake, L. J. (ed.) (1973) *Vision and Realisation: A Centenary History of State Education in Victoria*, Melbourne: Education Department of Victoria.
Burke, C. and Grosvenor, I. (2008) *School*, London: Reaktion Books.
Campbell, C. and Proctor, H. (2014) *A History of Australian Schooling*, Sydney: Allen & Unwin.
Darian-Smith, K. and Henningham, N. (2014) 'Site, School, Community: Educating Modern Girls at the J. H. Boyd Domestic College', *History of Education Review* 43, 2: 152–71.
Dickenson, J. (2016) *Australian Women in Advertising in the Twentieth Century*, Basingstoke: Palgrave Macmillan.
Elvery, D. (2006) 'Setting the Stage for Landcare', in R. Youl (ed.) *Landcare in Victoria: How Landcare Helped People, Government and Business in Victoria Work Together*, Melbourne: Mary Johnson, Victoria Mack, Sue Marriott and Horrie Poussard: 39–44.

Goozee, G. (2001) *The Development of TAFE in Australia*, Leabrook: National Centre for Vocational Education Research Ltd.

Harwood, E. (2010) *England's Schools: History, Architecture and Adaptation*, Swindon: English Heritage.

Harwood, E. (2013) 'School Buildings and the Architectural Heritage of Childhood: Designing Mid-twentieth Century Schools in England', in K. Darian-Smith and C. Pascoe (eds) *Children, Childhood and Cultural Heritage*, London and New York: Routledge: 190–206.

Healy, S. and Darian-Smith, K. (2015) 'Educational Spaces and the "Whole" Child: A Spatial History of School Design, Pedagogy and the Modern Australian Nation', *History Compass* 13, 6: 275–87.

Karmel, P. (1973) *Schools in Australia: Report of the Interim Committee for Australian Schools Commission*, Canberra: Interim Committee for the Australian Schools Commission.

Lake, M. (1987) *The Limits of Hope: Soldier Settlement in Victoria, 1915–38*, Melbourne: Oxford University Press.

Lawn, M. (1999) 'Designing Teaching: The Classroom as a Technology', in I. Grosvenor, M. Lawn and K. Rousmaniere (eds) *Silences and Images: The Social History of the Classroom*, New York: Peter Lang: 83–104.

Lewi, H. and Nichols, D. (eds) (2010) *Community: Building Modern Australia*, Sydney: New South Books.

Logan, G. (1981) *A Centenary History of Home Economics Education in Queensland 1881–1981*, Brisbane: Queensland Department of Education.

Mackinnon, A. and Proctor, H. (2013) 'Education', in S. Macintyre and A. Bashford (eds) *The Cambridge History of Australia*, Volume Two, Cambridge: Cambridge University Press: 429–51.

Main, H. and Scantlebury, V. (1926) 'Report to the Minister of Public Health on the Welfare of Women and Children', *Victorian Parliamentary Papers* 2: 239–43.

Marginson, S. (1993) *Education and Public Policy in Australia*, Cambridge, New York: Cambridge University Press.

Marginson, S. (1997) *Educating Australia: Government, Economy and Citizen Since 1960*, Cambridge: Cambridge University Press.

McLeod, J. (2012) 'Educating for "World-mindedness": Cosmopolitanism, Localism and Schooling the Adolescent Citizen in Interwar Australia', *Journal of Educational Administration and History* 44, 4: 337–57.

McLeod, J. and Wright, K. (2013) 'Education for Citizenship', *History of Education Review* 42, 2: 170–84.

Murray-Smith, S. (1966) 'A History of Technical Education in Australia: With Special Reference to the Period before 1914', PhD thesis, Faculty of Education, University of Melbourne.

Phillips, C. (2012) 'Seabrook & Fildes', in P. Goad and J. Willis (eds) *The Encyclopedia of Australian Architecture*, Melbourne: Cambridge University Press: 620–1.

Reiger, K. (1985) *The Disenchantment of the Home: Modernizing the Australian Family 1880–1940*, Melbourne: Oxford University Press.

Saint, A. (1987) *Towards a Social Architecture: The Role of School Building in Post-War England*, New Haven: Yale University Press.

Schoenheimer, H. (1980) 'School Out of School', in L. Allwood for the Australian Council of State School Organisations (ed.) *Schoenheimer on Education*, Melbourne: Drummond Publishing: 145–7.

Spaull, A. (2005) 'Education, Technical', in A. Brown-May and S. Swain (eds) *The Encyclopedia of Melbourne*, Cambridge: Cambridge University Press, available at: http://www.emelbourne.net.au/biogs/EM00510b.htm.

Stillman, C. G. and Castle Cleary, R. (1947) *The Modern School*, London: The Architectural Press.

Sydney Morning Herald (1933) 'Domestic Science', 22 August: 10.

Teese, R. (1989) 'Gender and Class in the Transformation of the Public High School in Melbourne, 1946–1985', *History of Education Quarterly* 29, 2: 237–59.

Tiffany, C. (1999) 'Victoria's Better Farming Train', *Victorian Landcare* 12 (Winter): 24–5.

Willis, J. (2014) 'From Home to Civic: Designing the Australian School', *History of Education Review* 43, 2: 138–51.

'Work and Production' (1925) *Mercury* (Hobart) 14 July: 5.

12

'WE MAKE NO DISCRIMINATION'

Aboriginal education and the socio-spatial arrangements of the Australian classroom

*Julie McLeod and Sianan Healy**

School space shapes pedagogical practice and student identities, yet how this happens has culturally differentiated significance and effects. This chapter develops a case for seeing school classrooms as racialised spaces, and does so by considering the aims and provision of education for Indigenous children in 1960s Australia. Widespread educational reforms were underway in Australia during this period, with rapid expansion in the building of state secondary and technical schools (Minister of Education 1968; Campbell and Proctor 2014) and renewed interest in progressive and child-centred education (Potts 2007; McLeod 2014). Both old and new progressive ideas were gaining ground concerning the freedom of the child, the space and openness of school environments and the role of pedagogies to foster self-discovery (Punch 1969). The 1960s was also a period during which the federal- and state-level policy of assimilation of Aboriginal people, in place from the 1930s, was officially enacted via a number of legislative and constitutional changes (Attwood and Markus 2007; McGregor 2011). Following a period of political agitation, other changes included giving Aboriginal people the right to vote federally and counting them in the national census. This happened alongside the continued forced removal of Aboriginal children from their families into state care or adoptive white families (Human Rights and Equal Opportunity Commission [HREOC] 1997; Haebich 2008), where they were to be assimilated into white domestic and social cultures.

School facilities, buildings and pedagogies were crucial in both mediating and contesting assimilationist projects, with the school environment reflecting and mobilising ideas about the type of education deemed appropriate for Aboriginal children. Edward Soja has argued that 'there is a growing awareness of the simultaneity and interwoven complexity of the social, the historical and the spatial, their inseparability and interdependence' (Soja 1996: 3). In the case of Indigenous education, however, acknowledging the 'influence of space' is not simply a corrective to an alleged over-reliance on temporality in understanding schooling. The form and impact of socio-spatial dynamics are enmeshed with the history and effects of colonisation. The inside and outside of classrooms and the spatial, rhetorical and material arrangements of

---

* The authors wish to advise Aboriginal and Torres Strait Islander readers that this chapter contains names and images of Indigenous persons who are deceased.

curriculum and pedagogy were critical factors, we suggest, in deliberations on whether or how to recognise Aboriginal children as a distinct category of students. Here, we seek to draw out the racialised and colonising dimensions of school space, and in doing so contribute to cultural histories of school design and environments in Australia.

The sources for analysis are published debates among teachers and educators across Australia in the 1960s (Gunton 1964; Roper 1969; Tatz and Dunn 1969) regarding how best to educate Aboriginal children, and reports from school inspectors' annual visits to schools in the state of Victoria. Teacher-led conferences conveyed strong criticisms of how the education of Aboriginal children was being managed by the various states, and many participants presented outspoken challenges to assimilationist thinking. While not always of the same voice, there was, especially among those with direct experience of working in Aboriginal schools, an openness to incorporating Aboriginal culture and language into schooling, practical suggestions for teaching strategies and some recognition of the ways in which the classroom and school environment itself could serve to alienate Aboriginal children and families. This contrasts with the predominantly pro-assimilationist views towards the education of Aboriginal children expressed in reports discussed here from school inspectors in the Victorian Department of Education. These reports reveal how assimilationist agendas were incorporated into judgements of the proper classroom, good pedagogy and the ideal student. In such texts, we argue, the racialisation of the classroom emerges in attempts both to not notice and to remediate difference through adoption of the cultural and domestic practices of white Australia.

Before turning to develop these arguments we provide, first, a summary account of current scholarship on space and schooling and its relevance to our concerns regarding the racialisation of school space and, second, a brief contextual discussion of twentieth-century race relations in Australia as background to educational debates in the 1960s.

Space, colonialism, schools

A flourishing scholarship has investigated how school design and spatial arrangements reflect understandings of the purposes of education, changing relations between schools and communities and conceptions of the child and adolescent (Kozlovsky 2010). Both historical and sociological studies of education have been influenced by the 'spatial turn' (for example, Massey 1994; McGregor 2004; Paechter 2004), with growing attention to the ways in which 'space, power and knowledge' intersect in the domain of education (for example, Gutman and de Coninck-Smith 2008; Burke 2010). School buildings, Burke and Grosvenor argue, 'should not be viewed merely as capsules in which education is located and teachers and pupils perform, but also as designed spaces that, in their materiality, project a system of values' (Burke and Grosvenor 2008: 8). Such work encompasses a focus on the material culture of schooling, which is 'taken to include the landscapes, buildings, rooms, furnishings, clothes, toys and many other objects and things that children [and all students] wear and use' (Gutman and de Coninck-Smith 2008: 3). Herman et al.'s (2011) study of the school desk illustrates how what are often unnoticed classroom objects, such as chairs, desks or blackboards and whiteboards, are in fact integral to the history of schooling and are usefully understood as the 'materialisation' of school culture (Herman et al. 2011: 98). Other work has given close attention to the affective dynamics of classroom objects and to the kind of normative student subjectivities and dispositions the spatial dynamics of schooling invites and makes possible (Rasmussen 2012; McLeod 2014). Accompanying this is an interest in rethinking the spatial boundaries of schooling in light of the impact of 'new mobilities' (Leander, Phillips and Taylor 2010). Leander et al. (2010: 329) argue that the idea of the 'classroom-as-container' remains a dominant discourse, even in educational discussions that seek to take account of space and place. This discourse 'constructs not only particular ways of speaking and writing in educational research, but also systems of rules concerning how meaning is made', functioning as an '"imagined geography" of education, constituting when and where researchers and teachers should expect learning to take place'. Additional questions are introduced in this chapter regarding the 'imagined geography' of education, ones that underscore the racialisation of school space and draw out the multiple resonances of 'geographies of education' to encompass the very land on which schools have been imagined, built, designed, inhabited and renovated under sway of any manner of pedagogical innovations.

Recent postcolonial scholarship has questioned understandings of the arrangement of spaces – and the bodies within them – as having emerged naturally over time, exploring the ways in which the 'the development of space is a process of uneven power inscription that reproduces itself in the creation of oppressive spatial categories' (Banivanua-Mar and Edmonds 2010: 5–6; see too Dovey 2014; Razack 1998; Read 2014; Wolfe 2001). Much of this scholarship has focused on mapping settler space onto and over the top of Indigenous lands during early periods of colonialism. We propose that such arguments regarding space and power are also relevant to understanding the socio-spatial organisation of schooling and pedagogies for Aboriginal children into the twentieth century. Such matters underwrote, for example, contestations over the merits and rationale for segregated or integrated schooling – all of which were materialised or silenced in the form and aspirations of school design.

Policies of Aboriginal assimilation in Australia were put in place by state governments, which were responsible for their Indigenous populations (as was education policy), on an ad hoc basis around the turn of the twentieth century. These policies were predicated on the social-Darwinist idea that Aboriginal people of full descent were destined to die out in the face of the superior European civilisation (McGregor 1997; Wolfe 2001; Anderson 2003). The growing population of mixed-descent Indigenous people, a cause of concern for state governments, were forcibly removed from the stations and reserves, and had welfare support removed in the hope that they would blend into the white population (*Aboriginal Welfare* 1937: 3). At the same time, Aboriginal people living under the various acts had their movements, working prospects, living arrangements and even marriage rights controlled by the state. The forced removal of Aboriginal people from the missions and reserves which had, for many, been their only home, did not lead to their absorption into white society, due to discrimination and lack of opportunity. Many Aboriginal people thus ended up living in fringe camps on the outskirts of towns and cities (Broome 1994: 139–40). In order to further facilitate the assimilation of Aboriginal people into the community, state and territory governments also removed children of mixed descent from their families and either put them into institutional care or adopted them out to white families (HREOC 1997). The responsibility for Aboriginal affairs passed to the Commonwealth following a constitutional referendum in 1967 (Attwood and Markus 2007).

Political protests during the 1960s era of civil rights cast a critical light on these discriminatory practices and brought into the foreground issues about educational and social possibilities for Aboriginal children, under models of either assimilationist or segregated schooling. Herbert describes the history of Aboriginal education in terms of dynamics between 'centre–periphery', with Aboriginal people deliberately positioned on the periphery, which she argues 'not only rendered people powerless but, the resolute retention of such systemic positioning until well into the 1970s, sustained perhaps even institutionalised such powerlessness' (Herbert 2012: 94). Moreover, she argues that although the 1960s saw changes in legal status and government involvement and financial commitment to Aborigines, 'little seemed to be happening in education for this was the era of the deficit model, where excuses such as lack of English language, cultural deprivation, poor health and low self-esteem' (Herbert 2012: 97) were offered as explanations and causes of educational disadvantage. By the mid-1960s, most Aboriginal children of primary school age were attending school, but the participation rate dropped drastically for secondary school. A survey by the New South Wales Teachers' Federation in 1964 found that 'only 9 per cent of Aboriginal children proceeded beyond second-year secondary school and over 58 per cent were rated as slow learners' (Duncan 1969: 30). Speaking on the situation in Queensland, at a conference on Aboriginal education in 1967, Joe McGinness, of Kungarakany descent and a founding member of the Board of the Centre for Research into Aboriginal Affairs at Monash University, asserted that '[t]ill very recently, the official attitude was that a standard education for a nine-year-old child was sufficient for an Aborigine or Islander to see him through life' (McGinness in Tatz and Dunn 1969: 52). He suggested 'it would be safe to say that less than one in every hundred Aboriginal or Islander children [in Queensland] . . . was receiving secondary education' (McGinness in Tatz and Dunn 1969: 51). At the same conference in 1967, Mr P. E. Felton, Superintendent Aborigines Welfare Board, estimated that in Victoria there were then approximately 750 Aboriginal children of school age, with 500 in primary and 250 in secondary schools (Felton in Tatz and Dunn 1969: 8).

Questions about the capacity and dispositions of Aboriginal children as learners and their sameness or difference from white peers fuelled discussions about the type of school environments that should be provided. At the same time, education was held up as providing important opportunities to orient Aboriginal children towards culturally dominant (white) norms. The status, potential for educability and future of Aboriginal children were all at stake, closely managed and monitored by the state, with education a central agency in mediating assimilationist policies and aspirations. To develop this proposition, we look in two directions: first to reports from conferences of educators and teachers held during the 1960s that debated and commonly repudiated education's role in assimilation; and second to reports of school inspectors from their visits to schools located within Aboriginal settlements or nearby Aboriginal communities. In the latter we see not simply the endorsement of assimilation projects but the active normalisation of a particular kind of domesticity and family life in and beyond the classroom – one that held up the classroom and the school as spaces for modelling desirable forms of family and social life.

On noticing and not noticing the Aboriginal child in 1960s schooling

While each mainland state and territory had some 'special' Aboriginal schools on stations and missions, from the 1950s state education departments began closing Aboriginal schools where there was a nearby 'normal' or mainstream school to absorb the pupils (and where there was no resistance or protest from the white community; see Fletcher 1989). In line with assimilationist policies, state departments of education did not keep separate statistics on Aboriginal children at these schools; statistics serve to mark out and reinscribe difference, which officially was meant to be receding. As a senior bureaucrat in the Victorian Education Department stated, in response to a request for statistical information on Aboriginal enrolments, 'we make no discrimination or segregation of pupils. Aboriginal children receive the same educational treatment as all other pupils. . . . We tend to avoid thinking of them as a separate group' (Tatz and Dunn 1969: 3). Insisting on not seeing Aboriginal children as a separate group and providing 'the same educational treatment' represents a form of 'progressive' thinking that does not hold onto racial hierarchies, yet it is also a telling instance of how 'sameness' discourse is mistaken for a politics of equality, as if difference is antithetical to equality (see famously Joan Scott's deconstruction of the equality/difference opposition in feminist politics; Scott 1990). Questions about the value and purpose of differentiating the student population troubled educators and bureaucrats alike, and not only in relation to Aboriginal pupils. On the one hand, such differentiation and recognition of specific group needs and interests can be seen as another kind of progressive response, a way of acknowledging identity claims (for example, of girls, or the migrant child). On the other hand, recognition of some groups was framed in the language of deficit and deprivation, naming 'backward children' or 'culturally deprived' children as warranting being singled out for special intervention, and as beyond the possibility of being included in 'sameness' discourses. In its 1968 annual report, the Victorian Department of Education described efforts to educate those they termed 'backward children', a category which included '"mentally handicapped" children' as well as a group of children who are 'socially handicapped or have suffered cultural deprivation', going on to say, 'Many of the culturally deprived are aborigines to whom special attention is given by the provision of carefully chosen teachers at Lake Tyers' (a school in East Gippsland and the site of a former mission; Minister of Education 1968: 12). Much educational debate thus pivoted on the status and recognition of the Aboriginal child as inherently different or potentially the same, with schools having a pivotal role in mediating these issues in and beyond the classroom.

In proceedings from teachers' conferences during this period, we see struggles over how and whether to name and recognise difference, without collapsing into deficit accounts, or refusing the politics of equality (construed as a politics of sameness) or ignoring the impact of historical legacies of race relations and dispossession. In this politically and affectively charged context, how might the social-spatial arrangements of schooling accommodate and recognise, or refuse to recognise, Aboriginal pupils? At a 1968 conference in Sydney on the role of the teacher in Aboriginal education organised by the National Union of Australian University Students, a strongly expressed position was that mainstream school curriculum did not provide space for Aboriginal cultural values and learning systems, and that the school culture was unselfconsciously white and Western-oriented. One presenter, G. W. L. McMeekin (a lecturer at the Australian School of Pacific Administration, Sydney), observed that attempts to assimilate Aboriginal children served to underscore their difference and separation from 'White Australia':

> Our schools have an inbuilt value system that is essentially 'White Australian' in its orientation. Within the school we have provided a place for the Aboriginal child, but does the school really admit such a child to the fullest participation? It demands of him a cultural conformity to standards that he cannot meet, activities that are wholly out of context in his life, experiences to which he cannot respond. The school can easily become not the means of involving the child in the wider Australian community but an effective means of accentuating the differences that mark off the Aborigine from the dominant socio-cultural group.
>
> (McMeekin 1969: 24)

A number of mission or reserve schools had predominantly or entirely Aboriginal students, and the curriculum was usually based on the mainstream curriculum, with some adaptation. In a report from a 1964 'in-service' conference for (non-Indigenous) teachers working in Aboriginal schools in South Australia, J. D. Gunton, Assistant Superintendent of Primary Schools (Special Schools), observed that 'one test of modern civilisation is the thought and care given to its members who are handicapped in any way (mentally, physically, colour of skin etc.)' (Gunton 1964: 15), articulating the language of deprivation as expressed in the Victorian annual reports noted above. On one hand, the conference aims were expressed in a progressive language of attending to 'Communication, Curricula, Community' (Gunton 1964: 8), and on the other, it rehearsed a familiar racial paternalism towards Aboriginal children and their capacities. Presentations at this conference included 'Reading Retardation among Half-Caste Children and Its Treatment', the removal of grading and an emphasis in the curriculum on creative arts – music, painting, oral communication – and 'outdoor activities'. Attention to these areas of schooling and to customising the standard curriculum (no testing, for example) suggested that the education of Aboriginal children lay properly outside the boundaries and functions of the regular classroom. In particular, teaching approaches had to be adapted to teach the basics such as literacy (see, for example, Roper 1969), and there was some interest in the value of teaching in the 'vernacular' (that is, teaching Aboriginal languages), a view at odds with the policy of departments of education, which mainly insisted on instruction in English throughout schools (Tatz and Dunn 1969: 34). S. B. Hill from Ernabella School in South Australia, for example, reported that in her experience of teaching Aboriginal children, teaching in the vernacular 'helps to retain their culture and gives a foundation on which to build. A respect for their culture is encouraged' (Hill quoted in Gunton 1964: 26).

Similar themes were echoed in the 1968 Sydney conference convened by the National Union of Australian University Students on the role of the teacher in Aboriginal education. In his introduction to the published proceedings, conference organiser Tom Roper observed:

> Where the people were primarily tribally oriented it was emphasized that part of any programme should have major sections on the Aborigine's own culture and elders should be involved. All Aboriginal people should have special sections on their own history and culture to enable them to have feelings, not of guilt or inadequacy but pride and self-respect.
>
> (Roper 1969: vi–vii)

Questions about how and under what circumstances to recognise difference – when to value, minimise or ignore – also arose in relation to deliberations on whether there was a need for special facilities, provision and settings. This encompassed customised school buildings as well as initiatives such as scholarships to support Aboriginal children to attend secondary school and extending the provision of preschool education.

Related matters were debated at a 1967 conference convened by the Monash Centre for Research into Aboriginal Affairs and held at Monash University. A conference presenter from South Australia noted: 'A quite extensive building programme has been undertaken, including new schools, residences for head teachers, showering facilities for children, a kitchen-dining room, a woodwork room and a "home management" unit in which older girls can be taught the rudiments of modern house-keeping' (Tatz and Dunn 1969: 34) (see Figure 12.1). The anticipated and already circumscribed destinies of Aboriginal children are materialised in the type of classroom spaces specially provided for them: manual training and domestic arts. The special facilities – kitchen-dining room, showering facilities – in elevating cleanliness and domesticity, convey concerns about their absence in Aboriginal families and show how the school room itself was positioned as a model for home and family life. Provision of such special facilities was questioned by others, such as A. P. Duncan, a lecturer in adult education at Sydney University, who saw them as damaging 'the self-concept of the Aborigine himself as a person and further strengthens his feelings of his inadequacy, his dependence and lack of self-confidence' (Tatz and Dunn 1969: 29). This view was challenged in the following discussion by another participant, Dr Colin Tatz, who argued that because Aboriginal people were not in an equal position, then 'programmes of discrimination in favour of Aboriginal people were necessary' (Tatz and Dunn 1969: 35), and that this might encompass special facilities and arrangements as part of a more affirmative (rather than assimilationist) agenda. We see in these debates among educators, then, a critique of assimilation as well as some uncertainty about what a progressive politics might look like in relation to how to recognise and name difference, in political and ethical terms and in the practical matter of how to organise schooling.

These concerns extended to the structure of school buildings for Aboriginal children and the appropriateness of their design and layout. Tatz, a white South African living in Australia, was a political scientist, a member of the Aboriginal Welfare Board in Victoria and a vocal contributor to conferences and public debates on Aboriginal rights and race relations. Tatz

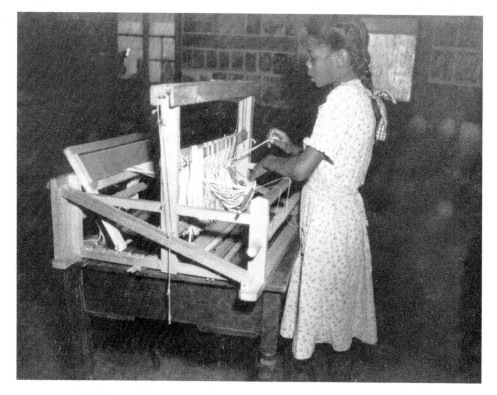

FIGURE 12.1   Girl Weaving, 1953. St Mary's School, Broome.

Source: State Library of Western Australia 010845D

condemned the symbolic violence of school buildings constructed for Aboriginal people, and in so doing brought into view the perspective of Aboriginal parents and families, not as the source of their children's cultural backwardness but as communities concerned about their cultural traditions – their 'tribal mores and values'. Such criticisms acknowledged cultural difference, not necessarily as a deficit to be remediated but as a difference to be recognised, valued and accommodated. He argued:

> The model for every Aboriginal school is the standard metropolitan or country town school with the same size classrooms, blackboards, and window sizes. Some times lip service is paid to an arid zone by building from some sort of brick material which is supposed to be heat-proof. One of the things that is very clear in the minds of Aborigines, particularly in northern reserves and Settlements, is that white men are simply collecting their children together early in the morning and the children are disappearing into this dreadful prison-like building for about seven or eight hours and the Lord alone knows what kind of indoctrination is going on there. The parents may well be rubbishing everything that takes place in that school during the day. If the school were held out in the open in such a way that the parents could sit around on the periphery and listen to what is going on so that they could see that there is no subversion of tribal mores and values.
> (Tatz and Dunn 1969: 86–7)

Here the conventional school building is lambasted not only for its inappropriateness for Aboriginal children but also for its restrictions for all students. The idea of the school as part of the community, as having a more open orientation and design, echoed discussions about alternative education taking place around the same time. The embrace of the 'open-plan' classroom, an interest in community-based schooling, respect for the culture and knowledge

FIGURE 12.2   State School, Lake Tyers Aboriginal Station, c. 1938.

Source: State Library of Victoria H99.170/5; reproduced with permission

children bring from home – these were strong emerging themes in the mainstream education of white Australian children. Yet, as Tatz's comments above suggest, they were far from commonplace in the imagination and design of school environments for Aboriginal children. The provision and design of schooling to accommodate Aboriginal children drew on the language of 'special schools' (as in the language noted above of catering for 'backward' or 'handicapped' children) and on missions and reserves imitated a somewhat older-style model of school environment, an almost nostalgic school house (see Figure 12.2); yet it was a classroom that was being radically reimagined and redesigned in other spheres of state education. Images of what classrooms and schoolhouses for Aboriginal children should look like are evoked in reports from school inspectors, which we now turn to consider.

Inspecting the organisation of schooling: designing a 'pleasant learning environment'

Throughout the 1960s and into the 1970s, inspectors in Victoria continued to make regular annual visits to all state schools, observing classrooms and teachers, documenting the atmosphere and physical environment of the school, evaluating teachers' lesson planning and conduct in the classroom, and describing the liveliness of classes, the perceived learning and achievement of pupils and the tone and activities of the school in general. While these reports represented a form of surveillance of teachers' work, they also provided rich documentation about what a good classroom was deemed to be at a particular time and place – how it should be arranged, how children should be behaving and what they ought to be learning. Inspectors' reports thus offer powerful insight into prevailing norms of students as learners and the pedagogic organisation of school space. In the case of the education of Aboriginal children in the 1960s, the reports also show how assimilationist agendas were incorporated into judgements of the proper classroom, good pedagogy and the ideal student. In such texts, we argue, the racialisation of the classroom emerges in attempts both not to notice and then to remediate difference through adoption of the cultural and domestic practices of white Australia. Here we consider reports from inspectors' visits to two schools – Club Terrace in Gippsland (in rural Victoria), which was located in a mill town just over an hour from Lake Tyers Aboriginal Mission and had a significant population of Aboriginal children, and a school on the former Aboriginal reserve of Framlingham in south-west Victoria ('School Records . . . 1934–1967').

Inspectors commented on aspects of the curriculum such as reading, composition, spelling, speech and arithmetic, but what is of particular interest here is their reporting on the classroom set-up, facilities and equipment. This included detailed notes on the condition of desks and chairs, light and ventilation, decoration and blackboard use, as well as approving acknowledgement when, for example, a teacher showed awareness of the importance of 'a pleasant learning environment' ('Club Terrace Inspectors Report Book 1954–1974': 17–18 June 1968). In 1968 the inspector for the Gippsland area of Victoria, reporting on the Club Terrace primary school, wrote:

> the two classrooms provide sufficient accommodation for the present enrolment. Both rooms are very attractively decorated, with child art, selections of compositions, Health and Nature charts and blackboard preparations of a very fine standard. The environment is thus highly suitable for learning and children are responding as well as can be expected.

(17–18 June 1968)

The school enrolment reflected the town population, which was a mix of Aboriginal and white, often transient (because of the need to follow mill work) and socioeconomically disadvantaged. The inspector's comments on children learning as 'well as can be expected' suggests race- and class-based judgements of the normative pupil and the idea of the school classroom as compensating for deprivation and educational backwardness.

A few years earlier an inspector had advised that the head teacher was 'to be commended on placing emphasis on the important needs of this school, i.e. the restoration of tone, discipline, pupil–teacher cooperation and the development of good personal and social habits' (27 November 1957). Reporting on the same school, an inspector commented in 1971: 'The problem of successfully stimulating children with a deprived cultural background and fostering a desire to learn still emerges as the greatest difficulty confronting teachers' (20 October 1971). The idea of inciting a desire to learn echoed through inspectors' reports, with lack of desire constructed as an object of pedagogical repair, which could be achieved by being in the right learning environment. Moreover, a desire for learning (or the potential for the realisation of desire) and the display and enactment of discernment were crucial markers in determining Aboriginal children's educability and their capacity for assimilation. This is evident in the frequent emphasis on the aesthetic and orderly arrangement of the classroom. 'The development in children of a pride in achievement and in their school should be the aim. This could be developed by making children aware of their role in ensuring a pleasant learning environment and gaining their cooperation in the maintenance of both classroom and grounds which are in an untidy state' (20 October 1971).

Repeated attention was given to the intrinsic educational value of floral arrangements and visual decorations, along with the uplifting effect of cultivated gardens. This was particularly striking in the annual reports of inspectors to Framlingham. From the first inspector's report in 1934 (5 October 1934), the school was described as 'enfenced'; 'large trees supply ample shade and shelter', clearly demarcating the stylised cultivation of the school environment and its visible separation from the surrounding community. 'Desks should be arranged differently to allow ready access to pupils, desk tops need to be cleaned and coloured, and pictures are necessary to make the room more attractive', one inspector opined. The pedagogic effect of a designed school garden was held to be very important, with the inspector in 1936 observing: 'The small lawns and garden beds make an attractive approach and the aim is to encourage similar improvements in the homes' (31 July 1936). Similar themes echoed inspectors' reports throughout the 1960s. In 1963, Inspector Emerson happily noted on his annual visit to Framlingham:

> The school entrance and surrounds have been transformed by the establishment of well-kept and colourful garden beds. A newly established vegetable garden is also making very good progress. Although of comparatively recent origin, the School Committee has developed a basketball court. Septic closets have been installed and garden seats have been purchased. Ground and pavilion are tidy, water is satisfactory and a new jungle gymnasium has been erected as a result of School Committee interest.
>
> (3 October 1963)

The exhortations and praise for orderly and contained horticulture is in one sense a celebration of the domestication or even taming of the natural environment. In relation to Aboriginal school environments, however, such exhortations could also suggest attempts to ward against perceived impulses towards a traditional way of life, of living in the uncultivated

natural environment, a mode of living that would threaten the assimilationist project of education. The inspector similarly commended the evident attention to the appearance of the
room, reflecting orderliness and discernment: 'Building: Close attention is paid to maintenance duties, and room appearance is enhanced by good prints, curtains, and tidy storage.
Monitors could be encouraged to keep an impressive array of sporting trophies bright and
shining. Furniture is well preserved' (23 July 1959). Instilling a desire for pride and encouraging obedient and docile bodies became evidence not of dull passivity but of educability (see
Figure 12.3). In this respect, children taking an active role, such as becoming a class monitor,
was seen as an important step. It demonstrated capacities for responsibility, but it can also be
seen as a kind of complicity in the teacherly and pedagogical aspects of assimilation.

It is important to acknowledge that school inspectors' reports from visits to mainstream
schools reveal a similar preoccupation with floral arrangements, paintings and the cleanliness and comportment of the classroom (see, for instance, the Inspectors Report Book for
Glengarry West Primary School in western Victoria, 9 December 1963, 30 July 1964). Yet,
such attention has a different resonance and consequence in relation to the schooling of
Aboriginal children, where the school's disciplining influence required scrupulous attention

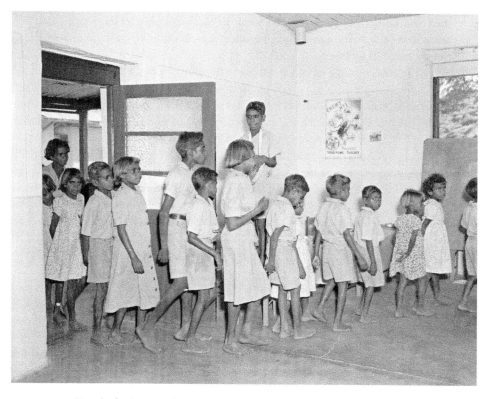

FIGURE 12.3   'Ready for lessons, children file into their class rooms to the beat of a drum in the
NT. They are well behaved little folk, work well and keep their books neat and
clean. They have a talent for drawing and percussion music. These children are of the
Arunta people'. 1958.

Source: National Archives of Australia NAA, A1200, L13745

to documenting evidence of pupil capacities, not only in the basics of curriculum but also in the manners of life. Demonstrating a keenness of eye for everyday aesthetics was evidence of educability and of capacities that could be cultivated in the service of assimilation. The focus on conventional forms and objects of classroom propriety – manners, floral arrangements, gardens, simple domestic symbols – was a reminder of difference, while also representing a set of pedagogical techniques to remediate such difference. Attention to these matters also underscores how classroom objects and spatial arrangements can be seen as the materialisation of cultural values and broader political projects (Herman et al. 2011). Training students to recognise the aesthetic and uplifting value of the floral design or the orderly cultivated garden was part of the pedagogical project of assimilation, and learning these cultural dispositions as motifs of a normative (non-Aboriginal) way of life was arguably as important as work-book diligence.

Conclusion

In examining discourses on the provision of education and organisation of school environments for Aboriginal children in the 1960s, we have argued that the classroom itself can be understood as a racialised space. Education was crucial in the project of assimilation, and we have canvassed some of the contestations over how school curriculum and classroom arrangements should respond to the politics of race and the education of Aboriginal children. As a backdrop to these arguments, we noted that the 1960s was a period of significant educational change as well as political activity and legislative reform in relation to the formal status of Aboriginal people – even so, assimilationist practices and attitudes continued. The type of education provided to Aboriginal children was thus a topic of considerable national importance, with more educators and teachers taking an interest, in both Aboriginal children entering mainstream schools and the role of non-Indigenous teachers in Aboriginal settings.

Debates among teachers and educators reveal fissures and fractures in assimilationist agendas as well as some uncertainty regarding how to negotiate and accommodate difference – that is, when to notice and not notice Aboriginal children. A key dilemma, articulated across diverse forums, was whether or how to recognise Aboriginal children as a distinct category of students: was noticing Aboriginal children as different a form of hierarchical racial discourse, an acknowledgement of the failed or doomed project of assimilation, or respectful recognition of (unassimilable) cultural difference? Discussions regarding the provision of special educational facilities and buildings for Aboriginal children revealed some of these tensions. In conferences dedicated to discussing Aboriginal education, we see a largely – but not entirely – critical view of then current educational and assimilationist agendas in relation to schooling provision for Aboriginal children. The physical environments and curriculum of schools were topics of concern, but, at the same time, proposals for special facilities – dining rooms, craft rooms, outdoor activities – underscored the differentiated futures anticipated for Aboriginal children, registering that their education did not easily belong in the spaces of regular, mainstream classrooms. In contrast, other educational discussions, such as the reports of school inspectors, reveal a concerted effort precisely to make Aboriginal children fit in to the spaces, norms and modes of conduct associated with the arrangements of conventional class rooms. We have analysed the importance the school inspectors attached to the aesthetic and orderly aspects of classroom design, which we argue were cast as vital in the pedagogic mission of cultivating the proper sensibilities and conduct of Aboriginal children and their assimilation into mainstream, white, Australian society.

The socio-spatial arrangements of schooling, including the seemingly ordinary objects of classrooms and the pedagogic work of cultivating pupil taste and comportment, not only are interconnected but form part of the processes by which classroom space is racialised and, as such, affectively charged and cut across with desires and anxieties about when to notice and not notice difference. In this way, the classroom is never simply a space of learning but also and always a space of learning to become a particular type of person. Finally, in the case of Aboriginal education, no matter how school buildings are designed and arranged, they are erected on colonised lands, and the repeated focus on the cultivation of domestic gardens, the ordinary 'pleasant' aesthetic of classroom settings, all these seemingly benign expressions of a caring pedagogy should also serve as reminders of how settler colonialism has insinuated itself into the micro and macro practices of schooling.

Acknowledgement

Research for this chapter has been supported by two grants from the Australian Research Council: 'Youth Identity and Educational Change since 1950: Digital Archiving, Re-using Qualitative Data and Histories of the Present' (Julie McLeod FT110100646) and 'Designing Australian Schools: A Spatial History of Innovation, Pedagogy and Social Change' (DP110100505).

Works cited

Aboriginal Welfare: Initial Conference of Commonwealth and State Aboriginal Authorities held at Canberra, 21st to 23rd April, 1937 (1937) Canberra: L.F. Johnston, Commonwealth Government Printer.

Anderson, W. (2003) *The Cultivation of Whiteness: Science, Health and Racial Destiny in Australia*, New York: Basic Books.

Attwood, B. and Markus, A. (2007) *The 1967 Referendum: Race, Power and the Australian Constitution*, Canberra: Aboriginal Studies Press.

Banivanua-Mar, T. and Edmonds, P. (eds) (2010) *Making Settler Colonial Space: Perspectives on Race, Place and Identity*, Basingstoke: Palgrave Macmillan.

Broome, R. (1994) *Aboriginal Australians: Black Responses to White Dominance, 1788–1994*, Sydney: Allen & Unwin.

Burke, C. (2010) 'Putting Education in Its Place: Mapping the Observations of Danish and English Architects on 1950s School Design', *Paedagogica Historica: International Journal of the History of Education* 46, 5: 655–72.

Burke, C. and Grosvenor, I. (2008) *School*, London: Reaktion.

Campbell, C. and Proctor, H. (2014) *A History of Australian Schooling*, Sydney: Allen & Unwin.

'Club Terrace Inspectors Report Book 1954–1974'. Education Department of Victoria. Public Records Office of Victoria, VPRS 9332/P/0001, Unit 1.

Dovey, K. (2014) *Framing Places: Mediating Power in Built Form*, Hoboken, NY: Taylor & Francis, 2014.

Duncan, A.T. (1969) 'Are Special Facilities Necessary?', in T. Roper (ed.) *Aboriginal Education: The Teacher's Role*, Melbourne: Abschol, National Union of Australian University Students.

Fletcher, J. (1989) *Clean, Clad and Courteous: A History of Aboriginal Education in New South Wales*, Carlton, NSW: np.

Gunton, J. D. (1964) *Aboriginal Schools Bulletin No. 1: A Record of the Conference of Teachers in Aboriginal Schools, Held in Port Augusta from 26–29 May 1964*, Adelaide: Education Department of South Australia.

Gutman, M. and de Coninck-Smith, N. (eds) (2008) *Designing Modern Childhoods: History, Space, and the Material Culture of Children*, New Brunswick, NJ: Rutgers University Press.

Haebich, A. (2008) *Spinning the Dream: Assimilation in Australia 1950–1970*, North Fremantle, WA: Fremantle Press.

Herbert, J. (2012) '"Ceaselessly Circling the Centre": Historical Contextualization of Indigenous Education within Australia', *History of Education Review* 41, 2: 91–103.

Herman, F., van Gorp, A., Simon, F. and Depaepe, M. (2011) 'The School Desk: From Concept to Object', *History of Education* 40, 1: 97–117.

Human Rights and Equal Opportunity Commission (1997) *Bringing Them Home: A Guide to the Findings and Recommendations of the National Inquiry into the Separation of Aboriginal and Torres Strait Islander Children from Their Families*, Sydney: Human Rights and Equal Opportunity Commission.

Kozlovsky, R. (2010) 'The Architecture of "Educare": Motion and Emotion in Postwar Educational Spaces', *History of Education* 39, 6: 695–712.

Leander, K. M., Phillips, N. C. and Headrick Taylor, K. (2010) 'The Changing Social Spaces of Learning: Mapping New Mobilities', *Review of Research in Education* 34, 1: 329–94.

Massey, D. (1994) *Space, Place and Gender*, Cambridge: Polity.

McGregor, J. (ed.) (2004) *Forum* 46, 1, Special Issue on Schools and Space.

McGregor, R. (1997) *Imagined Destinies: Aboriginal Australians and the Doomed Race Theory, 1880–1939*, Melbourne: Melbourne University Press.

McGregor, R. (2011) *Indifferent Inclusion: Aboriginal People and the Australian Nation*, Canberra: Aboriginal Studies Press.

McLeod, J. (2014) 'Experimenting with Education: Spaces of Freedom and Alternative Schooling in the 1970s', *History of Education Review* 43, 2: 172–89.

McMeekin, G. W. (1969) 'Race Relations in Aboriginal Education?', in T. Roper (ed.) *Aboriginal Education: The Teacher's Role*, Melbourne: Abschol, National Union of Australian University Students: 18–26.

Minister of Education (1968) *Education Report of the Minister of Education for the Year 1966–67*, Melbourne: Education Department.

Paechter, C. (2004) 'Metaphors of Space in Educational Theory and Practice', *Pedagogy, Culture & Society* 12, 3: 449–66. doi:10.1080/14681360400200202.

Potts, A. (2007) 'New Education, Progressive Education and the Counter Culture', *Journal of Educational Administration and History* 39, 2: 145–59. doi:10.1080/00220620701342304.

Punch, M. (1969) 'How to Be a "Progressive" School Now?', *New Society* 13, 328: 123–24.

Rasmussen, L. R. (2012) 'Touching Materiality: Presenting the Past of Everyday School Life', *Memory Studies* 5, 2: 114–30. doi:10.1177/1750698011412147.

Razack, S. H. (1998) *Looking White People in the Eye: Gender, Race, and Culture in Courtrooms and Classrooms*, Toronto: University of Toronto Press.

Read, P. (2014) *Settlement: A History of Australian Indigenous Housing*, Canberra: Aboriginal Studies Press.

Roper, T. (1969) *Aboriginal Education: The Teacher's Role*, Melbourne: Abschol, National Union of Australian University Students.

'School Records: Framlingham Settlement (Primary School No. 4532); Also Known as Framlingham Aboriginal Settlement 1934–1967'. Education Department of Victoria. Public Records Office of Victoria, VPRS 9063/P/0001, Unit 1.

Scott, J. (1990) 'Deconstructing Equality-Versus-Difference: Or, the Uses of Poststructuralist Theory for Feminism', in M. Hirsch and E. Fox Keller (eds) *Conflicts in Feminism*, New York: Routledge: 134–48.

Soja, E. W. (1996) *Thirdspace: Journeys to Los Angeles and Other Real-and-imagined Places*, Cambridge, MA: Blackwell.

Tatz, C. and Dunn, S. (eds) (1969) *Aborigines & Education*, Melbourne: Sun-Books in Association with Centre for Research into Aboriginal Affairs, Melbourne: Monash University.

Wolfe, P. (2001) 'Land, Labor, and Difference: Elementary Structures of Race', *The American Historical Review* 106, 3: 866–905.

13

A MODEL SCHOOL FOR A MODEL CITY

Shaw Junior High School as a monument
to planning reform

Amber Wiley

On 12 March 1967 at Cardozo High School in northwest Washington, DC, Dr Martin Luther King Jr delivered a speech titled 'On People and Shaw Urban Renewal' to a crowd of around 3,800 people (Haskins 2007/2008: 55). King had been invited to speak by Reverend Walter Fauntroy, head of New Bethel Baptist Church and president of the Model Inner City Community Organization (MICCO). The day's events started at Paul Laurence Dunbar High School with a parade of bands, floats and marching units through the Shaw School Urban Renewal Area, and ended with King's speech at Cardozo High School (see Figure 13.1) (Honsa 1967: C2). Here, in the heart of the nation's capital, one of the most well-known and influential political activists of the time was advocating for urban renewal in a predominately African-American neighbourhood.

This chapter examines the complexity involved in bridging the ideals espoused across the fields of architecture, education and urban planning to inform design in the Shaw School Urban Renewal Area in Washington, DC, in the context of the social upheaval and the politics of racial desegregation in the United States. The building campaigns in Washington in the late 1960s reflected new power dynamics in African-American community politics and urban renewal that emphasised a progressive agenda for education reform. Community leaders and activists took advantage of federal legislation put forth by Lyndon B. Johnson to counteract the devastating consequences of residential segregation, upper-middle-class and middle-class suburban flight and concentrated poverty. These clergy members, architects, planners, school board members and city council members used their political and social capital to transform their communities. The result was one of the most praised community–government collaborations of federal urban renewal planning. This renewal was markedly different from previous proposals, which had resulted in negative impacts on African-American neighbourhoods through wholesale demolition of neighbourhoods and displacement of communities. It was intended the new renewal would have African-American architects, planners, contractors and construction workers playing prominent roles. The renewal would be incremental and piecemeal, strategically building on under-utilised lots for larger construction, and rehabilitating rundown sectors instead of instigating extensive demolition. Central to the plan was a new Shaw Junior High School, a

FIGURE 13.1   MICCO flyer advertising Dr Martin Luther King Jr speech in support of Shaw School Urban Renewal Area.

Source: Washington DC Public Library, Washingtoniana Division

building with forward-looking design that would replace the old 'Shameful Shaw', an aging and overcrowded building constructed in 1902.

Just over a year after the speech King made at Cardozo High School in support of the Shaw School Urban Renewal Area, the area was ablaze with riots. King was assassinated in Memphis, Tennessee, on 4 April 1968. Urban unrest spread across the country with the news, as grief and anguish turned to anger in communities like Shaw. Shaw was a part of the much larger confluence of African-American neighbourhoods in Washington that included the U Street Corridor and LeDroit Park. This area was considered the heart of black Washington, with a bustling commercial corridor, several performance and movie theatres, black-owned and black-operated banks and newspapers, and respected black academic institutions such as Dunbar High School and Howard University (Green 1967; Gillette 1995; Ruble 2010; Wiley 2010). In Washington, one of the hardest hit cities in the 1968 riots, the situation and outlook were particularly bleak. Devastation was widespread, the estimated cost of damage to real estate was around $24.8 million, and 1,352 businesses experienced damage or theft (Levy 1969: C8). Before the riots, the Shaw Urban Renewal Area plan had stuttered along, with community activists trying to garner neighbourhood buy-in to the idea. This is one of the reasons King was called in to speak on behalf of the plan. After the riots renewal was no longer an option for the area; it was an imperative.

The post-riot building campaigns in the city reflected urban renewal that also emphasised a progressive agenda for education reform. Inspiration for this renewal came from a number of directions. The Educational Facilities Laboratory produced *The Schools and Urban Renewal: A Case Study from New Haven* (Ferrer 1964) to promote school construction as a method of community-informed renewal. The Community Research and Development Corporation's report, *The Education Park* (Corde Corporation 1967), argued for the creation of large-scale educational centres on the basis these would consolidate student populations in urban areas and revive the cultural capital of cities while promoting racial integration. Education policy expert Roald Campbell edited a volume titled *Education and the Urban Renaissance* (Campbell et al. 1968) that moved the conversation forward to engage Model Cities legislation, a federal initiative that promoted citizen participation in urban renewal plans.

Model school division

Shaw Junior High School was at the heart of two major initiatives that came out of federal attempts to address education and urban renewal in the inner city. The first was the Model School Division, a semi-autonomous subgroup in the Washington public school system that allowed for 'innovation and experimentation' within the curriculum, teacher training and programming of a target area – Cardozo High School and all its feeder schools, including Shaw. The second was the Model Cities program.

In the 1960s federal efforts to improve urban education resulted in legislative and monetary outcomes that were applied on an individual case basis and were tailored to the needs of local communities without clear indication of measures for success and perpetuation. Christopher T. Cross, historian of educational policy, characterises post–World War II educational reform during the Eisenhower years (1953–1961) as 'fraught with complications regarding the baby boom generation and the need to expand classroom space' (Cross 2004: 4). Many bills proposed for school construction in this period were struck down at the national level because of the fear that states would lose their pedagogical autonomy, and that schools receiving federal aid would be pushed into centralised and federally mandated national curricula. In the Kennedy era (1961–1963) the educational focus was on the expansion of maths and science programs, but during the Johnson era (1963–1969) there was a shift towards racial integration policies and compensatory education in impoverished areas as fundamental to social and educational reform. By the mid-1960s, major federal programs were created to give aid to schools in urban areas throughout the United States that were desperately competing with attractive suburban schools for students from middle-class and upper-middle-class families.

The reform agenda developed under President Lyndon B. Johnson, collectively referred to as the Great Society, worked to eradicate poverty, inequity and social injustice in cities across the United States. These sweeping social reforms included programs aimed at the healthcare system, education, civil rights, transportation and housing. One of the Great Society's main focuses (and indeed enduring legacy) was the War on Poverty, which was administered through the Office of Economic Opportunity. Some of the major legislative acts under the

Johnson presidency that were intended to aid urban education included the Civil Rights Act of 1964, the Elementary and Secondary Education Act of 1965 and the Demonstration Cities and Metropolitan Development Act of 1966, which created the Model Cities Program.

While the Civil Rights Act was more broadly focused on equalising the rights of minority citizens and women, it reaffirmed the federal government's commitment to the 1954 *Brown v. Board of Education* ruling against racial segregation in public schools. The Civil Rights Act remained a controversial piece in the history of desegregation since many policymakers believed it would support bussing school children in racially segregated neighbourhoods, a move that was characterised as unconstitutional by opponents of the bill.

The Elementary and Secondary Education Act was created to shape educational reform through a myriad of avenues that included increased funding for schools with a concentration of low-income students and the creation of supplementary educational programs. The legislation was also a reaction to earlier concerns about federal funding and the threat of a national curriculum, the imposition of which would encroach on states' rights to autonomy. It was clear in the legislation that no federal curriculum should be enforced – rather that state and local governments should have control over shaping the curricula for their schools. However, the legislation was criticised for allowing the federal government to distribute money for specific purposes, rather than assigning more block grants and general aid to federally funded schools (Milius 1969: A1). These concerns lasted years after the act was passed, even while curricula were undergoing rapid changes to embrace culturally diverse and individualised programs that focused on an ethnocentric approach to education.

The freedom for states to determine curriculum, however, was important for a nation that was wary of too much authority sitting with the centralised federal government. It is partially for this reason that Cross (2004: 4) characterises the 1960s as the peak of the open education movement, 'with its emphasis on tearing down classroom walls'. Cross's tone is slightly sinister as he describes the reform trends in which 'a core curriculum was abandoned and students were urged to enroll in whatever courses they wished to take, *whether or not they had any academic merit*' (emphasis added, Cross 2004: 4). The revolution of pedagogy and curriculum in the 1960s and 1970s reflected larger societal changes that not only questioned the status quo but also expanded it so notions of academic merit had a more humanistic and individual slant aimed at combating issues of failure within schools.

The Equality of Educational Opportunity Report of 1966, commonly referred to as the Coleman Report after its principal author James S. Coleman, was published two years after the Civil Rights Act. Its aim was to measure the success of improved educational opportunities for all students regardless of race. The Coleman Report has been critiqued as explaining black student underachievement in terms of social factors rather than resource allocation. James K. Kent, then a doctoral student at the Harvard Graduate School of Education, argued that the Coleman Report redefined how educational equality was characterised and evaluated. Instead of measuring good schools by quantifiable input such as resource allocation, student-to-teacher ratio, school expenditures per student and laboratory facilities, the report findings indicated that student achievement lay directly with the individual student and the school itself. This sentiment propagated the notion that student failure was not the fault of a larger system of societal neglect but a result of the student lacking enterprising spirit and exposure to other social classes (and therefore racial) examples. Educational policy reformers saw the Coleman Report as a call towards integration, where black students could succeed if placed within a majority white learning environment (Kent 1968: 242).

The findings of the Coleman Report did little to influence integration policy in Washington. The city had already tried its hand at integration through the implementation of federal legislation in the 1950s, but the school district was already black in majority at the time. Federal involvement in the educational policy of Washington was more direct than in other cities in the nation because, as it still is, the city was run by Congress and received most of its funds for public projects from congressional allocations. Federal officials hoped that Washington public school reform would be a model for the rest of the nation. Between 1963 and 1974 Washington implemented steps to develop and cultivate the Model School Division program, a collaborative project between the non-profit advocacy organisation Washington Action for Youth and the Board of Education.

The Model School Division used federally funded compensatory programs such as Head Start and Project Follow Through to improve student success in the early stages of childhood education. Program elements ranged from new reading, organisational and curricular plans to suit a diverse student body, summer programs, and employing the community school model for the neighbourhood by increasing accessibility to school facilities for neighbourhood residents before and after the school day. The overall goal was to create the 'greatest individual and collective student achievement possible . . . [helping] students to understand themselves, to have mature personal and social relationships in school, home, and community' (District of Columbia Public Schools 1966: 2). Clearly, in addition to the 'three Rs', the program was a staunch proponent of educational and sociological theories that schools should and could be incubators for responsible citizens and community benefit. Students received intense educational training, and neighbourhood residents were granted access to previously unavailable community facilities.

Model cities: Shaw school urban renewal area

Shaw Junior High School was named for Colonel Robert Gould Shaw, leader of the all-black 54th Massachusetts regiment that served during the American Civil War. The school was established in 1919 and was initially housed at the former M Street School before settling in a building previously constructed for the all-white McKinley Manual Training High School. The school was situated on a corner site, and the building form responded to the irregular intersection of Seventh Street and Rhode Island Avenue in the northwest quadrant of Washington. The three-storey building plan was V-shaped, with two wings arranged at about a 110-degree angle (see Figure 13.2). Both wings consisted of double-loaded classroom corridors. Classroom space dedicated to the industrial arts was situated in the basement nestled below the two 'V' wings. The imposing Romanesque facade was buff brick and limestone.

Once McKinley had outgrown the space, the building was handed over to the coloured school system, as Washington, DC, then operated a racially segregated school administration. Shaw Junior High School was congested from the start. The Shaw Parent-Teacher Association requested 'immediate relief from the overcrowded condition' as early as 1941 (Board of Education 1941: 2). A 1949 report on Washington public schools stated: 'The educational adequacy of the plant is so low that no reasonable amount of rehabilitation could correct its deficiencies' (Strayer 1949: 346).

The National Capital Planning Commission published a comprehensive plan for Washington in 1950 that called for the wholesale demolition of the neighbourhood around Shaw Junior High School, although the school remained untouched (National Capital Planning Commission 1950: 25). By 1959, however, the commission's plans included replacing the

FIGURE 13.2   Perspective sketch, McKinley Manual Training High School. Completed in 1902. Later Shaw Junior High School.

Architect: Henry Ives Cobb

Source: Washington DC Public Library, Washingtoniana Division

school (Board of Education 1959). In 1963 the Board of Education approved budget sketches for a new Shaw Junior High School at Seventh and P Street, NW. This site became problematic only a few years later when the John F. Kennedy Playground was constructed on the plot in memory of the slain president (Board of Education 1963). The site was valued as a community asset and was one of the first memorials to the president erected after his death. Alternative suggestions for this potential school site met with strong community opposition.

Washington had undertaken urban renewal in a different form before the Shaw Urban Renewal Area was established (see Figure 13.3). City planners envisioned the Southwest Urban Renewal project of 1955 as an icon of city revitalisation; instead it became the symbol of the destructive nature of large-scale city redevelopment plans. Just over a decade later, the nation's capital was considering a new approach to city planning through the Model Cities legislation passed by President Johnson in 1966. Walter Washington (former head of the National Capital Housing Authority), Reverend Walter Fauntroy (of the New Bethel Baptist Church) and Tom Appleby (head of the District of Columbia Redevelopment Land Agency) combined efforts to have the Shaw School Urban Renewal Area designated a Model Cities project in 1967 (Griffith 1969: 26; see also District of Columbia Redevelopment Land Agency 1970). Fauntroy stated in a January 1966 presentation to the three Washington commissioners and board members of the Redevelopment Land Agency and National Capital Planning Commission:

> There is a legitimate fear among many that one or more of the area's pockets of despair may simply explode if something isn't done soon to relieve conditions. People don't explode when they have *legitimate reason* to believe help is coming.
>
> (Griffith 1969: 27; italics in original)

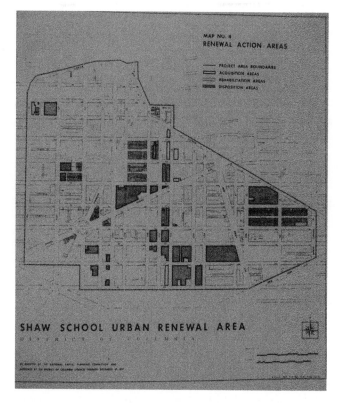

FIGURE 13.3 Shaw School Urban Renewal Area. Bounded to the east by North Capitol Street, south by M Street NW, west by 15th Street NW and north by Florida Avenue NW.

Source: District of Columbia Redevelopment Land Agency (1973) *NDP4 Summary of Proposed Modifications to Urban Renewal Plan. Shaw School Urban Renewal Area*; George Washington University Special Collections Washingtoniana

The help that Fauntroy sought in the form of a Model Cities designation for the neighbourhood would allow distribution of federal funds to the urban renewal project, with the strict requirement that local community organisations and agencies had a leading role in the project undertaking. Civic organisations with community leaders partnered with local planning agencies to carry out the redevelopment process. In Washington many of the key local organisers were affiliated with various churches in the Shaw School Urban Renewal Area.

Fauntroy's political and activist work bridged the gap between various racial and socioeconomic populations in Washington. In 1966 Fauntroy and a coalition of leaders from the Shaw neighbourhood formed the Model Inner City Community Organization (MICCO), which was the major conduit for coordinated community involvement with the Redevelopment Land Agency. Its leadership consisted of block club representatives, civic associations, chamber of commerce and business groups, health and welfare councils, job training programs, churches and fraternal groups and school parent-teacher associations (Griffith 1969: 28). MICCO was a powerful force in determining the direction of the Shaw School Urban Renewal Area project. It became the 'first citizens' group ever funded by the federal government to take part in determining the destiny of a neighborhood' (Meyer and Smith 1972: A1, D1). MICCO's involvement in the Shaw program was what urban political historian Howard W. Hallman calls 'equal-bargaining planning'; unlike other planning initiatives where communities were involved, the MICCO/Shaw example showed the community's 'political influence and independent professional competence – in other words, power and knowledge' (Hallman 1970: 176). Black architects and planners were consulted and, with black organisations, played a central role in the development of the Shaw School Urban Renewal plan. African-American architects, trained at Howard University, had established an influential presence near the Shaw neighbourhood and formed a coalition with a particularly strong voice in urban renewal (Mitchell 2003).

MICCO's director of planning, Reginald Griffith, was then completing a master's degree at the Massachusetts Institute of Technology. His thesis recorded a change in the atmosphere of the Shaw area after the 1968 riots that devastated the neighbourhood (see Figures 13.4). By August 1968 the Redevelopment Land Agency was acquiring land for the Shaw school site (Clopton 1968: A32; 'City Life: RLA Acts on New Shaw Site' 1968: B8). In January 1969 the National Capital Planning Commission and the city council approved the plans for the

FIGURE 13.4 'Shameful Shaw' seen through the broken glass of an empty automobile sales agency that was burned out in the 1968 riots.

Source: Washington DC Public Library, Washingtoniana Division

Shaw School Urban Renewal Area. Griffith noted that after the riots MICCO moved from operating as an ambiguous 'go-between' to an active advocate on behalf of Shaw's black community (Griffith 1969: 39–40):

> It must be noted that the flame of black self-awareness, pride, and united efforts to overcome the systematic exclusion of Blacks from the main stream of american [*sic*] life was agitated by the tragic assassinations of Malcolm X and Dr. King. With the passing of Dr. King, whose dedication to non-violent philosophy was respected by militants and conservatives alike, the agitated flame has moved toward the extremists and tended to embrace more and more of the black power philosophy.
>
> (Griffith 1969: 7)

MICCO pamphlets, brochures and annual reports declared the Shaw School Urban Renewal Area a project 'with the people, by the people, for the people'.

The pre-riot plans for a replacement Shaw Junior High School had not involved black architects, contractors, planners, construction workers or electricians. Although there was a higher concentration of black architects in Washington than in other cities, most of their commissions were smaller in scale than those of white architects. Churches, banks and the occasional residence were the staples of a black architect's oeuvre (Etheridge 1979). However, after the riots MICCO worked in conjunction with the Redevelopment Land Agency to ensure adequate representation of the black community in the design process. The architects and consulting engineers were African Americans, selected because black architects and other construction professionals demanded involvement. The physical impact of the riots that devastated Shaw and Columbia Heights in northwest Washington, as well as the H Street corridor in the northeast quadrant and the growing Black Power sentiment among members of the African American community added to the diversity of the plan. It was radical in mission and also in application – exhibiting a sensitivity to the urban fabric of the neighbourhood and supplanting the traditional notion of urban renewal, which focused on commercial or governmental edifices, with one that focused on an educational facility as the centrepiece.

Shaw school prototypes: the education park and the open plan

The post–World War II period in the United States was characterised by major demographic shifts in the student population as a result of racial desegregation education policies. Around the nation, urban school districts drew on highly conceptual models for school design and programming in attempts to alleviate such issues as overcrowding in black schools, under-enrolment in white schools and the loss of key tax-paying demographics to the suburbs due to white flight. The advent of integration policies in the late 1960s and early 1970s was so powerful that, in addition to bussing plans, school districts attempted to reconfigure school attendance zones of school districts in a way that would capture optimum enrolment numbers for the distressed areas. These concepts included the education park (or school park), community schools and free schools. These schools were not constrained by traditional neighbourhood boundaries, so they held potential to help integration policies.

The education park was not a new concept when it gained popularity among educational policy makers and administrators in the late 1960s. The idea of a shared park that acted as a community anchor was championed as early as 1894 when Preston Search, the superintendent of schools in Los Angeles, proposed a 'school park' for the city. All levels of primary and secondary education would be located centrally in an open campus-like setting and resources such as school facilities, administrators, faculty and supporting services would be pooled between the different levels of schools for optimum cost-efficiency. This model was compared to the functioning mechanisms of a small college campus (Corde Corporation 1967: 0). Edward A. Campbell, a consulting architect for the University of Chicago suggested a similarly situated conceptual complex – designed as a focal point in the community and set amid spacious walks, gardens, fountains and sculpture – would invite participation in education of many kinds (Campbell 1960). People of all ages might study astronomy or zoology or sketching, hear poetry or make music, and learn dancing or chess. The park was the setting for community facilities such as the library, museum, concert hall, theatre, art centre and school.

The education park and 'community school' concepts that catered to a larger population of students were promoted as a means to facilitate racial integration in schooling. In 1967 the Community Research and Development Corporation (Corde Corporation) published a report titled *The Education Park*. While the report was undertaken to determine the feasibility of the education park in New York, Philadelphia and Baltimore, other cities such as East Orange, New Orleans and Pittsburgh were also investigating school park applications (Corde Corporation 1967: 0). The report highlighted the benefits arising from the large size of the education park campus and structure, quoting an educational consultant 'who saw the park as giving schools a "dramatic new visibility" in the community by taking smaller schools "out of the back alleys of the city" and placing them on prominent sites' (Corde Corporation 1967: 8). The size and siting of the park would 'engender feelings of school pride and importance' (Corde Corporation 1967: 8). Size was particularly important, as school administrators who promoted the education park concept as a means of integration believed that the larger school could be placed in residential areas bordered by black and white neighbourhoods and capture students from both populations. Similar to the ideas of rezoning and bussing in school districts, this approach was based on the existing and segregated residential patterns of blacks and whites in the cities.

In Washington, DC, the education park was not considered a serious option for successful integration as it was in a variety of other cities. This was, according to A. Harry Passow, because the Washington public school system was in the majority black (Passow 1967: 13). Nonetheless, the Greater Washington Chapter of Americans for Democratic Action urged Granville F. Woodson, then assistant school superintendent for buildings and grounds, to adopt an educational park plan. This was to leave smaller school sites open for residential development, particularly for public housing that could be scattered throughout the city instead of being concentrated in one area where it would essentially create an 'urban ghetto' (Filson 1966b: C3). In 1966, William Cox, of the Board of Education's buildings and grounds department, did the preliminary sketch up for the Shaw replacement school in an education park. It was a six-storey tower with a one-storey building that included community services such as a swimming pool, two gyms, a multiservice centre, study rooms, a cafeteria, a meeting room and an auditorium (Hoffman 1966: A12).

Shaw neighbourhood activists also saw the educational park as an opportunity to 'provide things you couldn't have in any one school and at the same time reduce the cost of operation of all the schools involved' (Filson 1967: B4). One of several plans drawn up by local activist groups included coordinated efforts and resource sharing between the area elementary schools as well as Dunbar High School and Armstrong Vocational School (see Figure 13.5). The plan had a central building that included a city library, non-profit cafeteria, art exhibits, theatre, auditorium, gym, youth centre and senior citizens lounge (Filson 1967: B4).

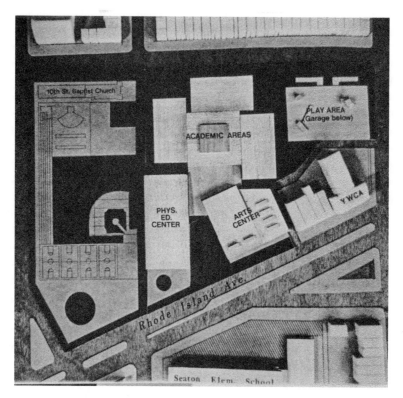

FIGURE 13.5 One of the MICCO conceptual proposals for the Shaw education park.

Source: Model Inner City Community Organization *Annual Report 1968–1969* (Washington, DC: MICCO, 1969); George Washington University Special Collections Washingtoniana

Another major trend in educational design and policy that influenced the scheme for the new Shaw Junior High School was the open school (also known as the open-plan school). This concept used team teaching and open-plan classrooms in an attempt to revolutionise and individualise the learning process. Schools within the Model School Division were already attempting new teaching techniques within the same confined spaces of early nineteenth-century schools. In 1966 school officials planned to do away with the highly criticised track system that kept students of various learning abilities separated and on distinct 'tracks' and replace it completely with team teaching that allowed for greater numbers of students to be instructed at the same time by more than one teacher. A major issue in introducing this new technique was a lack of classroom space. Flexible classrooms were needed (Filson 1966a: 1). The open-plan school, with its potential for individual curricula that addressed the needs of each student, was extremely attractive to a community that sought autonomy in all things social, educational and cultural. The extreme polarisation of race, economics and design concepts during the era of the urban crisis reinforces this idea. The construction of a new Shaw school would allow architects to respond to the 'innovative and experimental' curriculum of the Model School Division. The open-plan school, adopted from British models, was popular in the United States in the late 1960s, and its appeal was seen across a variety of racial and socioeconomic settings, as well as urban and rural environments, and it was used for both primary and secondary education (Wiley 2013). This open classroom prototype, along with a campus that reflected an educational park, was adopted for the design of Shaw Junior High School. The design of the new Shaw school was based on the 'house' model, which broke down a spacious open plan with movable partitions (Hoffman 1969: C1).

Although various architects and planners were involved with initial design schematics, the commission went to Sulton-Campbell architects, a black firm. John Dennis Sulton and Leroy Miller Campbell established Sulton-Campbell in 1964 'in response to the growing demand for greater African American participation in the design profession in the Washington, DC metropolitan area' (Sulton Campbell Britt Architects 2013). Campbell came from New York City and graduated from Howard University School of Architecture, while Sulton had architectural training from South Carolina State and Kansas State colleges ('Leroy Campbell, Area Architect for 26 Years' 1977: C4; 'John D. Sulton Dies, Washington Architect' 1994: D5.) Sulton-Campbell was selected for the project after major campaigning in Washington for more black involvement in the urban renewal area. This rise in the employment of black designers in the reconstruction work was the result of a combination of factors – including advocacy on the part of MICCO, and the presence of architect Charles Cassell on the Board of Education and architect Robert Nash in the Urban Planning Organization, one of the many bodies informing the work undertaken in the Model Cities area. Both Cassell and Nash were important figures in the struggle for greater representation of black architects in major design projects in Washington. Cassell founded the DC Council of Black Architects, while Nash and Campbell were founding members of the National Organization of Minority Architects.

Sulton-Campbell seized the opportunity to design an ambitious and forward-thinking Shaw Junior High School. The US$13 million school project, the city's first open-plan design for a secondary school, was a considerable contrast to its double-loaded corridor predecessor (Milloy 1977: C1). The new Shaw Junior High School design would be a fitting centrepiece for an area targeted for experimentation, as it was developed as part of both the Model School Division and the Model Cities project. It was a demonstration that school design could support non-traditional educational policy, curriculum and administration. The new Shaw school would also prove that federal legislation creating autonomy in struggling urban areas could have a powerful impact on educational opportunity for black communities. The burden was a heavy one, as a *Washington Post* article declared: 'A school can fulfil its whole responsibility to a neighborhood like Shaw's if it is much more than a school' ('Shaw School, At Last' 1966: A16). The replacement Shaw Junior High School, after decades of advocacy on behalf of neighbourhood residents, was completed in 1977.

The final design included three 'houses', or sub-schools, that would accommodate up to four hundred students each. These houses were physically distinct from each other, contained two floors, and had their own administration, dining areas, teaching areas, stairs, toilets and lockers. The architecture firm's proposal for the teaching areas noted that the teaching spaces were unobstructed by columns or permanent walls so that the greatest variety of teaching methods could occur as instructors reconfigured the space to meet their teaching needs. The houses were joined by a central common area designed to provide informal gathering spaces for students between classes and in moments of leisure.

The Shaw design also provided facilities that would be shared with students and the neighbourhood. These included tennis and basketball courts, an auditorium and spaces given over to technology workshops and industrial work. The plan also called for community offices where neighbourhood residents could seek information on employment, legal aid and welfare.

Conclusion

The *Washington Post* published a scathing editorial in 1965 bemoaning the condition of Washington's inner-city neighbourhoods and schools. It proclaimed:

> A public school is supposed to be the symbol of advancement and the avenue to equality.... But in Washington, the slums deform the schools faster and far more thoroughly than the schools can reform the slums. The leading example is Shaw Junior High School and the system of elementary schools within its ambit.
>
> ('The Schools of the Slums' 1965: A14)

In an effort to correct these ills, federally legislated programs such as the Model School Division and Model Cities allowed greater autonomy in the local decision-making process in school pedagogy and urban planning, though both programs were short-lived. The Nixon presidency from 1969 to 1974 was considered less friendly to minorities and the urban poor than the Johnson presidency, and Nixon came under fire from the press for not being responsive to or protective of prior reform. A *Washington Post* article from 1969 highlighted some of the concerns of Nixon's task force on education, stating that the president was 'not regarded as a friend by most of the Nation's Negroes, nor as a particularly "education-minded President" by the Nation as a whole' (Milius 1969: A1). The legislation created by Johnson during his presidency, such as the Model Cities and Model School Division programs, was rebuffed by the Nixon administration.

The Model Cities program ended in 1974 with varied results. The Washington, DC, example of the Shaw School Urban Renewal Area is often cited as the most successful partnership between local government agencies and community organisations for the use of federally appropriated resources to rehabilitate a marginalised, primarily African-American neighbourhood. The effectiveness of MICCO is at the forefront of success stories about the cultural and political empowerment of African-American communities in planning for renewal in their neighbourhoods. The concentration of social and political capital and professional skills held by the organisation's administrators are at the heart of this success. Washington has been unique in this aspect in regard to its African-American community, particularly in the twentieth century, as it was home to the largest concentration of African-American professionals in the country, including those well versed in architecture and planning.

Most of the early reviews of the Model School Division focused on its experimental nature and the plethora of compensatory, collaborative and community-focused programs that were executed as part of the school reform plan (Tunnell 1970: B1). Missing in the literature, however, was how these programs were coordinated, who the specific administrators were and what the long-term tactics were for sustaining and measuring the outcomes of the programs. Even though these factors were of considerable consequence in guaranteeing that the program worked past the initial stages of implementation, they were often neglected in reform policies across the nation on the local, state and federal levels. In the final report on the Model School Division, Larry Cuban surmised that the major failings of the initiative included no comprehensive planning, power struggles within the administration and between organisations overseeing the project, no long-term modes of measuring effectiveness and, finally, no diffusion of lessons learned from the project throughout the rest of the school district (Cuban 1972). Although the Model School Division and Model Cities Program increased funding to city centre initiatives and community action programs that coordinated federal and local leadership, the multiplicity of the approach hindered successful collaboration and guidance as the federal government bureaucracy expanded and lost its transparency.

Zoning restrictions put in place during the implementation of the Shaw plan are still in effect today, as the 1977 Shaw Junior High School sits abandoned and unused (see Figure 13.6). Schools like Shaw that once stood as icons for black empowerment and avant-garde school design with a Brutalist aesthetic are now considered relics of a bygone era. Administrators and teachers criticised the open plan of Shaw, along with many of its open-plan contemporaries like Dunbar High School in Washington, as impractical. In fact, the Shaw principal Percy Ellis was highly critical of the plan, worrying that the spaces would not be used in the way they were intended (Wiley 2013: 108). Ellis's fears were valid, as teachers operating in these new educational spaces did not readily adopt the open-plan and team-teaching techniques.

Shaw Junior High School became Shaw Middle School in the 1980s. From 2007 to 2010 the Washington public school district, under the direction first of Chancellor Michelle Rhee and then of Chancellor Kaya Henderson, systematically closed down elementary and middle schools, folding school histories into one another and deleting individual institutional histories altogether. This move was an increasing effort to consolidate resources as a response to falling student enrolment. A 2009 memorandum addressed to the District of Columbia Public School Office of Transformation Management and the Office of the State Superintendent of Education noted: 'The District of Columbia Public School (DCPS) enrollment peaked at 146,000 students in 1967. The total public school enrollment – DCPS and public charter schools – is down to only about half of that number today' (21st Century School Fund, Urban Institute, Brookings Institution 2009: 1). As a result, massive school closings took place. Shaw was consolidated with Garnet-Patterson Middle School (itself the result of a previous school consolidation) to become Shaw Middle School @ Garnet-Patterson. In 2013 Shaw Middle School @ Garnet-Patterson was closed. Its enrolment at the time of closure was 154 students.

FIGURE 13.6   Shuttered Shaw School, 2013.

Photograph: Amber Wiley

The open-plan Shaw School completed in 1977, in contrast, was designed to accommodate around twelve hundred students.

With the consolidation of school resources, the waves of school closures over the last decade and a top-down approach to managing community planning and education, the future for meaningful, community input and collective progress seems dim. The proliferation of charter schools in Washington is now seen as the next progressive educational reform movement. The Shaw neighbourhood, like many others in Washington, is undergoing rapid gentrification, but the public school district is not benefiting from this increase in social and political capital. New community members who have the economic and political means to advocate for their children send them to charter schools or private schools (Rosenblat and Howard 2015). Different community groups want to tear down the 1977 Shaw Junior High School building, calling it an eyesore. The previous building, constructed in 1902 and once dubbed 'Shameful Shaw', is now Asbury Dwellings, affordable housing for the elderly, and is included on the DC Inventory of Historic Sites.

Lost is the narrative of a moment when Washington was enfranchised to use urban renewal as a tool for community revitalisation and the construction of a new school. In the midst of gentrification and disregard for the African-American contribution to city in the 1960s and 1970s, here is a shining example of urban renewal in the hands of the community. When given opportunity, autonomy and funding, local activists – be they clergy, concerned citizens, designers, planners, militant or moderate – used the tools at hand to create a successful project. These activists were able to move up the political ladder and create positive change for the city in their respective fields, with generous federal programs funding. Architects Robert Nash and Leroy Campbell would go on to found the National Organization of Minority Architects along with several other African-American members of the American Institute of Architects in 1971. Walter Fauntroy served briefly on the city council and would later become the city's first congressional representative in over one hundred years. He served in that capacity from 1971 to 1991. Reginald Griffith, planning director for MICCO, was a commissioner and vice chair of the National Capital Planning Commission from 1975 to 1979. He was appointed executive director of the commission in 1979 and held that post until 2000. As Fauntroy stated in 1969:

> The people of Shaw, the development teams, and particularly the MICCO Planning Staff . . . take just pride in the skill in which we have taken urban renewal, a tool historically used to remove black people, and fashioned it into an instrument of non-violent land reform for the people of our neighborhood.
>
> (Model Inner City Community Organization 1969: 1)

The success of the Shaw Urban Renewal Area should be a standard taught in planning schools, architecture schools, schools of public policy and, finally, Washington, DC, public schools. It was a teachable moment in the larger civil rights movement that combines an African-American empowerment narrative with design and planning.

In the wake of the Black Lives Matter movement, many architects, planners and historians are rallying for design to have a social justice agenda (TenHoor and Massey 2015). In 2015 this is particularly evident in events such as the Black in Design conference held at the Harvard University Graduate School and the National Organization of Minority Architects annual conference titled 'Social Justice by Design'. African-American design students are searching for ways to make their work more meaningful to disenfranchised communities. They are hungry for lessons on how to make design a practice in equity and restorative justice (Griffin

2015; Mock 2015). The Shaw Urban Renewal Area illustrates how African-American architects, concerned citizens and civic leaders can redefine and reconfigure pre-existing power structures, policy and notions about urban planning to benefit the community at large.

Works cited

Board of Education of the District of Columbia (1941) Minutes of Board of Education of the District of Columbia Meeting 8 January 37: 2.

Board of Education of the District of Columbia (1959) Minutes of Board of Education of the District of Columbia Meeting 18 March 101: 44.

Board of Education of the District of Columbia (1963) Minutes of Board of Education of the District of Columbia Meeting 16 October 110: 2.

Campbell, E. A. (1960) 'New Spaces and Places for Learning', *School Review* 68, 3 (Autumn): 346–52.

Campbell, R. F., Marx, L. A. and Nystrand R. O. (eds) (1968) *Education and the Urban Renaissance*, New York: Wiley.

'City Life: RLA Acts on New Shaw Site' (1968) *Washington Post* (16 August): B8.

Clopton, W. Jr. (1968) 'Riot-Scarred 7th Street Area Gets Role in Shaw Renewal', *Washington Post* (24 November): A32.

Corde Corporation (1967) *The Education Park: Report to the School District of Philadelphia*, Philadelphia: The Corporation. Series 772–6, General Pamphlet Collection, Urban Archives, Temple University.

Cross, C. T. (2004) *Political Education: National Policy Comes of Age*, New York: Teachers College Press.

Cuban, L. (1972) *Reforms in Washington: The Model School Division, 1963–1972. Final Report*, Washington, DC: US Department of Housing, Education, and Welfare, Office of Education.

District of Columbia Public Schools (1966) *Development: First Year Evaluation of the Model School Division*, Washington, DC: District of Columbia Public Schools.

District of Columbia Redevelopment Land Agency (1970) *Annual Report*. Accession 93–008–2 Series 2: Annual Reports, Box 2, District of Columbia Redevelopment Land Agency Papers, District of Columbia Archives.

District of Columbia Redevelopment Land Agency (1973) *NDP4 Summary of Proposed Modifications to Urban Renewal Plan. Shaw School Urban Renewal Area*; George Washington University Special Collections Washingtoniana.

Etheridge, H. (1979) 'The Black Architects of Washington, 1900–Present', PhD thesis, Catholic University of America.

Ferrer, T. (1964) *The Schools and Urban Renewal: A Case Study from New Haven*, New York: Educational Facilities Laboratory.

Filson, S. (1966a) 'Shaw School Plans to End Track System', *Washington Post* (21 September): 1.

Filson, S. (1966b) 'Small School Policy Questioned – Educational Parks Discussed', *Washington Post* (5 December): C3.

Filson, S. (1967) 'Decision on a Site for Shaw Delayed by School Officials', *Washington Post* (30 March): B4.

Gillette, H. Jr. (1995) *Between Justice and Beauty: Race, Planning, and the Failure of Urban Policy in Washington*, Baltimore: Johns Hopkins University Press.

Green, C. M. (1967) *The Secret City: A History of Race Relations in the Nation's Capital*, Princeton, NJ: Princeton University Press.

Griffin, T. (2015) 'There Is a Syllabus for an Urban Design Course on Race and Justice in Harlem' *Next City* (27 May), available at: https://nextcity.org/daily/entry/design-for-the-just-city-a-curriculum-in-urban-justice (accessed 17 October 2015).

Griffith, R. W. (1969) 'The Influence of Meaningful Citizen Participation on the "Urban Renewal" Process and the Renewal of the Inner-City's Black Community. Case Study: Washington D.C.'s "Shaw School Urban Renewal Area" – MICCO, a Unique Experiment', Master's thesis, Massachusetts Institute of Technology.

Hallman, H. W. (1970) *Neighborhood Control of Public Programs: Case Studies of Community Corporations and Neighborhood Boards*, New York: Praeger.

Haskins, F. P. (2007/2008) 'Behind the Headlines: The *Evening Star*'s Coverage of the 1968 Riots', *Washington History* 19/20: 50–67.

Hoffman, E. (1966) 'New Shaw School Plan Has Six-floor Tower', *Washington Post* (23 July): A12.

Hoffman, E. (1969) 'Students View Plans for Shaw', *Washington Post* (10 January): C1.

Honsa, C. (1967) 'Shaw Groups to Air Views on Site for School', *Washington Post* (21 February): C2.

'John D. Sulton Dies, Washington Architect' (1994) *Washington Post* (2 March): D5.

Kent, J. K. (1968) 'The Coleman Report: Opening Pandora's Box', *Phi Delta Kappan* 49, 5 (January): 242–5.

'Leroy Campbell, Area Architect for 26 Years' (1977) *Washington Post* (31 August): C4.

Levy, C. (1969) 'April Riot Caused 4900 Workers to Lose Jobs, New Survey Says', *Washington Post* (9 May): C8.

Meyer, E. L. and Smith J.Y. (1972) 'Shaw: Blight Remains Despite Promises', *Washington Post* (20 February): A1, D1.

Milius, P. (1969) '$1 Billion Urged for Schools', *Washington Post* (5 February): A1.

Milloy, C. (1977) '$13 Million Junior High Replaces "Shameful Shaw"', *Washington Post* (5 September): C1.

Mitchell, M. L. (2003) *The Crisis of the African American Architect: Conflicting Cultures of Architecture and (Black) Power*, New York: Writers Advantage iUniverse.

Mock, B. (2015) 'There Are No Urban Design Courses on Race and Justice, So We Made Our Own Syllabus' *CityLab* (14 May), available at: http://www.citylab.com/design/2015/05/there-are-no-urban-design-courses-on-race-and-justice-so-we-made-our-own-syllabus/393335/ (accessed 17 October 2015).

Model Inner City Community Organization (1969) *Status Report: First Action Year*, Washington, DC: MICCO.

Model Inner City Community Organization *Annual Report 1968–1969* (Washington, DC: MICCO, 1969); George Washington University Special Collections Washingtoniana.

National Capital Planning Commission (1950) *Washington Present and Future: A General Summary of the Comprehensive Plan for the National Capital and Its Environs*, Washington, DC: National Capital Planning Commission.

National Capital Planning Commission and District of Columbia Redevelopment Land Agency, 'Civil Disturbances in Washington, D.C., April 4–8, 1968; A Preliminary Damage Report' (Washington DC: 1968).

Passow, A. H. (1967) *Toward Creating a Model Urban School System – A Study of Washington, D.C. Public Schools*, New York: Teachers College Columbia University.

Rosenblat, J. and Howard, T. (2015) 'How Gentrification Is Leaving Public Schools Behind', *U.S. News and World Report* (20 February), available at: http://www.usnews.com/news/articles/2015/02/20/how-gentrification-is-leaving-public-schools-behind (accessed 13 October 2015).

Ruble, B. (2010) *Washington's U Street: A Biography*, Washington, DC: Woodrow Wilson Center Press; Baltimore: The Johns Hopkins University Press.

'The Schools of the Slums' (1965) *Washington Post* (2 October): A14.

'Shaw School, At Last' (1966) *Washington Post* (19 September): A16.

Strayer, G. D. (1949) *The Report of a Survey of the Public Schools of the District of Columbia, Conducted under the Auspices of the Chairmen of the Subcommittees on District of Columbia Appropriations of the Respective Appropriations Committees of the Senate and House of Representatives*, Washington: US Government Printing Office.

Sulton Campbell Britt Architects (2013) *History*, available at: http://www.sultoncampbellbritt.com/history.html (accessed 28 March 2015).

TenHoor, M. and Massey, J. (2015) 'Black Lives Matter' *Aggregate* 2, available at: http://we-aggregate.org/project/black-lives-matter (accessed 17 October 2015).

Tunnell, G. (1970) 'Model Schools: Mixed Results', *Washington Post* 2 (December): B1.

21st Century School Fund, Urban Institute, Brookings Institution (2009) Memorandum to Abigail Smith, DCPS Office of Transformation Management; Stefan Huh, Office of the State Superintendent of Education: Analysis of the Impact of DCPS School Closings for SY2008–2009 (17 March).

Wiley, A. N. (2010) 'LeDroit Park: A Study of Contrasts', *Vernacular Architecture Newsletter* 123: 1–9.

Wiley, A. N. (2013) 'The Dunbar High School Dilemma: Architecture, Power, and African American Cultural Heritage', *Buildings & Landscapes* 20, 1: 95–128.

14

THE NIGERIAN 'UNITY SCHOOLS' PROJECT

A UNESCO-IDA school building program in Africa

Ola Uduku

A short history of Nigerian schools

West Africa has had a historical engagement with schools and Western education from early in the nineteenth century. Early missionary outposts in coastal African cities and islands such as Cape Coast, Bonny and São Tomé established basic primary schools from the late eighteenth century onwards. These first schools were missionary operated and catered for the Western-focused educational needs of the mixed race offspring of early European sailors, as well as the children of the emerging Indigenous coastal elite (Uduku 1992). This establishment of primary schools, and later secondary schools, followed the spread of missionary proselytising into the hinterland in parallel with the extension of colonial rule in West Africa. By the 1920s, a network of missionary and colonial schools existed across the British colonies in West Africa: Sierra Leone, the Gold Coast (Ghana) and the protectorates of Eastern, Western and Northern Nigeria (Ajayi 1965).

The absence of a 'white' settler population in West Africa, and the consequent early initiation of indirect rule which resulted in the delegation of administrative tasks to Western-educated indigenes, no doubt helped hasten the comparatively early establishment of West African schools. The early coastal schools founded by missions such as the Anglican Church Missionary Society (CMS) and the Catholic St Gregory's schools, along with the British colonial government-founded Kings College (see Figure 14.1), all in Lagos, quickly became part of a small group of schools that were attended by the colony's future intellectual elite. Thus, by the 1950s, with the emergence of self-rule or independence among British West African colonies, there was a small network of missionary and colonial government colleges that catered for some, but not all, of the new nations' educational needs (Ajayi 1965; Ayandele 1966; Fafunwa 1974; Uduku 1992).

The end of World War II in 1945 saw the establishment of the United Nations (UN) and its educational wing, the United Nations Educational, Scientific and Cultural Organization (UNESCO), and the founding of the International Development Agency (IDA), the development wing of the International Bank of Reconstruction and Development (IBRD; later the World Bank). These organisations led a global call for widened access to education. This

FIGURE 14.1 King's College, Lagos.

Photograph: Ola Uduku

was enshrined in the manifesto of the Conference of African States on the Development of Education in Africa, held by UNESCO and United Nations Economic Commission for Africa, in Addis Ababa in May 1961, which declared that all Africans needed increased access to education.[1]

In West Africa, the Gold Coast, renamed Ghana at independence in 1957, embraced this call early with its first and second national school building programs. A number of new colleges and schools in the colony were constructed, and a few of the historic missionary colleges and schools were upgraded and extended between 1945 and 1957 (Le Roux 2004; Uduku 2006; Jackson and Holland 2014). The British architectural firm Fry and Drew were tasked with carrying out the national programs, which produced the most extensive body of school buildings in Ghana. Most of these schools were designed in the Tropical International Style (Jackson and Holland 2014).

It was in this context that Nigeria, West Africa's largest and most populous country (with around 45 million people in 1961), negotiated an IDA loan to broaden its school building stock (Uduku 1992). The government proposed developing a number of demonstration or 'model' schools, which would showcase ideal school building design. This design arose from research undertaken through the UNESCO educational units and took into account local climatic features and the new systems of comprehensive education that were being developed around the world. These model schools would come to be called 'Unity Schools'.

It had been agreed at the 1961 Addis Ababa conference that such a system of schools would suit the African environment and broaden educational experiences and outcomes for Africans. This was important because reports and statistics from the development economists of bodies such as the International Labour Organisation (ILO) had identified a mismatch between the formal education being taught in Africa's Western-focused traditional high schools and the more technical and practical educational manpower needs of newly independent countries (Skapski 1966; Onu et al. 2013).[2] By the 1960s technical and commercially trained graduates

were badly needed to take up positions as technicians and in middle-management commercial and administrative areas, but there were very few of them, whereas there was no lack
of graduates in professions like medicine and law. This trend was exacerbated by 'diploma
disease' – the widespread aspiration for higher academic qualifications (see Dore 1976). Most
students aimed to study conventional academic subjects at secondary school and to go on to
gain university degrees in traditional professional areas, such as law, medicine or economics,
which they saw as a means to attain higher status and salaried jobs. There was thus limited
public interest in technical or commercial education. Nonetheless, this type of training was
the main pedagogic aim of international education policies in the 1960s. Policy changes supported comprehensive education, and funding was provided by bilateral aid and grants for the
building of new comprehensive schools.

In Nigeria, this resulted in several new school building initiatives. Some secondary schools
were expanded in response to growing student populations, while others were relocated from
crowded parts of central Lagos to suburban areas. These new buildings and campuses were
generally built by expatriate firms, such as the Architects Co Partnership (Ansar ud Deen
School, Lagos) or Godwin and Hopwood (CMS School, Lagos). Two comprehensive schools
were also built by the government in collaboration with the United States Agency for International Development (USAID), one at Aiyetoro in the Western Region, and the other at
Port Harcourt in the Eastern Region. These 'one-off' projects were precursors to the Unity
Schools (Uduku 1992).

The Unity Schools

Nigeria was successful in brokering a deal with the IDA to fund the construction of three
model schools, one each in the Northern, Eastern and Western regions of Nigeria to represent the geographical and ethno-cultural diversity of the country. These schools, conceived
and funded in 1964 and 1965, were to be designed and delivered by the Nigerian architectural firm Alex Ekwueme and Associates, with advice from UNESCO and further support
from the British architectural consultants Robert Matthew Johnson Marshall and Partners
(RMJM). They were to be designed with the facilities necessary for a comprehensive curriculum and were to be open to children on academic merit, with admission, as to other elite
schools in Nigeria, by entrance examination. Furthermore, as the schools were effectively
owned by the government, no fees were to be charged.

The first model school building was on its way towards successful completion in South
Eastern Nigeria when the Nigerian–Biafran civil war broke out in late 1966. All building
work stopped until the war ended in 1970. At the end of hostilities, Nigeria transformed its
regional administrative system to a 12-state federal structure. With this change, the model
schools that had been planned for the regions were renamed 'Unity Schools', possibly because
funding for them came from what was now a united federal government and also to reinforce
the government's desire that these schools demonstrate Nigeria's post–civil war 'unity' in
education. The government planned to build a Unity School in every state's capital city, with
the two leading former colonial government schools, King's College and Queen's College in
Lagos, becoming additional 'honorary' Unity Schools (Uduku 1992; Adekunle 2002: 426–9).

Originally, all the schools were to be coeducational secondary boarding schools. By the
early 1970s, however, each state was to have one coeducational and one girls' boarding school,
but no all-male schools. No records were found to explain this change, but Nigeria's northern

states, which were, and remain, predominantly Muslim in religious outlook, would have promoted segregated single-sex education for girls, and it is likely this influenced the decision.
There were also examples of successful girls' missionary and convent schools in southern
states, not to mention Kings College and Queens College, which were single-sex schools for
boys and girls respectively.

Architects and consultants

Nigeria, by the 1960s, had its own Western-trained architects (most of whom had studied in
Britain) who could design and deliver new schools and other infrastructure projects. The firm
Alex Ekwueme and Associates went on to design airport terminal facilities across Nigeria,
while other prominent architects included Olumuyiwa Olumide, notable for designing the
YWCA Headquarters, Lagos (1960), and Crusader House, Lagos (1958) (Le Roux 2002).[3]
Adedokun Adeyemi, instigator of the 1953 London conference on Tropical Architecture, was
another of Nigeria's pioneer architects (Immerhwar 2007: 167; Wakely 1983).[4]

In all, there were to be 24 new Unity Schools, with Kings College and Queens College
bringing the total to 26. All the schools were designed to deliver a seven-year secondary education program, from form one (ages 10 and 11 years) to form five (15 and 16 years), usually
with three classes at each year level, and to include a lower and upper sixth form stream (18 and
19 years). As previously planned, entrance would be through national examination and state
representation (Uduku 1992).

Unity School design

All the Unity Schools were built on government land, although some were initially located on
temporary sites, which the government acquired later. The typical building plan had groups
of single-storey classrooms arranged around courtyards; a larger 'assembly hall' building; single-
storey administration areas which included staff rooms, libraries and book stores; and further
wings housing science, technology, art and other specialist classrooms (see Figures 14.2A and
14.2B).

Classrooms were designed to be single-banked, their longer sides oriented north–south,
with large, opening window areas that took into account the prevailing West African south–
west and north–east wind directions to allow for maximum cross ventilation. The large windows, covering 20 per cent of the wall area, also ensured there was adequate natural light for
reading and working, conforming to the 2 per cent daylight factor value required by British
Building Research standards.

In keeping with tropical design guidelines, schools in the northern part of Nigeria made
greater use of courtyards to create shaded areas protected from external high temperatures
and sand-bearing winds. In contrast, southern schools were designed to be linear, allowing
maximum envelope access for cross ventilation and providing the most comfortable environment in the more humid climate.

The student dormitory blocks were usually single-storey buildings oriented north–south,
similar to the classroom blocks and also designed for maximum natural ventilation. Windows
in the dormitory blocks were designed so metal bunk beds could be placed in the wall spaces
between the windows. Ablution facilities, comprising showers and toilets, were oriented east–
west, at right angles to the dormitory wings.

KEY
1 Junior secondary school (JSS) block 1
2 JSS 2
3 Senior secondary school (SSS) block 1
4 SSS 2
5 JSS 3
6 SSS 3
7 Staff room / guidance and counselling / library
8 Administration
9 Physics laboratory
10 Fine arts room and temporary classrooms

11 Auditorium
12 Post office
13 Lecture theatres
14 Biology / chemistry / science labs
15 Home economics
16 Computer lab. / agriculture lab.
17 Technical drawing / applied economics
18 Woodwork / auto tech. / metal work
19 Original administration (burnt down)
20 Foundation, abandoned classroom block
21 Agricultural livestock pens

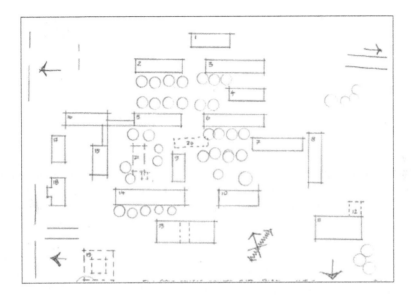

FIGURE 14.2A A Unity School: Federal Government College, Sokoto. Site plan.

Drawings: Ola Uduku

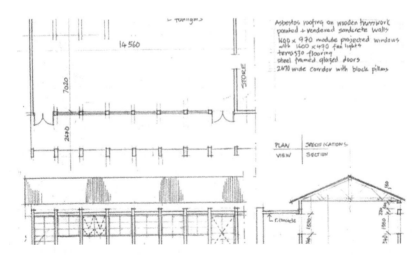

FIGURE 14.2B A Unity School: Federal Government College, Sokoto. Building plan and views.

Drawings: Ola Uduku

The Unity Schools' designs and layouts have clear similarities to the Ghanaian schools designed two decades earlier by Maxwell Fry and Jane Drew under the Gold Coast national school building programs (Jackson and Holland 2014). This is probably because the UNESCO-appointed consultants RMJM and the Nigerian lead architect, Alex Ekwueme, had access to the school building guidelines developed by the British Research Establishment (BRE) in association with the Architectural Association (AA) Tropical School (which had been headed by Maxwell Fry), and these had also been incorporated into the design guidelines brief that schools funded by the UNESCO were expected to follow (see De Raedt 2014). Further, a school building workshop had been held at the AA in the 1960s, which Nigerian delegates attended. It is likely that Fry and Drew's tropical schools were discussed there and may have featured as examples of good educational design (Arena 1966).

The classrooms were designed primarily for traditional forms of teacher-centred pedagogy. The teacher was positioned in front, facing the students, who sat in serried ranks viewing the teacher and blackboard. Science laboratory blocks were equipped in accordance to the UNESCO education specifications, designed for an optimum class size of 30 to 35 students, with storerooms for chemicals and other equipment, and side offices and 'preparatory' areas for teachers (Almeida 1988; Vickery 1988). Staffrooms, offices for bursars and head teachers, and libraries were provided in single-storey linear blocks similar to the classroom blocks. The libraries, designed for Unity Schools in the early 1970s, well before the computing revolution, stocked text books and books for borrowing. They also had ample reading spaces so students could use the library for their homework or 'prep' periods in the evenings.

The Unity Schools design policy, although developed in response to local climate conditions and to provide optimum thermal comfort, was also derived from the earlier design guides produced by the BRE and missionaries active in the tropics. The schools remained elitist; as boarding schools they charged higher fees than day schools, and the teaching focus aligned with that of the former missionary and colonial boarding schools already well established in Nigeria. These older colonial schools, in turn, had been designed and planned with infrastructure and layout arrangements that emulated the typical British grammar school with boarding facilities.

Educational theory and design implications for the Unity Schools

Nigeria had been engaged with the Western education curriculum since its pre-colonial days. By the early 1960s, as an independent African nation, it was a member of UNESCO and party to all conventions relating to the UN-backed 'Education for All' policy. More importantly, the country had been involved in the various UN-supported education conferences in Africa and globally. The UNESCO-funded 1961 Addis Ababa conference was the most significant of these to education in Nigeria to occur after 1960, when self-rule was established. It effectively called for the 'decolonisation' of African education and commitment to providing relevant education for all citizens of the continent. The most tangible outcome of this was that African history and literature textbooks were written, and African-based curricula in these subjects were developed to replace the colonial-based materials previously in place. In the sciences, also, a two-year integrated science program was developed for West African schools, where textbooks by Nigerian authors supported specialisation in the key areas of physics, chemistry and biology. These books provided experiments with local contextual examples, such as dissecting tropical insects in biology and exploring local chemicals and compounds in use in tropical industries in chemistry.

The Nigerian Government had also pledged to develop technical and vocational education in secondary schools in response to the ILO directive (Skapski 1966). The demonstration technical school built in Aiyetoro, Western Nigeria, with funds from USAID, the US development NGO active in Africa from the 1950s to the 1970s, was part of this drive (Uduku 1992). The intention was to expand Nigeria's national education policy to include a vocational stream in all secondary schools, thus creating a 'comprehensive' secondary system that taught both 'academic' and 'technical-vocational' subjects.

In practice, however, this was not immediately achieved. In the post-independence period, from the 1960s to the mid-to-late 1970s, only a few technical colleges were built to deliver post-secondary curriculum technical education. It was not until the entire Nigerian education system was restructured in 1979, to the 6–3–3–4 system (six years primary, three years junior and three years senior secondary education, with four years of tertiary education), that technical education was fully introduced into the secondary school curriculum at junior and secondary school level (Adesina and Ogunsaju 1984; Uduku 1992).

The design implications of providing technical and vocational facilities within typical Nigerian secondary schools proved difficult. Classrooms in the well-funded Unity Schools were altered in the mid-1970s to accommodate some vocational subjects, such as technical drawing, art and domestic science. Integrated science, which had been developed as a more relevant, non-specialist introduction to science for the junior secondary years, was taught in the appropriate physics, chemistry or biology laboratories.

Apart from this, little concession was made to non-traditional learning styles, and technical workshops were not constructed in the Unity Schools. Neither student-centred nor peer-to-peer learning was supported in the classroom design. Furthermore, despite the innovative environmental design standards for classrooms and the inclusion of courtyards and verandas in sympathy with the local climate, there was no encouragement of outdoor learning.

Reviewing the Unity Schools

The conceptualisation, design and construction of the Unity Schools in Nigeria represent a critical case study in African educational design. The schools were commissioned by an independent African country, with funding and consultation from international institutions (UNESCO and the IDA) and designed by a Nigerian architect. The aspirations behind the program to establish exemplar Unity Schools across Nigeria were partially realised. From the 1970s until the collapse of the Nigerian economy in the late 1980s, they were the schools of choice for the middle classes and those whose children could pass the selective entrance exams.

In design terms, however, the aspirations held by the Nigerian Government for these schools remained firmly embedded in a historical understanding of schools, educational practices and school buildings. In Western education, comprehensive secondary schooling had by this time been embraced, with the emphasis on examination success to determine children's futures at an early age increasingly rejected. In the United Kingdom, the abolition of the '11 plus' exam in the mid-1970s was part of this trend (Seaborne and Lowe 1974; Woolner 2010). Despite UNESCO's promotion of vocational education training and its early consultative role in the initial design of the Unity Schools, the Nigerian Government was not interested in comprehensive international education policies, and this was evident in the design of schools and their curriculum. This situation is not unique to Nigeria. In much of contemporary

Africa, the public notion of good education remains firmly associated with the missionary-colonial era. This past history of formal education delivered by missionary and colonial government organisations prior to national self-rule is valorised. In these pasts, school education was hierarchical – the teacher was the main conveyor of knowledge, education was centred around conventional academic subjects, and the classroom was designed and furnished to allow for this traditional learning process – and such a system is still largely seen as the ideal.

Today's parents and educationists are lukewarm about Nigerian national education policies, which from the 1970s have consistently called for an overhaul of the academically focused schools to create a fully comprehensive curriculum. In Nigeria and other African countries, since the neo-liberalisation of economic policies, a number of religious institutions have re-emerged as significant providers of fee-paying secondary education, focused, as schools had been in the past, on teaching an academic curriculum to children of the middle-class elites.[5] Vocational and technical education remains limited and tends to be only provided by the government; it is seen as second best by parents. This has resulted in the persistent lack of middle- to low-level technical expertise in Nigeria and the other African countries. Arguably, the widespread and enduring public view of the academic curriculum as higher in status than the comprehensive model has been reinforced by the reluctance of exemplar schools, like the Unity Schools, to expand their academic-focused curricula to fully incorporate technical-vocational subjects.

Thus, historic British educational design guidance has persisted in postcolonial West Africa. The region remains close to its colonial British origins, and much of the technical aid and expertise provided for educational expansion in the post-independence period is still British focused. In contrast, the comprehensive educational model and design guidance for schools had more success in Latin America and parts of South East Asia that had technical aid and advice from organisations such as UNESCO (UNESCO 1961).

A contemporary view

Nigeria is not alone in being unable to provide adequate education for all its children. Since the 1961 Addis Ababa conference on African education, a number of international conferences have taken place that have called for increased access to education for all children, particularly in Africa, the continent with the largest population of children who remain out of school. The failure of the second of the UN Millennium Development Goals (MDG) – to provide primary education for all children by 2015 – has been felt significantly in the poorer states of Africa. The post-MDG Sustainable Development Goals now include 'access to quality education' (UNDP 2015).

Paradoxically, however, as the Unity Schools case in Nigeria has highlighted, a cadre of postcolonial schools has evolved that catered to the educational aspirations of Africa's elite with little regard for the internationally supported curriculum changes towards comprehensive teaching or to infrastructure design that might support these changes. Thus Africa's current national education systems remains stuck within school design and academic curricula traditions inherited from the colonial past.[6] Possibly the most spectacular example of this is the late President Banda's Kamuzu Academy in Mtunthama, Malawi, known as 'The Eton of Africa'. Built in 1981 to Banda's personal specifications, Kamuzu Academy was designed to be Malawi's premier elite school. Initially staffed primarily by British expatriate teachers, it was to be open to all academically gifted Malawian students who could win scholarships.

Essentially, however, it has been run as a high-fee-paying school for children of expatriates and Malawi's elite (Carroll 2002; Britten 2006; Uduku 2015; Kamuzu Academy website).

No national or state school programs in Africa have evolved a truly contemporary indigenous-focused approach to designing schools to work with new learning theories and inclusive curricula. Julius Nyerere, leader of Tanzania from 1960 to 1985, established the 'Harambee' education program in the 1960s and 1970s to promote basic education for all Tanzanians (Bray and Lillis 1988; Onsomu et al. 2004). This followed more the philosophy of Brazilian educationist Paolo Freire (Freire 1970), in supporting a grassroots approach to building schools in rural areas, staffing them with a network of volunteer teachers to teach basic reading and arithmetic skills. There have also been some 'one-off' innovative school schemes in Africa, supported by NGOs or charitable organisations such as the Aga Kahn Foundation. The Aga Kahn Foundation used its schools as a soft approach to the promote Shi'a Islam in Africa, initially in Kenya but now also in other parts of the continent (Uduku 2015; Aga Khan Foundation website).

Since the 1990s, South Africa began to break with its apartheid-based school past, which not only stratified education by race, but also by skill levels, with emphasis on an academic education curriculum for white children, and commercial and technical education for non-whites. From 1992, new approaches to school planning, design and construction have been instituted. The devolved education departments of the post-apartheid system have had the independent provincial muscle to promote these approaches. They have employed architects who are willing to explore new parameters of learning and learning-space design. This has allowed architects to engage strongly with educationalists and others versed in education theory and the contemporary realities of high socioeconomic disadvantage in areas of South Africa. The work of architect Joe Noero in designing context-specific education infrastructure in Cape Town townships like Dunoon, Khayelitsha, is a good example of this development (see Figure 14.3) (Uduku 2010).

FIGURE 14.3 Dunoon School, Khayelitsha.

Photograph: Ola Uduku

The advent of mobile computing, including one laptop per child projects, and the rapid penetration of smartphones and tablets in Africa, however, is likely to offer the most significant challenge to the traditional school design models that remain intact across much of the continent. As education becomes more mobile and less tied to the classroom, the appeal of the old teaching methods and classroom arrangements could decline. Advances in technology may finally break the enduring aspiration towards, and commitment to, the replication of historic traditional school buildings by African teachers, policy makers and philanthropists (Uduku 2015).

Conclusions

The Unity Schools program demonstrated a successful strategy by the Nigerian Government to plan and execute a post-independence school building program across the country. The program was developed during a period when the government was financially and culturally disposed to promote new schools and education. At the same time, there was a significant expansion in tertiary education, with the upgrading of the infrastructure of the two historic universities, Ibadan and Nigeria, that had existed at independence in 1960. The foundation of 10 new 'federal' universities has since ensured each of the 12 states in the new Nigerian Federation has a tertiary institution (Fafunwa 1968; Akpan 1987).

The Unity Schools had significant sociocultural and economic symbolism. They were 'democratically' spread across Nigeria, and notionally students represented the then 12 states. In practice, some of the northern states had only a limited pool of children who had attained the educational level demanded by the schools, and these states often had lower levels of girls achieving secondary education. In addition, a number of elite families were able to acquire places for their offspring in the Unity Schools through non-academic means including political favours.

The design of the Unity Schools by a Nigerian architect, albeit with consultancy assistance from UNESCO, also showed Nigeria's independence from direct aid in architecture and construction, which set it apart from much of Eastern and Southern Africa. But there were problems with the process. Awarding the initial contract for more than 12 schools to one architect in some ways highlights the issue of the 'winner takes it all' project system that was then evolving in Nigeria. Unlike the design and building of the post-apartheid South African schools, only one architectural firm, Ekwueme and Associates, was involved in the Unity Schools project. This limited the design possibilities to only one firm's design philosophy and ideas.

Further, that the Unity Schools did not deliver the infrastructure or teaching needed to fulfil the Nigerian Government's technical and vocational curriculum reflects both the elitist aspirations of the parents of children who attended the Unity Schools and the government's willingness to ignore its commitment to provide comprehensive education in its exemplar schools. While the government was making considerable investment in universities during this period, it paid only lip service to the responsibilities implicit in its pledges to provide more infrastructure and teaching in technical and vocational education.

From the 1980s, the school landscape in Nigeria began to change, with a distinct hierarchy appearing. The collapse of the Nigerian economy from the mid-1980s, along with the wholesale revision of the educational curriculum and the introduction of a neoliberal approach to education, led to the establishment of a number of privately funded schools from this period onwards, some of the best being 'faith-based' institutions. These schools are regulated by the Federal Ministry of Education, but individual schools set their own selection criteria, which often explicitly target fee-paying students. The Unity Schools still exist, but they are poorly funded by the federal government and are no longer the schools of choice for the middle classes. There are also some local 'state' schools, which receive even less funding than the nationally funded schools.

Even lower in this hierarchy are private schools that operate at the lower socioeconomic level. These schools are usually run 'in-house' by independent proprietors and from very basic structures. These schools often produce better student results than underfunded 'state' schools, in part because of their lower class sizes, but, as their facilities and teacher qualifications are limited, they rarely perform as well as the better-funded private schools.[7] The design and environmental performance of these classrooms is poor and rarely meets the historic school design guidelines, which remain modelled on the UNESCO school building standards of the 1960s.

This stratified educational system has not replicated the design ideals of the Unity Schools. Contemporary pedagogic concepts related to vocational learning have still not yet reached government school level, although secondary technical colleges for senior secondary students do now exist. The elite and middle-class aspirational schools of choice are now the private schools, which have effectively, if not physically, replaced the Unity Schools. There are far fewer of these private schools, and their buildings do not form a body of design that can be compared with that of the Unity Schools. As with the Unity Schools, however, their emphasis remains on providing the education and academic infrastructure to produce secondary school graduates who will go on to a tertiary education in classic academic subject areas and professions – much like the private education system found elsewhere throughout Africa and the rest of the world, and much like Nigeria's schools before independence.

This persistent design and curriculum link with past highlights that the aspirations of post-independence governments and the parents of the elite beneficiaries of these model institutions remain strongly influenced by colonial and missionary models of traditional academic education and their associated historic educational infrastructure. New, international models of contemporary education – which international aid and funding bodies such as UNESCO and the IBRD had aimed to promote – have for decades remained unrealised.

Notes

1   The delegates from this conference came from 37 countries across West, Central East and Southern Africa; the Republic of South Africa was invited to attend as was Portugal, France, the United Kingdom and Brazil (the latter in observer status). The conference resolved, among other things, to create an African education system, increase the number of schools built in rural areas, develop technical and vocational education, and request US$4 million investment from the UN for technical aid and assistance to do this.
2   Dr Adam Skapski developed the first Technical Curriculum for Nigeria titled 'National Plan of Vocational and Technical Education in the Republic of Nigeria' in 1966.
3   Ekwueme obtained his architectural education at the University of Washington, USA, in the late 1950s, while Olumide was educated in the United Kingdom during the 1950s.
4   Adedokun Adeyemi (1920–2000) was educated at Manchester University, United Kingdom.
5   In Nigeria these institutions abound and include Loyola College, a Jesuit-run institution, founded in Western Nigeria in 1953–56 (http://www.loyolajesuit.org/ljchome_ie.htm) and Covenant College, founded in the 1990s as an evangelical institution and now a feeder institution to Covenant University (http://www.cusscanaanland.com/).

6   Often these trends were internationally backed, as seen in the UNESCO school design guidelines and the establishment of a West African school building design office in Dakar, Senegal (UNESCO 1989).
7   However, *The Economist*, in an article titled 'The-$1-A-Week School' (2015), notes that Nigeria has one of the more regulated private school economies in the emerging world.

Works cited

AA Department of Tropical Studies (1965) 'An Issue Largely on Education', *Architectural Association Journal* 80, 891: 286–8.

Adekunle, J. O. (2002) 'Nationalism, Ethnicity, and National Integration: An Analysis of Political History', in Oyebade, A. (ed.) *The Transformation of Nigeria: Essays in Honor of Toyin Falola*, Asmara: Africa World Press, Inc: 405–33.

Adesina, S. and Ogunsaju, S. (1984) *Secondary Education in Nigeria*, Ille-Ife: University of Ife Press.

Aga Khan Foundation (2015) 'Education', available at http://www.akdn.org/akf_education.asp.

Ajayi, J. F. A. (1965) *Christian Missions in Nigeria, 1841–1891*, London: Longmans.

Akpan, P. A. (1987) 'The Spatial Aspects of Higher Education in Nigeria', *Higher Education* 16, 5: 545–55.

Almeida, R. (1988) *Handbook for Educational Buildings Planning*, Paris: UNESCO.

Ayandele, E. A. (1966) *The Missionary Impact on Modern Nigeria, 1842–1914*, London: Longmans.

Bray, M. and Lillis, K. (1988) *Community Funding of Education: Issues and Policy Implications in Less Developed Countries*, London: Commonwealth Secretariat/Pergamon Press.

Britten, N. (2006) 'The Man Who Saved the Eton of Africa', *Telegraph* (26 December), available at: http://www.telegraph.co.uk/news/worldnews/1537859/The-man-who-saved-the-Eton-of-Africa.html.

Carroll, R. (2002), 'The Eton of Africa', *Guardian Online* (24 November), available at: http://www.theguardian.com/education/2002/nov/25/schools.uk.

Covenant College website (2015) http://www.cusscanaanland.com/.

De Raedt, K. (2014) 'Between "True Believers" and Operational Experts: Unesco Architects and School Buildings in Post-colonial Africa', *Journal of Architecture* 19, 1: 19–42.

Dore, R. (1976) *The Diploma Disease: Education, Qualification and Development*, Berkeley: University of California Press.

Fafunwa, A. B. (1968) *Over a Hundred Years of Higher Education for Nigerians*, Lagos: Federal Ministry of Information.

Fafunwa, A. B. (1974) *A History of Education in Nigeria*, London: Longmans.

Freire, P. (1970) *The Pedagogy of the Oppressed*, London: Penguin.

Immerhwar, D. (2007) 'The Politics of Architecture and Urbanism in Postcolonial Lagos, 1960–1986', *Journal of African Cultural Studies* 19, 2 (December): 165–86.

Jackson, I. and Holland, J. (2014) *The Architecture of Edwin Maxwell Fry and Jane Drew: Twentieth Century Architecture, Pioneer Modernism and the Tropics*, Farnham, Surrey: Ashgate.

Le Roux, H. (2002) 'Critical Approaches to the Discourse of Climatic Responsiveness in Modern Architecture in West Africa', M.Arch thesis, University of the Witwatersrand.

Le Roux, H. (2004) 'Modern Architecture in Post-Colonial Ghana and Nigeria', *Architectural History* 47: 361–92.

Loyola College website (2015) http://www.loyolajesuit.org/ljchome_ie.htm.

Onsomu, E. N., Mungai, J. N., Oulai, D., Sankale, J. and Mujidi, J. (2004) *Community Schools in Kenya: Case Study on Community Participation in Funding and Managing Schools*, London: International Institute for Educational Planning, available at: http://www.unesco.org/iiep/PDF/pubs/Kenya_B185.pdf.

Onu, G., James, J., Onwughalu, V. C. and Chiamogu, A. P. (2013) 'Redesigning Education Curricula as a Panacea for Unemployment and Poverty Reduction in Nigeria', *Public Policy and Administration Research* 3, 4: 43–57.

Seaborne, M. and Lowe, R. (1974) *The English School: Its Architecture and Organization*, London: Routledge, Kegan Paul.

Skapski, A. (1966) *Report of the Comparative Technical Education Seminar Abroad and Recommendation for a National Plan of Vocational and Technical Education in the Republic of Nigeria*, Lagos: Federal Ministry of Education.

'The-$1-A-Week School' (2015) *The Economist*, 1 August.

Uduku, O. (1992) 'Socio-Economic Factors Affecting Secondary School Design in Nigeria', PhD thesis, University of Cambridge.

Uduku, O. (2006) 'Modernist Architecture and "The Tropical" in West Africa: The Tropical Architecture Movement in West Africa, 1948–1970', *Habitat International* 30: 397–8.

Uduku, O. (2010) *Designing School Buildings as Development Hubs for Learning: Final Project Report for EdQual Project*, Bristol: University of Bristol.

Uduku, O. (2015) Designing Schools for Quality: An International Case Study-Based Overview, *International Journal of Educational Development* 44: 56–64, doi:10.1016/j.ijedudev.2015.05.005.

UNESCO (1989) *Educational Spaces* 1 (July): 1–4.

UNESCO and the United Nations Economic Commission for Africa (1961) *Conference of African States on the Development of Education in Africa, Addis Ababa 16–25 May 1961: Final Report*, Paris: UNESCO; available at: http://unesdoc.unesco.org/images/0007/000774/077416e.pdf.

United Nations Development Programme (UNDP) (2015) *Introducing the 2030 Agenda for Sustainable Development*, available at: http://www.undp.org/content/undp/en/home/librarypage/corporate/sustainable-development-goals-booklet.html.

Vickery, D. S. (1988) *Facilities Design Guide*, Paris: UNESCO.

Wakely, P. I. (1983) 'The Development of a School: An Account of the Department of Development and Tropical Studies of the Architectural Association', *Habitat International* 7, 5–6: 337–46.

Woolner, P. (2010) *The Design of Learning Spaces*, London: Continuum.

PART IV

School spaces

15

QUIET STORIES OF EDUCATIONAL DESIGN

Catherine Burke

> *People and things require nooks and crannies to inhabit in space. An essential quality in this respect is what we might call 'cupboardness', with the kangaroo as our ideal.*
>
> (Herman Hertzberger 2008)

Herman Hertzberger, quoted here, is a contemporary architect who applies an understanding of the value for young children of quiet withdrawal spaces in the schools he designs. The 'little library' at the Montessori Apollo school in Amsterdam is a case in point: it is just one of a wide range of carefully placed retreat areas positioned throughout the general open areas of the school. Tucked under a flight of stairs is a recessed carpeted area furnished with a single child-scaled chair that invites a pupil to enter this cosy space and read for a while (see Figure 15.1). But such attention to the detailed planning of quiet intimate spaces is rare in school design today. The hegemony of the classroom has re-emerged alongside regimes of learning that limit so-called 'off-task behaviour' (Roberts 2001: 1). This chapter explores how and why such attention to the provision of intimate spaces such as quiet rooms, sitting rooms, bedrooms and child-sized openings was seen as indicative of best practice in the design of schools in the middle decades of the twentieth century. It also argues that the intention of designers can only be realised fully if inhabitants of schools – especially teachers – fully understand and support the pedagogical principles informing the provision of these spaces.

In England and – as a result of international visits by designers and educationalists and exchanges of the ideas – later in the United States of America, Australia, New Zealand and other parts of Europe, the decades from the 1930s to the 1970s saw the image of the school child expand to include and embrace freedom of movement, choice of activities and dispositions of isolated quiet concentration, contemplation and thoughtfulness. This reflected new ways of seeing childhood, education and the built environment that established what came to be called a 'Revolution in Primary Education' (Clegg 1971). I argue here that discourses of quietness and withdrawal became part of a common vocabulary of design shared by progressive educators and school designers in Britain and other nations seeking to redefine and strengthen democracy against the challenges posed by the development of industrial

FIGURE 15.1 The 'little library' at the Apollo Montessori School, Willemspark, Amsterdam, 1981–83.

Architect: Herman Hertzberger

Photograph: Herman Hertzberger

capitalism and the rise of Fascism. These discourses, while on the face of it about the control of noise, were less concerned with designing for acoustical variation and more with the exercise of freedom that they believed should be at the heart of the child's experience of modern schooling. For a time, at a high point of investment in public schooling in England, quiet spaces were thought by some leading designers and educators to be essential components of the built-in variety and educationally driven schools designed for the young child.

A sensory theory of education

Historians of education have recently taken a cue from Mark Smith's *Sensory History* (2008) to begin to pay attention to an analysis of the senses in the history of education. Drawing from Henri Lefebvre, Sue Middleton has suggested we begin to chart a sensory theory of education (Middleton 2013). Scholars interested in school design and the nature of the relationship between materialities and ideology have started to chart histories of schooling via the senses. Catherine Burke and Ian Grosvenor, in an article titled 'The Hearing School', have interpreted some acoustical dimensions of school design past and present as a means of entering 'the black box of the classroom' and deepening our understanding of the everyday (Burke and Grosvenor 2011). From the perspective of social geography, Michael Gallagher has explored the uses of sound and silence in the contemporary primary school with particular reference to discipline and surveillance (Gallagher 2011).

Here, I want to consider quietness not so much as an absence of sound or an imposition of silence but as a dimension of curriculum design associated strongly with a vision of a new kind of school 'to fit the child'. Such an environment was an essential component of the international effort to strengthen individual citizenship and collective democracy in the postwar decades. In this sense, the construction of quiet spaces was less an acoustic detail and more a political statement. While the provision of quiet areas in schools was of course one aspect of the 'built-in variety' of spaces for teaching, learning and play espoused by architects working for the Department of Education for England and Wales in the middle decades of the twentieth century, they have until now been mostly overlooked as minor details of a wider picture (Franklin 2012). But a review of educational and architectural discourse during this period reveals a striking generosity of engagement with the idea of the young child in quiet thought, alone or within a small group, with or without the teacher, and having made a free choice to take time out.

The provision of quiet spaces envisaged and celebrated a view of the child as a self-directed individual, capable and free to exercise choice and occasionally to choose to access some available space and time to concentrate, think, consider and even dream. In England, during the 1950s and 1960s in particular, teachers, school inspectors and architects began to develop a shared vocabulary of design, and quiet spaces were also commonly referred to by each of these as 'opt-out' or 'withdrawal areas'. These might have been roughly fashioned by teachers (sometimes with pupils) out of materials readily available; they might have been carefully reconstituted from recycled materials; they might have been a single object associated with withdrawal and imagination such as the rocking horse; and they might have been determined by architects in collaboration with educators in the planning of new school buildings.

Quiet rhythms of school design

Thinking is often associated with, and arguably supported by, rhythmic movement – walking, rocking, swinging, moving – and children are inclined towards these kinds of activities as any close observation will demonstrate. Yet the rhythmic movement of children has long been anathema to the traditional model of schooling established in the nineteenth century. Progressive educators have recognised the importance of voluntary bodily movement, wherever possible building it into schooling through opportunities for children to experience the sense of retreat, withdrawal and temporary removal. This explains the many tree houses that in the twentieth century became emblematic of progressive schooling. Here we can think about King Alfred's school in Hampstead, London, with its tree-house classroom which it was claimed produced 'not young Tarzans, but young citizens' (British Pathe 1946) or John Aitkenhead's 'holly hut' at Kilquhanity House school in Scotland (f. 1940) or the 'cubbies' that continue to be built by children at Preshil school in Melbourne, Australia. The swing bench at Prestolee school, Lancashire (see Figure 15.2), designed by head teacher Edward F. O'Neill to encourage reading while swinging, is a case in point (Holmes 1952: 71). Not only did the swing bench, along with a complete refabrication of the school furniture, contribute towards the deinstitutionalisation of this elementary school, but it provided a withdrawal space designed to fit the child and respect its longing for comfort and movement (Burke 2005).

FIGURE 15.2 The swing bench at Prestolee primary school, Kearsley near Bolton, England, 1940s.

Source: Manchester Evening Chronicle

In more orthodox educational environments, opportunities for rhythmic movement might have been provided by a rocking horse, desired by a small child as a place to think, imagine and recreate. Rocking horses were commonplace in infant schools and nurseries during the postwar decades. In a survey carried out in the 1960s by Boston schools architect Walter Hill which asked English pupils what their schools should have, they responded with the suggestion 'give us a rocking horse where we can think' (see Figure 15.3). One expectation of the modern primary school was that large numbers of children would be occupied in the same general work area carrying out a range of different tasks. Spaces of withdrawal from the general hubbub were designed not merely as acoustic devices to enable quieter exchanges between pupils and their teachers but also as aspects of the deinstitutionalisation of school where ebb and flow would be expected to occur at unpredictable intervals.

With this in mind, we can understand why the term 'withdrawal' peppers architectural discourse in these middle decades of the twentieth century. Contingent on so many activities envisaged to be happening synchronously, the architect David Medd, who with his wife Mary Medd was to revolutionise school design in England and Wales, queried, 'what does the designer do about this? . . . some spaces will be for quiet work, withdrawal or concentration; others for dirty processes' (Medd 1984: 11). Designers were encouraged to think about the polarities that might be expected to occur between noisy and quiet alongside other terms of contrast such as large and small, clean and dirty, inside and outside (Medd 1984).

FIGURE 15.3   Rocking horse, Middleton Infant School, West Yorkshire, England, 1950s.

The turn towards quietness and withdrawal

What factors explain the turn towards quietness and withdrawal in the design of the postwar primary school? An explanation can be found on both sides of the Atlantic, in Britain and the United States, in schools that modelled and envisaged an entirely new form of pedagogy associated with progressive values of individual freedom and collective democracy. The traditional classroom arrangement of seated silent individuals, passively listening to the single voice of the teacher, was challenged as representing the autocratic past. Pioneering postwar schools were designed to celebrate and strengthen democracy by supporting active learning, freedom of movement and varied sizes of group activities. This fundamentally altered the sound of schooling and created a situation whereby day-to-day learning was generally more likely to be hectic and noisy. This outcome has usually been considered in terms of teachers' experience of open-plan school design and their frustrations with noise (Shield, Greenland and Dockrell 2010), but there is another important story to be told from a progressive view of childhood.

Progressive philosophies grew out of the international New Education movement which flourished during the interwar years as a worldwide aspirational movement primarily associated with private or independent fee-paying schools. Members of the New Education Fellowship (NEF), founded 1921, and its sympathisers were partly influenced by the emergence of educational psychology, but many educationalists were also interested in new forms of arrangements for everyday living, including school design. Some were motivated by spiritual leanings, and many key individuals associated with the ideas of NEF belonged to the Society of Friends. In Britain and Europe these included highly influential architects such as Mary

Medd (nee Crowley) (1907–2005); school inspectors such as Robin Tanner (1904–1988); and influential head teachers such as George Baines in England and Kees Boeke in the Netherlands. In the United States, an important and influential figure in the design of a new form of school for young children was the educational administrator Carleton Washburne, also a Quaker. Quakers recognise the active power of silence, and their quiet service to the public good is characteristic of their faith. Quietness is for Quakers not an absence of noise but an active choice and a statement of their commitment to public well-being. Alongside this is held a positive view of human nature and a decision to focus on the good and the best in order to bring insight and uplift the whole. The efforts of many Quakers to improve the quality of public education during these years was highly influential in establishing the general atmosphere of schooling that represented best practice.

Other influences include the education through art movement, which began to take root during the 1930s through the work of art educators such as Arthur Lismer in Canada and Gordon Tovey in New Zealand, and the impact of art critics such as Herbert Read in England (Read 1943). European émigrés who travelled to the United States or Australia were also highly influential in the development of new forms of art education. These included in England the architect Walter Gropius, the dance educator Rudolf Laban, the photographer Edith Tudor Hart and in Australia the artist Ludwig Hirschfeld Mack. The notion that young children might better appreciate the beauty of objects and things if they were able to view them in a quiet space took hold. Drawing from her experience in infant schools, Alice Yardley described the quiet room as where (unsupervised) children might develop their aesthetic sensitivities and 'make their own relationship with what they find' – part of her mission to support what she calls 'education of feeling' (Yardley 1970: 49). As she later explained,

> they could choose to go there, they could ask their teacher, not more than two from each class, and to keep it quiet, and they could just go and enjoy doing what they did in there, but it was always to be quiet.
>
> (Brooks 2006: 273)

Creating domestic spaces of schooling

The English primary school was born out of the education reforms that followed the end of World War II. From its beginning, the primary school was strongly associated with a national project to renew democracy (Middleton 2013: 58). Part of the answer to the problem of preparing the next generation to resist any resurgence of Fascism, it was argued, was to be found in changing the relationship between home, community and school. Countless references are made during World War II and immediately after to this aspect of educational and social change. For Carleton Washburne, 'the way to combat autocracy is through strengthening democracy (while) strengthening democracy is a primary goal in progressive schools' (Washburne 1952: 38). To meet this goal, a completely different attitude was required toward the meaning and possibilities of the dispositions of schooling. According to Washburne, in the traditional school, the three commandments were 'sit still, keep quiet, do as you're told'. Now quietness was to become the result of free movement by pupils enabled by the design of school environments that not only permitted quiet contemplation but also built this into the fabric supporting an activity-based curriculum.

The evacuation of large numbers of urban children to be hosted temporarily by rural families during the first years of the war brought to the attention of English society the inadequacy of many children's home environments. The homes that pupils came from were to become much more a concern of teachers, and it was realised that these were often inadequate in supporting strong educational development. Therefore the school should become less like an institution and more like a home complete with comfortable domesticated spaces and furnishings. As the first staff inspector for primary education for the British Ministry of Education between 1946 and 1955, Christian Schiller, put it, 'we began to talk of working spaces, noisy spaces, a quiet home space, an environment in which children could live and learn' (Schiller 1971: Introduction). Reflecting on changes taking place in English primary education, Schiller observed, 'there is a growing awareness that the very young need help in their growing up beyond the capacity of most homes, and that school and home must be more closely related' (Schiller 1972: 96). Simply put, the majority of English children lived in houses or lesser dwellings that had limited space, and it was common for children to have no easy access to spaces where they might read or study at home. This put them at a relative disadvantage to children occupying wealthier, more spacious homes. School, particularly the primary school, should therefore come close to resembling a comfortable and nurturing home where one might find warmth and space enough to rest, work and play at liberty (Marsh 1970: 106). The school, in this sense, would through its transformation bring about a strengthening of civic life and play a part in reducing social and cultural inequalities.

British educationalist Alice Yardley's justification for providing the quiet room confirms the perceived value of these spaces as going some way to make up for the deficit experienced by many children from poorer homes. During the 1950s Yardley kept a notebook reflecting on her practice in Nottingham City schools, and laying out her plans and goals for educational reform. The notebook for 1955–56 includes reflections on the value of the quiet room:

> In a world of speed and noise it is essential to provide opportunities for peace and meditation. Few if any of our estate homes have a quiet corner of any kind. Homes where art, beauty and culture find a space are rare. Can we wonder then, that our children are tense, neurotic and disintegrated. It is up to the school to provide this ingredient so essential for sound education for living. If we can give each child a little inner peace we have done well.
>
> (Yardley in Brooks 2006: 273)

Therefore, it can be suggested from this evidence that something so small, quiet and overlooked such as a room designed for reflection and thought was an integral part of a spirit of engagement across school and community boundaries at this time.

Quietness as a matter of choice

> *Childhood is the only period of life when a man can exercise his choice between the branches of a tree and his drawing room chair.*
>
> (Rabindranath Tagore 1933)

World War II stimulated developments among the nations that had defeated Fascism in thinking about how to support the next generation as democratic citizens capable of critical thought and independence of spirit. Freedom of spirit was a characteristic of school practices that were celebrated in Europe and North America by progressive educators keen to exploit the opportunities offered by the need to build for the next generation. So much had been destroyed during the war including, in Britain, many hundreds of school buildings. Building began in the heavily populated home counties including Hertfordshire, whose architects developed new models of system construction resulting in modern, light, open environments (Saint 1983). Learning to manage freedom was essential to the democratic project and was at the heart of the changes envisaged in schools for the young. It was agreed, by those striving for a new transatlantic vision of the primary school, that it was only through exercising freedom that children would learn to use it without abusing it (Washburne 1952: 41). Managing sound was a prominent characteristic of the new experience that would be offered in postwar schooling, where it was expected that individuals and small groups of children would be learning in a whole variety of ways in large open general work areas. Reference to the auditory field was fundamental to the exposition of student self-direction in the new learning environment. On this point, Washburne commented:

> Even very little children can learn through experience and a little guidance that one set of actions may have results that prevent them from achieving what they really want to achieve. A child in the first grade can readily see that if he or his fellows continue a noisy activity in which they are having fun, they will not be able to hear an interesting story the teacher is going to read to them ... that if one wants to be listened to quietly when telling an experience one has to be equally considerate when others are telling their experiences and so on.
>
> (Washburne 1952: 42)

That same freedom of spirit might extend to architecture whereby

> the expanding energies of the new education, bursting that stubborn box, have found their way ... into outward expression ... that liberating spirit which is making the art of teaching (the greatest of all arts) articulate in the art of architecture.
>
> (Hudnut 1941: 83)

Crow Island school at Winnetka, on the North Shore of Chicago, was to render Washburne's 'Philosophy in Brick'. At Crow Island, quietness was not so much confined to particular areas as infusing the whole and characteristic of the tone of principal architects and educators. For example, the first director, Frances Presler, remarked that the classrooms 'express inner tranquility which can be sustained' (Presler 1941: 80) while courtyards were used for 'quiet readings' (Herbert 1990: 37). It is notable how the language of school design in the postwar era in both Britain and the United States is infused with sensory allusions toward quietness.

The first *Building Bulletin* published by the British Ministry of Education in 1949, and written by the architects David and Mary Medd, referred to 'the right kind of spaces in which small groups of children may rest quietly' ('New Primary Schools' 1949). The Medds, certainly the most influential school designers in Britain in the 1950s and 1960s, aimed to create 'built-in variety' in design, with quiet bays for children rather than discrete quiet rooms (Burke 2013: 124). They believed in designing 'from the inside out, that is, starting from the observable educational needs of the children and teachers and designing from that starting point' (Grosvenor and Burke 2008: 132–3). This was also true of designs for schools for the very young. Mary Medd recognised the child's desire to retreat from others and seek solace. She noted in *A Right to Be Children*:

> What he likes is to get away sometimes though to a comfortable place on his own, where he can curl up – under a table or a rug, in a box or a barrel, along a wide low window ledge with a cushion or two.
>
> (Medd 1976: 27)

At Eynsham primary school in Oxfordshire, which opened in 1966, a series of eight 'home bases' were positioned at each corner of two large general work areas. Its design was influenced by the work of the Development Group at the Department of Education but was carried out by architects at Oxfordshire County Council. Each home base was visited at the start and end of each day when children could meet in 'family groups' (of mixed ages) with their teacher. Each home base then doubled up as a subject area, but one base was always kept as a quiet bay or 'opt-out' area (see Figure 15.4). This was the intention of the head teacher, George Baines, who had in a previous school fashioned such an area using rugs and soft furnishings. Baines, a great observer of pupils, recognised the need of some to occasionally withdraw from the general work area. His wife, Judith Baines, who also taught at the school, later recalled:

> if a teacher went into the withdrawing bay to do something often a child would creep in too and just have a peaceful one-to-one moment. We also took anyone there who

FIGURE 15.4 'Opt-out' bay, Eynsham primary school, Oxfordshire, 1980s.

Photograph: David Medd

was in a state of some sort – rage, fear, offended, poorly – to comfort them or sort out the difficulty. We automatically talked quietly in those bays and privacy was respected.

(Judith Baines, pers. corr.)

The highpoint of designing with quietness and expectations of withdrawal in mind was realised at Eveline Lowe primary school, Southwark, London, which opened in 1966. This was a school designed by the Development Group of the Department of Education and Science in collaboration with the Inner London Education Authority. The *Building Bulletin* associated with this school sets out the rationale for the design realised through research over the previous fifteen years. A pen drawn plan of village schools ('Eveline Lowe Primary School' 1967: 4) underlined the intention to achieve the same order of intimacy in this urban setting. An outline drawing of an 'old two-room classroom' at Brize Norton, Oxfordshire (where George Baines had fashioned a quiet 'opt-out' space), coupled with a drawn plan of a new school at Finmere, Oxfordshire, served this purpose. The drawing contained careful detail of quiet domesticated spaces; even a rocking horse was included (see Figure 15.5).

As an explanation of the variety of spaces it was thought necessary to provide for this age of school pupil, the designers mused on their observations of primary classrooms in practice elsewhere in England:

at one table a boy sat absorbed in a page of sums, oblivious of the swirl of activity around him (while) . . . at his side sat another chewing his pencil, unable to shut out the

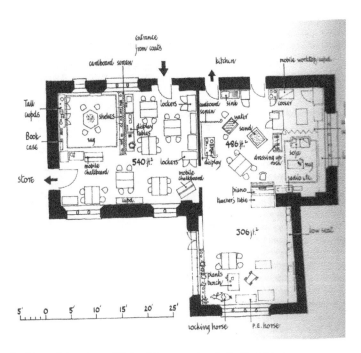

FIGURE 15.5 Architects' drawing of Brize Norton school, Oxfordshire.

Source: Building Bulletin 36

counter-attractions. The teacher said she would have liked a quieter retiring space, as some children needed to be able to get away from it all occasionally.

('Eveline Lowe Primary School' 1967: 13)

The final design for Eveline Lowe school was achieved through a series of detailed drawings imagining life at its fullest expression in the various linked group spaces. While each group area was to be furnished with some form of quiet or withdrawal space, each would have its own character (see Figure 15.6). Such detail was necessary in this humanising architecture that sought to recognise and celebrate the growth, change and movement of children and their learning. The architects explained their working method in the following terms: 'A drawing which records the plants growing on the windowsills, the corrugated cardboard folded out to form a screen, the settee, rug, low tables and radio . . . do more to show how different is a classroom today' ('Eveline Lowe Primary School' 1967: 19). Drawn plans included a specific quiet space, including a Kiva, as well as a 'story telling retreat, a 'sitting room' and a 'bedroom' complete with turned-down bedding. ('Eveline Lowe Primary School' 1967: 21). The Kiva was a twelve-foot (3.6-metre) square carpeted space furnished with bunks where up to forty

FIGURE 15.6 The Kiva, one of seven quiet spaces at Eveline Lowe primary school, Southwark, London.

Photograph: UCL Institute of Education archives. REF Architect and Buildings Branch

children might gather with their teacher, or where children might retreat for a while, either individually or in pairs. It was connected by an open entrance to the rest of the spaces and was described by the team of architects as 'a small snugly furnished enclosed space' where children might 'sit on their haunches to hear a story told by their teacher, or read quietly'.

Another group-space in the design for Eveline Lowe school was furnished with 'a curtained recess . . . carpeted and wall-papered . . . (and containing) a divan bed with pillows and rug, a rocking chair and round table' ('Eveline Lowe Primary School' 1967: 31). Other student groups would 'make do' with arrangements of furniture and fittings as well as utilising varieties of levels. The authors of the *Building Bulletin* paid serious attention to these quiet spaces, often featuring them in illustrations. The Kiva featured in no less than three full size images, including that used for the front cover ('Eveline Lowe Primary School' 1967: 35, 36).

In the appraisal of Eveline Lowe school carried out by the Department of Education after three years of operation, it is striking how the commitment to the several quiet and withdrawal spaces is unshaken ('Eveline Lowe Primary School Appraisal' 1972). The appraisal suggests that the success in the use of these spaces was directly related to the degree to which they were generously supplied in the design. Once again the Kiva featured in illustration, with the caption: 'The first priority in shared spaces is for quiet withdrawal areas provided on a generous enough scale to make withdrawal a workable reality' ('Eveline Lowe Primary School Appraisal' 1972: 7). The building had 'provided opportunities for quiet withdrawal, for quiet and concentrated practice, for practical work requiring varying amounts of space for vigorous, noisy or messy play' ('Eveline Lowe Primary School Appraisal' 1972: 6). Educational commentary about progressive schools more generally highlighted quiet areas when indicating what was innovative at Eveline Lowe (Marsh 1970).

School designers across the world were influenced by the English experience. In 1980, the Wellington-based architect Gerald Melling explored the interpretation of 'open learning' in New Zealand's primary schools. He noted how in the 1970s,

> the 'enclosed room' began to steadily appear under a variety of guises – as 'quiet room' or 'seminar room' or more commonly, 'withdrawal room' . . . for small groups of children to withdraw into when the task or the temperament demands it.
>
> (Melling 1980: 52)

In his book *Open Schoolhouse*, Melling discussed Karori West primary school, whose planning formalised the Kiva for the first time: 'an introverted small-group meeting place made up of carpeted "steps" or "tiers"'. Two were provided in each open classroom block. The essence of the Kiva, Melling suggested, was in its relative seclusion and cosiness. With a nod to the English primary school, he concluded that the Kivas at Karori West 'show an encouraging tendency towards the Eveline Lowe philosophy of particular bays' (Melling 1980: 59).

Outside spaces

It was not only in the interior arrangements that architects such as David and Mary Medd of the Department of Education in England and Wales were concerned. They also observed children's expressed desire for intimate spaces in the outdoor environment of the schoolyard. Characteristic of the Medd's planning was close observation, and they were encouraged by educationalists such as Christian Schiller to 'see that the children's experience and activities, take full advantage of all the facilities available, and especially outdoors' (Schiller in Griffin-Beale 1979: 2). Careful observation of English primary schools' play-time recess in the early 1950s led the Medds to remark:

> It was striking to see how little real provision there usually was for the children who did not care to play in large groups. Three or four were noticed, for instance, taking chairs and arranging themselves round a small and still bare laburnum tree ... a solitary child was reading amongst the coats and wellingtons.
>
> ('Woodside Junior school at Amersham' 1958: 71)

Teachers agreed that there was a need for more private or intimate spaces. The Medds noted that one teacher requested 'corners' and another recalled 'the fascination for a child of a secluded corner of the garden, with a seat under a tree, of summerhouses, garden sheds, mazes and queer shapes'. They concluded that the layout of the garden as well as the interior of the building could 'provide better opportunities for these smaller, quieter groups to entertain themselves in reasonable comfort and amenity' ('Woodside Junior school at Amersham' 1958: 712). In her book about designing nursery spaces for the under-fives, Mary Medd suggested a range of simple devices to support active and imaginative play. There should be 'grassy mounds and hollows ... enough for a child to fit and have the "illusion of aloneness" with grass near by above eye level' (Medd 1976).

Conclusion

This discussion about the postwar interest from educationalists and architects in spaces designed to support children's need for quietness or withdrawal is more concerned with intention than effect. There is evidence that the original purpose of quiet spaces was lost as they became underused because of their inability to host whole classes or the challenges of supervision. There is evidence of this from the site visits I have made to Eveline Lowe school (renamed Phoenix Primary School). As school administration became more complex, the quiet spaces were often the first resort when teachers needed spaces for storage. From the early 1970s, in England at least, there was a shift of interest toward the inner child considered in terms of cognitive development, and the environment came to be thought of as more of an impediment than a nurturing influence (Burke 2013: 199). Nevertheless, it is a remarkable episode in school design when quietness, thoughtfulness and contemplation were essential components of the common vocabulary shared among a generation of progressive educators and architects.

Works cited

British Pathe (1946) *Treetop School*. A Short Film about King Alfred's School, available at: www.british pathe.com.
Brooks, P. (2006) 'The Travelling Spark: Alice Yardley and Child-Centred Education, the Development of Her Educational Thought, 1913–2002', PhD thesis, Lesley University, USA.
Burke, C (2005) '"The School without Tears": E. F. O'Neill of Prestolee School', *History of Education* 3: 263–75.
Burke, C. (2013) *A Life in Education and Architecture: Mary Beaumont Medd*, London: Ashgate.
Burke, C. and Grosvenor, I. (2011) 'The Hearing School: An Exploration of Sound and Listening in the Modern School', *Paedagogica Historica: International Journal of the History of Education* 47, 3: 323–40.

Clegg, A. B. (1971) *Revolution in the British Primary Schools*, Washington: National Association of Elementary School Principals.

'Eveline Lowe Primary School' (1967) *Building Bulletin* 36, London: Department of Education, HMSO.

'Eveline Lowe Primary School Appraisal' (1972) *Building Bulletin* 47, London: Department of Education, HMSO.

Franklin, G. (2012) '"Built-in Variety": David and Mary Medd and the Child-Centred Primary School, 1944–80', *Architectural History* 55: 321–67.

Gallagher, M. (2011) 'Sound, Space and Power in a Primary School', *Social & Cultural Geography* 12, 1 (February): 47–61.

Griffin-Beale, C (1979) *Christian Schiller in His Own Words*, London: A & C Black publishers.

Grosvenor, I. and Burke, C. (2008) *School*, London: Reaktion Books.

Herbert, E. (1990) 'Crow Island: A Place Built for Children', in E. Herbert and A. Meek, *Children, Learning and School Design*, Winnetka, IL: The Winnetka Public Schools: 33–8.

Herzberger, H. (2008) *Notes from Space and Learning: Lessons in Architecture*, Rotterdam: 010 Publishers.

Holmes, G. (1952) *The Idiot Teacher: A Book about Prestolee School and Its Headmaster E. F. O'Neill*, London: Faber.

Hudnut, J. (1941) 'Crow Island School', *The Architectural Forum* (August): 83.

Marsh, L. (1970) *Alongside the Child: Experiences in the English Primary School*, New York: Praeger Publishers.

Medd, M. (1976) *A Right to be Children: Designing for the Education of the Under-Fives*, London: RIBA Publications.

Medd, M. (1984) 'An Attitude to School Design: In Retrospect', London: UCL Archives ME/M/4/4 27–28 April.

Melling, G. (1980) *Open Schoolhouse: Environments for Children in New Zealand*, Dunedin: Caveman Press.

Middleton, S. (2013) *Henry Lefebvre and Education: Space, Theory, History*, London: Routledge.

'New Primary Schools' (1949) *Building Bulletin* 1, London: Department of Education, HMSO.

Presler, F. in Washburne, C. (1941) 'Notes on Planning', *The Architectural Forum* (August): 80.

Read, H. (1943) *Education through Art*, London: Faber.

Roberts, M. (2001) 'Off-Task Behaviour in the Classroom', National Association of School Psychologists, USA, available at: http://www.nasponline.org/communications/spawareness/Off-Task%20 Behavior.pdf (accessed 22 January 2015).

Saint, A. (1983) *Towards a Social Architecture: The Role of School Building in Post War England*, New Haven and London: Yale University Press.

Schiller, L. C. (1971) 'Designing New Primary Schools', *The Froebel Journal* 19 (Spring): 5.

Schiller, L. C. (1972) 'Changing Needs in the Design Context', *Built Environment* 1, 2 (May): 96–102.

Shield, B., Greenland, E. and Dockrell, J. (2010) 'Noise in Open Plan Classrooms in Primary Schools: A Review', *Noise Health* 12: 225–34.

Smith, M. (2008) *Sensory History*, London: Berg.

Tagore, R. (1933) 'My School', *Personality*, London: Macmillan.

Washburne, C. (1952) *What Is Progressive Education? A Book for Parents and Others*, New York: John Day Co.

'Woodside Junior School at Amersham' (1958) *Building Bulletin* 16, London: Department of Education, HMSO.

Yardley, A. (1970) *Senses and Sensitivity (Young Children's Learning)*, London: Evan Brothers.

16

HANS COPER AND PAUL RITTER

Tactile environments for children in postwar Britain and Australia

Geraint Franklin and David Nichols

The decades following World War II saw a slow change within learning environments in many parts of the Anglophone world, from streamlined, passive versatility to 'active' and individualistic learning models. In certain respects this might be reflected most markedly by the rise, in the 1960s, of the adventure playground movement, initiated through Danish forays into children's agency in play space and quickly picked up in other nations. However, novel advances are also to be found in key innovators' important experiments in surface treatment of school buildings and their surroundings.

This chapter explores the work of two very different men born five years and 160 kilometres apart: Hans Coper (1920–1981) and Paul Ritter (1925–2010). Both created tactile environments for children, both worked across disciplines and cultures and both were Jewish émigrés to Britain in the 1930s. Their forays into design for schools and their environments – for instance, a child's walk to and from school – provide an insight into the understanding and design of children's sensory worlds in the postwar decades. While both Coper and Ritter were to evolve forms, techniques and ways of collaborating that were unquestionably idiosyncratic, their work provides insights into broader themes, including the enrichment of modern architecture; the balance of power between designer, manufacturer and patron; and the locus of collaboration in the postwar school design adventure. Here, we recover the parallel work of the two men and situate it within the broader turn to collaborative and creative spaces for children.

Hans Coper at Digswell

> *The artist has a vital part to play in our modern world of mass production. William Morris was defeated by the problem of the machine; Walter Gropius in our own time, has worked out a solution. . . . The prototype of the articles that are manufactured by the thousand must be designed by artists. . . . What we have to do is to relate the artist and the craftsman in a realistic way to the community.*
> Henry Morris, 'The Contemporary Artist and the Community'[1]

English school building after 1945 faced a singular and urgent set of circumstances. The acute shortages of places for students, skilled designers, materials and funds created an acute need for school buildings which could not be met by a resumption of interwar practice.

Local education authorities (LEAs) evolved a strategic approach to providing school build-ings, coordinating whole programs of schools, rationalising construction through the use of prefabrication and consolidating expertise and buying-power through the formation of school building consortia such as the Consortium for Local Authorities Special Programme (CLASP). Given the exigencies of the national situation and the relatively technocratic solu-tions adopted, it is perhaps surprising that so much attention was paid by LEAs to qualitative aspects of school design, such as the relationship between learning and planning and the ways the visual environment could be ameliorated.

Decorative art was one way in which school spaces could be enhanced. The value of art in its application to school buildings, the architectural historian Andrew Saint suggests, was 'not so much as absolute cultural statements, more as attempts, like the colour schemes and the visible landscape, to develop children's visual experience' (Saint 1992: 27). Ideas of 'visual edu-cation' were promoted by Herbert Read's *Education Through Art* (1943) and organisations such as the Society for Education in Art (established in 1940) and the Arts Council of Great Britain (1945). There were many media through which visual education could be achieved. Some authorities built up loan collections of art works, others subsidised site-specific sculpture or murals, while still others believed that well-designed school buildings could themselves imbue their occupants with an aesthetic sensibility.

Henry Morris (1889–1961), Director of Education at Cambridgeshire County Council from 1922 to 1954, was an enthusiastic collaborator with designers and artists who believed that art and architecture were 'silent teachers', instrumental in creating a rounded and lib-eral education (Maclure 1984: 45). Morris can be considered a 'bridge' between pre- and postwar educational thinking. He inculcated a younger generation to give new shape to his ideas, including the architect Stirrat Johnson-Marshall and the educationists John Newsom and Stewart Mason (Rée 1973: 79, 92). The Cambridgeshire 'village colleges' he introduced from the 1920s, integrating secondary education with social and cultural amenities for adults, influenced the postwar community schools movement. Morris's final project was the Digswell Arts Trust, founded in 1957. Its aim was to reintroduce artists into the centre of the local community while bringing them into contact with those involved in postwar reconstruction, including town planners, architects and manufacturers (Bimrose 1965).

So it was that on Saturday 24 May 1958, four men – Morris, the German-born potter Hans Coper, Stirrat Johnson-Marshall and Bill Allen (another architect) – met to discuss a new venture. Notwithstanding their different backgrounds, all shared common aspirations: to give prefabricated building a humane face, to recast the artist as consultant designer and to reconcile the crafts and industrial production. It was the start of what Coper termed 'my architectural period', an idealistic but ultimately flawed collaboration that, although today obscure, repre-sents key cultural ambitions, inheritances and networks in postwar Britain (Birks 1983: 44). Coper worked with a network of architects and manufacturers under the aegis of the Dig-swell Arts Trust to develop new ranges of ceramic tiles, acoustic bricks and other building components. These were designed with prefabricated schools and similar public buildings in mind, although they were also available for purchase on the open market for any purpose.

Coper was born in Saxony, the second son of a prosperous Jewish family. His childhood and adolescence were blighted by increasing anti-Semitism, and he moved to England in 1939. After wartime service with the Pioneer Corps he met émigré Viennese potter Lucie Rie and, with no experience of pottery, joined her studio as an assistant. Coper's wheel-thrown early pots attracted attention when exhibited at the Festival of Britain in 1951 and in subsequent joint exhibitions with Rie. By the time he commenced work at Digswell in

January 1959, Coper had built a reputation as one of the most exciting studio potters work-ing in Britain. His sparse yet sculptural mature style was based upon a vocabulary of con-trasting and often compound forms, with patinated surfaces and black manganese and pale cream slips. A modest yet enigmatic figure, Coper identified with sculptors such as Constantin Brâncuşi, Alberto Giacometti and the anonymous potters of the prehistoric past (Birks 1983: 8; de Waal 2004).

Coper came into contact with Morris's circle of educationists in 1952, when he and Rie attended a craft conference at Dartington Hall School, a progressive coeducational boarding school. He was to meet the school's founders Dorothy and Leonard Elmhirst, the educationist Robin Tanner and Morris, all fervent believers in the educational value of the arts and crafts (Birks 1983: 27). Morris first invited Coper to Digswell in March 1958, and in May attended Coper's first one-man show at the Primavera Gallery in London, enthusing, 'I have never seen any contemporary work that is so powerful' (Morris 1958). Coper's time at Digswell Arts Trust, during which making pots continued on a reduced scale alongside the architectural projects, represents one of his most creative and influential periods.

The location of Digswell Arts Trust in Welwyn, the second garden city in England and among the first generation of new towns, was no accident. In 1946, Morris was appointed cultural advisor on new towns to the Ministry of Town and Country Planning. Perennially anti-urban in outlook, he advocated a 'diaspora' of artists outside the London art scene, serv-ing and educating local communities (Bimrose 1965: 8). With the sculptor Ralph Brown and the weaver Peter Collingwood, Coper was among the first artists to be offered a residency by the trust. Studio and living accommodation was provided at Digswell House, a Regency mansion leased from the Welwyn Garden City Development Corporation. In winter 1959 Coper moved into 'Annex Cottage No. 20', a studio with attached bed-sit where he worked and lived in characteristically Spartan conditions for about five years.

A mile from Digswell House lived Morris's friend Stirrat Johnson-Marshall (1912–81), then deputy architect to Hertfordshire County Council and later architect to the Ministry of Education and co-founder of Robert Matthew Johnson-Marshall & Partners. He wanted to introduce to the Digswell project the same spirit of collaboration between architects and educationists, manufacturers and designers that had characterised Hertfordshire school build-ing. There, crude prefabricated systems were taken up and manipulated into informal, child-scaled layouts; colour, light and furniture were reconceived with profound implications on postwar design. Johnson-Marshall's designers engaged and cajoled manufacturers and were not afraid to get their hands dirty in the process. His co-conspirator was Bill Allen (1914–98), the Canadian-born director of scientific and industrial research at the Building Research Station nearby at Garston. As one of the first national organisations undertaking research in construction, the Building Research Station was instrumental in introducing to school design a continuous cycle of design, manufacture and appraisal.

At Digswell, Morris gathered together the key actors in the industrial design process – designer, manufacturer and consultant architects – in pursuit of a common goal: improving the visual environment of schools and other public buildings. Here is Coper's account:

> The development group based on the Digswell work-shop, consisting of a number of architects concerned with school and public buildings, two heavy-clay manufacturers, and occasionally technical consultants, and myself as design consultant, is continuing to function; the main pre-occupation being the development of clay products for pre-fabricated application in housing and school building . . .

> This work, if brought to a practical conclusion, will produce the 'face' of much of future public building. . . . So far a number of products have been developed at Digswell and are being successfully produced. Cladding tiles, which might be regarded as an intermediate step – between traditional and pre-fabricated usage – acoustic tiles and bricks and, rather outside the actual group work, cladding tiles and bricks for traditional application and some sanitary ware.
>
> (Bimrose 1965: 59)

Mass-produced relief cladding for schools offered a means to enrich the exteriors of pre-fabricated buildings without resorting to expensive site-specific commissions of artistic work. An earlier example was the precast concrete tiles designed by Birkin Haward for Ipswich schools, the diamond patterns of which recall East Anglian vernacular buildings, but which *Concrete Quarterly* thought possessed 'an irregularity reminiscent of some primitive African work' ('Precast Concrete Profiled' 1958: 31). Hampshire County Council designed 'shadow blocks', modular concrete blocks with low-relief surface modelling, for the Second Consortium of Local Authorities (SCOLA), which in 1961 followed CLASP's lead (Martin 1970). Factory-made patterned or profiled blocks and ceramic or concrete 'motif tiles' were easily available from the mid-1960s. Brian Goldsmith, an architect at the Greater London Council, included the tiles in a tactile mural that enlivened a corridor at the Richard Cloudesley School for physically disabled children in central London (Pearson 2007: 127).

The Digswell group started with a series of extruded cladding tiles based on the eighteenth-century principle of mathematical tiles. Coper received grants of £500 from the Dartington-based Elmgrant Trust and – after much cajoling by Allen – £1000 from the manufacturers, the Maidenhead Brick and Tile Company of Burgess Hill, Sussex. Johnson-Marshall hoped the tiles would be adopted by CLASP, the first of the school-building consortia set up to coordinate the efforts and purchasing power of the local authorities. He brought on board Henry Swain, deputy architect at Nottinghamshire and a leading advocate of prefabricated school design.

Coper's tiles were intended as an addition to CLASP's 'cocktail solution' to component design, where a wide variety of cladding options were accommodated within a framework of common dimensions. Tile-hanging was much used in early CLASP buildings for the handicraft appearance which warmed up the prefabricated structures, and, because the system was developed for areas where mining had occurred, it was thought that the tiles would shift on their battens in the event of subsidence (Saint 1987: 157–83). Coper's tiles were thicker than normal and were screwed rather than nailed to their battens for extra resistance. They could also be bonded onto prefabricated panels or bedded directly into concrete.

The Keymer range, as it was known, included about six designs, available in several colours and dimensions (see Figure 16.1). The range was launched with advertising in the trade journals and a stand, apparently designed by Coper himself, at the 1965 International Building Exhibition at London Olympia. The Coper tiles were used on at least two Nottinghamshire schools, Nettleworth Infant and Nursery School, Mansfield Woodhouse, Mansfield (1964–65, job architect David Meylan) and Newark Orchard School, Appletongate, Newark, of roughly similar date (see Figure 16.2). It is likely that others exist.

That was not all. With Allen, Coper developed a range of acoustic facing bricks that combined sound absorbency with a sculptural appearance. Inspired by the brickwork of a Finnish

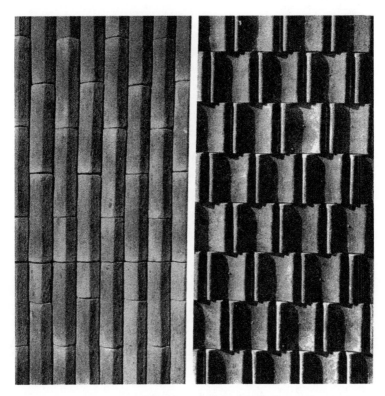

FIGURE 16.1   Series KP1 (left) and KP2 (right) from the Keymer range, designed by Hans Coper and manufactured by the Maidenhead Brick and Tile Company.

Source: Tony Birks, *Hans Coper* (Catrine, Ayrshire: Stenlake Publishing, 2013)

church, they were manufactured by the Maidenhead Brick and Tile Company and, later, Blockleys of Telford (see Figure 16.3). Coper designed a relief panel for 'Laingspan', a prefabricated system of pre-stressed concrete components. It was trialled at Robert Matthew Johnson-Marshall's additions to the Royal Russell School, an independent school in Croydon. And for SGB Ltd of Dudley, Coper designed a series of frost-proof tiles in vitreous glazed fireclay, and the 'Curlew' washbasin and lavatory. He joked that the taps were initialled 'H' and 'C' in his honour. Other photographs show Coper at work on a plaster mould for large, bowl-like planters, perhaps intended for use in the civic quarters of the New Towns (Birks 1983: 42–8).

Coper's acoustic bricks were still commercially available in the early 1980s, but production of the mathematical tiles ceased in 1969 and stocks were run down (Clay Cladding Products Ltd 1969). Swain later puzzled, 'the photographs of the cladding look so nice that I don't see why we did not go on using them' (Swain 1983). One reason was the limited take-up of the products in schools, the key market for which they were developed. As the 1960s wore on, inflationary pressures meant that pre-cast concrete and brick were increasingly favoured in school building. There were supply-side problems, too; the design patents for the products were retained by the manufacturers, effectively anonymising Coper's designs and tying them to the uncertain fortunes of the British ceramic manufacturing industry.

FIGURE 16.2 Coper tiles at Nettleworth Infant and Nursery School, Mansfield Woodhouse, Mansfield, Nottinghamshire, UK, 1964–65.

Architect: Nottinghamshire County Council Architect's Department, job architect David Meylan

Source: Tony Birks, *Hans Coper* (Catrine, Ayrshire: Stenlake Publishing, 2013)

FIGURE 16.3 A selection of Coper-designed acoustic facing bricks.

Source: Tony Birks, *Hans Coper* (Catrine, Ayrshire: Stenlake Publishing, 2013)

The obscure fate of Coper's designs for architectural ceramics contrasts with the prestigious site-specific commissions he also completed while at Digswell Arts Trust (Graves 2012). For Basil Spence he made candlesticks for the altar at Coventry Cathedral and for the Meeting House at Sussex University (now installed on a Henry Moore altar at the church of St Stephen Walbrook in London). Coper's sculptural, burnished pots sell for five-figure sums today, and his 1961 ceramic installation for the Swinton Technical High School in Yorkshire was sold at auction in 2011 for £181,250, after the school realised that they were in possession of a 'Coper' (Phillips de Pury & Company 2011).

The reasons for the failure of the Digswell project are less likely to relate to material shortcomings than to unresolved tensions and contradictions in the relations of production. The economics of Coper's pots were straightforward: they were bought by a collector, perhaps with a cut going to an art dealer or commercial gallery. The Digswell development group brought together designer and maker, but the relation between client and user was more ambiguous. The identity of the patron remained unclear: was it the welfare state (as represented by Johnson-Marshall and Swain), the industrialists who funded Coper's work or a nascent 'third sector' represented by the Digswell Arts Trust? The Digswell project represents a notable, if ultimately unsuccessful, attempt to align the shifting interests of the public-sector client, the building industry and the design consultant.

While it saw limited application, Coper's work for Digswell Arts Trust highlights broader and perhaps underappreciated trends in postwar school design. Many designers sought to improve children's visual environments and present a new face to the welfare state by enlivening exterior and interior surfaces with relief, pattern and colour. Coper's use of prefabricated components to fulfil this role represents an intriguing alternative to the commissioning of 'one-off' relief mural schemes, such as those of Paul Ritter.

Ritter and Sculp-crete

Paul Ritter emerged into architecture, planning and education at a time when postwar reconstruction enabled the reimagining of places and institutions to compound processes and disciplines previously considered discrete. He was an eccentric, controversial and provocative figure in the United Kingdom and then in Australia after 1965, where he became the first city planner for Perth, the capital of Western Australia, affecting extant plans in ways widely lauded since and contributing numerous features to his adopted city. A factotum, he qualified as an architect while maintaining a strong on-going interest in education; he helped develop a range of patented processes particularly for the creation of modelled concrete, known as 'Sculp-crete'. It is perhaps unsurprising, given the scope of his activities, that he adopted as his own a principle of Wilhelm Reich's espousing the 'unity of the world, the way that it all "hangs together"' (Ritter 1982: 5). In his 1981 book, *Concrete Renaissance*, Ritter recommended the 'three-beat, creative rhythm' of 'Attraction-Fusion-Liberation', stemming from this conception. He was a devoted father of seven, who maintained an interest in childhood experience and environment throughout his life.

Ritter moved as a refugee from Czechoslovakia to Britain in the late 1930s. He claimed to have fallen into architecture and then planning by default, egged on initially by his (divorced) single mother, who was determined her son have a prestigious career. Ritter's ideas about the built environment were informed by his childhood and the lives of children – his own and those of others. 'I was always spatially related to things around our home', he remembered, recalling scenes from his birthplace in suburban Prague as 'very very deeply embedded' in his memory and work: 'I dream about them a lot, in pleasant ways' (Ritter 2007).

Ritter married fellow University of Liverpool architecture graduate Jean Finch in 1946, and the two produced research and analysis under the banner of the Planned Environment and Education Research Institute for over sixty years. The year 1959 was seminal: it saw the publication of a book credited to Jean and Paul Ritter, *The Free Family*, on their philosophy of 'self-regulated' child rearing and the staging of Paul Ritter's 'Child's Eye View' exhibition, mounted in Nottingham. On this, he wrote:

> The Child's Eye View Exhibition made vivid differences in scale. One section, domestic interior, designed so that its size and detail were to the adult as the normal house is to the toddler, led to the town planning section where this lesson was applied.
>
> (Ritter 1964: 11)

Ritter later remembered:

> We learnt a great deal. We had a two-and-a-half times size toilet, and one of my most vivid memories is of a mother looking at this and saying 'Gawd, no wonder 'e doesn't want to sit on this'. . . . It got enormous publicity in England, and we showed part of it here in Perth and at Cottesloe showground, with the kindergarten association helping us and so on. So this sort of orientation towards children, as you can see, was pretty total.
>
> (Ritter 2007)

Ritter's *Planning for Man and Motor* (1964) was a far-reaching survey of the accommodation of pedestrian and automobile in the postwar urban world, through which he advocated for the separation of road from pathway via 'Radburn'-styled residential environments which saw residents gain easy access to shared open space. It highlighted the importance of children to Ritter's vision. His interest in children's experience of the environment was similarly applied in his development of 'educreation', a concept that, like many of Ritter's ideas, was largely explicable from its name ('learning and teaching, thinking and doing') (Ritter 1982: 6). The essence of this approach to both learning and design, he wrote, signalled its 'diametric departure from education' and lay in its 'combination of the three tenets – self-regulation, co-operation, therapy'. He continued:

> It will emerge from any system, based on this attitude. What is more, the system itself will have the capacity and tendency to grow with the times, to act as a catalyst to the advances of society so that the young ask questions and are not afraid to act according to the answers they discover.
>
> (Ritter 1966: 38–9)

Like much of Ritter's work, it encompassed and encouraged a tactile engagement between children and the built environment; engagement with surfaces and space would foster personal growth and creativity. In his 1966 book, *Educreation*, Ritter implores the reader:

> Stroke sculpture; caress architecture with your eyes; feel the spaces and the floors, the temperature and the quality of the air; note the faces of the people moving about; hear

the noises, touch the materials; sense the movement; sit on seats; and become aware of the delight and the frustrations.

(Ritter 1966: 319)

The educational philosophies espoused in *Educreation* pertained in large part to the education of architectural students at tertiary level. Certainly Ritter did not hold back in his criticisms of the way teenagers were prepared (or not) to enter professional training by the dreariness of inert rote learning; however, he had not yet embarked on architectural work to address specific classroom deficiencies as he saw them.

In 1964 Paul and Jean Ritter and their seven children migrated to Perth, where, as a result of the success of the 'Child's Eye View' exhibition, he had been offered the position of city planner. His tenure in this position was short lived, and he was dismissed in 1967, though not before successfully calling to a halt the vigorous demolition of nineteenth-century buildings and the freeway-centred development programs of his contemporaries. The Ritters remained in Perth, and Paul continued in private practice. His commissions were varied and, as shall be seen, often exotic and wide-ranging.

He suggests in his 1981 book *Bio-Building* that he was inspired to explore what would become Sculp-crete by the request from a developer to make good on a claim in *Planning for Man and Motor* that pedestrian underpasses could be 'the brightest spots in town' (Ritter 1981: 13). 'Neighbourhoods planned with footpath and cycle systems and accessible activity space for all age groups', he wrote, 'DO WORK and make a decisive difference in every way' (Ritter 1971: 59). Bungaree, the developer of the new Perth suburb of Rockingham, was directed by progressive planner-architects George Clarke and Don Gazzard, who were open to Ritter's child-oriented ideas. Driven by what one journalist called a 'desire to make pedestrian sub-ways bright places where children can play instead of dark blackboards for graffiti' (Sanders 1969), Ritter created 'seven sculptured underpasses' for Rockingham (Ritter 1971: 95). Here, he later wrote, he utilised 'vague memories on the use of polystyrene as liners' – that is, the carving of moulds from polystyrene – as initially practiced by the British sculptor William Mitchell (Ritter 1981: 13).

The Rockingham underpasses – many of which still exist over forty years later – were tactile, designed to encourage interactivity and inspire imaginative play among children walking to and from school or otherwise engaging freely in environments that were modelled on the neighbourhood unit: that is, with the school at the centre of residential areas (see Figures 16.4a and 16.4b). Ritter's intention was to blur the distinction between school – ideally a place of experiential and creative learning, rather than merely grim induction – and the surrounding environment; he hoped to prevent the 'ways home from school' being 'anxiety ridden' (Ritter 1971: 59). At Rockingham, one of the underpasses had surfaces which encouraged games of skill with ball-bearings in channels in the wall; another, known as 'Fort Brave', was a 'series of iron windows in walls' with projecting footholds that allowed children to climb through the tunnel without touching the ground (Ritter 1981: 57). Mitchell's modernist, concrete climbing wall on Hockley flyover (1968) in Birmingham is conceptually related to Ritter's design, as both are artworks that also serve as play equipment. Another of Ritter's underpass walls featured life-size native marsupials, including a kangaroo pouch which could be used for a stone-throwing game; on yet another was an 'underwater scene' of dangerous and thrilling sea creatures.

Ritter recalled in 2007 that as an architecture student he had designed a kindergarten with 'little posts around the fence; on the outside of each one a little brass animal for the kids to

FIGURE 16.4A   Paul Ritter, sculpted concrete interior, underpass, Rockingham, Western
Australia, 1971: 'Fort Brave'.

Photograph: Julian Williams, 2013

FIGURE 16.4B   Paul Ritter, sculpted concrete interior, underpass, Rockingham, Western
Australia, 1971: Australian native animals.

Photograph: Julian Williams, 2013

stroke', which was rejected by his teachers beholden to a rigid 'Le Corbusier type of formalism'. Revisiting his Rockingham underpasses some time after their construction, Ritter commented:

> I saw a little kid put his finger in the mouth of a shark, and I remember that's what I used to do to some lions that were on a statue, in Czechoslovakia. And I felt ever so brave – I saw this kid doing the same thing and I thought, 'well I'll be damned' – that's why I did it.
>
> (Ritter 2007)

The Rockingham underpasses had been created to Ritter's designs by a local firm, and, while they were not true Sculp-crete, he later co-opted them into his discussions of this innovation. The next step towards creating the new process was developed by Ritter with a consultant and collaborator, Ralph Hibble. The two also worked together in 1971 on the 'Harmony of Minerals Obelisk', an iconic (if not notorious, seemingly loved and hated in equal measure and often referred to as 'the kebab') structure near Perth's Council House.

Sculp-crete was the realisation of a Ritter principle of learning and creation through group activity: he advocated 'Participation sculpture' (Ritter 1982: 6). Its technical capacities were outlined in two books with almost identical content (perhaps better described as the same book published under two different titles): *Bio-Building* (1981) and *Concrete Renaissance* (1982). The concern here was primarily the potential uses and adaptability of the versatile and plastic Sculp-crete process as a form: for instance, in creating vertical 'bio-walls' – surfaces on which small plants could grow – or even roof gardens atop textured beds named 'ritterings'.

It is in collaborations with children, however, that Ritter and Hibble's Sculp-crete was most innovative. *Bio-Building* relates the recruitment of sixty-four eight-year-old children to produce Sculp-crete panels for a veranda wall at their school in Canning Shire (Ritter 1981: 84–6). This process, Ritter claimed, was a success on almost every level imaginable – including the outcome, unusual perhaps from a contemporary point of view, that positive parental involvement was obtained through adults seeing their children's work on commercial television. *Bio-Building* contains many pages of illustrations of concrete surfaces attributed to groups of schoolchildren in 1979 for the 150th anniversary of the establishment of Western Australia. These were created, the text suggests, using the Sculp-crete school kit, developed 'by the P.E.E.R Institute' in 1979. Ritter writes:

> In tribute to the fourteen schools it must be said that they co-operated fully with only 24 hours notice on this project and in response to just one enthusiastic phone call to the Principal, by Paul Ritter. . . . We co-ordinated the efforts of small country towns and capital city, of primary schools to final year university students, self-regulated community school to highly disciplined state and private colleges: the project showed that the idea is widely applicable.
>
> (Ritter 1981: 85)

The process of making moulds, involving searing a polystyrene mould with a low-voltage electronic carving tool, was both simple and accessible to all: 'From consultants to kids, artists professional and amateur to folks who never draw or sculpt, the method enticed them all to participate on the same surface' (Ritter 1981: 85).

Ritter's enthusiasm for his own creations notwithstanding, the essential message of the Sculp-crete project is clear. Ritter sought to tie his interest in community, in artistic development and expression, and in the therapeutic value of art and design to individuals and groups, into a process by which individually expressive and tactile works could be combined in projects celebrating local natural environment and historic endeavour, as well as providing an interactive place which was created by and for children. The success of this work, at least briefly, is made evident in the text of *Bio-Building* and *Concrete Renaissance*.

Conclusion

In 1970 Anthea Holme and Peter Massie, in their extensive British study *Children's Play*, quoted Ritter's analysis of the school-centred neighbourhood unit and its benefit to child development (Holme and Massie 1970: 77). In the same year, American architectural professor and specialist in early childhood facility design Robert Utzinger published a critical investigation into playgrounds and 'nursery schools' in Europe. He found of greatest interest those playgrounds, and the structures within them, which reflected children's interests and desires: Tingnjerg in Copenhagen, for instance, or the 'Robinson' playgrounds of Switzerland (Utzinger 1970: 52, 66–74). A brick folly in London, he wrote, was 'something that the youngsters like because it is their own creation' (Utzinger 1970: 28). Utzinger's feeling was that children's facilities 'should constitute a true children's environment' and eschew 'slick and shiny wall surfaces that inhibit both the teacher and the child'; he advocated for wall surfaces that were 'usable, touchable and colourful' (Utzinger 1970: 75, 76).

Utzinger did not directly address Coper's work, and Ritter, of course, was no longer working in Europe. Yet Utzinger's observations and values relate to a wider movement in which both men made substantial contributions. Coper's relief tiles and Ritter's Sculp-crete can be situated in a liminal space between 'art' and 'architecture'. Both projects could be interpreted as a reintroduction of a socially motivated architectural decoration to the civic realm, a concept that coexisted uneasily with the architectural Modern movement. The relief sculptor Anthony Hollaway spoke for many collaboration-minded artists when he said: 'I feel someone really ought to unsort the tangle of what is "decorative" and what is "art"'. Coper and Ritter integrated industrial techniques of production to their work, as did many others. 'My life-long dream', the artist Mitzi Cunliffe wrote in 1967, 'is a world where sculpture is produced by the yard in factories and used in buildings as casually as bricks' (Pearson 2007: 131).

Coper sought to improve the 'face' of social architecture through industrialised production of decorative and tactile cladding components. His exploration of the role of design consultant in industry can be seen in terms of an engagement with social architecture and as an implicit critique of his normative mode of production – the crafting of one-off art objects or site-specific commissions. There is irony, then, in the fact that Coper's ceramic products are today obscure, whereas the one-offs are among the most precious commodities on the art market. His project is emblematic of the limitations of the postwar school building program: the focus on supply and provision at the expense of user need and participation.

Ritter's legacy is far more problematic, not least because of a damaging professional 'blip' in the late 1980s when he was imprisoned on charges of making misleading representations to gain an export grant, which has affected how he is now seen in Western Australia. As regards his (and Hubble's) Sculp-crete work, Ritter's interest was more in the process of its collaborative potential – children were to be vested in the creation of their daily surrounds – than in the pursuit of a certain style, other than that which was derived from contingencies of the Sculp-crete process. This work must necessarily be seen as a part of the wider output of a principled thinker and technician, facilitating for others rather than pursuing a unique vision.

Despite their philosophical affinities, the work of Coper and Ritter provides some illuminating contrasts. Both men were approaching the same humanising objective – the enrichment of children's environments through relief sculpture – from opposing standpoints. Coper sought a supply-side solution, collaborating with industry in the manufacture of a series of products intended for schools and other public buildings. Ritter's Sculp-crete, by contrast, was created in collaboration with the children for whom the works were intended, and their participatory and site-specific nature can be seen as a celebration of the creative and communal aspects of education. In this regard, both should be seen as important progressive contributors, in the postwar decades, to an understanding of children's play and learning space.

Acknowledgement

Research for this chapter has been supported by a grant from the Australian Research Council: 'Designing Australian Schools: A Spatial History of Innovation, Pedagogy and Social Change' (DP110100505).

Note

1   Cited in Bimrose 1965: 7.

Works cited

Bimrose, D. (1965) *Digswell: A Matter Done*, Welwyn: Digswell Arts Trust.

Birks, T. (1983) *Hans Coper*, London: Collins.

Birks, T. (2013) *Hans Coper*, Catrine, Ayrshire: Stenlake Publishing.

Clay Cladding Products Ltd (1969) Letter of 26 June 1969 to the CLASP Development Group. Box 139, 'Wall Coverings – Tiles includes (296)/f, (296)/g', CLASP collection, Nottingham: Nottinghamshire Archives.

de Waal, E. (2004) 'Coper, Hans Joachim (1920–81)', in *Oxford Dictionary of National Biography*, Oxford: Oxford University Press, available at: http://www.oxforddnb.com/view/article/58507.

Graves, A. (2012) 'Hans Coper: Sculpture in Architecture', *Interpreting Ceramics* 14, available at: http://interpretingceramics.com/issue014/articles/05.htm.

Holme, A. and Massie, P. (1970) *Children's Play: A Study of Needs and Opportunities*, London: Michael Joseph.

Maclure, S. (1984) *Educational Development and School Building*, Harlow: Longman.

Martin, B. (1970) 'Facing the Wall', *Official Architecture and Planning* 33, 7 (July): 611–13.

Morris, H. (1958) Letter of 12 May 1958 to David Hardman, DE/DAT/5/1/10, Hertford: Hertfordshire Archives.

Pearson, L. (2007) 'Roughcast Textures with Cosmic Overtones', *Decorative Arts Society Journal* 31: 117–37.

Phillips de Pury & Company, London Design auction, 27 September 2011, Lot 50, 'Hans Coper: Swinton School Wall Mural, 1960', available at: https://www.phillips.com/detail/HANS-COPER/UK050211/50.

'Precast Concrete Profiled and Pierced Slabs Make a Notable Contribution to the Face of Architecture' (1958) *Concrete Quarterly* 38: 27–37.

Read, H. (1943) *Education Through Art*, London: Faber & Faber.

Rée, H. (1973) *Educatory Extraordinary: The Life and Achievements of Henry Morris*, London: Longman.

Ritter, P. (1964) *Planning for Man and Motor*, London: Pergamon Press.

Ritter, P. (1966) *Educreation*, London: Pergamon Press.

Ritter, P. (1971) 'Community in the Expanding Metropolis', in *Perth: The Expanding Metropolis, a Seminar*, Perth: Australian Institute of Urban Studies: 59–61.

Ritter, P. (1981) *Bio-Building*, Perth: Down to Earth Bookshop Press.

Ritter, P. (1982) *Concrete Renaissance: Through Building Technology*, Perth: Down to Earth Bookshop Press.

Ritter, P. (2007) Interview by D. Nichols, Kalamunda, 9 June.

Saint, A. (1987) *Towards a Social Architecture*, New Haven: Yale University Press.

Saint, A. (1992) 'Historical Background on Post-War School Buildings' in General Principles for the Selection of Post-1939 Education Buildings for Listing, unpublished report, post-war steering group collection, London Region Historians' files collection, London: Historic England.

Sanders, R. (1969) 'He Wants Us All to Co-operate', *Age* 26 May: 10.

Swain, H. (1983) *Letter of 6 June 1983 to David Medd. ME/M/1/20*, London: Institute of Education Archives.

Utzinger, R. C. (1970) *Some European Nursery Schools and Playgrounds*, Ann Arbor, MI: University of Michigan Press.

17

BRISTLING WITH OPPORTUNITY

Audiovisual technology in Australian schools from the 1930s to the 1980s

David Nichols and Hannah Lewi

> *The printing-press is the oldest and still the most widely used device for spreading knowledge and explaining the world. But the modern devices beyond the chalk-board, the model and the picture – the projector, the film, the radio, television, the tape recorder – are powerful means of enabling learners to look and see, to listen and hear, more fully and discriminately.*
>
> (E. J. Perry [Visual Education Officer of Victoria] 1973: 1048)

This chapter discusses the way a range of interlinked technologies – film, radio and television and their precedents – has been used in the Australian classroom since the beginning of the twentieth century, and the impact of such technologies on the idea of a classroom itself. The extent to which these technologies have *brought* change is, perhaps, up for question: their adoption may merely *reflect* change. Yet the apprehension about, antipathy towards or fervent embrace of new technologies in teaching practice has led to changes in classroom design, use and culture for over a century.

To investigate the uptake of technology in the classroom, we have consulted a range of education practice papers and parliamentary reports, and have interviewed technicians and teachers involved with developing and screening resources in Australia. We have also immersed ourselves in films of the era that depict school and technological advances. The inclusion of such documentary evidence offers an additional way to illuminate aspects of classroom and school spaces that gradually became infused with audiovisual technologies (Wormington et al. 2011: 458). As Inés Dussel has suggested, studying the history of visual technologies of all types is integral to understanding classrooms as visual spaces. Recent international scholarship attends to the early and sometimes marginal adoption of pathoscopes, magic lanterns, slides and film (Dussel 2013: 41).

The passive nature of most media consumption before the arrival of interactive media in the late twentieth century has no doubt contributed to the ambivalence felt by educator and layperson alike towards audiovisual technology in schools. One anonymous cynic in the *Newcastle Sun* in 1931 can stand in for a million commentators on this topic. 'Listener-in', wary of his or her radio entertainment being intruded upon by dry lectures, opined that 'a young man or woman would not stand much of a loud-speaker dissertation on inferiority complex or some other such subject before he or she in desperation twisted the dials to pick up some dance music' ('Listener-in' 1931).

The 1940s classrooms in three short films

In Australia, the principles of broadcasting education, particularly to remote areas, were a matter of great interest and subject to significant innovation. The Australian Broadcasting Commission's commitment to education via radio broadcast – *School of the Air*, for instance – was a first in the English-speaking world, and perhaps beyond. Stanley Hawes's 1946 film *School in the Mailbox*, produced for the National Film Board, serves both as a documentary on and as propaganda for this practice. It focuses on those children – 'wise to the ways of the land', yet not required to undertake formal education if living further than three miles (4.8 kilometres) from a school – for whom correspondence schooling was established. The film shows the elaborate communication technologies adopted by teachers and pupils; lessons were literally delivered in a mailbag, and a map of Australia illustrating the extensive network of deliveries from cities outwards is shown to convey broader themes of national cohesiveness. We see weekly lessons carried by bike, buggy, rail, truck and even, in isolated Western Australia, camel. The bricks and mortar correspondence centres in each city feature an army of correspondence teachers in an enlarged staff room instead of children sitting in rows of desks. Paper-based lesson books are enhanced with radio broadcasts, illustrated by scenes of families attentively gathered around the wireless in their country living rooms and kitchens. *School in the Mailbox* vividly shows the routines, technologies and tools enacted for a complex system of distance education delivery that took the classroom to the country.

1947's *Australia at School*, from the same production body, was seemingly produced to assuage fears among postwar migrants about Australian educational practices. Throughout the film, a headmaster and a concerned mother tour a range of schools to explore modern education. They view an attentive class through a small window as the children are told by an announcer that 'Britain is building more and more ships', a sequence which perhaps resonated with audiences familiar with the use of news media for war propaganda earlier in the 1940s. The preteen students are shown stiffly sitting at their desks, concentrating on the words from a small speaker at the front of the class – there is no danger of enjoyment in this process. The film, however, does espouse the development of the senses through artistic expression and play for younger children, followed by more formal studies after the age of eleven years. It is possible, we are told, to 'bring the outside world into the classroom by the use of aids like film and radio'.

In the same year as *Australia at School* was released, Launceston headmaster R. L. Maslin recommended that students themselves be enabled to take the reins of radio, to give schools 'a new sense of purposeful realism'. He wrote that the new field of internal school broadcasting 'opens up a field of educational enterprise that is bristling with opportunity' (Whitford 1947: 7). Maslin saw a downside to broadcast radio as it had evolved under commercial imperatives. In 1945, he had bemoaned the 'nauseating' commercial radio clubs that had turned 'education's greatest asset, the radio, into its enemy' ('Teachers Opposed to Radio Clubs' 1945). In proposing that radio be put into the hands of students, Maslin was predictive. Technology was not only being harnessed to receive educational materials; it was also becoming recognised as an educational and creative tool in itself.

Over a decade later, there was a greater range of technologies – at least in some showcase schools. The Victorian Education Department's 1959 film *Building for Learning* depicts how Australian primary schools were being modernised to 'prepare the citizens of tomorrow'. The narrative is charted through a story focused on prefabrication and new school construction, which the audience is led through the visual cue of a school plan drawing. Sound is a very important device in setting the scenes of the film and depicting 'children at work' in one of these new primary schools. We hear marching anthems and school songs, busy chatter, the piano as 'an essential part of new school equipment', and music and drama classes. In particular, the technology of the classroom is highlighted in sound and image: we see children using lightweight, flexible furniture; a teacher operating a bi-fold door divider in two classrooms allowing for free drama and movement classes; the chalkboard in active use (green to prevent glare); and movable library book shelving. Thus, there is a strong emphasis on the operation of the classroom and its furniture as a vital part of the new technology available to the teacher. When the audience moves on to view the higher year levels, we see a long sequence of a teacher bringing out a projector to show a film to students, pulling down a portable screen and drawing blackout curtains to darken the room's ample daylight. The problem of classroom ventilation is ingeniously overcome by holes carefully cut out of the curtains to accommodate the mechanical air vents. We then move to a Grade 5 class, where a pre-recorded radio broadcast, turned on by one of the boys, plays through the classroom speaker. Recording and amplification equipment, stored in the school office, is also demonstrated. Another class is shown recording their own play using this recording equipment, as children gather around the microphone reading their lines. Children, we are told, gain instant satisfaction by hearing their own voices played back to the class while the teacher is given an opportunity for 'correcting speech problems'. The scene ends with one child's long recorded speech.

All three films, but *Building for Learning* in particular, capture visual and non-visual atmospheres and ideologies of technology in the classroom of the postwar era. Sound is used to evoke the routines and familiarities of the school day (Burke and Grosvenor 2013), and it is made clear within the films that objects of everyday schooling now begin to include not just pen and paper, and chalk and board (Rasmussen 2012: 114), but also audiovisual aids. However, although technology was enthusiastically showcased on films about schools, it would take time and debate before it was adopted in its many iterations between 1900 and the 1970s.

The beginnings of audiovisual education in Australia

The educational profession, from coalface teacher to theorist, grappled with the potential for audiovisual education in the classroom from the outset when, in the first decades of the twentieth century, the twin prongs of radio and cinema were explored for their educational potential. Staff at the Victorian Teachers College prepared optical lantern slides for consideration by schools in 1901, and by 1906 the Victorian Department of Education began to experiment with magic lantern slides, distributing stereoscopes and accompanying explanatory booklets such as one titled *Schoolroom Travel* which created stereoscopic maps of the world.

On the eve of World War I, C. R. Herschell, the Victorian manager of Pathé Films, demonstrated the cinematograph to the Education Office in Melbourne with a film of children in action at the Melbourne Cricket Ground. It was a clear prediction that the moving image would indeed become a powerful tool in the classroom. The audience agreed that this medium could enable students to 'in imagination travel to distant countries, to assist in historical ceremonies, and to take part in expeditions of peril' (Blake 1973: 1041).

In 1921, as a result of Australians' experience of film as a wartime news, education and information tool, the Victorian Council for Public Education (VCPE) appointed a committee to investigate the 'moving image in its relation to the child'. The VCPE concluded that film had potential for education but needed to be tested. By the end of the 1920s, some schools were incorporating film into their curriculum.

The year 1921 was also when radio broadcasting was formally introduced to Australia, and at the end of the 1920s state organisations regularly produced broadcasts for schools, exposing them to 'distinguished visitors' and 'noteworthy gatherings' ('Broadcasting a Music Lesson' 1924) or, as happened in late 1929, an 'educational orchestral programme for State school children by the University Symphony Orchestra' ('Broadcasting' 1929). Compared to film, actual delivery of radio was simple once the set was purchased and the loudspeaker system connected, but control over content was not so easy. This lack of control over programming is surely the most important aspect of considering radio in schools.

In 1930 the Victorian Education Department declared that, in combination with a teacher, film was an acceptable – indeed, an irresistible – component of a rounded education that 'induced concentration' (Blake 1973: 1041; Bertrand 1982: 4–5). The following year, the Visual Education Committee, recently established to conduct experiments into film's value to education ('Films to Teach' 1930), reported that screening a film to Grade 8 children (thirteen- to fourteen-year-olds) imparted knowledge, and that students retained this knowledge more successfully than that learned through conventional teaching. However, many other experiments, reports and opinions presented the counter view and acknowledged that the benefit of the technology was largely contingent on the quality of the content (Blake 1973: 1042). Another consideration was that projectors were difficult to obtain and operate, and suitable films were not easy to come by, with local content particularly hard to source. These issues were to dog the introduction of films into school for another fifty years and made it a difficult and often unrewarding medium for classroom use.

A midway device, the 'filmstrip', was for many decades an efficient and simple method of image delivery, perhaps closest in form to the very common twenty-first-century mode of the PowerPoint slide show than to either radio or film. The main difference is that with rare exceptions the filmstrip, a sequence of images on sprocketed film which was stored in a roll and manually moved frame-by-frame in a projector, was purchased pre-made. 'They do not talk, which is an advantage in teaching', declared the Darwin *Army News* in 1945, announcing the arrival of this compact 'cinematic technique' to replace the textbook ('"Film Strip" for Schools' 1945). Three years later, an American author declared them the 'simplest, most direct, and least expensive mass medium of communication yet invented' (Falconer 1948: 1). The technology was adopted across Australia. Production of the strips in Victoria began at the Melbourne Technical College in 1939, with topics including the search for the Komodo Dragon ('Visual Aids in Schools: Experiment Succeeds' 1938) and a geography lesson that compared Victoria with the Yosemite Valley ('Visual Aids in Schools' 1939). By 1949 the Visual Education Centre, which was the primary educational lending service, reported a lending rate of an average of 1,200 copies of filmstrips across Victoria (Blake 1973: 1048).

The number of titles available continued to grow markedly from around one thousand in 1949 to five thousand in 1971 (Blake 1973: 1051). The parents and citizens' associations for schools in the tiny New South Wales towns of Frogmore and Rye Park, north of Yass, each purchased filmstrip projectors in late 1952. They were battery-operated because the district was not yet serviced with electricity. The NSW Education Department responded to the Frogmore purchase by forwarding '87 films' for the students – an embarrassment of riches, though how content or topic was decided is not detailed in the *Boorowa News* ('Frogmore News' 1952).The newspaper speculated that the advantage of such a device over film projectors was the ease with which appropriate media could be obtained ('Purchase Strip-Film Projector' 1952).

In 1969, tape recording services were established to record Australian Broadcasting Commission (ABC) transmissions and provide them to schools; soon afterwards, the ABC began promoting an educational tool it called Radiovision. This combined filmstrips with audio programs delivered by broadcast. The ABC claimed it was

> a combination of radio programs, colour filmstrips and printed text. Professionally-prepared audio commentary, sound effects and music are integrated with projected pictures to provide an experience in sight and sound more flexible than the television program, since the components can be used together, separately and in segments.
>
> (ABC 1977: 22)

Once again, the 'flexible' nature of this visceral form presaged the PowerPoint-based learning that would become common in the twenty-first century. The most unpredictable and, frankly, inadequate element of Radiovision was surely the audio broadcast. Teachers had to order the filmstrip component and an explanatory booklet, and then record the program from the air. The option of simply operating the filmstrip for the class to accompany the program 'live' was discussed in ABC literature, but this would clearly negate the 'flexibility' of, for instance, stopping and starting programs for discussion or learning exercises.

The filmstrip's 'flexibility' was important. Viewing did, however, require the same dedicated dark space as other forms of projected film. *Building for Learning* features a long sequence in which a classroom is prepared for a (moving) film show. The late 1940s pamphlet series *News in Visual Aids in Education* reported on the production and use of film technology in schools: a two-page instructional article and diagram was featured on the subject of 'Darkening Classrooms'. Timber baffles and canopies fitted to windows, an appropriate length of curtain material and an electric fan for additional ventilation were all required (*News of Visual Aids in Education* 1949).

It may have been because of these contingencies of viewing space that many news and journal discussions of filmstrip education did not distinguish between moving film and filmstrips. All were 'films for schools', in some instances discussed more in terms of the storage space required (filmstrips, naturally, were preferable by this rubric; notably, the dangers of flammability had been largely counteracted with advances in 'safety film' in the late 1940s). Boxes of slides with accompanying explanatory and/or lecture text were also a feature of classroom education, the advantage over filmstrips being a higher visual definition and the ability to rearrange images.

In the field of audio-based education, too, changes were afoot. Whereas films and film-based forms were commonly shown in the conventional classroom, these – particularly in the development of language learning – led to the provision of dedicated classrooms and facilities.

Audiolingualism and language labs

Warren Roby discusses forays into language learning through dedicated arrangements of phonographic equipment at the beginning of the twentieth century in the United States and

Europe (Roby 2004: 524). But it was much later, between the 1950s and 1970s in Australian primary and high schools, that there were sporadic moves towards creating dedicated laboratories for language learning rather than relying on media technology brought temporarily into the everyday classroom.

The gradual availability of audio, and sometimes visual, systems of recording technology, as well as teacher-operated 'listening posts' connecting students and instructors, coincided with new ideas in behaviourist psychology. This led to an investment in sensory resources other than printed text material, and in reshaping approaches to the learning of languages towards 'audiolingualism', a technique built on the individual repetition of phrases and words (Lo Bianco 2009).

What really demarcated the term 'laboratory' was the provision, in the 1950s, of acoustically separated booths – sometimes called 'roomlets' or 'cabins' – for individual learners; shared tables connected to a central recording device were often substituted in Australian schools. This is seen in Figure 17.1, where pupils demonstrate the newly built classroom facilities for Grade 5 and 6 children at Fitzroy Primary School in Victoria in 1973.

A 1968 photograph accompanying a news story about a display at Lyneham, Canberra, shows a dedicated technician demonstrating dials, cords and microphones, which evoke ideas of technological advancement ('Language Lab at Lyneham' 1968). Laboratory and dedicated classroom facilities were also provided for remedial English tuition, with Commonwealth Government programs explicitly targeting inner-city primary schools in the 1970s to bolster English literacy among the burgeoning migrant population.

FIGURE 17.1   Pupils demonstrate the newly built classroom facilities, Fitzroy Primary School, Victoria, 1973.

Photograph: Alan K. Jordan

Source: Courtesy Caroline Jordan and State Library Victoria

The 1960s saw the development and increased use of video, as well as film, along with the recognition that re-recordable media had great value in facilitating students' own forays into the audiovisual field. The 1970s would herald new changes in both technology and its distribution and uptake in the classroom.

'It was the process that was important'

Tim Thorpe's experience in audiovisual technology in the 1970s and 1980s is similar to that of many who worked in the field. Thorpe was at turns creator, distributor and facilitator: his entrée into this world came after three years of teaching primary school in Melbourne. 'In 1978', he says:

> I bluffed my way into the audiovisual education centre, initially applying to be in the TV unit – I'd gained experience borrowing a Portapak from, and doing rudimentary editing at, Dandenong Audiovisual, which was the best of the audiovisual centres.
>
> (Thorpe 2015)

His experience, it transpires, was the tail end of a media supply system for Victorian schools that was soon to be superseded by the arrival of video and computer-based media. *Vision and Realisation* outlines the origins of some of the institutions Thorpe witnessed in their final years: the 'motion film circuit', which began in Brunswick in 1945, and in-house production of films about and for schools (Blake 1973: 1047, 1048).

The Visual Education Centre's circuit library at 450 Burke Road, Camberwell, Melbourne, was established in 1965. Thorpe recalls 'a bunch of old blokes downstairs' in charge of the 16mm films:

> They would pack 'em up every morning, put 'em on the train, then they'd have a cup of tea and chat about the war.
> The Circuit Library guys were 'public servants', whereas us in the education centre were 'teachers'. . . . We had an array of slides, charts, posters. The best seller was a wood-working chart, with pictures of screwdrivers, boldly titled 'screwing techniques'. There was a dark room, a whole bunch of projectors, some cameras to lend out, charts, slides, audio tapes of all the *For Schools* programs for the last 10 years.
>
> (Thorpe 2015)

Teachers who wished to show films to their classes were required to be trained and certified to operate a projector, a two-day course, according to Thorpe, for which 'you were only awarded a certificate for the brand of projector you learnt on'. Many teachers were not thus qualified, and 'circuits' of touring projectionists had been in existence since the mid-1940s. Thorpe was one of the last to work on these, visiting areas just beyond the periphery of Melbourne's conurbation:

> When I first started in '78, we used to take on the role of circuit projectionist. It wasn't teachers who showed the film, it was people like me, a guy in a dustjacket. Not every school could afford a projector. . . . Two delightful days a month I received travelling money, to go to places like Kinglake, Diamond Creek, Hurstbridge and later beachside

schools on the Mornington Peninsula. The kids would enthusiastically greet you at the gate, to help you lug in the projector, stand, screen and precious cans of film. A bit of a spiel, the light monitor flicks the switch and the show begins.

(Thorpe 2015)

Soon after starting at the centre, Thorpe became involved in two aspects of production: the generation of materials for schools commissioned by the Education Department, and that by students and teachers at schools as part of learning exercises.

> The teaching aspect of being an audiovisual officer was far more enjoyable for me than classroom teaching. I dived in and dived out, I didn't have to suffer the consequences of razzing up the students. Teaching video production I tried to devise ways to involve the whole class. . . . I didn't want kids sitting round doing nothing, I'd probably have ten or eleven people, then rotate them. . . . I didn't really care about the result, it was the process that was important.
>
> (Thorpe 2015)

Thorpe also made a series with producer Sue Gallagher, *Theatre in Schools*, which he shot on one video camera: 'we were bold and we were terrible!' As a young man working in this field, Thorpe's impression is that the systems and technologies – and staff – in place at his arrival had largely adhered to the same essential pattern for thirty years. By the 1990s, the process of ordering 16mm films from the 'circuit library' utilising the expertise of the circuit librarian ('You'd say, "I want an animated film about cats but I particularly want one about ginger cats" . . . and he'd say, "try #10563"') was being superseded. The time of tangible media would also soon fade. Thorpe says:

> Most of us were in another world of old movies that still existed. I had one foot in that and one foot in the new world of video. My demise was the coming of computers – in that 12 years it went from ancient history through to the future and unfortunately I was a young thing 12 years before and able to adapt and I wasn't one of the young things with new technology.
>
> (Thorpe 2015)

TVeaching

> The television teacher is using an audio-visual medium. He must balance with subtlety and purpose the visual image and the spoken word and each in its proper order, judging with his producer when each or both are demanded by the development of the theme. The eye is the more immediately informative organ of reception and in any competition with the ear is likely to dominate. The ear however, is the more critical and demanding organ and through the ear the impressions conveyed by the eye can be filled out, deepened and clarified. Hence the television teacher and producer have to know how to marshal and combine the two approaches.
>
> (Bull 1964: 180)

When Charles Bull wrote these words, television had been a feature of Australian life for a decade, but its use in disseminating information had been discussed long before it arrived.

In 1924, at the conclusion of a report of a musical lecture given by radio to ten thousand British schoolchildren, an Adelaide *Register* journalist espoused the advantages of 'wireless television' which would 'enable teachers and children in remote centres to benefit directly by the instruction and help of experienced and capable lecturers' ('Broadcasting a Music Lesson' 1924). Thirty years later, readers of the Adelaide *Chronicle* were told of a pilot program in Britain described as 'TVeaching', to intersperse students' 'ordinary syllabus ... with TV lessons in science, travel, aesthetic appreciation, industry and current affairs' ('Television May Replace Blackboards' 1951).

Australian schools were involved in television production experiments long before the advent of regular television broadcasts. In early 1950, Waratah Boys School and Cooks Hill Primary students each performed fifteen-minute dramas for a 'television demonstration' at Newcastle's City Hall ('Televised Plays for Children' 1950). Melbourne's *Argus* in October 1951 envisaged 'a large scale upheaval' in classroom design:

> For a start, nearly all classrooms will be obsolete for TV instruction. Architects will probably design rooms with sloping floors and high windows.
>
> Educationists have already opposed any move in TV schools to have children sitting in darkened rooms, but this could be overcome by using large daylight viewing screens.
>
> Meanwhile, technical developments by TV manufacturers show that it will be possible for one master receiver to channel transmissions to a dozen independent screens in different classrooms.
>
> ('The Blackboard Is on Its Way Out' 1951)

'There is no limit', this unnamed *Argus* contributor enthused, 'to the bounds of TV and its place in education'.

Television arrived in Australia in 1956. For the next decade, educational programs mainly concentrated on secondary science and maths, then in the 1960s extended to social studies, English and subjects aimed at primary levels (Thompson 1969: 70). At this stage, television was regarded as a teaching aid and not a surrogate teacher, although it was often grudgingly admitted that the use of audiovisuals provided respite for teachers.

Televisions were portable and could be transported around the school relatively easily; additionally, their use did not need dedicated training and/or technicians coming into the classroom, as was the case with film technology. That said, any classes using television programming had to be structured around broadcast schedules – an issue for timetabling in many schools. In weighing up television over filmstrips, it was thought that an advantage was that television could 'reach the four corners of the state at the one time' (Thompson 1969: 71). Thus, television and radio became and remained significant technologies in audiovisual education in Australian schools, only to be ultimately usurped again by the ubiquitous connective of the digital media age in the twenty-first century.

Conclusion

Despite superficial technological differences, the effectiveness, nominal cheapness and sensory value of the audiovisual experience has changed little over the twentieth century – nor have the hopes and predictions invested in more effective tools and techniques (a 2015 report in the Melbourne *Age* stating that PowerPoint had 'let teachers introduce technology into the classroom' notwithstanding) (Park 2015). As many historians of education and modern architecture have noted, the association with light and modernity was particularly acutely observed in construction of new schools in the mid-twentieth century. This focus on light was not just about improving the physical conditions of old, inadequate facilities through extensive windows and glazed walls that connected students to the outside; light also became a powerful metaphor for newness and intellectual illumination. Catherine Burke suggests that light is 'fundamental to the visual culture of the classroom' (Burke 2005: 129). However, with the gradual adoption of audiovisual material into the school and classroom, visual technology intervened in this metaphor. Slides, film, filmstrips and television all required a state of (temporary) darkness. Room darkening became part of the process and ritual of setting up these devices for classroom use by teachers or technicians. This was at its most extreme in the dedicated language laboratory with its isolated booths that closed down both light and space.

In all such schemes, technology has aspired to 'bring the outside world into the classroom', whether through radio, filmstrip, television, film or, more recently, internet and other computer-based learning. All provide an additional, up-to-date resource capable of creating an 'atmosphere' through a multisensory medium stimulating imagination and provoking ideas. These technologies project information beyond the teacher's reach – with a heightened value in bringing learning to remote areas of Australia.

But although media of all kinds was certainly invested with hopes of bringing the outside world into the classroom, it was always treated with some circumspection – in part perhaps because this world was now mediated and somehow artificial – produced by neither the teacher nor the child, and consumed in a fairly passive mode. The challenges of introducing digital media technologies – including laptops, iPads and whiteboards – into the classroom are still apparent. Although digital mobile devices are now being issued to individual children in the classroom, debates around appropriate lighting, ergonomic furniture and acoustic separation are still very much alive in the design and retrofitting of classrooms.

Perhaps ultimately the value of teaching with such technology lies in the abilities of the student to obtain perspective on input from a multitude of sources, and to distinguish experience from what is merely witnessed. The distinction between media as entertainment and media as educator has been a difficult enough one for many teachers and education policymakers – the use of media as source material is perhaps a bridge too far for some. While we are often told that 'millennials' (those born in the 1980s and 1990s), in particular, are far more media-savvy than preceding generations, concerns continue about their ability to distinguish types of information on a spectrum from credible to fabricated. It is here, perhaps, that educators once again must reinvent the wheel in the classroom, enabling students to go beyond the stiff, attentive desk-dwellers of *Australia at School*, to sceptical, yet engaged, cultural consumers.

Acknowledgements

Research for this chapter has been supported by a grant from the Australian Research Council: 'Designing Australian Schools: A Spatial History of Innovation, Pedagogy and Social Change' (DP110100505). The authors would like to thank Bernard McMahon and Sari Wawn for information provided during research for this chapter.

Works cited

ABC (1977) *Media in the Classroom: The Use of ABC Radio and Television for Schools*, Sydney: New Century Press.

Bertrand, I. (1982) 'Film and History: The International Context', in A. Hutton (ed.) *The First Australian History and Film Conference Papers*, Sydney: Australian Film, Television and Radio School: 3–22.

'The Blackboard Is on Its Way Out' (1951) *Argus* (Melbourne) 26 October: Education Supplement 2S.

Blake, L. J. (ed.) (1973) *Vision and Realisation: A Centenary History of State Education in Victoria*, Melbourne: Education Dept. of Victoria.

'Broadcasting' (1929) *Canberra Times* 17 September: 2.

'Broadcasting a Music Lesson' (1924) *Register* (Adelaide) 22 September: 8.

Bull, C. (1964) 'Teaching by Television', *Australian Journal of Education* 8, 3: 171–82.

Burke, C. (2005) 'Light: Metaphor and Materiality in the History of Schooling', in M. Lawn and I. Grosvenor (eds) *Materialities of Schooling: Design, Technology, Objects and Routines*, Oxford: Symposium Books: 12–43.

Burke, C. and Grosvenor, I. (2013) 'The Hearing School: An Exploration of Sound and Listening in the Modern School', *Paedagogica Historica: International Journal of the History of Education* 47, 3: 323–40.

Dussel, I. (2013) 'The Visual Turn in the History of Education', in T. S. Popkewitz (ed.) *Rethinking the History of Education*, London: Palgrave: 29–49.

Falconer, V. M. (1948) *Filmstrips: A Descriptive Index and User's Guide*, New York: McGraw-Hill.

'"Film Strip" for Schools' (1945) *Army News* 27 January: 3.

'Films to Teach School to Children' (1930) *Register News-Pictorial* (Adelaide) 22 April: 5.

'Frogmore News' (1952) *Boorowa News* 17 October: 3.

'Language Lab at Lyneham' (1968) *Canberra Times* 16 February: 12.

'Listener-In' (1931) 'What People Think', *Newcastle Sun* 16 December: 4.

Lo Bianco, J. (2009) 'Second Languages and Australian Schooling', *Australian Education Review* 9, available at: http://research.acer.edu.au/aer/8.

News of Visual Aids in Education 3 (1949).

Park, K. (2015) 'Powerpoint Should Be Banned: This Powerpoint Presentation Explains Why', *Age* (28 May), available at: http://www.theage.com.au/digital-life/digital-life-news/powerpoint-should-be-banned-this-powerpoint-presentation-explains-why-20150528-ghbbpt.html.

Perry, E. J. (1973) 'Audio-visual Technology: Bringing the World into the Classroom', in L. J. Blake (ed.) *Vision and Realisation: A Centenary History of Education in Victoria*, Melbourne: Education Department of Victoria: 1041–8.

'Purchase Strip-film Projector for Rye Park School' (1952) *Boorowa News* 26 September: 3.

Rasmussen, L. R. (2012) 'Touching Materiality: Presenting the Past of Everyday School Life', *Memory Studies* 5, 2: 114–30.

Roby, W. B. (2004) 'Technology in the Service of Foreign Language Teaching: The Case of the Language Laboratory', in D. Jonassen (ed.) *Handbook of Research on Educational Communications and Technology*, 2nd edn, Bloomington, IN: AECT.

'Teachers Opposed to Radio Clubs' (1945) *Mercury* (Hobart) 12 January: 11.

'Televised Plays for Children' (1950) *Newcastle Herald and Miners' Advocate* 23 February: 7.

'Television May Replace Blackboards' (1951) *Chronicle* (Adelaide) 11 October: 25.

Thompson, L. (1969) *Looking Ahead in Education*, Melbourne: Education Dept. of Victoria, 1969.

Thorpe, T. (2015) Personal communication with the authors, February.

'Visual Aids in Schools' (1939) *Argus* (Melbourne) 26 May: 4.

'Visual Aids in Schools: Experiment Succeeds' (1938) *Argus* (Melbourne) 18 June: 9.

Whitford, R. L. (1947) 'The School Radio Station', *Tasmanian Education* 2, 6 (December).

Wormington, P., Van Gorp, A. and Grosvenor, I. (2011) 'Education in Motion: Uses of Documentary Film in Educational Research', *Paedagogica Historica: International Journal of the History of Education* 47, 4: 457–72.

18

DIGITAL CLASSROOMS AND THE NEW ECONOMIES OF ATTENTION

Reflections on the end of schooling as confinement

Inés Dussel

Introduction

> *The idea of special places for special stages of life is fading.*
> (Joshua Meyrowitz 1985: 157)

In 1985, Joshua Meyrowitz wrote a book on how television and electronic media were changing social and communicative behaviour. One of his main arguments was that media was not only blurring the boundaries between adults and children but also flattening out the differences between domestic and public spaces. If buildings or rooms had been able to confine people 'not only physically, but emotionally and psychologically as well', Meyrowitz considered that electronic media such as TV, which allow information to 'flow through walls and rush across great distances', altered time and space and made room for more egalitarian and fluid relationships (Meyrowitz 1985: viii).

Since that time, generations of digital devices have come one after another that make these older changes look pale in comparison. Personal computers and the internet introduced digital networking and created the possibility of virtual navigation and exploration, real-time collaboration networks and conversations, and production and sharing of multimodal texts (Coleman 2011). More recently, social media and smartphones have taken the 'personal, portable and pedestrian' media (Ito, Matsuda and Okabe 2005) to a new level. While in Meyrowitz's canvass there were still recognisable, even if fading, boundaries between adults and children, scholars today talk about situations where these differentiations are no longer relevant, underscoring the deterritorialisation and disembodiment of space in the digital landscape (Castells 2000).

How is this new context affecting the spatial organisation of schooling? In particular, smartphones and netbooks as permanent artefacts in classrooms, with individualised screens and internet or intranet connectivity, seem to significantly challenge the organisation of the power/knowledge relations in the classroom, and the centralised management and control by institutional authorities of the configuration of time and space. Considering the possibility of separating a space for a special task is not only harder to realise but also increasingly perceived as pedagogically unsound and questionable. Indeed, questions arise about whether schools will continue to be 'another place', different from home, cafeterias or other social gatherings. And if the acts of separating and confining bodies in a peculiar space, and suspending some space-time to produce scholarly performances, is ever more difficult, does it mean they have to be abandoned or that new conditions have to be recreated?

This chapter discusses these questions, reflecting on qualitative research conducted between 2011 and 2015 in Argentinean schools that have implemented a one-computer-per-child program. The research focused on investigating how hierarchies of knowledge and organisations of space and time are being reconfigured in the context of high availability of digital devices in classrooms. In my analysis, I bring together historical and pedagogical perspectives with a spatial and architectural approach (Healy and Darian-Smith 2015). I argue that there is much to be gained by considering the contemporary transformation of schools and classrooms as part of a longer series of changes and continuities in the social and spatial organisation of education and schooling, and by addressing the challenges that the new attention economies of digital media pose to the institutionalised production and reproduction of knowledge in our societies.

Instead of celebrating these challenges as the triumph of freedom over discipline, I suggest it is more productive to take the perspective of the 'pharmakón', that which is simultaneously venom and remedy (Stiegler 2010). Thus, my analysis remains ambivalent about the effects that digital technologies are having on classrooms, distancing itself both from the generalised optimism that is perceived in the edubusiness rhetoric and from the pessimism of school reformers that denounce the continuity of traditional schooling. As will be made clear in my final remarks, this ambivalence should not be confused with care-less-ness, or with being 'incurious' and irresponsible towards what is changing. As Bernard Stiegler (2010) says, there is need for a new politics of care and of curiosity that takes seriously the challenges posed by the digital programming industry and the short circuiting of intergenerational connections, and that promotes a reinvention of democracy and the institutions of knowledge such as schools and universities.

Thinking historically about classroom space and design

A starting point for this chapter is a critical analysis of how we think about schooling and school spaces now and in recent times, informed by 'the spatial turn' that has brought a new awareness of the distribution, organisation and scale of the social world (Thrift 2006). Under this new theorising, 'space' has implied an invitation to look at the materiality of institutions, discourses and other practices, and to break free of moulds and boundaries that fixed space to particular territories. The spatial turn has drawn on Foucault (1986) to historicise space and interrogate the discourses (including those of knowledge institutions such as museums and schools) that have shaped our experience of it.

Historically, modern schools were thought as spaces for 'a special stage of life' – childhood, as Meyrowitz said – and for accumulating and distributing cultural knowledge and social experience (Hamilton and Zufiaurre 2014). In terms of design, for the last two centuries school buildings have borrowed much from 'military functionalism', with 'its mechanical landscapes and calculated artifices' (Daniel-Lacombe 2015: 84, 94). While styles varied over and within time periods, eggcrate classrooms were the norm, with buildings organised around the imperatives of discipline and moral training (Hunter 1994; Markus 1996).

This organisation has been subjected to heavy criticism, first by progressive education at the turn of the twentieth century and later by radical pedagogies of the 1960s and 1970s that experimented with open spaces and alternative dispositions and ordering of the bodies of students and teachers (Ogata 2013; McLeod 2014; Willis 2014). Echoing and amplifying this structure of feeling, Foucault (1977) wrote one of the sharpest and well-known critiques of schooling as a disciplinary institution, questioning the confinement of bodies produced by this arrangement. He considered classrooms and school desks as individual cells that sought to isolate and sedentarise children and turn them into docile subjects. His arguments have since become almost commonsensical, and their echoes can be heard in current architectural concerns that do not endorse Foucault's radical critique of modern societies but share his denunciation of disciplinary institutions. As Lippman puts it:

> the school setting has been organized to control behaviour. Schools, like prisons, have been designed with classrooms adjacent to one another along either single or double loaded corridors. This arrangement limits the types of activities that can occur and symbolically reinforces for children that they have little power to make changes in their daily lives, affect their environment, or opportunities to examine alternative ways of living.
>
> (Lippman 2002)

Today, talk about ubiquitous learning, learning landscapes, personalised pods or zoned workflow spaces has entered the field of school design (Rudd et al. 2006) and given a new language for these long-term critiques of the 'outdated industrial-age classrooms' (Fisher and Newton 2014: 905). In a literature review commissioned by the Department of Education and Early Childhood Development of Victoria (Australia), Blackmore et al. (2011) show that there is a growing consensus that school spaces have to be redesigned following the principles of flexible learning, moving from a teacher-centred disposition to a student-centred environment. The 'Next Generation Learning Environments' (Fisher and Newton 2014) are no longer called schools or classrooms, and are designed to meet the needs of the new learners and the emergent technologies.

Interestingly, with the exception of Blackmore et al. (2011), there is almost no debate on the historicity of these claims, or about the political implications of claims about open spaces or neutral arenas of participation that is a common thread within the rhetoric of social media and internet corporations. Similarly to previous movements in the second half of the twentieth century for school reform and open-plan schools that wanted to transform school space and experience and make it flexible and customised to the individual (see Gyure 2011; also Amy Ogata's and Cameron Logan's contributions to this book), the current corporate discourse of social media and internet mega-corporations advocate for connectivity and openness, and for just-in-time and tailor-made content.[1] The 1960s claims for greater freedom and less rigidity have been appropriated today by the cultural forms and business models of the large corporations of creative or cognitive capitalism, which appear as 'freedom fighters' against the centralised authorities of the nation-states and Fordist, industrial modes of organising society, including schools. The cries about the oppression of the learner, the lack of play and humour, and the inflexibility of space and time in disciplinary institutions have been adopted and extended in a new wave of reforms that claim to remove these grievances and that produce an unexpected alliance of the 1960s cultural critique with corporate capitalism (Boltanski and Chiapello 2007).[2]

The assumptions upon which these shifts and displacements from spatial control to flexibility, and from teaching to learning, are based need to be historicised and problematised, as is proposed in several chapters of this book. But there is another thread that I follow in this chapter, related to the critique of the global jargon that surrounds much talk of digital classrooms and the renewal of school design. In many cases, these new learning environments appear to be technologically determined, universal experiences, showing few variations across different localities. The 'flattening out of differences' pointed to by Meyrowitz assumes a positive outlook, and placelessness and distancelessness appear as the solution to the rigidity of modern institutions and also to the inequalities created by boundaries and uneven relations.[3] However, as Arjun Appadurai argues, 'different forms circulate through different trajectories, generate diverse interpretations, and yield different and uneven geographies . . . so globalization is never a total project capturing all geographies with equal force' (Appadurai 2013: 67). Digital culture, although promoted and sold as placeless and homogenising, deterritorialised and unbounded, 'remains thoroughly socialized and materially entangled with spatial experience' in its actual practices (DeNicola 2013: 83).

There are two localities to which my argument pays attention. One is the classroom as a particular space where digital culture is reconfigured and reinscribed, which will be discussed in the next section. The other is a geopolitical consideration of schooling experience in a location such as contemporary Argentina where, until recently, a politically radical agenda for education in schools prevailed. In the policies that have promoted digital inclusion, and particularly in the program that has delivered netbooks to every secondary school student in the public system in Argentina, tellingly named Connect Equality (*Conectar Igualdad*) (I have analysed this program elsewhere; see Dussel, Ferrante and Sefton-Green 2013; Dussel 2014a; http://www.conectarigualdad.gob.ar/), there is almost no use of catchwords like individualism, liberal freedom and economic competitiveness that are so common elsewhere. Egalitarianism, democratic participation and entitlement, pedagogical innovation, and state-centred policies instead of market-driven strategies are some of the traits that made the country an interesting laboratory for radical politics until very recently (see McGuirk 2014).

These two localities – the classroom as a generalised space and the case of digital educational technologies in Argentina in particular – provide important keys to understand how digital media is affecting the configuration of time and space in classrooms, and call for nuanced arguments about how the institutions of schooling are relating to digital challenges in different parts of the world.

Changes and continuities in digital classrooms in Argentinean schools

In reflecting on observations from fieldwork in Argentinean schools in recent years, I focus on three aspects of classroom design and pedagogy that appear to be changing: the organisation of space and time, the grouping of students and the new attention economies brought by new digital media, that point to the idea of the 'end of confinement' of bodies in modern schooling. This research was done in several stages. In 2011, I followed the implementation of the federal program Connect Equality in one school in the city of Buenos Aires throughout the year, through meetings with the school principal and teachers, in-depth interviews with three teachers, and collection of students' multimodal productions (videos, blog postings, school assignments). In 2012 and 2013, with a research team at the Universidad Pedagógica de la

Provincia de Buenos Aires, I did research in four public secondary schools that were enrolled in the same program. The team observed two classrooms in each school, interviewed teachers about their perspectives and the difficulties and advantages of using netbooks in the classroom, and interviewed four students in each classroom. We also collected students' audiovisual productions that were part of their school assignments. Finally, in 2015 and with another team, I conducted research on ten public secondary schools also involved in the digital inclusion program.[4] While this research was not part of a longitudinal study and did not follow the same schools throughout these years, it produced a significant amount of knowledge of registers of school life and classroom interactions and gives hints about what is going on in these 'connected classrooms' in Argentina.[5]

My analysis uses a pedagogical and historical perspective that takes into account architectural and design approaches to schooling, and it includes an anthropological sensibility about the workings of agents and artefacts in the assemblage of the social (Latour 2005). As Jan Nespor says:

> The temporal organization of something like a classroom isn't entirely given by clock and calendars, but it is also produced by the ways in which teachers and students organize their work and referential practices in terms of alternate spatial and temporal orders (which means disagreement and struggle revolve at some level around how to position the here-and-now in competing histories and geographies).
>
> (Nespor 2006: 303)

Considering that the interactions in digital classrooms are shaped not only by the physical space but also by visual technologies and media, I claim that any understanding of classroom space has to take into account the sights, perspectives and technologies that organise social life. Thus, my analysis is also grounded on visual studies (Crary 1999; Mirzoeff 2005; among many others) and media studies (Gitelman 2008, 2014). This grounding leads me to explore if and how new organisations of visual technologies are deployed in classrooms, looking particularly at changes in the regimes of attention and of the media that are present in the school setting, and how images are part and parcel of school knowledge. I consider that the space of classrooms is, among other things, the arena of a clash between different media devices that organise perceptions and promote cultural forms and modes of address that differ radically from each other (Zielinski 2008).[6] But this clash is not complete or over-encompassing: there are ambivalences and continuities with previous organisations of bodies and knowledge, as will be seen in the next sections.

Changes in classroom organisation of space and time

Classrooms can be considered as porous, precarious spaces, which have been shaped historically (Hamilton 1989; Nespor 1996; Thrift 2006). Since Comenius (1592–1670), the classroom was structured on the basis of a frontal method. This is a disposition of disciplined bodies looking at the front of the classroom, with a focal point of attention in an adult figure, and based on visual technologies such as the blackboard, printed illustration or religious image, that ordered the social interchanges and established an asymmetrical and radial relationship between the adult teacher and the students. Years later, the simultaneous shifts in pedagogy and the introduction of grade-specific schools ended up shaping what we know today as a classroom, as a group of students who basically learn similar things at the same time, and who pay attention to a teacher who has a central program that structures her or his teaching.[7]

This way of organising the classroom, based on the simultaneity and homogeneity of groups, on a centralised visual technology and control of content and interchanges, on a space and time that was bounded by school legislation, is being fractured, and it has been so for some decades now. Twentieth-century child-centred pedagogies claimed that teachers needed to address diversity and singularity, challenging the notion of uniform pedagogies and simultaneous teaching. More recent has been the emergence of other technologies that appeared 'from below' in classrooms, such as the cell phone. In classroom observations, it is evident that students and teachers are dividing their attention between what happens in the classroom and the calls – or interruptions – from their mobile phones. It could even be said that the idea of 'divided attention' in schools might be an overstatement, and that the battle has already been lost by the school in favour of cell phones and other screens, which are much more appealing not only to young people but also to adults.

The notion of culture and of a shared, collective and public memory is also changing. These changes are quite evident in the use of visual technologies not only during school breaks but also in classroom time. Most students take pictures all the time of any social situation, and they do it for fun, for 'laughing out loud', and not for producing lasting memories. Photographic historian Joan Fontcuberta calls them 'Kleenex-images', disposable images (Fontcuberta 2010: 29), which constitute a different kind of archive, one intended not to memorialise events to nurture a common culture but to produce a sign in a fluid situation. For students, experiencing the world through digital technologies becomes equivalent to posing, and they are over-attentive to the recording and public display of one's image (Adatto 2008). There is a different disposition of bodies and gazes in these landscapes overpopulated with cameras. A teacher from Buenos Aires interviewed in 2011 reported that she takes it as a given that students might be taping or filming her with their cell phones. 'Now I dress up and take more care of myself', she said, as if she was on stage daily.

It is noteworthy that some years ago Jane Gallop discussed the notion of 'impersonation', of putting up another persona, of acting a different role, as a central one for teaching and teachers (Gallop 1995). Yet, it is now unclear the extent to which the presence of cameras is taking this to another level, because teachers are acting for audiences that they might not know and who see their 'acts' in totally different contexts – and, probably, in different series or texts: digitalisation allows much more intervention with images and voices. If classroom interactions used to be monitored only by supervisors or parents, who mostly knew about them through oral reconstructions, there are now many more records available that can also be shared and known almost immediately. In the interviews conducted in 2012 and 2015, teachers complained that parents were informed of problems, punishments or low grades even before the end of the school day, and that this immediacy caused interruptions and a constant pressure on their work that was perceived as overwhelming. There is an obvious connection between these digital visual technologies and a new global panopticon (Levin et al. 2002).

What emerges throughout the observations and interviews is that there is a shrinking of space and an acceleration of time brought about by digital cameras and mobile media in classrooms. The boundaries between school and out-of-school are becoming much more insecure, and the limits of the space and time of schools, its walls and its bells seem not to hold power to organise experiences as they did in the past. There is a lot of 'out-of-school' life in schools already, such as the massive practice of taking pictures or uploading content in social networks, texting messages or being on Facebook during school hours. This is a movement that has become almost impossible to control, particularly in settings where teachers' authority was already highly questioned. In addition, the 'school' (as a social organisation of knowledge practices) continues to exist beyond its own timeframes – for example, in the Facebook accounts that are now the platform for school teaching or the blogs that are promoted by schools and the writing of which is evaluated as a school production. In this way, the school has 'glass walls' through which interactions can be constantly surveilled by parents, authorities and social media.

In terms of rhythm and pace, in the observed classrooms the interaction seems, at first sight, very fragmentary and chaotic. There is constant noise, and it is difficult to discern a common thread or topic of conversation in the group. The class is fragmented into activities to be done individually or by groups organised by one screen; if breaking in small groups was common practice, the presence of individual screens opens up new possibilities for conversations that connect to other spaces outside the classroom. In terms of time, the class does not have a clear beginning, nor does it reach an end; there seems to be continuing work on a given assignment that runs through several days. Class work seems to gain some features of online participation – for example, of Wikis. Not surprisingly, Wikipedia defines itself as 'work in progress', and perhaps some of its ethos and practice of content production is reaching schools. When interviewed, teachers complain that the time slot they have in the school timetable is not enough to attain their educational goals (a complaint that is hardly new but has newer resonances). Some of these problems might be related to the novelty of artefacts, and the need to have new teaching repertoires that acknowledge time and technical constraints, but they might also be related to what comes with digital interaction, which demands more involvement and dedication from both teachers and pupils. Due to the intensity of the engagement, classes usually take up the break time, and students continue working on their productions or assignments, particularly when these are videos or photo collections. The 'deep time' of digital media (Zielinski 2008), willing to intensively mobilise bodies and affects, clashes with the school schedule of fixed and fragmented time frames for each school subject, and as a result the forty- or eighty-minute slot for lessons might be too much or too little, depending on students' engagement with a particular task.

What these findings show is that the experience online cannot be easily separated or segregated from the experience offline; there are patterns of interaction, tones and styles that move from one site to the other. Beth Coleman, in her book *Hello Avatar!*, states that physical presence is today technologically mediated: 'Instead of isolated, discrete incidents of virtual play or real work, what is growing in scale are the experiences of connected selves that get involved with multiple sites of agency' (Coleman 2011: 107). These multiple sites of agency can be experienced almost simultaneously, as in digital classrooms, when connecting to other spaces and conversations is very easy. There is a need to theorise another 'ontology of the presence' that takes into account mobile media and actors (Aranzueque 2010). Decupeyre, Masschelein and Simons (2012) call this new ontology an 'absent presence', which devalues the importance and depth of face-to-face relationships and promises an instant connection and feedback with a distant other.

The reconfiguration of classroom space and time with high availability of digital devices significantly challenges the possibility of intergenerational conversations, being so easy to switch off from adults' talk and demands and engage instead in conversations with peers. It also becomes more difficult to introduce students to languages and references that are not proximal or immediately comprehensible. 'Difficult', 'dense', 'tiresome' become negative associations for tasks or texts that require more complex operations. With the fall of disciplinary institutions and the centrally managed control of space and time, other authorities and power relations emerge; as Foucault said, each new liberty comes at the price of new subjections (Foucault 1978).

Classroom groups: the form and content of interactions

The clash between different modes of address and pedagogical organisation in classrooms and new media is quite evident in the way participants are grouped. In his study of videogames, James Paul Gee states that game platforms privilege learning from others who are not necessarily what the school would consider peers (Gee 2007). He calls these new kinds of social affiliation 'affinity spaces' and suggests that schools should learn from these sites. Affinity spaces are organised around a common task, limited in time and depend on the will of the participants. They are not defined primarily by age, gender or class, and have flexible boundaries that allow entering and leaving without much trouble. This approach emphasises two aspects: the heterogeneity of the groups and their common interest around a task. What goes unquestioned in this literature when it addresses space and flows is that, for most of the users, these affinity spaces propose segmented and encapsulated paths within groups organised around interests or friendship, which might deepen current social divisions or solidify what cultural industries define as common.[8]

In one of the schools included in the research, some strategies had been put in place to produce different kinds of groupings inside connected classrooms, which shows that the media clash can be negotiated in different ways, related to different trajectories. It is a school that constitutes a singular case both because of its recent history and because of its enthusiastic leadership, aligned with the left-leaning policies that are able to mobilise resources and support for their own projects. The school is in an expensive neighbourhood in the city of Buenos Aires and has received students from aristocratic families in the past; however, in the last twenty years the student population has changed because of the middle- and upper-class flight to private schools and the inclusion of urban poor students in public ones. The students now come from the slums located near the railway station. The school, however, retains a small group of middle-class students, who basically come from the National Ballet School located two blocks away. The leaders of the school consider it to be a laboratory for egalitarian educational policies and refer to Freire and Rancière in their projects and discussions.[9]

School staff started to implement the program with an interest-driven strategy. When they received the laptops, they regrouped students according to their interests in subjects and new media. But staff soon realised that the kids from the slums were not making academic progress and that the divisions in the groups went as deep as ever. So they consciously began to mix groups, assigning tasks that combined different knowledge (such as map the neighbourhood, write a song, produce a video) but also explicitly sitting kids from different groups together. Nespor (1996) calls this a typical strategy of teachers to control space and movement in the classroom, but in this case the crossing of students' perspectives and tastes, likes and dislikes, with social fragmentation and the politics of fear, gives other meanings to the action of regrouping students and leaving aside their elective affinities. The philosophy teacher recalls the first days:

> I was talking and I saw that a kid in the corner was saying hi to a girl, one of the ballet students, on this other corner, and then others were saying, '*hey you José, I didn't know your name*'. . . . I didn't get it in the beginning . . . but then they told me that they were

starting to get to know each other. . . . I assumed they already did. . . . It was a kind of re-cognition, or may be cognition, getting to look at each other, getting to know their names. Funny that it happens through the screens. In the end, we even got romance in the class, one of the ballet dancers and a kid from the slums.

The teachers at this school perceive gains in students' enthusiasm from laptop use, but also acknowledge a concurrent set of challenges. They see that while laptops might succeed in increasing interest in content, students do not necessarily want to engage with complex texts, whether visual or written. As the same teacher argues:

> These students lack basic literacy skills because they had such a poor primary school, so when I tell them to read something relatively complex, they complain and refuse to do it. If I could just sit with each of them and read it together line by line, I would probably be able to break this resistance. But given a 20- or 30-student classroom, it becomes almost impossible. But I want to get there. . . . We have to find other ways to do it.

This teacher acknowledges that an individualised teaching program – which the technology promises – is almost impossible in current classroom conditions. The students that already have the will and the skills to interact with complex texts can use the tools and possibilities offered by digital platforms more successfully and richly. However, this teacher sees that even those students who are not getting the most out of it make some gains. For example, he acknowledges that all students are forced to participate in digital platforms; keeping up with blogs makes their production visible and thus more accountable. The technology certainly makes it easier for teachers to track students' writing and provide feedback about it. Compulsory participation, thus, has the effect of forcing students to get used to more rigorous language and to overcoming the difficulties they encounter in its appropriation, but this requires pedagogical strategies and agents that care about what each one of the students is actually achieving.

The experience of this school shows the complex negotiations that are taking place between the new demands posed on pedagogy and design to make room for individual interests and voluntary participation, and the old ways of grouping students and organising classroom interaction. It also makes it evident that the concerns and strategies of teachers at this school are related to an assemblage of pedagogies and agents (including artefacts) that is inscribed in a particular geopolitical location. The content of these interchanges also suggests that taking for granted the interests and choices of students might curtail the possibilities of opening new paths for sociability and for power/knowledge relations different from the ones prevalent in digital social media.

Classrooms and pedagogical technologies in the new attention economy

The third set of reflections relate to what some scholars are calling a new 'attention economy', a new visual regime that is profoundly changing human relationships to other humans and to the world (Stiegler 2010; Citton 2014). In the era of the wealth of information, attention has become a scarce resource and has been commodified and annexed to the circulation of goods. Economists, philosophers, sociologists, media analysts and others are theorising how to understand this transition from 'time as labour to time as attention' (Crogan and Kinsley 2012: 6). For George Franck, the attention economy is a further development of the industrialisation of a 'knowledge society', as it can be calculated and monetised through the 'esteem' obtained through cultural leadership (in Crogan and Kinsley 2012: 6), mainly through popularity in social media.

Among these theorisations, the approach taken by Bernard Stiegler is of particular relevance to education. Stiegler considers attention as a psychic and social capacity that is historically and technically shaped. Rewriting Foucault's biopower, he defines *psychopower* as the contemporary form in which power operates on the self (Crogan and Kinsley 2012).

In an essay eloquently titled 'The Carnival of the New Screen', Stiegler states that we are living an irreversible rupture with the cultural industries that dominated throughout the twentieth century, which could also be applied to schooling as part of the same centralised, broadcast media. For Stiegler, there will no longer be a 'calendar organization of programmed access' to some images produced and distributed centrally, with a social synchronisation provided by television or the movies (Stiegler 2009: 52). While it could be said that this synchronisation did not start with the cinema and that it could be traced back to the schools and other institutions concerned with the governing of populations, Stiegler signals that this organisation of attention is today challenged by what he calls a 'cardinal' mode of access to images. The public has access to stocks of discrete audiovisual objects that are severed from the programmed flux of narrative contents that has characterised television over the last sixty years. Stiegler says that there is a battle for people's attention, especially for children's attention. The new visual regime intents to capture or, better, to produce a 'time of available brains' (Stiegler 2009: 47) – that is, a psychological and social disposition to pay attention, preferably to consume or buy something immediately afterwards. This fragmentation of the centralised audiovisual program poses similar challenges to TV producers and to teachers, because they both have to face the interaction with a consumer or prosumer whose exclusive attention is very difficult to obtain. And even though attention and distraction should be thought of more as a continuum than as opposites, it should be noted that there is a shift from a centralised attention, organised frontally or vertically, to an attention dispersed in multiple screens and windows, both in schools and in cultural industries. According to Stiegler, there will be no longer a community of spectators focused on a singular point but horizontal networks with multiple fluxes that will be impossible to control centrally.

In this context, however, cultural leadership is not evenly distributed, and the institutions of knowledge are having a hard time competing with the entertainment industry. An example of these tensions can be found in a literature class that was observed in my research. The teacher wanted the students to read an early modern Spanish romance that deals with death and love, and she decided to ask her students to do a short video clip on what they would do if they had only one more hour to live. However, the actual content that was produced by students took different paths and, according to the literature teacher, had no dialogue with the piece of literature. The tone of the students' clips was ironic or melodramatic and imitated the genres and icons of television programs. As this teacher reported: 'We never got to the reading; they were very motivated to do a video clip but I think it would have been the same to do it without the literary work, as they didn't use it'. The reading was considered too complex and difficult, while producing the video clip was 'fun' and entertaining. The teacher could not break the boundaries defined by the cultural industries about what is 'fun' or 'entertaining' or challenge their association with easy content or immediate accessibility and quick operations and feedback.

Another entry to this battle for attention can be seen in students' visual culture. In 2012, we asked students about what images they recalled as being powerful and which had produced valuable learning for them. The images referred to came overwhelmingly from popular culture and from a visual regime that values shock and impact above other things (Jaguaribe 2007), and that produces intense engagements, described by Henry Jenkins as the 'wow effect' (Jenkins 2007). For example, a student said that she became aware of the disaster caused by Haiti's earthquake after seeing shocking pictures on Facebook asking for donations. There is a global visual Esperanto (Mirzoeff 2005) that is punctuated by pictures of catastrophes and a loose humanitarianism.

In other interviews, the value of 'impact' or 'emotional shock' emerged when students were asked what kind of images they bring to the school and share with their friends. While there are certainly some constraints in the method (that is, students 'not willing/not able/not prepared' to talk about their private consumptions or uses of images; see Gleeson and Frith 2004), in the interviews students referred to the emotional impact of the images they keep or share. A young male student recounted how a social science teacher had asked them to bring pictures of catastrophes, hunger, poverty and solidarity. He recalled it as a moving experience and one occasion in which he felt he learned something valuable; however, when asked about the particular image he had chosen for that activity, the student could not remember it. Emotions seem to taint what is learned, and the content seems to be reduced to a good or bad feeling – which takes us back to what has already been mentioned about the kind of operations produced by digital social media, and also to Stiegler's point about this new psychopower.

Concluding remarks

There are operations of language that demand to be critiqued.

(Georges Didi-Huberman, 2014: 162)

My approach to the changes brought by digital media in classrooms and to the end of the confinement of bodies and centrally managed control of the traditional institutions of knowledge that these media imply is pharmacological – that is, simultaneously pointing to the venom and remedy that they carry. The fading of disciplinary institutions and the redesigning of classrooms as open, flexible spaces has brought more freedom to talk and broader cultural references to classrooms, and has reversed the old hierarchies of knowledge and culture, but they do not necessarily make room for a more democratic politics or for a critique of existing power/knowledge relations. In fact, what can be seen in the research presented in this chapter is that the new cultural hierarchies seem to reinforce what is already prevalent in new digital media, and that schools, particularly the ones that want to be a laboratory for more egalitarian policies, have a hard time challenging those hierarchies.

Keeping an ambivalent stance is meant not to be careless but rather to engage with a new politics of care that confronts the challenges posed by the digital programming industry and the short-circuiting of intergenerational connections, and seeks to reinvent the institutions of knowledge in order to reinvent democracy in these new times. One central point in this new politics of care is to reclaim the notion of the public, as distinct from the audience of the media. The public seems more and more co-opted by the media discourses that claim it is the audience of consumers, of individual interests and tastes, or of the opinion polls. The public is made of monitorial citizens who conceive their social and political participation as a surveillance of the themes and topics that affect them, and who react from this individualised point of view or interest (Papacharissi 2010).

Yet the school has been, and continues to be, organised on a different basis; as was said earlier in this chapter, schools are particular localities in which digital media are inscribed. Schools are public institutions that can 'open up an experience of a new beginning' (Masschelein and Simons 2010: 544) if they do not renounce the opportunity to make available words, movements, objects or thoughts that might not be immediately accessible, so that students can appropriate them and create something entirely new and unforeseen by the teachers. Through classroom interactions, teachers are required to introduce discussions about truth and common knowledge, about justice and the common good, about beauty and abjection – unlike media culture, which is the realm of fame and popularity. In some classrooms observed in Argentinean schools, and this is probably related to a political climate that allows experimentation and creativity for a more egalitarian politics, it seems that there are complex strategies to make room for popular media culture, but at the same time there are struggles to bring other languages and references to the conversation. And this is particularly important today, when, as Siegfried Zielinksi says, 'not all conversations must inevitably be markets' (Zielinski 2013: 252). Attention can resist commodification, and personal interests cannot be monetised or sold as part of a popular profile; but in order for this to happen, specific strategies have to be set up, and conditions have to be created for these strategies to be sustainable.

School design and architecture are important to create such conditions. School design might need to facilitate, from the architectural disposition of space and objects, the possibility of studying; of students being exposed to things, languages or objects that are not immediately available outside; of being part of an intergenerational connection and dialogue (Masschelein and Simons 2013). Schools might need to provide, more than ever before, a space of suspension, a space that affords a different pace and rhythm from enhancement or acceleration, and also a space that makes it possible to talk but also to listen to others. As Masschelein and Simons say, this kind of space might be 'boring for the utopianist – and the reforms she has in mind' (2010: 552); it is less concerned with style than with what it makes it possible to do and set in motion.

Maybe, as these authors suggest, this design has to be more like a vacant space, a free space, a space that can be inhabited by pedagogical strategies that do not endorse the spectacularisation of everyday life but promote a different kind of work with culture and knowledge. In this way, design might contribute to the end of schooling as confinement but also to a new beginning for more democratic interactions with knowledge and with the new cultural hierarchies that are emerging.

Notes

1   José van Dijck (2013) discusses the corporate ideology, promoted by Zuckerberg and others, that everything must be social and that users or participants have to build a 'truly open and connected space'. In social media such as Facebook and Twitter, the imperative to share and annotate all life experiences online so that people become more popular is based on the push to make all data available to companies that benefit from it (van Dijck 2013: 58).

2   This can be related to a more general movement described by Jacques Rancière:

> Have not all the forms of critique, play, and irony that claim to disrupt the ordinary circulation of images been annexed by that circulation? . . . The procedures of cutting and humor have themselves become the stock-in-trade of advertising, the means by which it generates both adoration of its icons and the positive attitude towards them created by the very possibility of ironizing it.
>
> (Rancière 2007: 27–8)

3   There is a promise, in digital technologies, of an endless development that is a continuation of the religious narratives on eternal life, as Stanley Fish poignantly discusses (2012). It is noteworthy that Meyrowitz, in more recent work, has moved away from 'placelessness' to discuss how *glocality* produces new senses of place and identities (2005).
4   This research was done at the Organización de Estados Iberoamericanos (OEI), and with the collaboration of Delia González. The analysis of findings is still under way.
5   The results of the first two projects have been published in Dussel (2014b) and Dussel, Ferrante, González and Montero (2015).
6   As said before in relation to Meyrowitz's argument, this clash is anything but recent. See Walter Benjamin's discussion of the opposition between critique and publicity and cinema (Benjamin 2002).
7   The organisation of attention involves a pedagogy, and the history of pedagogy can also be read as the history of particular regimes of attention. See Jonathan Crary (1999) for a thorough study of régimes of attention.
8   Also, it can be said that this approach seems more platform-driven than user-driven. Research on gaming communities in Latin America shows that there are hierarchies, that advanced players find ways to exclude novices, and that more excluded than novices are those with slow connections that would affect the pace of the game – basically those who connect in cybercafés or public places, obviously less advantaged economically. There is suffering and exclusion in gaming, as much as there is pleasure and anxiety and passion (Piracón 2015).
9   The experience of the school has been portrayed in a recent documentary, *Después de Sarmiento* (dir. Francisco Márquez 2015). More information is available at: http://www.pensarconlasmanos. com/#!despuesdesarmiento/c19qd.

Works cited

Adatto, K. (2008) *Picture Perfect: Life in the Age of the Photo Op*, Princeton, NJ: Princeton University Press.
Appadurai, A. (2013) *The Future as Cultural Fact: Essays on the Global Condition*, London: Verso.
Aranzueque, G. (ed.) (2010) *Ontología de la distancia: Filosofías de la comunicación en la era telemática [Ontology of Distance: Philosophies of communication in the telematics era]*, Madrid: Abada Ediciones.
Benjamin, W. (2002 [1933]) 'Se alquilan estas superficies', in *Calle de mano única* (trans. J.J. Del Solar), Madrid: Editorial Nacional. [English edition: 'This Space for Rent', in *One-Way Street: and Other Writings*, London: Harcourt Brace Jovanovich, 1978: 89–90.]
Blackmore, J., Bateman, D., Loughlin, J., O'Mara, J. and Aranda, G. (2011) 'Research into the Connection between Built Learning Spaces and Student Outcomes: Literature Review' (Paper 22), Research and Innovation Centre, Department of Education & Early Childhood Development, Victorian Government, available at: www.learningspaces.edu.au/docs/learningspaces-literature-review.pdf.
Boltanski, L. and Chiapello, E. (2007) *The New Spirit of Capitalism* (trans. G. Elliot), London: Verso.
Castells, M. (2000) *The Rise of the Network Society*, Oxford: Blackwell.
Citton, Y. (ed.) (2014) *L'économie de l'attention: Nouvelle horizon du capitalisme?* Paris: Editions La Découverte.
Coleman, B. (2011) *Hello Avatar! The Rise of the Networked Generation*, Cambridge, MA: The MIT Press.
Crary, J. (1999) *Suspensions of Perception: Attention, Spectacle, and Modern Culture*, Cambridge, MA and London: The MIT Press.
Crogan, P. and Kinsley, S. (2012) 'Paying Attention: Towards a Critique of the Attention Economy', Culture Machine 13: 1–29, available at: http://www.culturemachine.net/index.php/cm/article/view/463/500.
Daniel-Lacombe, E. (2015) 'Des écoles pour les enfants', in T. Paquot (ed.) *La ville récréative: Enfants joueurs et écoles buissonières*, Clermont-Ferrand: Infolio.
Decupeyre, M., Masschelein, J. and Simons, M. (2012) '"Where Are You?" Cell Phones and Environmental Self-Understanding amongst Students', *International Journal of Qualitative Studies in Education* 25, 6: 705–22.
DeNicola, L. (2013) 'Geomedia: The Reassertion of Space within Digital Culture', in H. Horst and D. Miller (eds) *Digital Anthropology*, London: Bloomsbury Academic: 80–98.
Didi-Huberman, G. (2014) 'Savoir Trancher', in *Foucault contre lui-même*, sous la direction de Par François Caillat, Paris: Presses Universitaires de France: 156–75.

Dijck, J. van (2013) *The Culture of Connectivity: A Critical History of Social Media*, Oxford and New York, Oxford University Press.

Dussel, I. (2014a) 'Programas educativos de inclusión digital: Una reflexión desde la Teoría del Actor en Red sobre la experiencia de Conectar Igualdad (Argentina) [Educational programs for digital inclusion: A reflection from ANT theory on the experience of Connect Equality], *Versión: Estudios de Comunicación y Política*, 34: 39–56.

Dussel, I. (2014b) 'Una escuela contra el abandono, o contra el abandono de la escuela' [A school against drop out/abandonment, or against the abandonment of schooling], in I. Dussel and L. Reyes-López, *La dimensión social de la lectura. La escuela: un espacio que no se puede abandonar [The social dimension of reading: The school: a space that cannot be abandoned]*, México DF: Conaculta.

Dussel, I., Ferrante, P., y González, D. and Montero, J. (2015) 'Transformaciones de los saberes y participación cultural a partir de la introducción de las netbooks en escuelas secundarias' [Transformations of knowledge and cultural participation since the introduction of netbooks in secondary schools], in A. Pereyra et al. (eds) *Prácticas pedagógicas y políticas educativas: Investigaciones en el territorio bonaerense [Pedagogical practices and educational policies: Research in the Province of Buenos Aires]*, Gonet, La Plata: UNIPE Editorial Universitaria.

Dussel, I., Ferrante P. and Sefton-Green, J. (2013) 'Changing Narratives of Change: Unintended Consequences of Educational Technology Reform in Argentina', in N. Selwyn and K. Facer (eds) *The Politics of Education and Technology*, London: Palgrave Macmillan.

Fish, S. (2012) 'The Digital Humanities and the Transcending of Mortality', blog entry posted 9 January 2012, 9:00 pm, available at: http://opinionator.blogs.nytimes.com/2012/01/09/the-digital-humanities-and-the-transcending-of-mortality/ (accessed 5 July 2015).

Fisher, K. and Newton, C. (2014) 'Transforming the Twenty-first-century Campus to Enhance the Net-generation Student Learning Experience: Using Evidence-based Design to Determine what Works and Why in Virtual/Physical Teaching Spaces', *Higher Education Research & Development* 33, 5: 903–20.

Fontcuberta, J. (2010) *La cámara de Pandora: La fotografí@ después de la fotografía [Pandora's Camera: Photogr@phy after photography]*, Barcelona: Ediciones Gustavo Gilli.

Foucault, M. (1977) *Discipline and Punish: The Birth of the Prison* (trans. Alan Sheridan), New York: Pantheon Books.

Foucault, M. (1978) *The History of Sexuality Volume I: An Introduction* (trans. Robert Hurley), New York: Vintage Books.

Foucault, M. (1986) 'Of Other Spaces (1967)', *Diacritics* 16, 1: 22–7.

Gallop, J. (ed.) (1995) *Pedagogy: The Question of Impersonation*, Bloomington and Indianapolis: Indiana University Press.

Gee, J. P. (2007) *Good Video Games + Good Learning: Collected Essays on Video Games, Learning and Literacy*, New York: Peter Lang.

Gitelman, L. (2008) *Always Already New: Media, History and the Data of Culture*, Cambridge, MA: MIT Press.

Gitelman, L. (2014) *Paper Knowledge: Toward a Media History of Documents*, Durham and London: Duke University Press.

Gleeson, K. and Frith, H. (2004) 'Pretty in Pink: Young Women Presenting Mature Sexual Identities', in A. Harris (ed.) *All About the Girl: Culture, Power and Identity*, New York & London, Routledge: 103–44.

Gyure, D. A. (2011) The Chicago Schoolhouse: High School Architecture and Educational Reform, 1856–2006, Chicago, IL: University of Chicago Press.

Hamilton, D. (1989) *Towards a Theory of Schooling*, London, New York & Philadelphia: The Falmer Press.

Hamilton, D. and Zufiaurre, B. (2014) *Blackboards and Bootstraps: Revisioning Education and Schooling*, Rotterdam: Sense Publishers.

Healy, S. and Darian-Smith, K. (2015) 'Educational Spaces and the "Whole" Child: A Spatial History of School Design, Pedagogy and the Modern Australian Nation' *History Compass* 13, 6: 275–87.

Hunter, I. (1994) *Rethinking the School: Subjectivity, Bureaucracy, Criticism*, Sydney: Allen & Unwin.

Ito, M., Matsuda M. and Okabe, D. (eds) (2005) *Personal, Portable and Pedestrian: Mobile Phones in Japanese Life*, Cambridge, MA: MIT Press.

Jaguaribe, B. (2007) *O choque do rea: Estética, mídia e cultura* [*The shock of the real: Aesthetics, media, and culture*], Rio de Janeiro: Rocco.

Jenkins, H. (2007) *The Wow Climax: Tracing the Emotional Impact of Popular Culture*, New York and London: New York University Press.

José van Dijck (2013) *The Culture of Connectivity: A Critical History of Social Media*, Oxford: Oxford University Press.

Latour, B. (2005) *Reassembling the Social*, Oxford: Oxford University Press.

Levin, T.Y., Frohne, U. and Weibel, P. (eds) (2002) *CTRL [SPACE]: Rhetorics of Surveillance from Bentham to Big Brother*, Karlsruhe: ZKM Centre for Art and Media.

Lippman, P. C. (2002) 'Practice Theory, Pedagogy, and the Design of Learning Environments', *CAE Net. The Quarterly Newsletter of the Committee of Architecture for Education*, 2, available at: http://network. aia.org/HigherLogic/System/DownloadDocumentFile.ashx?DocumentFileKey=c6d686b8–1265–4904-b45d–437769e426f0&forceDialog=0 (accessed on 13 November 2015).

Markus, T. (1996) 'Early Nineteenth-Century School Space and Ideology', *Paedagogica Historica: International Journal of the History of Education* 32: 9–50.

Masschelein, J. and Simons, M. (2010) 'Schools as Architecture for Newcomers and Strangers: The Perfect School as Public School?', *Teachers College Record* 112, 2: 533–55.

Masschelein, J. and Simons, M. (2013) *In Defence of the School: A Public Issue* (trans. J. McMartin), Leuven: Education, Culture and Society Publishers.

McGuirk, J. (2014) *Radical Cities: Across Latin America in Search of a New Architecture*, London and New York: Verso.

McLeod, J. (2014) 'Experimenting with Education: Spaces of Freedom and Alternative Schooling in the 1970s', *History of Education Review* 43, 2: 172–89.

Meyrowitz, J. (1985) *No Sense of Place: The Impact of Electronic Media on Social Behavior*, Oxford, UK: Oxford University Press.

Meyrowitz, J. (2005) 'The Rise of Glocality: New Senses of Place and Identity in the Global Village', in K. Nyiri (ed.) *A Sense of Place: The Global and the Local in Mobile Communication*, Vienna: Passagen Verlag: 21–30.

Mirzoeff, N. (2005) *Watching Babylon: The War in Irak and Global Visual Culture*, New York & London, UK: Routledge.

Nespor, J. (1996) *Tangled Up in School: Politics, Space, Bodies, and Signs in the Educacional Process*, Mahwah, NJ: Lawrence Erlbaum Associates.

Nespor, J. (2006) 'Finding Patterns with Field Notes', in Green, J. L., Camilli, G. and Elmore, P.B. (eds), *Handbook of Complementary Methods in Education Research*, Mahwah, NJ: Lawrence Erlbaum and AERA: 297–308.

Ogata, A. F. (2013) *Designing the Creative Child: Playthings and Places in Midcentury America*, Minneapolis: University of Minnesota Press.

Papacharissi, Z. (2010) *A Private Sphere: Democracy in a Digital Age*, Cambridge, UK: Polity Press.

Piracón, J. (2015) 'Videojuegos y escuela: Tensiones, actores y sus objetos' [Videogames and schooling: tensions, actors, and their objects], MA thesis, Latin American School for the Social Sciences, Argentina.

Rancière, J. (2007) *The Future of the Image* (trans. G. Elliott), New York: Verso.

Rudd, T., Gifford, C., Morrison, J., Facer, K. (2006) *What if . . . ? Reimagining Learning Spaces*, Bristol: Futurelab.

Stiegler, B. (2009) 'The Carnival of the New Screen: From Hegemony to Isonomy', in P. Snickers and P. Vonderau (eds) *The YouTube Reader*, Stockholm: National Library of Sweden: 40–59.

Stiegler, B. (2010) *Taking Care of Youth and the Generations*, Palo Alto, CA: Stanford University Press.

Thrift, N. (2006) 'Space', *Theory, Culture & Society* 23, 2–3; 139–55.

Willis, J. (2014) 'From Home to Civic: Designing the Australian School', *History of Education Review* 43, 2: 138–51.

Zielinski, S. (2008) *Deep Time of the Media: Towards an Archeology of Hearing and Seeing by Technical Means*, Cambridge, MA: MIT Press.

Zielinksi, S. (2013) *[. . . After the Media]* (trans. G. Custance), Minneapolis, MN: Univocal.

INDEX